Database Modeling & Design

Third Edition

TOBY J. TEOREY

Morgan Kaufmann Publishers, Inc.
San Francisco, California

Senior Editor: Diane D. Cerra
Director of Production and Manufacturing: Yonie Overton
Assistant Production Manager: Julie Pabst
Production Editor: Edward Wade
Copyeditor: Jennifer McClain
Text Design, Illustration, & Composition: Rebecca Evans & Associates
Cover Design: Martin Heirakuji Design
Indexer: Ty Koontz
Cover Photograph: Jason Hawkes/Tony Stone Images
Printer: Edwards Brothers, Inc.

Morgan Kaufmann Publishers, Inc.
Editorial and Sales Office
340 Pine Street, Sixth Floor
San Francisco, CA 94104-3205
USA

Telephone	415/392-2665
Facsimile	415/982-2665
Email	*mkp@mkp.com*
WWW	*http://www.mkp.com*
Order toll free	800/745-7323

Published 1990. Third edition 1999

Printed in the United States of America

03 02 01 00 99 5 4 3 2 1

Library of Congress Cataloging-in-Publication Data

Teorey, Toby J.
Database modeling & design / Toby J. Teorey. — 3rd ed.
p. cm.
Includes bibliographical references and index.
ISBN 1-55860-500-2
1. Relational databases. 2. Database design. I. Title.
QA76.9.D26T45 1999
005.75′6—dc21 98-42150
CIP

To Matt, Carol, and Marilyn

Database Modeling & Design

Third Edition

The Morgan Kaufmann Series in Data Management Systems

Series Editor, Jim Gray

Database Modeling and Design, Third Edition
Toby J. Teorey

Web Farming for the Data Warehouse
Richard Hackathorn

Management of Heterogeneous and Autonomous Database Systems
Edited by Ahmed K. Elmagarmid, Marek Rusinkiewicz, and Amit P. Sheth

Object-Relational DBMSs: Tracking the Next Great Wave, Second Edition
Michael Stonebraker and Paul Brown with Dorothy Moore

A Complete Guide to DB2 Universal Database
Don Chamberlin

Universal Database Management: A Guide to Object/Relational Technology
Cynthia Maro Saracco

Readings in Database Systems, Third Edition
Edited by Michael Stonebraker and Joseph M. Hellerstein

Understanding SQLs Stored Procedures: A Complete Guide to SQL/PSM
Jim Melton

Principles of Multimedia Database Systems
V. S. Subrahmanian

Principles of Database Query Processing for Advanced Applications
Clement T. Yu and Weiyi Meng

The Object Database Standard: ODMG 2.0
Edited by R. G. G. Cattell and Douglas K. Barry

Introduction to Advanced Database Systems
Carlo Zaniolo, Stefano Ceri, Christos Faloutsos, Richard T. Snodgrass, V. S. Subrahmanian, and Roberto Zicari

Principles of Transaction Processing
Philip A. Bernstein and Eric Newcomer

Distributed Algorithms
Nancy A. Lynch

Active Database Systems: Triggers and Rules For Advanced Database Processing
Edited by Jennifer Widom and Stefano Ceri

Joe Celkos SQL for Smarties: Advanced SQL Programming
Joe Celko

Migrating Legacy Systems: Gateways, Interfaces, and the Incremental Approach
Michael L. Brodie and Michael Stonebraker

Database: Principles, Programming, and Performance
Patrick ONeil

Atomic Transactions
Nancy Lynch, Michael Merritt, William Weihl, and Alan Fekete

Query Processing for Advanced Database Systems
Edited by Johann Christoph Freytag, David Maier, and Gottfried Vossen

Transaction Processing: Concepts and Techniques
Jim Gray and Andreas Reuter

Understanding the New SQL: A Complete Guide
Jim Melton and Alan R. Simon

Building an Object-Oriented Database System: The Story of O_2
Edited by François Bancilhon, Claude Delobel, and Paris Kanellakis

Database Transaction Models for Advanced Applications
Edited by Ahmed K. Elmagarmid

A Guide to Developing Client/Server SQL Applications
Setrag Khoshafian, Arvola Chan, Anna Wong, and Harry K. T. Wong

The Benchmark Handbook for Database and Transaction Processing Systems, Second Edition
Edited by Jim Gray

Camelot and Avalon: A Distributed Transaction Facility
Edited by Jeffrey L. Eppinger, Lily B. Mummert, and Alfred Z. Spector

Readings in Object-Oriented Database Systems
Edited by Stanley B. Zdonik and David Maier

Contents

Preface

Data modeling and database design have undergone significant evolution in recent years since the domination of business applications by the relational data model and relational database systems. Before the relational era, however, the dominating data models were the hierarchical and network models, characterized by IMS and CODASYL-style database systems, respectively. Database design for these systems depended on knowledge of both the logical and physical characteristics of the data model. More recently, however, the relational model has allowed the database designer to focus on these characteristics separately. Object-oriented databases, the next generation, are also based on a separation of the logical and physical aspects, but go further by integrating the data manipulation and data definition mechanisms. Other new technologies such as data warehousing, OLAP, data mining, and spatial, temporal, and multimedia databases have also had an important impact on database design.

In this third edition we continue to concentrate on techniques for database design in relational database systems, starting with the entity-relationship (ER) approach for data requirements specification and conceptual modeling; but we also look ahead to the common properties in data modeling and operations between the relational model and advanced database technologies such as the object-oriented, temporal, and multimedia models. We cover the database life cycle from requirements analysis and logical design to physical design for local, distributed, and multidatabases. The discussion of basic principles is supplemented with a common example—a company personnel and project database, based on real-life experiences and thoroughly classroom tested.

Organization

The database life cycle is described in Chapter 1. We also review the basic concepts of database modeling. Entity-relationship (ER) modeling is a popular method for the conceptualization of users' data requirements. Currently, there is no standard ER model, and published articles and textbooks have introduced an enormous variety of constructs and notation to represent fundamental modeling concepts. In Chapter 2 we present the most fundamental ER concepts and provide a simple set of notational constructs—that is, the Chen notation—to represent them. We then provide guidance to reading some of the most common alternative notations used in the literature. We look at ER models at two levels: the simple level that is currently used in most computer-aided software engineering (CASE) tools and that satisfies requirements for end-user readability, and a complex level that is useful to database designers who want to clearly define complex relationships.

Chapters 3 and 4 show how to use ER concepts in the database design process. Chapter 3 is devoted to direct application of ER modeling in logical database design. Chapter 4 explains the transformation of the ER model to the relational model and to SQL syntax specifically.

Chapter 5 is devoted to the fundamentals of database normalization through fifth normal form, showing the functional equivalence between the ER model and the relational model for the higher normal forms. Chapter 6 introduces the concepts of physical design, access methods, and join strategies and illustrates how to modify a relational schema to be more efficient when usage for specific applications is well known. The case study in Chapter 7 summarizes the techniques presented in Chapters 1 through 6 with a new problem environment.

Chapter 8 presents the fundamentals of fragmentation and data allocation in a distributed database system. Chapters 9 and 10 are entirely new. Chapter 9 describes the main database design issues in data warehousing and gives some examples of how OLAP and data mining are being used today to get new information from old data. Chapter 10 discusses the new database technologies, such as spatial, temporal, multimedia, object-oriented, and object-relational, and how they overlap and interact in terms of the database design life cycle.

An extensive review of the popular relational database query language SQL is presented in Appendix A for those readers who lack familiarity with database query languages. Appendix B takes a brief look at the major database parameters controlled by either the user or database administrator that affect performance in a significant way and can be tuned to improve efficiency. The relationship between database reliability and performance is explored in Appendix C, leading to a new way to compute mean transaction (response) time for any database application. As a supplement to Chapter 9, Appendix D lists many of the major vendors associated with data warehousing, including those specifically selling software for OLAP and data mining. Since a complete list is impossible to make, given the dynamics of the industry, several key Web sites are given to lead the reader to more up-to-date listings. Finally, Appendix E summarizes some recent research in the various ways databases can be integrated with the World Wide Web.

This book can be used by the database practitioner as a useful guide to database modeling and its application to database designs from business and office environments to scientific and engineering databases. Whether you are a novice database user or an experienced professional, this book offers new insights into database modeling and the ease of transition from the ER model to the relational model, including the building of standard SQL data definitions. Thus, whether you are using DB2, Oracle, Sybase, Informix, SQL Server, NonStop SQL, or any other SQL-based system, the design rules set forth here will be applicable. The case studies used for the examples throughout the book are from real-life databases that were designed using the principles formulated here. This book can also be used by the advanced undergraduate or beginning graduate student to supplement a course textbook in introductory database management or for a stand-alone course in data modeling or database design.

Typographical Conventions

For easy reference, entity names (Employee, Department, and so on) are capitalized from Chapter 2 forward. Throughout the book, table names (**product**, **product_count**) are set in boldface for readability.

Acknowledgments

I wish to acknowledge colleagues and students that contributed to the technical continuity of this book: Mike Blaha, Deb Bolton, Joe Celko, Jarir Chaar, Nauman Chaudhry, John DeSue, Yang Dongqing, Ron Fagin, Carol Fan, Jim Fry, Jim Gray, Bill Grosky, Wei Guangping, Wendy Hall, Paul Helman, Nayantara Kalro, John Koenig, Ji-Bih Lee, Marilyn Mantei, Bongki Moon, Wee-Teck Ng, Dan O'Leary, Kunle Olukotun, Dave

Roberts, Behrooz Seyed-Abbassi, Dan Skrbina, Rick Snodgrass, Il-Yeol Song, Dick Spencer, Amjad Umar, and Susanne Yul. I also wish to thank the Department of Electrical Engineering and Computer Science (EECS) and the Center for Information Technology Integration (CITI) the University of Michigan, the Computer Science Department at the University of Arizona, and the Department of Electronics and Computer Science at the University of Southampton for providing computer resources for writing and revising. The entire manuscript was written using Microsoft Word and MacPaint. Pat Corey and Ann Gordon provided excellent detailed critiques of the original manuscript, and Rosemary Metz was always there for anything that needed fixing. Finally, thanks to Julie for offering Ludington and for not giving up.

Solutions Manual

A solutions manual to all exercises is available. Contact the publisher for further information.

1 Introduction

Database technology began to replace file systems in the mid-1960s. Since that time database modeling and design has slowly evolved from an art to a science that has been partially implementable as a set of software design aids. Many of these design aids have appeared as the database component of computer-aided software engineering (CASE) tools, and many of them offer interactive modeling capability using a simplified data modeling approach.

In this chapter we review the basic concepts of database management and introduce the role of data modeling and database design in the database life cycle.

1.1 Data and Database Management

The basic component of a file in a file system is a *data item*, which is the smallest named unit of data that has meaning in the real world—for example, last name, first name, street address, id number, and political party. A group of related data items treated as a unit by an application is called a *record*. Examples of types of records are order, salesperson, customer, product, and department. A *file* is a collection of records of a single type. Database systems have built upon and expanded these definitions: In a relational database, a data item is called an *attribute*, a record is called a *row* or *tuple*, and a file is called a *table*.

A *database* is a more complex object; it is a collection of interrelated stored data that serves the needs of multiple users within one or more organizations, that is, interrelated collections of many different types of tables. The motivation for using databases rather than files has been greater availability to a diverse set of users, integration of data for easier access and update for complex transactions, and less redundancy of data.

A *database management system* (DBMS) is a generalized software system for manipulating databases. A DBMS supports a logical view (schema, subschema); physical view (access methods, data clustering); data definition language; data manipulation language; and important utilities such as transaction management and concurrency control, data integrity, crash recovery, and security. Relational database systems, the dominant type of systems for well-formatted business databases, also provide a greater degree of data independence than the earlier hierarchical and network (CODASYL) database management systems. *Data independence* is the ability to make changes in either the logical or physical structure of the database without requiring reprogramming of application programs. It also makes database conversion and reorganization much easier. Relational (and object-oriented) DBMSs provide a much higher degree of data independence than previous systems; they are the focus of our discussion on data modeling.

1.2 Data Modeling and the Entity-Relationship Approach

Schema diagrams were formalized in the 1960s by Charles Bachman. He used rectangles to denote record types and directed arrows from one record type to another to denote a one-to-many relationship among instances of records of the two types. The *entity-relationship* (ER) approach for conceptual database modeling, the approach emphasized in this book, was first described in 1976 by Peter Chen. The Chen form of ER models uses rectangles to specify entities, which are somewhat analogous to records. It also uses diamond-shaped objects to represent the various types of relationships, which are differentiated by numbers or letters placed on the lines connecting the diamonds to the rectangles. Since the original definition of entities and relationships, the ER modeling technique has undergone a variety of changes and extensions, including the implementation of experimental database management systems using the ER data model.

The overriding emphasis in ER modeling is on simplicity and readability. The goal of conceptual schema design, where the ER approach is most useful, is to capture real-world data requirements in a simple and meaningful way that is understandable by both the database designer

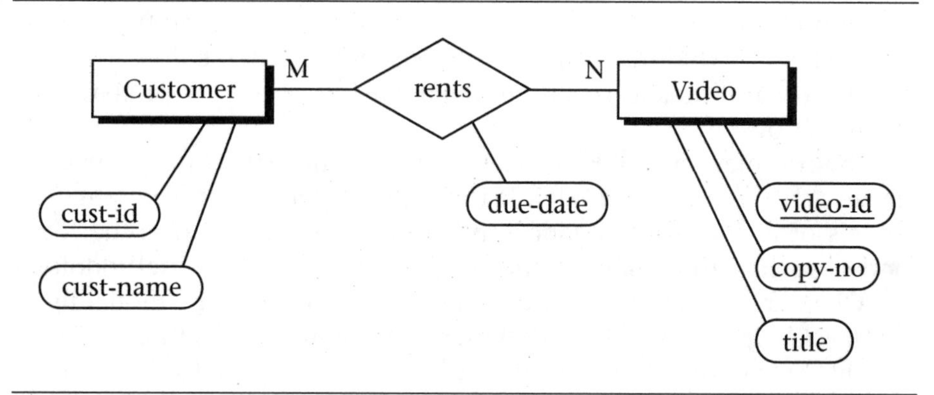

Figure 1.1 Example of ER model

and the end user. The end user is the person responsible for accessing the database and executing queries and updates through the use of DBMS software, therefore having a vested interest in the database design process.

The ER model has two levels of definition—one that is quite simple and another that is considerably more complex. The simple level is the one used by most current CASE tools. It is quite helpful to the database designer in communicating with end users about their data requirements. At this level you simply describe, in diagram form, the entities, attributes, and relationships that occur in the system to be conceptualized and whose semantics are definable in a data dictionary. Specialized constructs, such as "weak" entities or mandatory/optional existence notation, are also usually included in the simple form. But very little else is included, in order to avoid cluttering up the ER diagram while the designer's and end user's understandings of the model are being reconciled.

An example of a simple form of ER model is shown in Figure 1.1. We use the Chen notation for this example and throughout the rest of this book because it is the most common form in the literature today. In this example we want to keep track of videotapes and customers in a video store. Videos and customers are represented as entities Video and Customer, and the relationship "rents" shows a many-to-many association between them. Both Video and Customer entities have a few attributes that describe their characteristics, and the relationship "rents" has an attribute due date that represents the due date for a particular video rented by a specific customer.

From the database practitioner's standpoint, the simple form of the ER model is the preferred form for both database modeling and end-user verification. It is easy to learn and it is applicable to a wide variety of design problems we might encounter in industry and small businesses. We will also see that the simple form is easily translatable into SQL data definitions, and thus it has an immediate use as an aid for database implementation.

The complex level of ER model definition includes concepts that go far beyond the original model. It includes concepts from the semantic models of artificial intelligence and from competing conceptual data models such as the binary relationship model and NIAM methodology (see Chapter 2 for an overview of some NIAM concepts). ER modeling at this level helps the database designer capture more semantics without having to resort to narrative explanations. It is also useful to the database application programmer because certain integrity constraints defined in the ER model relate directly to code—code that checks range limits on data values and null values, for example. However, such detail in very large ER diagrams actually detracts from end-user understanding. Therefore, the simple level is recommended as a communication tool for database design verification.

1.3 The Database Life Cycle

The database life cycle incorporates the basic steps involved in designing a global schema of the logical database, allocating data across a computer network, and defining local DBMS-specific schemas. Once the design is completed, the life cycle continues with database implementation and maintenance. This chapter contains an overview of the database life cycle. In succeeding chapters we will focus on the database design process from the modeling of requirements through distributed data allocation (steps I through IV below). We illustrate the result of each step of the life cycle with a series of diagrams in Figures 1.2 through 1.4. Each diagram shows a possible form of the output of each step so the reader can see the progression of the design process from an idea to actual database implementation. These forms are discussed in much more detail in succeeding chapters.

I. *Requirements analysis.* The database requirements are determined by interviewing both the producers and users of data and producing a formal requirements specification. That specification includes the data required for processing, the natural data relationships, and the software platform for the database implementation. As an example, Figure 1.2 (step I) shows the concepts of products, customers, salespersons, and

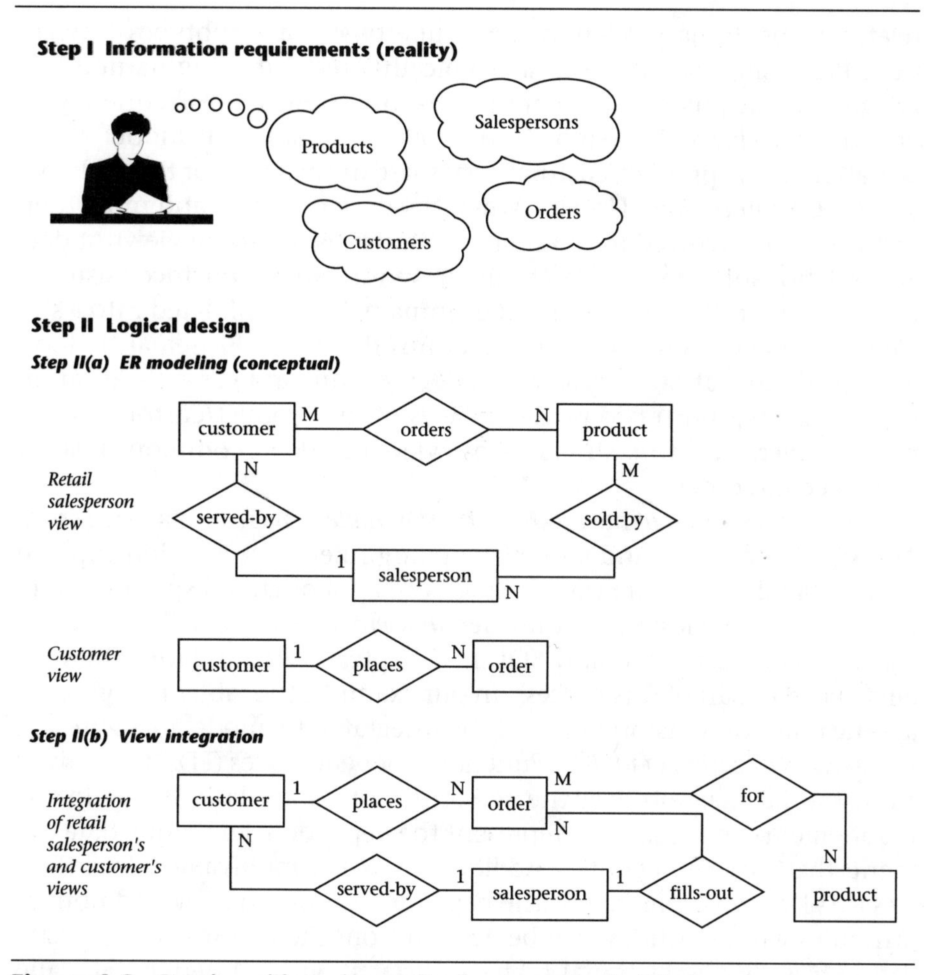

Figure 1.2 Database life cycle: requirements and logical design

orders being formulated in the mind of the end user during the interview process.

II. *Logical design.* The *global schema*, which shows all the data and their relationships, is developed using conceptual data modeling techniques such as ER. The data model constructs must ultimately be transformed into normalized (global) relations, or tables. The global schema development methodology is the same for either a distributed or centralized database.

a. *ER modeling.* The data requirements are analyzed and modeled by using an ER diagram that includes, for example, semantics for optional relationships, ternary relationships, supertypes, and subtypes (categories). Processing requirements are typically specified using natural language expressions or SQL commands along with the frequency of occurrence. Figure 1.2 (step II(a)) shows a possible ER model representation of the product/customer database in the mind of the end user.

b. *View integration.* Usually, when the design is large and more than one person is involved in requirements analysis, multiple views of data and relationships result. To eliminate redundancy and inconsistency from the model, these views must eventually be consolidated into a single global view. View integration requires the use of ER semantic tools such as identification of synonyms, aggregation, and generalization. In Figure 1.2 (step II(b)) two possible views of the product/customer database are merged into a single global view based on common data for customer and order.

c. *Transformation of the ER model to SQL tables.* Based on a categorization of ER constructs and a set of mapping rules, each relationship and its associated entities are transformed into a set of DBMS-specific candidate relational tables, called the *external user schema.* We will show these transformations in standard SQL in Chapter 4. Redundant tables are eliminated as part of this process. In our example, the tables in Figure 1.3 are the result of transformation of the integrated ER model in Figure 1.2.

d. *Normalization of tables.* Functional dependencies (FDs) are derived from the ER diagram and the semantics of data relationships in the requirements analysis. They represent the dependencies among data elements that are keys of entities. Additional FDs and multivalued dependencies (MVDs), which represent the dependencies among key and nonkey attributes within entities, can be derived from the requirements specification. Candidate relational tables associated with all derived FDs and MVDs are normalized (i.e., modified by decomposing or splitting tables into smaller tables) to the highest degree desired using standard normalization techniques. Finally, redundancies in the data that occur in normalized candidate tables are analyzed further for possible elimination, with the constraint that data integrity must be preserved. An example of normalization of the Salesperson table into the new Salesperson and Sales-vacations tables from step II(c) to step II(d) is shown in Figure 1.3.

III. *Physical design.* The last step in the design phase for centralized databases is to produce a physical structure for the database. The physical design step involves the selection of indexes (access methods) and clustering of data. The logical design methodology in step II simplifies the approach to designing large relational databases by reducing the number

Step II(c) Transformation of the ER diagram to SQL tables

Customer

cust-no	cust-name	. . .

Product

prod-no	prod-name	qty-in-stock

```
create table customer
    (cust_no integer,
    cust_name char(15),
    cust_addr char(30),
    sales_name char(15),
    prod_no integer,
    primary key (cust_no),
    foreign key (sales_name)
        references salesperson,
    foreign key (prod_no)
        references product);
```

job-level	vacation-days

ust-no

Order-product

order-no	prod-no

. tables

oval of update anomalies

job-level

Sales-vacations

job-level	vacation-days

:luding denormalization)

Customer / refined

cust-no	cust-name	sales-name

st-no

Physical design parameters:
indexing, access methods, clustering

Figure 1.3 Database life cycle: ER-to-SQL, normalization, and physical design

of data dependencies that need to be analyzed. This is accomplished by inserting ER modeling and integration steps (steps II(a) and II(b)) into the traditional relational design approach. The objective of these steps is an accurate representation of reality. Data integrity is preserved through normalization of the candidate tables created when the ER model is transformed into a relational model. The purpose of physical design is to then optimize performance as closely as possible.

As part of the physical design, the global schema can sometimes be refined in limited ways to reflect processing (query and transaction) requirements if there are obvious large gains to be made in efficiency. This is called *denormalization*. It consists of selecting dominant processes on the basis of high frequency, high volume, or explicit priority; defining simple extensions to tables that will improve query performance; evaluating total cost for query, update, and storage; and considering the side effects, such as possible loss of integrity. Denormalization is illustrated in Figure 1.3 (step III), with the extension of the Customer table to include "sales-name" for greater efficiency with database queries such as "Who is the salesperson for a customer named Pamela Wilson?"

IV. *Data distribution.* Data fragmentation and allocation are also forms of physical design because they must take into account the physical environment, that is, the network configuration. This applies only to distributed databases.

A *fragmentation schema* describes the one-to-many mapping used to partition each global table into fragments. Fragments are logical portions of global tables that are physically located at one or several sites of the network. A data *allocation schema* designates where each copy of each fragment is to be stored. A one-to-one mapping in the allocation schema results in nonredundancy; a one-to-many mapping defines a replicated distributed database. An example of the allocation of a fragmented and partially replicated database is shown in Figure 1.4, where various subsets of the whole database are allocated to different sites in a computer network.

Three important objectives of data distribution are

- the separation of data fragmentation and allocation,
- control of redundancy, and
- independence from local database management systems.

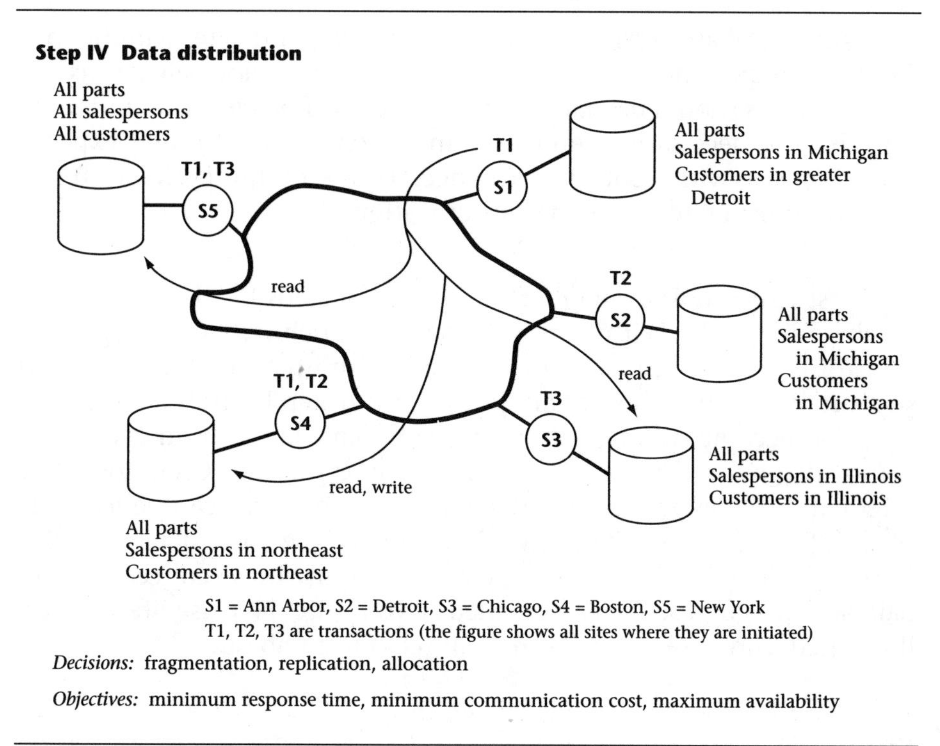

Figure 1.4 Database life cycle: data distribution

The distinction between designing the fragmentation and allocation schema is important: The first one is a logical, the second a physical mapping. In general, it is not possible to determine the optimal fragmentation and allocation by solving the two problems independently since they are interrelated. However, near-optimal solutions can be obtained with separable design steps, and this is the only practical solution available today.

V. ***Database implementation, monitoring, and modification.*** Once the design is completed, the database can be created through implementation of the formal schema using the data definition language (DDL) of a DBMS. Then the data manipulation language (DML) can be used to query and update the database, as well as to set up indexes and establish constraints such as referential integrity. The language SQL contains both DDL and DML constructs; for example, the "create table" command represents DDL, and the "select" command represents DML.

As the database begins operation, monitoring indicates whether performance requirements are being met. If they are not being satisfied, modifications should be made to improve performance. Other modifications may be necessary when requirements change or end-user expectations increase with good performance. Thus, the life cycle continues with monitoring, redesign, and modifications.

Most CASE tools available today focus on steps II, III, and V of the database life cycle. Within step II, the ER modeling, view integration, transformation to SQL, and normalization substeps are all commonly supported by many (but not all) tools. Within step III, transaction modeling has become commonplace, and automatic application generation is provided by some tools. An excellent survey of both CASE tools that offer database design and purely database design tools can be found in [BCN92]. In the next chapter we look first at the basic data modeling concepts, then—starting in Chapter 3—we apply these concepts to the database design process. The detailed steps in the database life cycle are illustrated using examples taken from real-life databases.

1.4 Summary

Knowledge of data modeling and database design techniques is important for database practitioners. Among the variety of data modeling approaches, the ER model is arguably the most popular in use today because of its simplicity and readability. A simple form of the ER model is used in most CASE tools and is easy to learn and apply to a variety of industrial and business applications. It is also a very useful tool for communicating with the end user about the conceptual model and for verifying the assumptions made in the modeling process. A more complex form, a superset of the simple form, is useful for the more experienced designer who wants to capture greater semantic detail in diagram form and avoid having to write long and tedious narrative to explain certain requirements and constraints over and over again.

The database life cycle shows what steps are needed in a methodical approach to database design from logical design, which is independent of the system environment, to local physical design, which is based on the details of the database management system chosen to implement the database, and to data distribution in a computer network.

Literature Summary

Much of the early data modeling work was done by Bachman, Chen, Nijssen, Senko, and others [Bach69, Bach72, Senk73, Chen76]. Database design textbooks that adhere to a significant portion of the relational database life cycle described in this chapter are [TeFr82, Yao85, Wied87, Flvo89, Hawr90, BCN92, CBS96, Hern97]. For recent general textbooks on database systems, consult [Maci89, Mitt91, ElNa94, ONei94, Date95, Kroe95, SiTe95, BoSa96, KSS97, Rama97, UlWi97]. Some of the early research in CASE tools for the ER model was done by [TeHe77, CFT84, Rein85, BCN92]; more up-to-date surveys on CASE tools can be found in recent issues of *DBMS* or *Database Programming and Design.*

[Bach69] Bachman, C.W. "Data Structure Diagrams," *Database* 1, 2 (1969), pp. 4–10.

[Bach72] Bachman, C.W. "The Evolution of Storage Structures," *Comm. ACM* 15, 7 (July 1972), pp. 628–634.

[BCN92] Batini, C., Ceri, S., and Navathe, S. *Conceptual Database Design: An Entity-Relationship Approach,* Benjamin/Cummings, Redwood City, CA, 1992.

[BoSa96] Bontempo, C.J., and Saracco, C. *Database Management: Principles and Products,* Prentice Hall, Upper Saddle River, NJ, 1996.

[CBS96] Connolly, T., Begg, C., and Strachan, A. *Database Systems: A Practical Approach to Design, Implementation, and Management: Version 2,* Addison-Wesley, Reading, MA, 1996.

[CFT84] Cobb, R.E., Fry, J.P., and Teorey, T.J. "The Database Designer's Workbench," *Information Sciences* 32, 1 (Feb. 1984), pp. 33–45.

[Chen76] Chen, P.P. "The Entity-Relationship Model—Toward a Unified View of Data," *ACM Trans. Database Systems* 1, 1 (March 1976), pp. 9–36.

[Codd90] Codd, E.F. *The Relational Model for Database Management,* Version 2, Addison-Wesley, Reading, MA, 1990.

[Date89] Date, C.J. *A Guide to the SQL Standard* (2nd Ed.), Addison-Wesley, Reading, MA, 1989.

[Date95] Date, C.J. *An Introduction to Database Systems,* Vol. 1 (6th Ed.), Addison-Wesley, Reading, MA, 1995.

[ElNa94] Elmasri, R., and Navathe, S.B. *Fundamentals of Database Systems* (2nd Ed.), Benjamin/Cummings, Redwood City, CA, 1994.

[FlvH89] Fleming, C.C., and von Halle, B. *Handbook of Relational Database Design,* Addison-Wesley, Reading, MA, 1989.

[Hawr90] Hawryszkiewycz, I. *Relational Database Design,* Prentice Hall, Upper Saddle River, NJ 1990.

[Hern97] Hernandez, M.J. *Database Design for Mere Mortals,* Addison-Wesley, Reading, MA, 1997.

[Kroe95] Kroenke, D.M. *Database Processing: Fundamentals, Design, and Implementation* (5th Ed.), Prentice Hall, Upper Saddle River, NJ, 1995.

[KSS97] Korth, H.F., Silberschatz, A., and Sudarshan, S. *Database System Concepts* (3rd Ed.), McGraw-Hill, New York, 1997.

[Maci89] Maciaszek, L. *Database Design and Implementation,* Prentice Hall, Upper Saddle River, NJ, 1989.

[Mitt91] Mittra, S.S. *Principles of Relational Database Systems,* Prentice Hall, Upper Saddle River, NJ, 1991.

[ONei94] O'Neil, P. *Database: Principles, Programming, Practice,* Morgan Kaufmann, San Francisco, 1994.

[Rama97] Ramakrishnan, R. *Database Management Systems,* McGraw-Hill, New York, 1997.

[Rein85] Reiner, D., Brodie, M., Brown, G., Friedell, M., Kramlich, D., Lehman, J., and Rosenthal, A. "The Database Design and Evaluation Workbench (DDEW) Project at CCA," *Database Engineering* 7, 4 (1985), pp. 10–15.

[Senk73] Senko et al. "Data Structures and Accessing in Data-base Systems," *IBM Syst. J.* 12, 1 (1973), pp. 30–93.

[SiTe95] Simovici, D.A., and Tenney, R.L. *Relational Database Systems,* Academic Press, San Diego, CA, 1995.

[TeFr82] Teorey, T., and Fry, J. *Design of Database Structures,* Prentice Hall, Upper Saddle River, NJ, 1982.

[TeHe77] Teichroew, D., and Hershey, E.A. "PSL/PSA: A Computer Aided Technique for Structured Documentation and Analysis of Information Processing Systems," *IEEE Trans. Software Engr.* SE-3, 1 (1977), pp. 41–48.

[UlWi97] Ullman, J., and Widom, J. *A First Course in Database Systems,* Prentice Hall, Upper Saddle River, NJ, 1997.

[Wied87] Wiederhold, G. *File Organization for Database Design,* McGraw-Hill, New York, 1987.

[Yao85] Yao, S.B. (editor). *Principles of Database Design,* Prentice Hall, Upper Saddle River, NJ, 1985.

The ER Model: Basic Concepts

This chapter defines all the major entity-relationship concepts that can be applied to the database life cycle. In Section 2.1, we will look at the simple level of ER modeling described in the original work by Chen and extended by others. In particular, we will use the Chen ER notation throughout the text. The simple form of the ER model is used as the basis for effective communication with the end user about the conceptual database. Section 2.2 presents the more advanced concepts that are less generally accepted but useful to describe certain semantics that cannot be constructed with the simple model.

2.1 Fundamental ER Constructs

2.1.1 Basic Objects: Entities, Relationships, Attributes

The basic ER model consists of three classes of objects: entities, relationships, and attributes.

Entities

Entities are the principal data objects about which information is to be collected; they usually denote a person, place, thing, or event of informational interest. (This book drops the older term "entity set" and uses entities to represent entity types.) A particular occurrence of an entity is called an *entity instance*, or sometimes an *entity occurrence*. In our example, employee, department, division, project, skill, and location are all

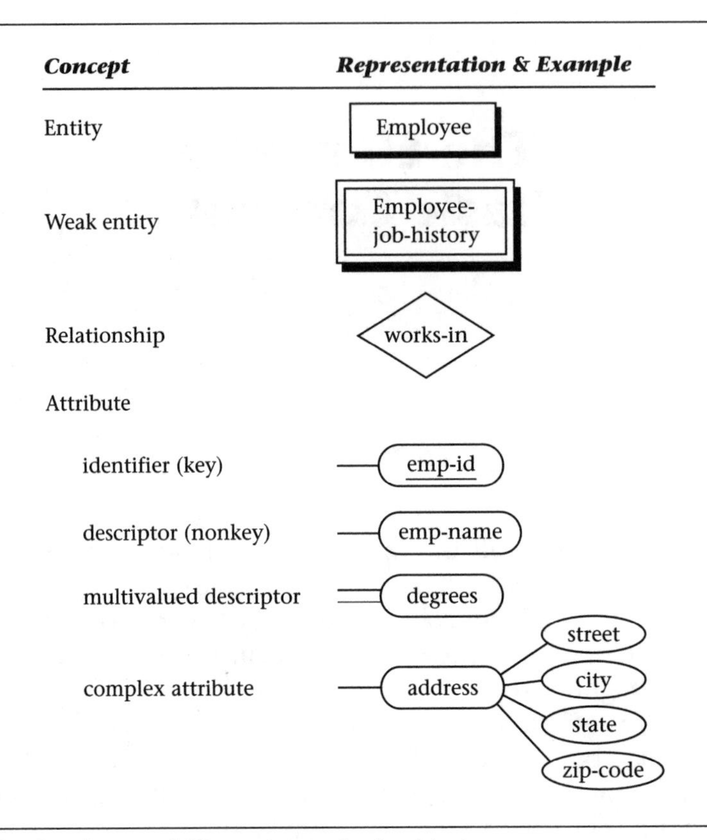

Figure 2. Fundamental ER constructs: basic objects

examples of entities. For easy reference, entity names will henceforth be capitalized throughout this text: Employee, Department, and so forth. The entity construct is a rectangle as depicted in Figure 2.1. The entity name is written inside the rectangle.

Relationships

Relationships represent real-world associations among one or more entities, and as such, have no physical or conceptual existence other than that which depends upon their entity associations. A particular occurrence of a relationship is called a *relationship instance* or, sometimes, *relationship occurrence*. Relationships are described in terms of degree, connectivity, and existence. These terms are defined in the sections that follow. The most common meaning associated with the term *relationship* is indicated by the connectivity between entity occurrences: one-to-one,

one-to-many, and many-to-many. The relationship construct is a diamond that connects the associated entities, as shown in Figure 2.1. The relationship name is written inside the diamond.

A *role* is the name of one end of a relationship when each end needs a distinct name for clarity of the relationship. In most of the examples given in Figure 2.2, role names are not required because the entity names combined with the relationship name clearly define the individual roles of each entity in the relationship. However, in some cases role names should be used to clarify ambiguities. For example, in the first case in Figure 2.2, the recursive binary relationship "manages" uses two roles, "manager" and "managed," to associate the proper connectivities with the two different roles of the single entity. Role names are typically nouns.

Attributes

Attributes are characteristics of entities that provide descriptive detail about them. A particular occurrence of an attribute within an entity or relationship is called an attribute value. Attributes of an entity such as Employee may include emp-id, emp-name, emp-address, phone-no, fax-no, job-title, and so on. The attribute construct is an ellipse with the attribute name inside (or oblong as shown in Figure 2.1). The attribute is connected to the entity it characterizes.

There are two types of attributes: identifiers and descriptors. An identifier (or key) is used to uniquely determine an instance of an entity; a descriptor (or nonkey attribute) is used to specify a nonunique characteristic of a particular entity instance. Both identifiers and descriptors may consist of either a single attribute or some composite of attributes. For example, an identifier or key of Employee is emp-id, and a descriptor of Employee is emp-name or job-title. Key attributes are underlined in the ER diagram, as shown in Figure 2.1.

Some attributes, such as specialty-area, may be multivalued. The notation for multivalued attributes is shown with a double attachment line, as shown in Figure 2.1. Other attributes may be complex, such as an address that further subdivides into street, city, state, and zip code. Complex attributes are constructed to have attributes of their own; sometimes, however, the individual parts of a complex attribute are specified as individual attributes in the first place. Either form is reasonable in ER notation.

Entities have internal identifiers that uniquely determine the existence of entity instances, but weak entities derive their identity from the

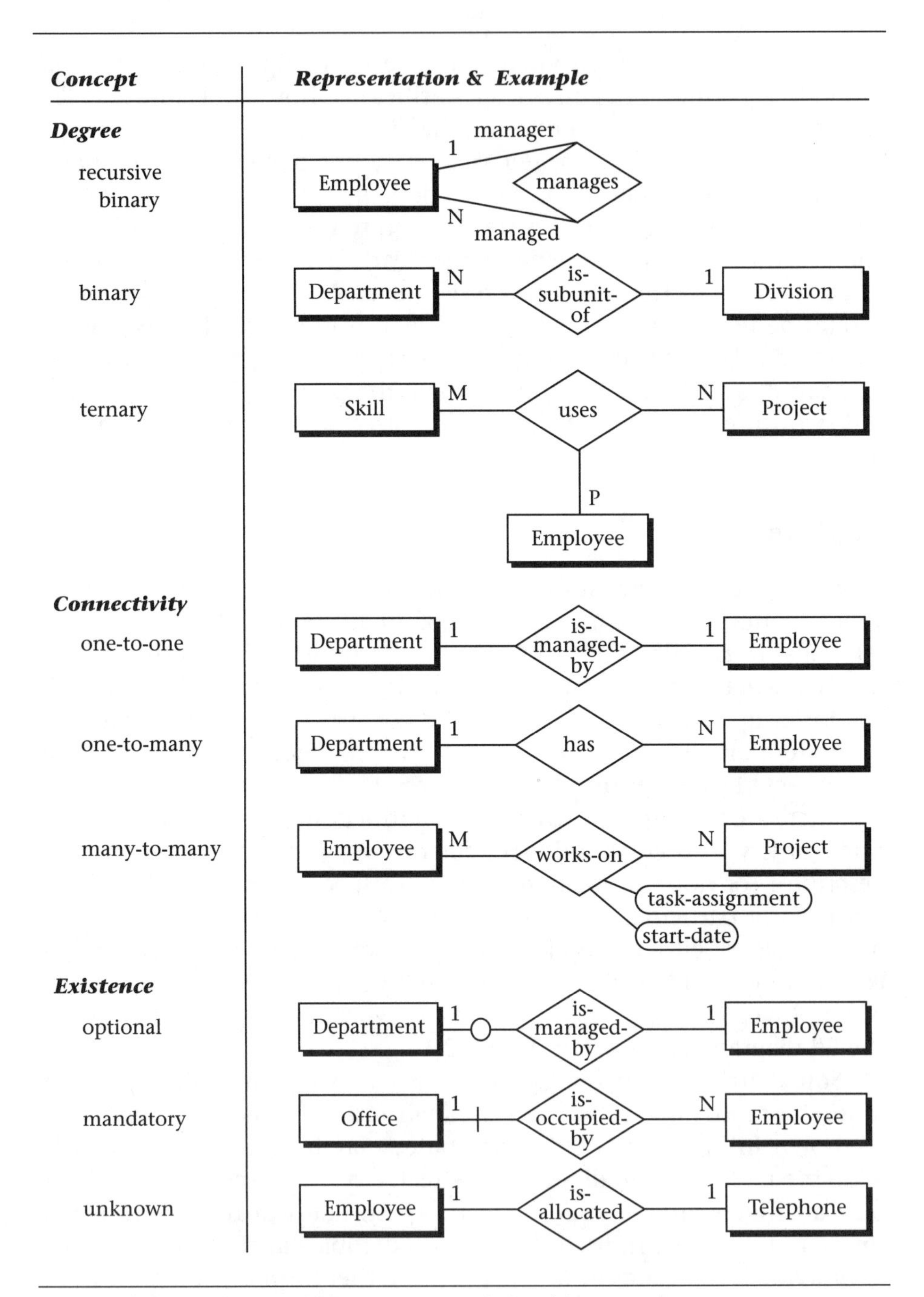

Figure 2.2 Fundamental ER constructs: relationship types

identifying attributes of one or more "parent" entities. Weak entities are often depicted with a double-bordered rectangle (see Figure 2.1), which denotes that all occurrences of that entity are dependent for their existence in the database on an associated (strong) entity. For example, in Figure 2.1, the weak entity Employee-job-history is related to the entity Employee and dependent upon Employee for its own existence. Another typical form for a weak entity is a multivalued attribute associated with an entity or a many-to-many relationship between two entities, so that the identity dependence is more obvious. As an example, in Figure 2.2 the relationship "works-on" between Employee and Project could be redefined as a weak entity Works-on, having a one-to-many relationship with Employee and a one-to-many relationship to Project. Note that Works-on must be the "many" side of each of the two new relationships (see Section 2.1.3).

2.1.2 Degree of a Relationship

The degree of a relationship is the number of entities associated in the relationship. Binary and ternary relationships are special cases where the degree is 2 and 3, respectively. An n-ary relationship is the general form for any degree n. The notation for degree is illustrated in Figure 2.2.

The binary relationship, an association between two entities, is by far the most common type in the natural world. In fact, many modeling systems use only this type. In Figure 2.2 we see many examples of the association of two entities in different ways: Division and Department, Department and Employee, Employee and Project, and so on. A binary recursive relationship—for example, "manages" in Figure 2.2—relates a particular Employee to another Employee by management. It is called recursive because the entity relates only to another instance of its own type. The binary recursive relationship construct is a diamond with both connections to the same entity.

A ternary relationship is an association among three entities. This type of relationship is required when binary relationships are not sufficient to accurately describe the semantics of the association. The ternary relationship construct is a single diamond connected to three entities as shown in Figure 2.2. Sometimes a relationship is mistakenly modeled as ternary when it could be decomposed into two or three equivalent binary relationships. When this occurs, the ternary relationship should be eliminated to achieve both simplicity and semantic purity. Ternary relationships are discussed in greater detail in Sections 2.2.3 and 5.5.

An entity may be involved in any number of relationships, and each relationship may be of any degree. Furthermore, any two entities may have any number of binary relationships between them, and so on for any n entities (see n-ary relationships defined in Section 2.2.4).

2.1.3 Connectivity of a Relationship

The *connectivity* of a relationship describes a constraint on the mapping of the associated entity occurrences in the relationship. Values for connectivity are either "one" or "many." For a relationship between entities Department and Employee, a connectivity of one for Department and many for Employee means that there is at most one entity occurrence of Department associated with many occurrences of Employee. The actual count of elements associated with the connectivity is called the *cardinality* of the relationship connectivity; it is used much less frequently than the connectivity constraint because the actual values are usually variable across relationship instances.

Figure 2.2 shows the basic constructs for connectivity for binary relationships: one-to-one, one-to-many, and many-to-many. On the "one" side, the number 1 is shown on the connection between the relationship and one of the entities, and on the "many" side, the letter N (and sometimes another letter like M or P) is used on the connection between the relationship and the entity to designate the concept of many. In the one-to-one case, the entity Department is managed by exactly one Employee and each Employee manages exactly one Department. Therefore, the minimum and maximum connectivities on the "is-managed-by" relationship are exactly one for both Department and Employee.

In the one-to-many case, the entity Department is associated with ("has") many Employees. The maximum connectivity is given on the Employee (many) side as the unknown value N, but the minimum connectivity is known as one. On the Department side the minimum and maximum connectivities are both one, that is, each Employee works within exactly one Department.

In the many-to-many case, the entity Employee may work on many Projects and each Project may have many Employees. We see that the maximum connectivity for Employee and Project is M and N, respectively, and the minimum connectivities are each defined as 1.

Some situations are such that the actual maximum connectivity is known. Let us assume, for example, in Figure 2.2 that the entity Employee in the many-to-many relationship may be a member of a maximum of three Projects (N = 3); thus, the maximum connectivity is 3 on the Project side of the "works-on" relationship. Reading from right to left in the same relationship, we may be told that the entity Project may contain a maximum of 15 Employees (M = 15). Thus, 15 is the maximum connectivity of Employee in the "works-on" relationship. The minimum connectivities in all relationships of any type are either zero or one, depending on whether the relationship is optional or mandatory, respectively (see Section 2.1.5). In this example the minimum connectivities are one for both Employee and Project.

2.1.4 Attributes of a Relationship

Attributes can be assigned to relationships as well as to entities. An attribute of a many-to-many relationship such as the "works-on" relationship between the entities Employee and Project (Figure 2.2) could be "task-assignment" or "start-date." In this case, a given task assignment or start date is common only to an instance of the assignment of a particular Employee to a particular Project, and it would be multivalued when characterizing either the Employee or the Project entity alone. Performance and storage utilization would be optimized at database implementation time by assigning these attributes to the relationship rather than the entities, because each instance of a "task-assignment" associated with an Employee must carry information about the Project with it, creating redundancy of data.

Attributes of relationships are typically assigned only to binary many-to-many relationships and to ternary relationships. Attributes are not normally assigned to one-to-one or one-to-many relationships because at least one side of the relationship is a single entity and there is no ambiguity in assigning the attribute to a particular entity instead of assigning it to the relationship. For example, in the one-to-many binary relationship between Department and Employee, an attribute "start-date" could be applied to Department to designate the start date for that department, or to Employee to be an attribute for each Employee instance to designate the employee's start date in that department. If the relationship changes to many-to-many, so that an employee can belong to many departments, then the attribute "start-date" must shift to the relationship so that each instance of the relationship that matches one employee with one department can have a unique start date for that employee in that department.

2.1.5 Existence of an Entity in a Relationship

Some enterprises have entities whose existence depends on the existence of another entity. This is called *existence dependency*, or just *existence*. Existence of an entity in a relationship is defined as either mandatory or optional. If an occurrence of either the "one" or "many" side entity must always exist for the entity to be included in the relationship, then it is mandatory. When an occurrence of that entity need not exist, it is considered optional. For example, in Figure 2.2 the entity Employee may or may not be the manager of any Department, thus making the entity Department in the "is-managed-by" relationship between Employee and Department optional.

Optional existence, defined by a 0 on the connection line between an entity and a relationship, defines a minimum connectivity of zero. *Mandatory existence*, defined by a line perpendicular to the connection line between an entity and a relationship, defines a minimum connectivity of one. If neither a 0 nor a perpendicular line is shown on the connection line between a relationship and an entity, then the type of existence, optional or mandatory, is unknown. For example, in Figure 2.2 it is not known whether all employees at a given instant are allocated a telephone, but normally each employee has one. When existence is unknown, we assume the minimum connectivity is one.

Maximum connectivities are defined explicitly on the ER diagram as a constant (if a number is shown on the ER diagram next to an entity) or a variable (by default if no number is shown on the ER diagram next to an entity). For example, in Figure 2.2 the relationship "is-occupied-by" between the entity Office and Employee implies that an Office may house from zero to some variable maximum (N) number of Employees, but an Employee must be housed in exactly one Office, that is, mandatory.

Existence is often implicit in the real world. For example, an entity Employee associated with a dependent (weak) entity, Dependent, cannot be optional, but the weak entity is usually optional. Using the concept of optional existence, an entity instance may be able to exist in other relationships even though it is not participating in this particular relationship.

2.1.6 Alternative ER Notations

At this point we need to digress briefly to look at other ER notations that are commonly used today and compare them with the Chen approach selected for this book. A popular alternative form for one-to-many and

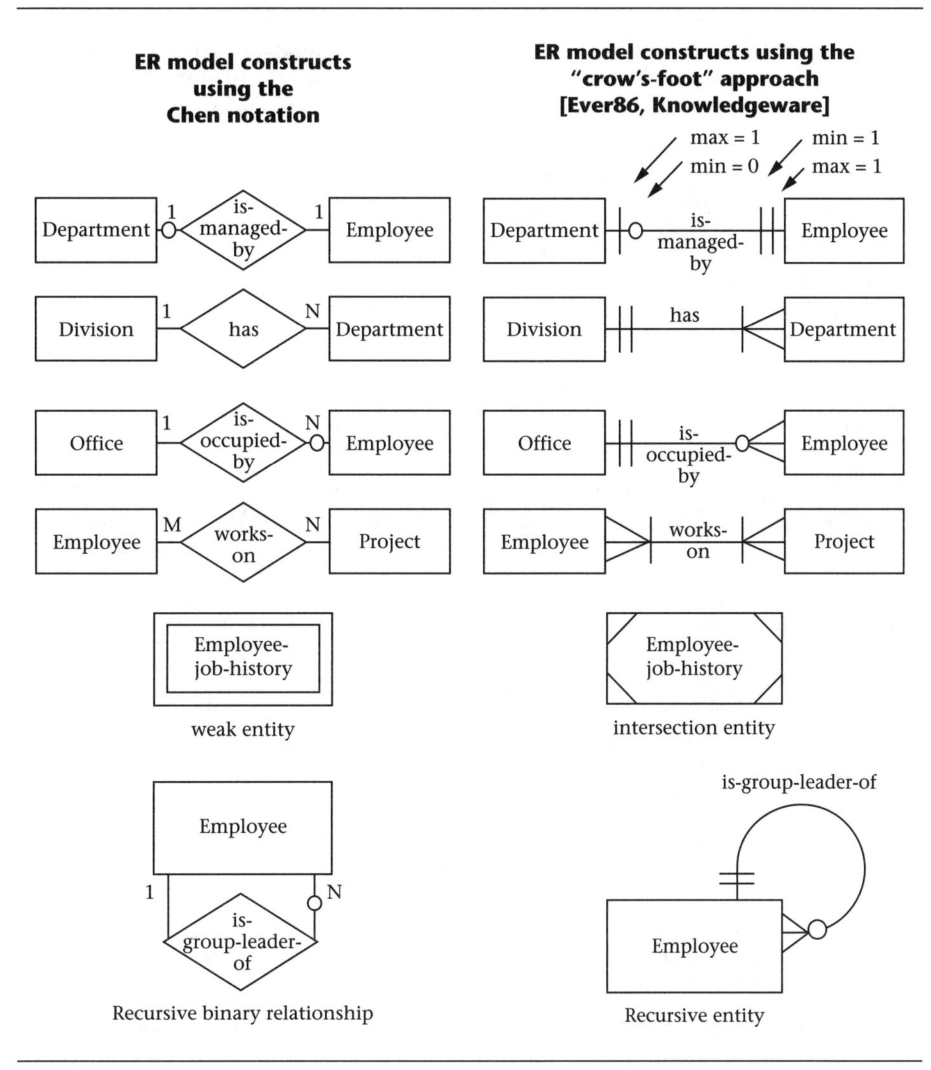

Figure 2.3a Comparison of ER construct conventions: Chen versus crow's-foot

many-to-many relationships uses "crow's-foot" notation for the "many" side (see Figure 2.3a). This form was popularized by Gordon Everest [Ever86] and used by some CASE tools such as Knowledgeware's Information Engineering Workbench (IEW). Relationships have no explicit construct but are implied by the connection line between entities and a relationship name on the connection line. Minimum connectivity is specified by either a 0 (for zero) or perpendicular line (for one) on the connection lines between entities. The term *intersection entity* is used to

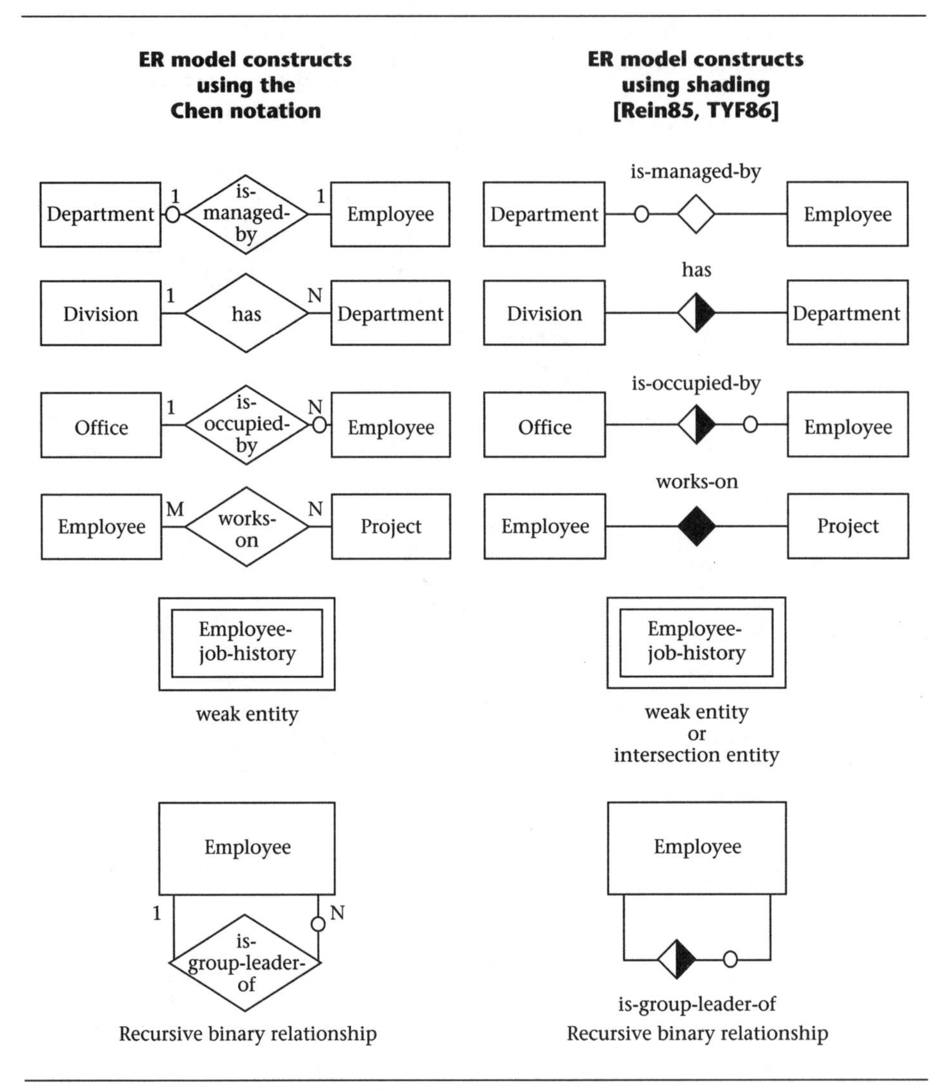

Figure 2.3b Comparison of ER construct conventions: Chen versus shading

designate a weak entity, especially an entity that is equivalent to a many-to-many relationship.

Connectivity in the ER model is sometimes expressed by the relationship shading approach in [Rein85,TYF86]. The shaded side of the relationship diamond implies "many" and the unshaded side implies "one." The circle on the connection line between a relationship and entity denotes optional existence of a particular entity instance; mandatory exis-

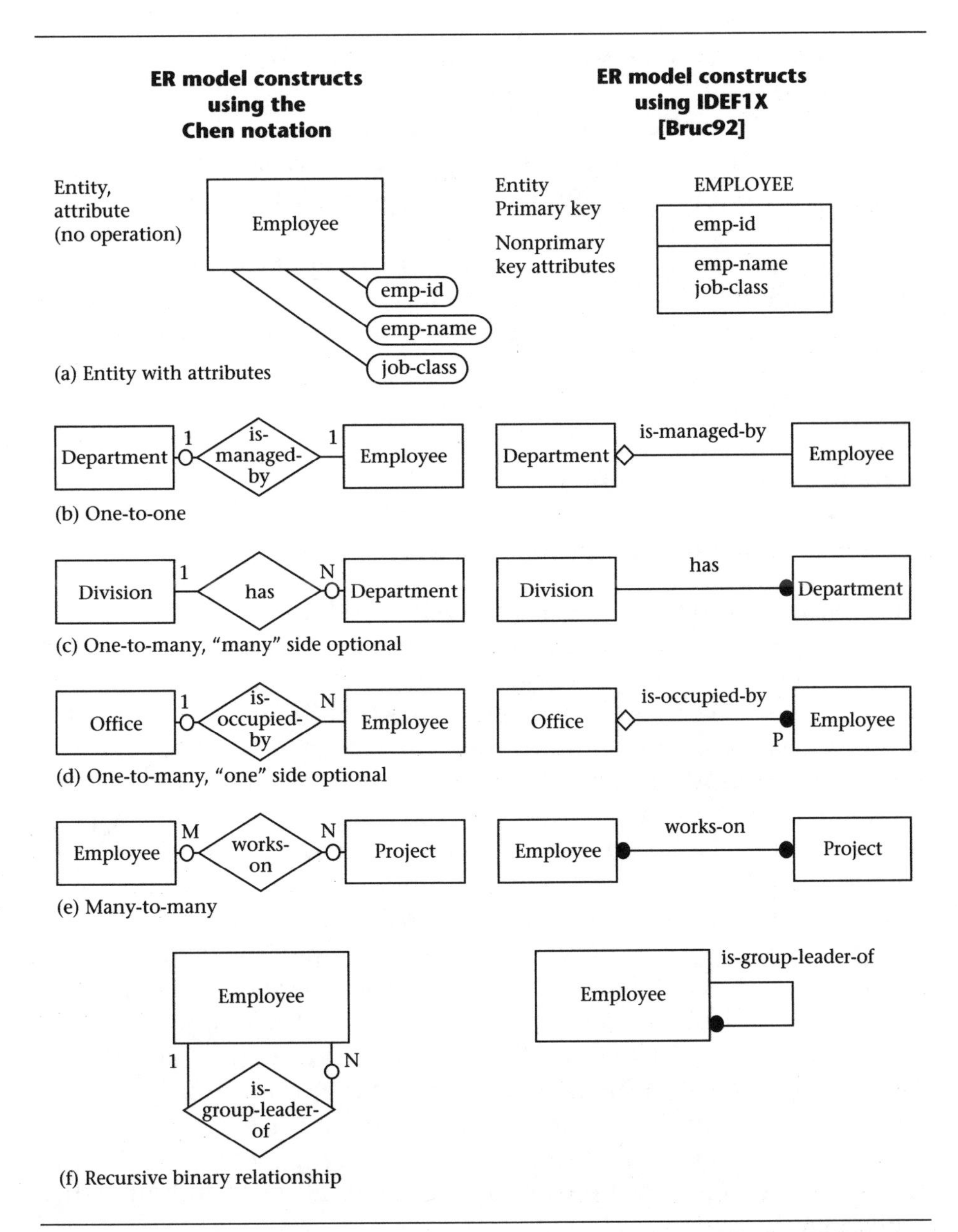

Figure 2.3c Comparison of ER construct conventions: Chen versus IDEF1X

tence is implied by the absence of the optional symbol. The constructs for entities, weak entities, and attributes are basically the same as in the Chen notation (see Figure 2.3b). Another popular form used today is the

IDEF1X notation, conceived by Robert G. Brown [Bruc92]. The similarities with the Chen notation are obvious from Figure 2.3c.

Fortunately, any of these forms is reasonably easy to learn and read, and the equivalence for the basic ER concepts is obvious from the diagrams. Without a standard for the ER model, however, many other constructs are being used today in addition to the three types shown here. Although standards efforts are currently under way, it will be years before standardization will be achieved, if ever. Developers of new CASE tools would certainly benefit from standardization, and in turn most database developers should welcome it.

2.2 Advanced ER Constructs

2.2.1 Generalization: Supertypes and Subtypes

The original ER model has been effectively used for communicating fundamental data and relationship definitions with the end user for a long time. However, using it to develop and integrate conceptual models with different end-user views was severely limited until it could be extended to include database abstraction concepts such as generalization. The *generalization* relationship specifies that several types of entities with certain common attributes can be generalized into a higher-level entity type: a generic or superclass entity, which is more commonly known as a *supertype* entity. The lower levels of entities—*subtypes* in a generalization hierarchy—can be either disjoint or overlapping subsets of the supertype entity. As an example, in Figure 2.4 the entity Employee is a higher-level abstraction of Manager, Engineer, Technician, and Secretary—all of which are disjoint types of Employee. The ER model construct for the generalization abstraction is the connection of a supertype entity with its subtypes using a circle and the subset symbol on the connecting lines from the circle to the subtype entities. The circle contains a letter specifying a disjointness constraint (see following discussion). *Specialization* is the same concept, but it is the reverse of generalization; it indicates that subtypes specialize the supertype.

A supertype entity in one relationship may be a subtype entity in another relationship. When a combination of supertype/subtype relationships comprise a structure, the structure is called a *supertype/subtype hierarchy*, or *generalization hierarchy*. Generalization can also be described in terms of inheritance, which specifies that all the attributes of a super-

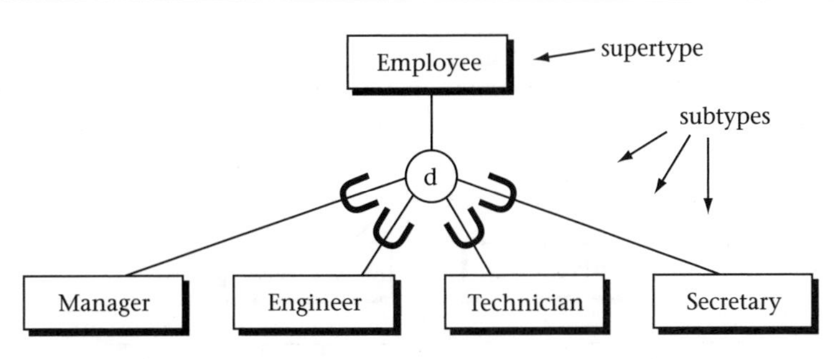

(a) Generalization with disjoint subtypes

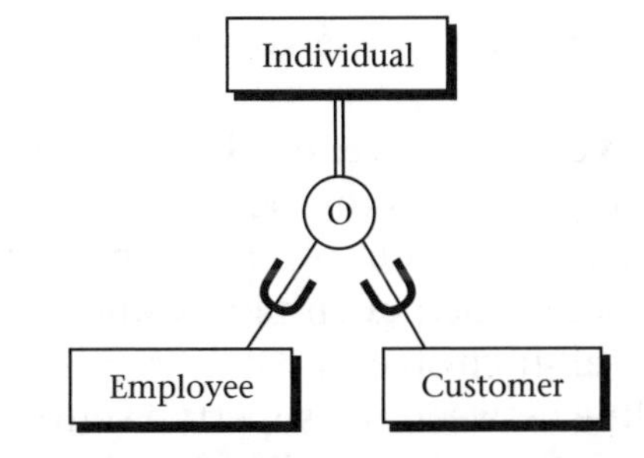

(b) Generalization with overlapping subtypes and completeness constraint

Figure 2.4 Generalization

type are propagated down the hierarchy to entities of a lower type. Generalization may occur when a generic entity, which we call the supertype entity, is partitioned by different values of a common attribute. For example, in Figure 2.4 the entity Employee is a generalization of Manager, Engineer, Technician, and Secretary over the attribute "job-title" in Employee.

Generalization can be further classified by two important constraints on the subtype entities: *disjointness* and *completeness*. The disjointness constraint requires the subtype entities to be mutually exclusive. We denote this type of constraint by the letter "d" written inside the generalization circle (Figure 2.4a). Subtypes that are not disjoint (i.e., overlapping) are designated by using the letter "o" inside the circle. As an example, with the supertype entity Individual that has two subtype entities, Employee and Customer, the subtypes could be described as overlapping or not mutually exclusive (Figure 2.4b). Regardless of whether the subtypes are disjoint or overlapping, they may have additional

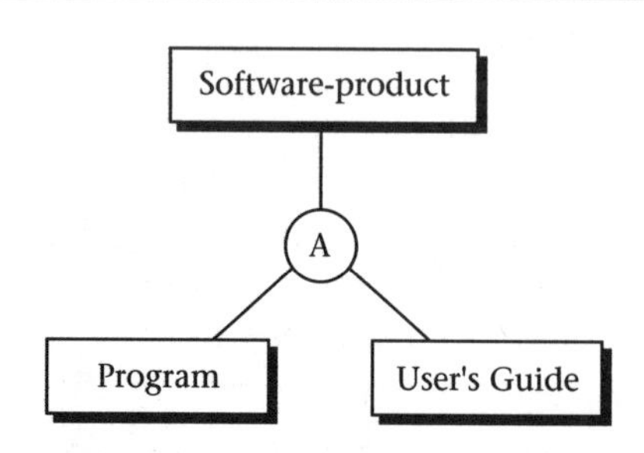

Figure 2.5 Aggregation

special attributes in addition to the generic (inherited) attributes from the supertype.

The completeness constraint requires the subtypes to be all-inclusive of the supertype. Thus, subtypes can be defined as either total or partial coverage of the supertype. For example, in a generalization hierarchy with supertype Individual and subtypes Employee and Customer, the subtypes may be described as all-inclusive or total. We denote this type of constraint by a double line between the supertype entity and the circle. This is indicated in Figure 2.4b, which implies that the only types of individuals to be considered in the database are employees and customers.

2.2.2 Aggregation

Aggregation is a form of abstraction between a supertype and subtype entity that is significantly different from the generalization abstraction. Generalization is often described in terms of an "is-a" relationship between the subtype and the supertype—for example, an Employee is an Individual. Aggregation, on the other hand, is the relationship between the whole and its parts and is described as a "part-of" relationship; for example, a report and a prototype software package are both parts of a deliverable for a contract. Thus, in Figure 2.5 the entity Software-product is seen to consist of component parts Program and User's Guide. The construct for aggregation is similar to generalization in that the supertype entity is connected with the subtype entities with a circle; in this case, the letter "A" is shown in the circle. However, there are no subset symbols because the "part-of" relationship is not a subset. Furthermore, there are no inherited attributes in aggregation; each entity has its own unique set of attributes.

2.2.3 Ternary Relationships

Ternary relationships are required when binary relationships are not sufficient to accurately describe the semantics of an association among three entities. Ternary relationships are somewhat more complex than binary relationships, however. The ER notation for a ternary relationship is shown in Figure 2.2 with three entities attached to a single relationship diamond, and the connectivity of each entity is designated as either "one" or "many." An entity in a ternary relationship is considered to be "one" if only one instance of it can be associated with one instance of each of the other two associated entities. It is "many" if more than one instance of it can be associated with one instance of each of the other two associated entities. In either case, one instance of each of the other entities is assumed to be given.

As an example, the relationship "manages" in Figure 2.6c associates the entities Manager, Engineer, and Project. The entities Engineer and Project are considered "many;" the entity Manager is considered "one." This is represented by the following assertions.

Assertion 1: One engineer, working under one manager, could be working on many projects.

Assertion 2: One project, under the direction of one manager, could have many engineers.

Assertion 3: One engineer, working on one project, must have only a single manager.

Assertion 3 could also be written in another form, using an arrow (→) in a kind of shorthand called a *functional dependency*. For example:

emp-id, project-name → mgr-id

where emp-id is the primary key (unique identifier) associated with the entity Engineer, project-name is the primary key associated with the entity Project, and mgr-id is the primary key of the entity Manager. In general, for an n-ary relationship, each entity considered to be a "one" has its key appearing on the right side of exactly one functional dependency (FD). No entity considered "many" ever has its key appear on the right side of an FD.

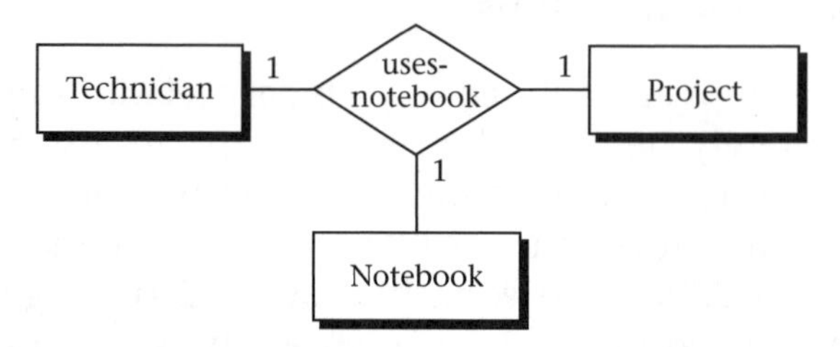

A technician uses exactly one notebook for each project. Each notebook belongs to one technician for each project. Note that a technician may still work on many projects and maintain different notebooks for different projects.

Functional dependencies

emp-id, project-name → notebook-no
emp-id, notebook-no → project-name
project-name, notebook-no → emp-id

(a) One-to-one-to-one ternary relationship

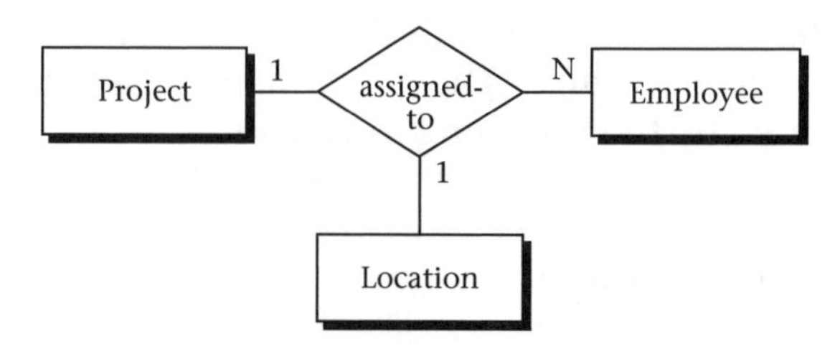

Each employee assigned to a project works at only one location for that project but can be at different locations for different projects. At a particular location, an employee works on only one project and many employees can be assigned to a given project.

Functional dependencies

emp-id, loc-name → project-name
emp-id, project-name → loc-name

(b) One-to-one-to-many ternary relationship

Figure 2.6 Types and properties of ternary relationships

All four forms of ternary relationships are illustrated in Figure 2.6. In each case the number of "one" entities implies the number of FDs used to define the relationship semantics, and the key of each "one" entity appears on the right side of exactly one FD for that relationship.

Ternary relationships can have attributes in the same way as many-to-many binary relationships can. These are attributes whose values are uniquely determined by some combination of the keys of the entities associated with the relationship. For example, in Figure 2.6d the relationship "skill-used" might have the attribute "tool" associated with a

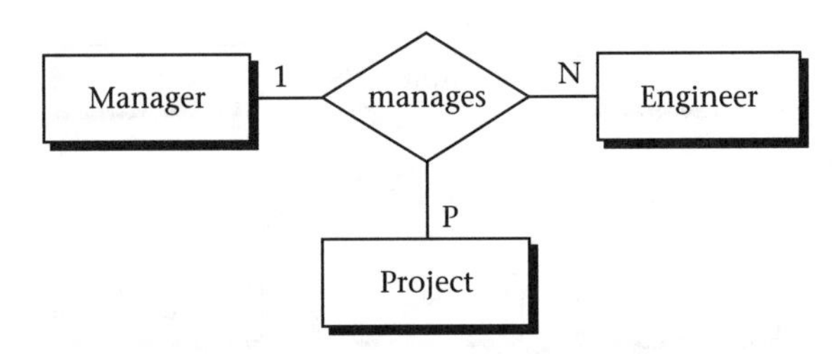

Each engineer working on a particular project has exactly one manager, but each manager of a project may manage many engineers, and each manager of an engineer may manage that engineer on many projects.

Functional dependencies
project-name, emp-id → mgr-id

(c) One-to-many-to-many ternary relationship

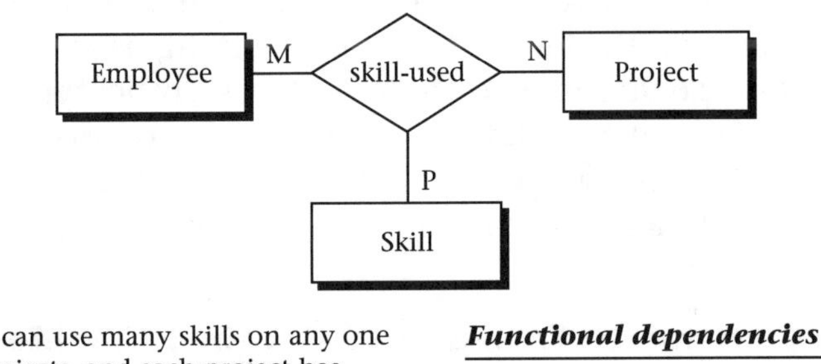

Employees can use many skills on any one of many projects, and each project has many employees with various skills.

Functional dependencies
none

(d) Many-to-many-to-many ternary relationship

Figure 2.6 *Continued*

given employee using a particular skill on a certain project, indicating that a value for tool is uniquely determined by the combination of employee, skill, and project.

2.2.4 General n-ary Relationships

Generalizing the ternary form to higher-degree relationships, an n-ary relationship that describes some association among n entities is represented by a single relationship diamond with n connections, one to each entity (see Figure 2.7). The meaning of this form can be best described in terms of the functional dependencies among the keys of the n associated

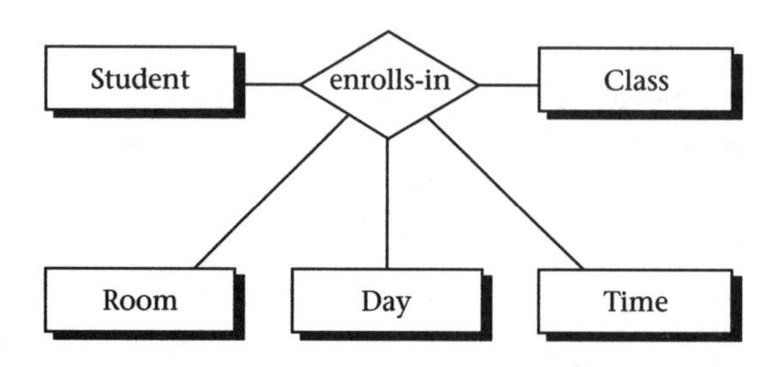

Figure 2.7 An n-ary relationship

entities. There can be anywhere from zero to n FDs, depending on the number of "one" entities. The collection of FDs that describe an n-ary relationship must have n components: n-1 on the left side (determinant) and 1 on the right side. A ternary relationship (n = 3), for example, has two components on the left and one on the right, as we saw in the example in Figure 2.6. In a more complex database, other types of FDs may also exist within an n-ary relationship. When this occurs, the ER model does not provide enough semantics by itself, and it must be supplemented with a narrative description of these dependencies.

2.2.5 ER Constraints: Extensions from the NIAM Model

Conceptual modeling of databases is by no means confined to the ER approach. A number of other schools of thought have received attention, and some offer a richer semantic base than the ER model. The binary relationship approach is the basis of the information analysis method called *Nijssens Information Analysis Method* (NIAM) [VeVa82]. This approach, which develops normalized (fifth normal form) tables from basic semantic constructs, provides low-level primitive constructs such as lexical object type, nonlexical object type, and role. These roughly correspond to the attribute, entity, and relationship concepts, respectively, in the ER model. However, unlike the ER approach, the binary relationship model tries to avoid making entity-attribute decisions early in the conceptual modeling process. The binary relationship model also includes the semantic concepts of subtyping (generalization), relationship connectivity, and membership class (mandatory or optional existence).

One obvious difference between the binary relationship model and the ER approach is that role names in the binary relationship model are directional between two lexical object types (attributes) and between a

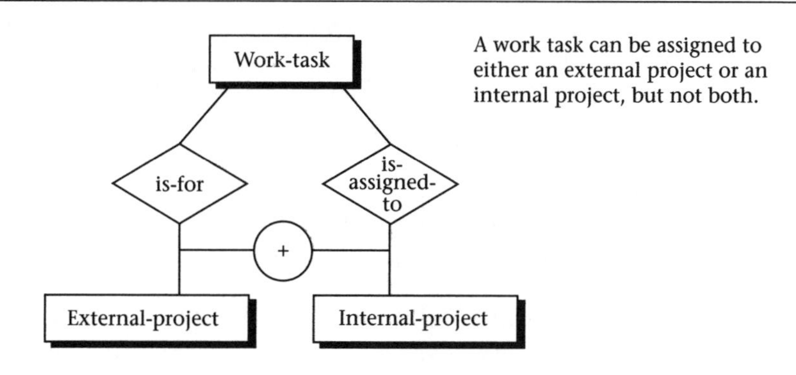
Work-task
is-for
is-
assigned-
to
+
External-project
Internal-project
A work task can be assigned to either an external project or an internal project, but not both.

Figure 2.8 Exclusion constraint

lexical (attribute) and nonlexical object type (entity). In fact, directional role names could easily be added to the ER model, but the designer would have to consider whether or not the added role names would degrade the readability of the ER diagram.

One of the most interesting aspects of the binary relationship model is the inclusion of integrity constraints on role occurrences. Some of the NIAM constraints such as exclusion and uniqueness can be easily adapted to the ER model. In the following paragraphs we illustrate how this could be done with some nonstandard ER notation.

Exclusion Constraint

The normal, or default, treatment of multiple relationships is the *inclusive OR,* which allows any or all of the entities to participate. In some situations, however, multiple relationships may be affected by the exclusion (*disjoint* or *exclusive OR*) constraint, which allows at most one entity instance among several entity types to participate in the relationship with a single root entity. For example, in Figure 2.8 suppose the root entity Work-task has two associated entities, External-project and Internal-project. At most one of the associated entity instances could apply to an instance of Work-task.

Uniqueness Constraint

The uniqueness constraint in the NIAM model combines three or more entities such that the combination of roles for the two entities in one direction uniquely determines the value of the single entity in the other direction. This, in effect, defines an FD from the composite keys of the entities in the first direction to the key of the entity in the second direction, and thus partly defines a ternary relationship. The ER constructs for ternary relationships are equivalent to the uniqueness constraint in NIAM.

2.2.6 Entity Integrity, Referential Integrity, and ID Dependency

Entity integrity, as defined in the relational model, requires that if an entity exists and it has a primary key, then its primary key must also exist. A foreign key is an attribute of a table, not necessarily a key of any kind (see Section 5.1.2 for definitions of the types of keys), that relates to a primary key in another table. *Referential integrity* requires that for every foreign key instance that exists in a table, the row (and thus the primary key instance) of the parent table associated with that foreign key instance must also exist. Both the entity integrity and referential integrity constraints have become so common in relational systems that they are not explicitly described in the ER model; they are usually implied as requirements for the resulting relational database implementation. (Chapter 4 discusses the SQL implementation of integrity constraints.)

ID dependency is a special case of existence dependency in which there is an additional constraint that the primary key of the weak entity must include the key of the associated strong (parent) entity. This could be indicated by including the letters "id" in the corner of the box for the weak entity.

2.3 Object-Oriented Data Modeling

Object-oriented programming languages and database systems are rapidly becoming a major part of the information systems industry. They have incorporated many new ideas and other well-established concepts, such as information hiding, into a coherent set of rules for data structure and data operations: data abstraction, encapsulation of data structure and behavior (operations) into the same object, and sharing of data structure and code. The object-oriented (OO) approach views classes (or types) as collections of methods, that is, operations on specific classes of objects. The ER model, on the other hand, is limited to viewing classes (supertypes and subtypes) as relationships among objects (entities) and ignores the dynamic behavior of the objects. Thus, to compare ER and object modeling, we need to understand both the differences and the similarities. In this section we first look at the basic OO concepts and then compare the data modeling constructs of the two approaches.

2.3.1 Object-Oriented Concepts

The object-oriented approach generally includes the following four characteristics [Rumb91]: identity, classification, polymorphism, and inheritance. *Identity* means that data is composed of discrete things called objects; objects can be things in the real world in the same way entities can be, but they can also be operations, or processes, on other objects. *Classification* is the grouping of objects with the same structure (attributes) and behavior (operations) into a class. Each object is then considered an instance of a class, and each instance of a class has its own value for each attribute but shares attribute names and operation names with other objects in that class. Operations that pertain to a particular class are called *methods*. Classification includes the concepts of data abstraction and encapsulation—the separation of the object's identity and function from the implementation details of that function.

Polymorphism is the characteristic that a given operation may behave differently on different object classes. For instance, a copy command has different implementations for buffers, disk files, and tape files. Finally, *inheritance* is the characteristic that attributes and operations among object classes can be shared in a hierarchical relationship. Each class can be divided into subclasses; each subclass inherits all the properties of the superclass in addition to defining its own unique properties. In OO programming, inheritance is often referred to in terms of code reuse because similar classes can be made to use common code in certain situations. *Multiple inheritance* permits a class to inherit all properties from more than one superclass and therefore allows you to mix information from many sources.

Some of the most popular object-oriented analysis (OOA) and design (OOD) techniques are OOA by Shlaer and Mellor [ShMe88] and by Coad and Yourdon [CoYo90], OOD by Booch [Booc91], object-oriented structured design (OOSD) by Wasserman [WFM89], the fusion method by Coleman [Cole94], the object modeling technique (OMT) by Rumbaugh and Blaha [Rumb91, BlPr98], unified modeling language (UML) by Booch and colleagues [BRJ98, FoSc97, TeWi97], Jacobsen [Jaco87], Meyer [Meye88], and others. OMT, for instance, is a methodology for object-oriented system development and a notation for representing OO concepts. It includes details for object analysis, system design, object design, and implementation. A good summary and comparison of techniques can be found in [FiKe92].

2.3.2 Object Modeling versus ER Modeling

Object modeling is a necessary discipline for object-oriented databases in the same way ER modeling is needed as a front end for designing relational databases. The object model describes the individual objects in the system, their identity, attributes, and behavior, and their relationships to other objects. The object diagram is a conceptual representation of the object model in the same way an ER diagram represents an ER model. Let us look at the basic concepts of object-oriented database (OODB) structure and compare it to the ER concepts we have already introduced in this chapter.

An *object* is a concept or thing in the real world. It has meaning for the data-oriented environment we are studying, and it has identity [Rumb91]. An *object class* is a meta-object that describes a group of objects with similar properties (attributes), common behavior (operations), and common relationships (associations) to other objects. An *object instance* is a single instance of an object class; for example, Bill Clinton is an instance of the object class President. An *attribute* of an object is a descriptive property of an object in the same way an attribute describes an entity in the ER model. An attribute also has a specific value that has the same data type within an object class it describes. A *link* is a connection between object instances, and an *association* is an abstraction of this linkage at the level of object classes. A *method* is an implementation of an operation for an object class, denoting that an operation such as "sort data" may be applied to many classes, with many possible implementations.

The correspondence between the ER model and an object model is easily illustrated by showing equivalent (or nearly equivalent) constructs side by side (Figure 2.9). In Figure 2.9a we see how an entity can be represented in an object model as an object class. Note that object classes in the UML notation and the Blaha and Premerlani variations [BRJ98, BlPr98] have names in boldface in the upper section of the box, a list of attributes and their data types in the middle section, and the names of operations on that object class in the lower section. The ER model only specifies data structure and not data behavior.

Associations in the object model are shown by straight lines between the object classes they connect, with the lower bound of zero and upper bound of one on connectivity shown with a zero at the end of the association line adjacent to the appropriate object class (Figure 2.9b). The absence of a zero (or any other symbol) on the association line represents a lower and upper bound of one (Figure 2.9b). The upper bound of

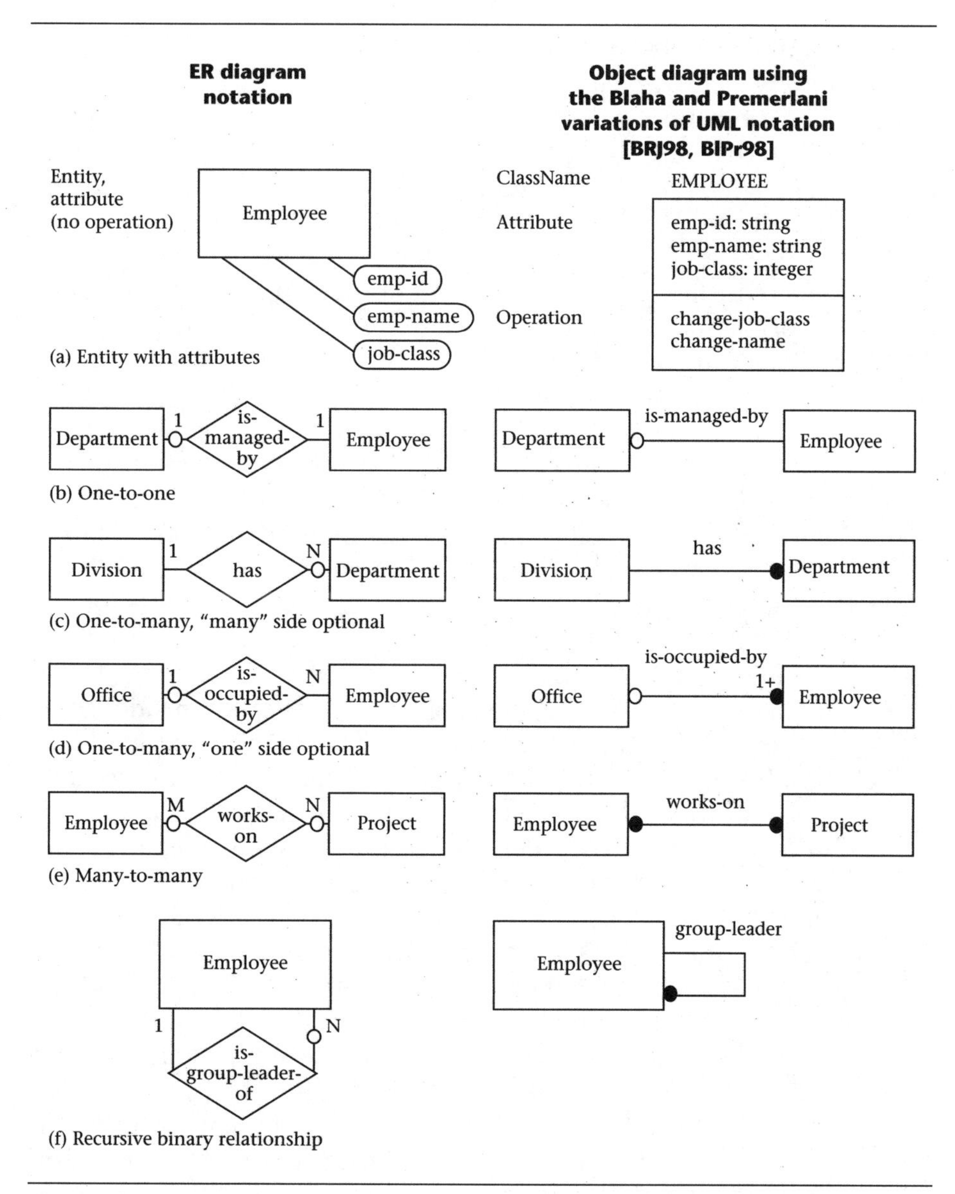

Figure 2.9 ER versus OO diagram notation: basic constructs

"many" and lower bound of zero is normally shown by a darkened circle adjacent to the appropriate object class (Figure 2.9c and e), whereas an upper bound of "many" and a lower bound of one has the association line with a number "1+" adjacent to the appropriate object class (Figure 2.9d). A binary recursive relationship has the same connectivity notation as binary relationships, except that the two ends of the association line are connected to a single object class (Figure 2.9f).

Object diagrams represent a concept of *multiplicity*, similar to the ER concept of connectivity of entities, by allowing the modeler to specify zero, one, many, an explicit range of values, or an explicit set of values for any object instance associated with another object instance. They also allow for the specification of association names when they are helpful to understanding the diagram and for role names that specify the role of each object class in a particular association.

Some of the more advanced ER constructs such as generalization, aggregation (an abstraction based on the "part-of" explosion idea), and ternary relationships are illustrated in Figure 2.10. The generalization hierarchy in an object model is similar to the ER model, except that the object model uses a triangle and states the name of the attribute in the superclass (supertype) object that is used to separate subclass (subtype) objects (Figure 2.10a). While generalization is used to refer to the "is-a" relationship among object classes, inheritance refers to the sharing of attributes and operations among classes using the generalization relationship.

The aggregation abstraction is modeled in the same way for entities and objects, however (Figure 2.10b). Ternary associations for objects do not have semantics that are as strong as the ER ternary relationships defined in this book (Figure 2.10c), but the object model does allow you to specify the candidate keys of the ternary association, which has the same semantics in most cases (see Chapter 5 for the subtleties of semantics for higher normal forms associated with ternary relationships).

Object model concepts that have similarities in the ER model, but are not shown explicitly here, include link attributes (such as attributes of many-to-many relationships in the ER model), constraints based on the NIAM model, and grouping (see clustering in Section 3.4). Object concepts that do not have ER equivalencies include role names, link attributes for one-to-many associations, ordering, derived objects, and homomorphisms (see [BlPr98]).

The OMT approach includes two other types of models in addition to object models to describe OO systems. One is the dynamic model, which specifies the dynamic aspects of a system such as events and the changing states of objects through state diagrams. The other type of model is the functional model, which describes the data value transformations that occur during execution of a system through the use of data

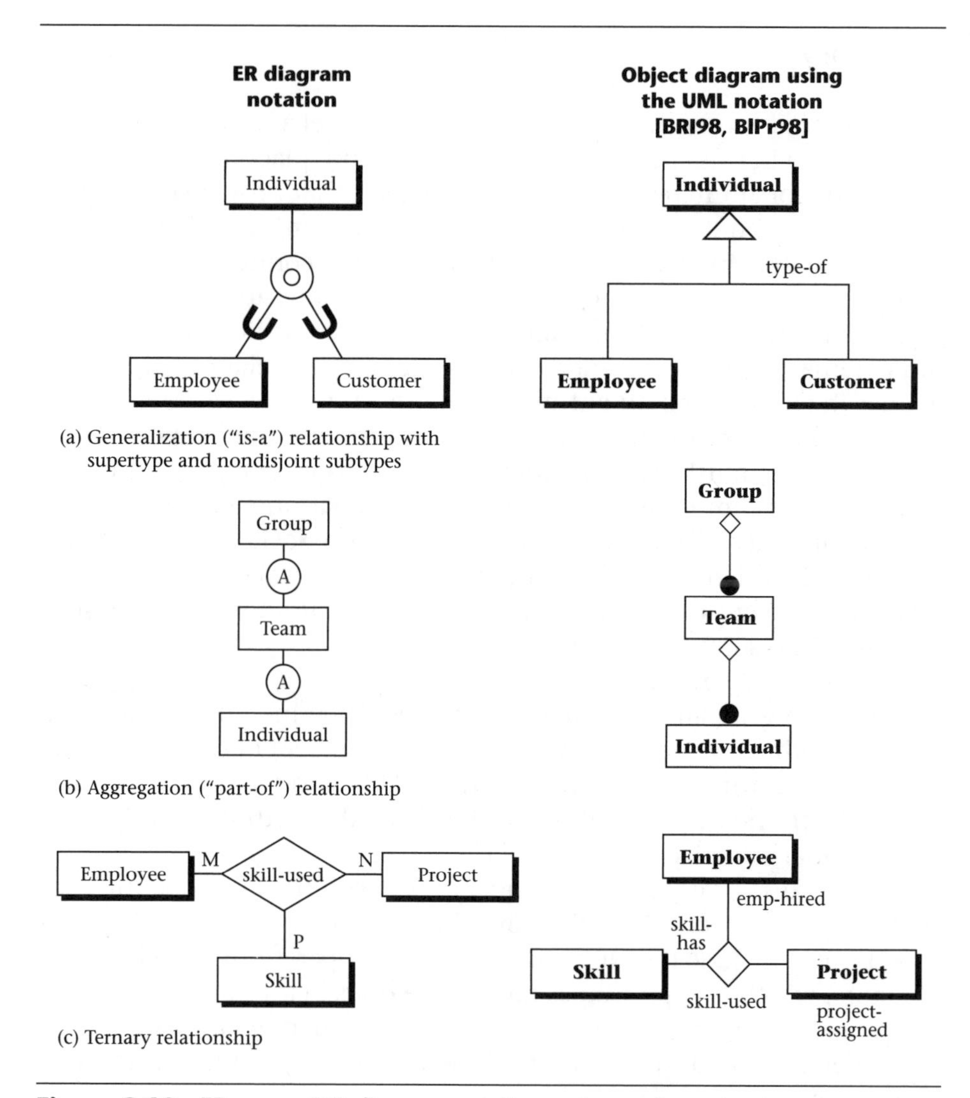

Figure 2.10 ER versus OO diagram notation: advanced constructs

flow diagrams. Neither of these types of models are included in the ER model, but they represent useful information in the OO approach needed to capture the correspondence between data objects and their behavior. Triggers, or the propagation of operations to one or multiple objects based on the application of an operation to a starting object, are also defined in this methodology.

2.4 Summary

The basic concepts of the entity-relationship model and their constructs are described in this chapter. An entity is a person, place, thing, or event of informational interest. Attributes are objects that provide descriptive information about entities. Attributes may be unique identifiers or nonunique descriptors. Relationships describe the connectivity between entity instances: one-to-one, one-to-many, or many-to-many. The degree of a relationship is the number of associated entities: two (binary), three (ternary), or any n (n-ary). The role (name), or relationship name, defines the function of an entity in a relationship.

The concept of existence in a relationship determines whether an entity instance must exist (mandatory) or not (optional). So, for example, the minimum connectivity of a binary relationship—that is, the number of entity instances on one side that are associated with one instance on the other side—can either be zero if optional or one if mandatory. The concept of generalization allows for the implementation of supertype and subtype abstractions.

The more advanced constructs in ER diagrams are sporadically used and have no generally accepted form as yet. They include ternary relationships, which we define in terms of the FD concept of relational databases; constraints borrowed from the NIAM model (exclusion and uniqueness); and the implicit constraints from the relational model such as referential integrity and primary key integrity.

There exists a very close relationship between the ER modeling concepts and the object-oriented approach, with the major exception that objects must include the encapsulation of data operations as well as data structure, which is expressed as part of the object class definition. Constructs such as entities, attributes, binary and ternary relationships, and the generalization abstraction are shown to be very similar in the two approaches.

We are now ready to apply the basic ER concepts to the life cycle database design steps.

Literature Summary

Most of the notation in this book is taken from the original ER definition by Chen [Chen76], with the shaded relationship coming from the Database Design and Evaluation Workbench project at CCA [Rein85]. The concept of data abstraction was first proposed by Smith and Smith [SmSm77] and applied to the ER model by [SSW80, NaCh83, TYF86, ElNa94, Shee89, Bruc92], among others. The application of the semantic network model to conceptual schema design was shown by [Bach77, McKi79, PoKe86, HuKi87, PeMa88], and the binary relationship model concepts, including the NIAM model, were studied by [Abri74, BPP76, NvS79, ISO82, VeVa82, Kent84, Mark87]. Other extensions to the original ER model such as the inclusion of the time dimension have also been described elsewhere [Bube77, ClWa83, Ferg85, Aria86, Ever86, MTM91]. Object-oriented data modeling schemes and issues are discussed in [Booc86, Bane87, Jaco87, Meye88, ShMe88, WPM89, CoYo90, Booc91, Rumb91, CACM92, IEEE92, FiKe92, FoSc97, TeWi97, BRJ98, BlPr98].

[Abri74] Abrial, J. "Data Semantics," Data Base Management, *Proc. IFIP TC2 Conf.*, North-Holland, Amsterdam, 1974.

[Aria86] Ariav, G. "A Temporally Oriented Data Model," *ACM Trans. Database Systems* 11, 4 (Dec. 1986), pp. 499–527.

[Bach77] Bachman, C.W. "The Role Concept in Data Models," *Proc. 3rd Intl. Conf. on Very Large Data Bases*, Oct. 6–8, 1977, IEEE, New York, pp. 464–476.

[Bane87] Banerjee, J., Chou, H.T., Garza, J.F., Kim, W., Woelk, B., and Ballou, N. "Data Model Issues for Object-Oriented Applications," *ACM Trans. on Office Information Systems* 5, 1 (Jan. 1987), pp. 3–26.

[BlPr98] Blaha, M., and Premerlani, W. *Object-Oriented Modeling and Design for Database Applications,* Prentice Hall, Upper Saddle River, NJ, 1998.

[Booc86] Booch, G. "Object-Oriented Development," *IEEE Trans. on Software Engineering* SE-12, 2 (Feb. 1986), pp. 211–221.

[Booc91] Booch, G. *Object Oriented Design with Appications*, Benjamin/Cummings, Redwood City, CA, 1991.

[BPP76] Bracchi, G., Paolini, P., and Pelagatti, G. "Binary Logical Associations in Data Modelling," *Modelling in Data Base Management Systems,* G.M. Nijssen (editor), North-Holland, Amsterdam, 1976.

[BRJ98] Booch, G., Rumbaugh, J., and Jacobson, I. *UML User's Guide,* Addison-Wesley, Reading, MA, 1998.

[Bruc92] Bruce, T.A. *Designing Quality Databases with IDEF1X Information Models*, Dorset House, New York, 1992.

[Bube77] Bubenko, J. "The Temporal Dimension in Information Modelling," *Architecture and Models in Data Base Management*

Systems, G. Nijssen (editor), North-Holland, Amsterdam, 1977.

[CACM92] *Comm. ACM* (Special Issue: *Analysis and Modeling in Software Development*) 35, 9 (Sept. 1992), pp. 35–171.

[Chen76] Chen, P.P. "The Entity-Relationship Model—Toward a Unified View of Data," *ACM Trans. Database Systems* 1, 1 (March 1976), pp. 9–36.

[Chen87] Chen and Associates, Inc. *ER Designer* (user manual), 1987.

[ClWa83] Clifford, J., and Warren, D. "Formal Semantics for Time in Databases," *ACM Trans. Database Systems* 8, 2 (1983), pp. 214–254.

[Cole94] Coleman, D., Arnold, P., Bodoff, S., Dollin, C., and Gilchrest, H. *Object-Oriented Development: The Fusion Method*, Prentice Hall, Upper Saddle River, NJ, 1994.

[CoYo90] Coad, P., and Yourdon, E. *Object-Oriented Analysis*, Prentice Hall, Englewood Cliffs, NJ, 1990.

[ElNa94] Elmasri, R., and Navathe, S.B. *Fundamentals of Database Systems* (2nd Ed.), Benjamin/Cummings, Redwood City, CA, 1994.

[Ever86] Everest, G.C. *Database Management: Objectives, System Functions, and Administration*, McGraw-Hill, New York, 1986.

[Ferg85] Ferg, S. "Modeling the Time Dimension in an Entity-Relationship Diagram," *Proc. 4th Intl. Conf. on the Entity-Relationship Approach*, IEEE Computer Society Press, Silver Spring, MD, 1985, pp. 280–286.

[FiKe92] Fichman, R.G., and Kemerer, C.F. "Object-Oriented and Conventional Analysis and Design Methodologies," *IEEE Computer* 25, 10 (Oct. 1992), pp. 22–39.

[FoSc97] Fowler, M., with Scott, K. *UML Distilled: Applying the Standard Modeling Language*, Addison-Wesley, Reading, MA, 1997.

[HuKi87] Hull, R., and King, R. "Semantic Database Modeling: Survey, Applications, and Research Issues," *ACM Computing Surveys* 19, 3 (Sept. 1987), pp. 201–260.

[IEEE92] *IEEE Computer* (Special Issue: *Inheritance and Classification in Object-Oriented Computing*) 25, 10 (Oct. 1992), pp. 6–90.

[ISO82] ISO/TC97/SC5/WG3-N695 Report. "Concepts and Terminology for the Conceptual Schema and the Information Base," J. van Griethuysen (editor), ANSI, New York, 1982.

[Jaco87] Jacobsen, I. "Object Oriented Development in an Industrial Environment," OOPSLA'87 as *ACM SIGPLAN* 22, 12 (Dec. 1987), pp. 183–191.

[Kent84] Kent, W. "Fact-Based Data Analysis and Design," *J. Systems and Software* 4 (1984), pp. 99–121.

[Mark87] Mark, L. "Defining Views in the Binary Relationship Model," *Inform. Systems* 12, 3 (1987), pp. 281–294.

[McKi79] McLeod, D., and King, R. "Applying a Semantic Database Model," *Proc. 1st Intl. Conf. on the Entity-Relationship Approach to Systems Analysis and Design*, North-Holland, Amsterdam, 1979, pp. 193–210.

[Meye88] Meyer, B. *Object-Oriented Software Construction*, Prentice Hall, Hertfordshire, England, 1988.

[MTM91] Moyne, J.R., Teorey, T.J., and McAfee, L.C. "Time Sequence Ordering Extensions to the Entity Relationship Model and Their Application to the Automated Manufacturing Process," *Data and Knowledge Engr.* 6, 5 (Sept. 1991), pp. 421–433.

[NaCh83] Navathe, S., and Cheng, A. "A Methodology for Database Schema Mapping from Extended Entity Relationship Models into the Hierarchical Model," *The Entity-Relationship Approach to Software Engineering*, G.C. Davis et al. (editors), Elsevier, North-Holland, Amsterdam, 1983.

[NvS79] Nijssen, G., van Assche, F., and Snijders, J. "End User Tools for Information Systems Requirement Definition," *Formal Models and Practical Tools for Information System Design*, H. Schneider (editor), North-Holland, Amsterdam, 1979.

[PeMa88] Peckham, J., and Maryanski, F. "Semantic Data Models," *ACM Computing Surveys* 20, 3 (Sept. 1988), pp. 153–190.

[PoKe86] Potter, W.D., and Kerschberg, L. "A Unified Approach to Modeling Knowledge and Data," *IFIP WG 2.6 Working Conf. on Knowledge and Data*, Elsevier, North-Holland, Amsterdam, Sept. 1986.

[Rein85] Reiner, D., Brodie, M., Brown, G., Friedell, M., Kramlich, D., Lehman, J., and Rosenthal, A. "The Database Design and Evaluation Workbench (DDEW) Project at CCA," *Database Engineering* 7, 4 (1985), pp. 10–15.

[Rumb91] Rumbaugh, J., Blaha, M., Premerlani, W., Eddy, F., and Lorensen, W. *Object-Oriented Modeling and Design*, Prentice Hall, Englewood Cliffs, NJ, 1991.

[Shee89] Sheer, A.-W. *Enterprise-Wide Data Modeling*, Springer-Verlag, Berlin, 1989.

[ShMe88] Shlaer, S., and Mellor, S. *Object-Oriented Systems Analysis: Modeling the World in Data*, Yourdon Press, Englewood Cliffs, NJ, 1988.

[SmSm77] Smith, J., and Smith, D. "Database Abstractions: Aggregation and Generalization," *ACM Trans. Database Systems* 2, 2 (June 1977), pp. 105–133.

[SSW80] Scheuermann, P., Scheffner, G., and Weber, H. "Abstraction Capabilities and Invariant Properties Modelling within the Entity-Relationship Approach," *Entity-Relationship Approach to Systems Analysis and Design*, P. Chen (editor), Elsevier, North-Holland, Amsterdam, 1980, pp. 121–140.

[TeWi97] Texel, P.P., and Williams, C.B. *USE CASES Combined with BOOCH/OMT/UML: Process and Products,* Prentice Hall, Upper Saddle River, NJ, 1997.

[TYF86] Teorey, T.J., Yang, D., and Fry, J.P. "A Logical Design Methodology for Relational Databases Using the Extended Entity-Relationship Model," *ACM Computing Surveys* 18, 2 (June 1986), pp. 197–222.

[VeVa82] Verheijen, G., and Van Bekkum, J. "NIAM: An Information Analysis Method," *Information Systems Design Methodologies,* T.W. Olle, et al. (editors), North-Holland, Amsterdam, 1982, pp. 537–590.

[WPM89] Wasserman, A.I., Pircher, P.A., and Muller, R.J. "An Object-Oriented Structured Design Method for Code Generation," *Software Eng. Notices* 14, 1 (Jan. 1989), pp. 32–55.

Exercises

Problem 2-1

Construct an ER diagram (including important attributes) for a bank database that shows the basic relationships among customers, checking accounts, savings accounts, loans, and the bank branches where various accounts and loans are taken out. You also want to keep track of transactions on accounts and loans and maintain the current balance in each account and the balance of the loan. Remember that each entity in the ER diagram represents a simple file of data of which you want to keep track.

Problem 2-2

Construct an ER diagram (including important attributes) for a car insurance database that includes data about customers (car owners), cars, accidents, drivers involved in accidents, and injured drivers and/or passengers. Note that any customer can insure many cars, each car may have different drivers at different times, and accidents typically involve one or more cars.

For this problem, show at least one use of generalization and at least one use of a ternary or higher n-ary relationship. Also, show two separate ER diagrams (without attributes), where the concept "accident" is an entity and a relationship, respectively. One of these two ER diagrams may be satisfied with the first diagram with attributes.

Problem 2-3

There is a business that owns a softball complex. It organizes league and tournament play over several seasons per year. The people associated with this business are represented as players or employees. An employee may also be a player. Most of these people play for teams that compose the leagues of this organization. These teams are not allowed to register into multiple leagues. Each season consists of several leagues and teams, with each team playing several games each season. Once a team and a league have entered the organization, they are invited to participate in each season thereafter.

Construct an ER diagram for this organization that keeps track of leagues, teams, individual players, and employees.

Please see page 347 for the solution to Problem 2-3.

3 ER Modeling in Logical Database Design

This chapter shows how the ER approach can be applied to the database life cycle, particularly in steps I through II(b) (as defined in Section 1.3), which include the requirements analysis and conceptual modeling stages of logical database design. The example introduced in Chapter 2 is used again to illustrate the ER modeling principles developed in this chapter.

3.1 Introduction

Logical database design is accomplished with a variety of approaches, including the top-down, bottom-up, and combined methodologies. The traditional approach, particularly for relational databases, has been a low-level, bottom-up activity, synthesizing individual data elements into normalized relations (tables) after careful analysis of the data element interdependencies defined by the requirements analysis. Although the traditional process has had some success for small- to medium-sized databases, its complexity for large databases can be overwhelming to the point where practicing designers do not bother to use it with any regularity. In practice, a combination of the top-down and bottom-up approaches is used; in some cases, tables can be defined directly from the requirements analysis. A new form of the combined approach has recently become popular because of the introduction of the ER model into the process.

The ER model has been most successful as a tool for communication between the designer and the end user during the requirements analysis and logical design phases. Its success is due to the fact that the model is easy to understand and convenient to represent. Another reason for its effectiveness is that it is a top-down approach using the concept of abstraction. The number of entities in a database is typically an order of magnitude less than the number of data elements because data elements usually represent the attributes. Therefore, using entities as an abstraction for data elements and focusing on the interentity relationships greatly reduces the number of objects under consideration and simplifies the analysis. Though it is still necessary to represent data elements by attributes of entities at the conceptual level, their dependencies are normally confined to the other attributes within the entity or, in some cases, to those attributes associated with other entities that have a direct relationship to their entity.

The major interattribute dependencies that occur in data models are the dependencies between the *entity keys*, the unique identifiers of different entities that are captured in the ER modeling process. Special cases such as dependencies among data elements of unrelated entities can be handled when they are identified in the ensuing data analysis.

The logical database design approach defined here uses both the ER model and the relational model in successive stages. It benefits from the simplicity and ease of use of the ER model and the structure and associated formalism of the relational model. In order to facilitate this approach, it is necessary to build a framework for transforming the variety of ER constructs into tables that are already normalized or can be normalized with a minimum of transformation. Before we do this, however, we need to first define the major steps of the relational design methodology in the context of the database life cycle.

3.2 Requirements Analysis and ER Modeling

Requirements analysis is the most important step (step I) of the database life cycle and is typically the most labor intensive. The database designer must interview the end-user population and determine exactly what the database is to be used for and what it must contain. The basic objectives of requirements analysis are

- to delineate the data requirements of the enterprise in terms of primitive objects;
- to describe the information about the objects and the relationships among objects needed to model these data requirements;

- to determine the types of transactions that are intended to be executed on the database and the interaction between the transactions and the data objects;
- to define any performance, integrity, security, or administrative constraints that must be imposed on the resulting database;
- to specify the hardware and software platform for the database implementation; and
- to thoroughly document all of the preceding in a detailed requirements specification. The data objects can also be defined in a data dictionary system, often provided as an integral part of the database management system.

The ER model helps designers to accurately capture the real data requirements because it requires them to focus on semantic detail in the data relationships, which is greater than the detail that would be provided by FDs alone. The semantics of ER allow for direct transformations of entities and relationships to at least first normal form tables. They also provide clear guidelines for integrity constraints. In addition, abstraction techniques such as generalization provide useful tools for integrating end-user views to define a global conceptual schema.

Let us now look more closely at the basic objects and relationships that should be defined during requirements analysis and conceptual design. These two life cycle steps are often done simultaneously.

Consider the substeps in step II(a), ER modeling:

- Classify entities and attributes.
- Identify the generalization hierarchies.
- Define relationships.

The remainder of this section discusses the tasks involved in each substep.

3.2.1 Classify Entities and Attributes

Though it is easy to define entity, attribute, and relationship constructs, it is not as easy to distinguish their roles in modeling the database. What makes an object an entity, an attribute, or even a relationship? For example, project headquarters are located in cities. Should "city" be an entity or an attribute? A vita is kept for each employee. Is "vita" an entity or a relationship?

The following guidelines for classifying entities and attributes will help the designer's thoughts converge to a normalized relational database design.

- Entities should contain descriptive information.
- Classify multivalued attributes as entities.
- Attach attributes to the entities they most directly describe.

Now we examine each guideline in turn.

Entity Contents

Entities should contain descriptive information. If there is descriptive information about an object, the object should be classified as an entity. If an object requires only an identifier and does not have relationships, the object should be classified as an attribute. With "city," for example, if there is some descriptive information such as "country" and "population" for cities, then "city" should be classified as an entity. If only the city name is needed to identify a city, then "city" should be classified as an attribute associated with some entity, such as Project. Examples of objects in the real world that are typically classified as entities are employee, task, project, department, company, customer, and so on.

Multivalued Attributes

Classify multivalued attributes as entities. If more than one value of a descriptor attribute corresponds to one value of an identifier, the descriptor should be classified as an entity instead of an attribute, even though it does not have descriptors itself. A large company, for example, could have many offices, some of them possibly in different cities. In that case, "office" could be classified as a multivalued attribute of "company," but it would be better to be classified as an entity, with "office-address" as its identifier. If attributes are restricted to be single valued only, the later design and implementation decisions will be simplified.

Attribute Attachment

Attach attributes to the entities they most directly describe. For example, attribute "office-building-name" should normally be an attribute of the entity Department instead of the entity Employee.

The procedure of identifying entities and attaching attributes to entities is iterative: Classify some objects as entities and attach identifiers and descriptors to them. If you find some violation of the preceding guidelines, change some objects from entity to attribute (or from attribute to entity), attach attributes to the new entities, and so forth.

3.2.2 Identify the Generalization Hierarchies

If there is a generalization hierarchy among entities, then put the identifier and generic descriptors in the generic or supertype entity and put the same identifier and specific descriptors in the subtype entities.

For example, suppose three entities were identified in the ER model shown in Figure 2.4b:

- Individual, with identifier indiv-id and descriptors indiv-name, address, and date-of-birth
- Employee, with identifier emp-id and descriptors emp-name and job- title
- Customer, with identifier cust-no and descriptors cust-name and organization

We determine, through our analysis, that Individual is a generalization of Employee and Customer. Then we put identifier indiv-id and generic descriptors indiv-name, address, and date-of-birth in the generic entity Individual; identifier emp-id and specific descriptor job-title in the entity Employee; and identifier cust-no and specific descriptor organization in entity Customer. Later, if we decide to eliminate **Individual** as a table, the generic attributes can be redistributed to the subtype tables **Employee** and **Customer**. (Note that we put table names in boldface throughout the book for readability.)

3.2.3 Define Relationships

We now deal with objects that represent associations among entities, which we call relationships. Examples of typical relationships are "works-in," "works-for," "purchases," "drives," or any verb that connects entities. For every relationship the following should be specified: degree (binary, ternary, etc.), connectivity (one-to-many, etc.), optional or mandatory existence, and any attributes that are associated with the relationship and not the entities. The following are some guidelines for defining the more difficult types of relationships.

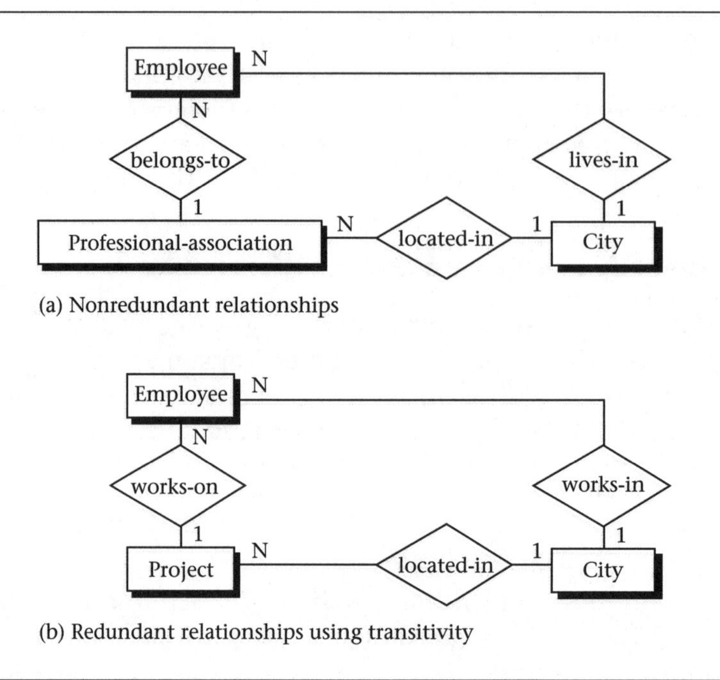

Figure 3.1 Redundant and nonredundant relationships

Redundant Relationships

Analyze redundant relationships carefully. Two or more relationships that are used to represent the same concept are considered to be redundant. Redundant relationships are more likely to result in unnormalized tables when transforming the ER model into relational schemas. Note that two or more relationships are allowed between the same two entities as long as the two relationships have different meanings. In this case they are not considered redundant.

One important case of nonredundancy is shown in Figure 3.1a. If "belongs-to" is a one-to-many relationship between Employee and Professional-association, if "located-in" is a one-to-many relationship between Professional-association and City, and if "lives-in" is a one-to-many relationship between Employee and City, then "lives-in" is not redundant because the relationships are unrelated. However, consider the situation shown in Figure 3.1b. The employee works on a project located in a city, so the "works-in" relationship between Employee and City is redundant and can be eliminated.

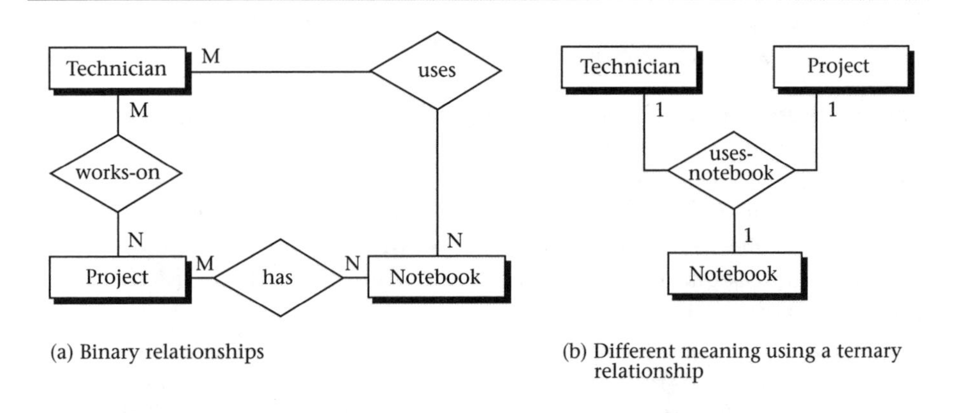

(a) Binary relationships

(b) Different meaning using a ternary relationship

Figure 3.2 Comparison of binary and ternary relationships

Ternary Relationships

Define ternary relationships carefully. We define a ternary relationship among three entities only when the concept cannot be represented by several binary relationships among those entities. For example, let us assume there is some association among entities Technician, Project, and Notebook. If each technician can be working on any of several projects and using the same notebooks on each project, then three many-to-many binary relationships can be defined (see Figure 3.2a). If, however, each technician is constrained to use exactly one notebook for each project and that notebook belongs to only one technician, then a one-to-one-to-one ternary relationship must be defined (see Figure 3.2b). The approach to take in ER modeling is to first attempt to express the associations in terms of binary relationships; if this is impossible because of the constraints of the associations, try to express them in terms of a ternary.

The meaning of connectivity for ternary relationships is important. Figure 3.2b shows that for a given pair of instances of Technician and Project, there is only one corresponding instance of Notebook; for a given pair of instances of Technician and Notebook, there is only one corresponding instance of Project; and for a given pair of instances of Project and Notebook, there is only one instance of Technician. In general, we know by our definition of ternary relationships that if a relationship among three entities can be expressed by a functional dependency involving the keys of all three entities, then it cannot be expressed by binary relationships, which only apply to associations between two entities.

3.2.4 Example of ER Modeling: Company Personnel and Project Database

Requirements Analysis and ER Modeling of Individual Views

Let us suppose it is desirable to build a companywide database for a large engineering firm that keeps track of all full-time personnel, their skills and projects assigned, department (and division) worked in, engineer professional associations belonged to, and engineer desktop computers allocated. During the requirements collection process—that is, interviewing the end users—we obtain three views of the database.

The first view, a management view, defines each employee as working in a single department and a division as the basic unit in the company, consisting of many departments. Each division and department has a manager, and we want to keep track of each manager. The ER model for this view is shown in Figure 3.3a.

The second view defines each employee as having a job title: engineer, technician, secretary, manager, and so on. Engineers typically belong to professional associations and might be allocated an engineering workstation (or computer). Secretaries and managers are each allocated a desktop computer. A pool of desktops and workstations is maintained for potential allocation to new employees and for loans while an employee's computer is being repaired. Any employee may be married to another employee, and we want to keep track of this relationship to avoid assigning an employee to be managed by his or her spouse. This view is illustrated in Figure 3.3b.

The third view, shown in Figure 3.3c, involves the assignment of employees, mainly engineers and technicians, to projects. Employees may work on several projects at one time, and each project could be headquartered at different locations (cities). However, each employee at a given location works on only one project at that location. Employee skills can be individually selected for a given project, but no individual has a monopoly on skills, projects, or locations.

Global ER Schema

A simple integration of the three views just defined results in the global ER schema (diagram) in Figure 3.3d, which becomes the basis for developing the normalized tables. Each relationship in the global schema is based upon a verifiable assertion about the actual data in the enterprise, and analysis of those assertions leads to the transformation of these ER constructs into candidate SQL tables, as Chapter 4 shows.

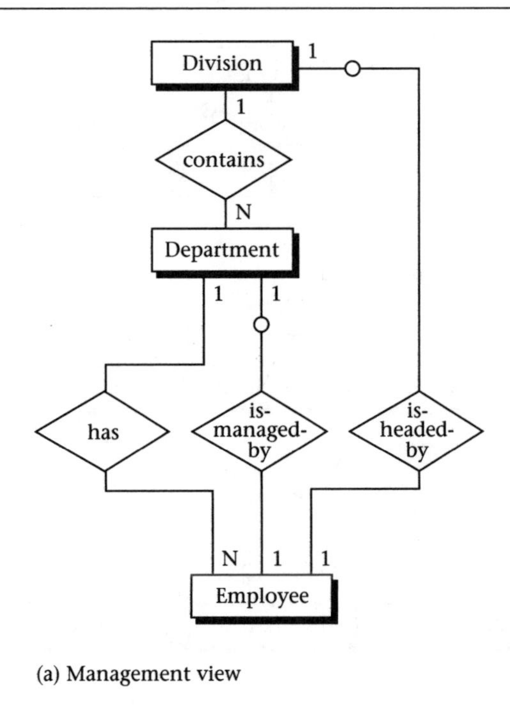

(a) Management view

Figure 3.3 Global ER schema: company personnel and project database

The diagram shows examples of binary, ternary, and binary recursive relationships; optional and mandatory existence in relationships; and generalization with the disjointness constraint. Ternary relationships "skill-used" and "assigned-to" are necessary because binary relationships cannot be used for the equivalent notions. For example, one employee and one location determines exactly one project (a functional dependency). In the case of "skill-used," selective use of skills to projects cannot be represented with binary relationships (see Section 5.5).

The use of optional existence, for instance, between Employee and Division or between Employee and Department, is derived from our general knowledge that most employees will not be the manager of any division or department. In another example of optional existence, we show that the allocation of a desktop to an engineer may not always occur, nor will all desktops necessarily be allocated to someone at all times. In general, all relationships, optional existence constraints, and generalization constructs need to be verified with the end user before the ER model is transformed to SQL tables.

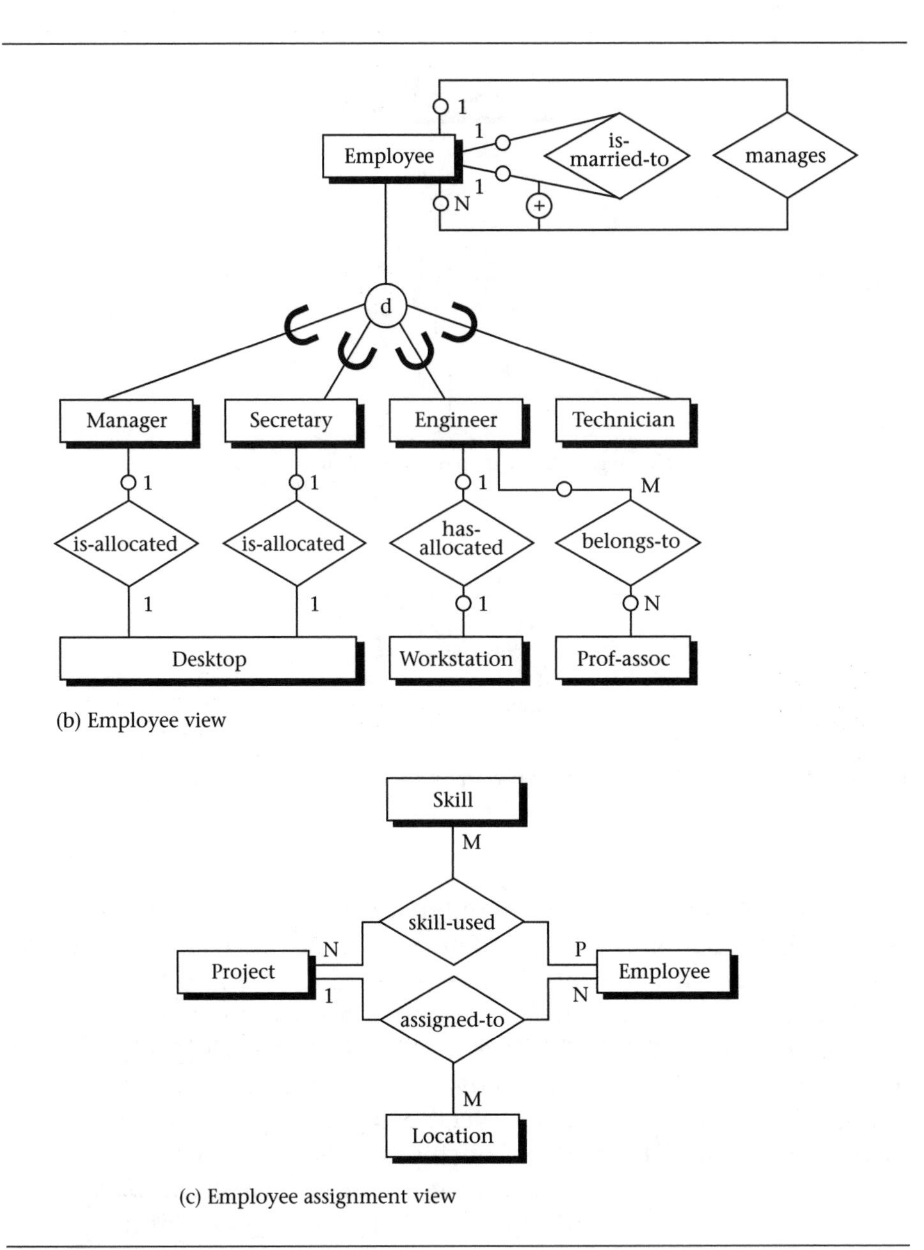

(b) Employee view

(c) Employee assignment view

Figure 3.3 *Continued*

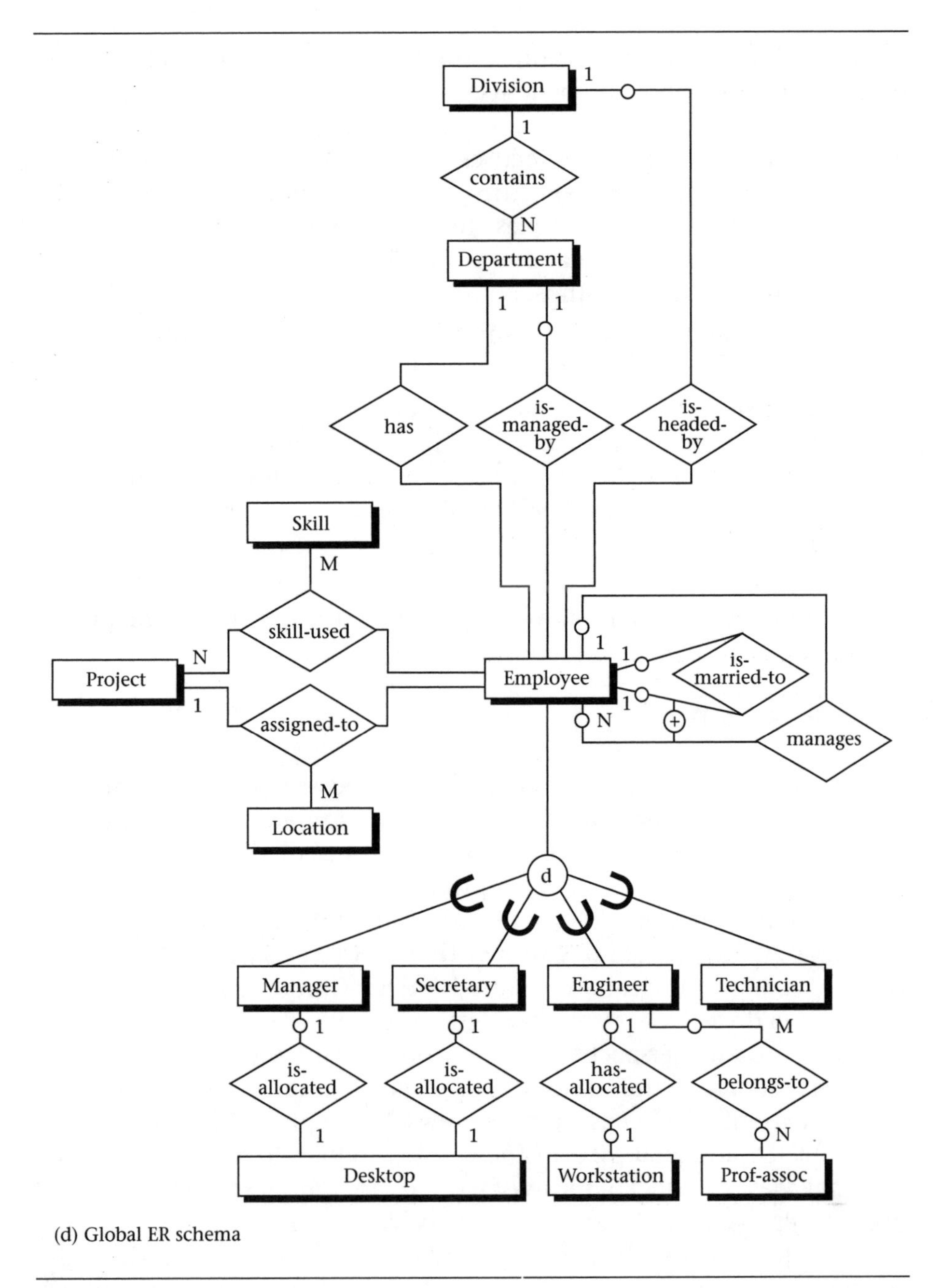

(d) Global ER schema

Figure 3.3 *Continued*

In summary, the application of the ER model to relational database design offers the following benefits:

- Use of an ER approach focuses end-user discussions on important relationships between entities. Some applications are characterized by counterexamples affecting a small number of instances, and lengthy consideration of these instances can divert attention from basic relationships.
- A diagrammatic syntax conveys a great deal of information in a compact, readily understandable form.
- Extensions to the original ER model, such as optional and mandatory membership classes, are important in many relationships. Generalization allows entities to be grouped for one functional role or to be seen as separate subtypes when other constraints are imposed.
- A complete set of rules transforms ER constructs into candidate SQL tables, which follow easily from real-world requirements.

3.3 View Integration

A most critical part of the database design process is step II(b), the integration of different user views into a unified, nonredundant conceptual schema. The individual end-user views are represented by ER conceptual models, and the integrated conceptual schema results from sufficient analysis of the end-user views to resolve all differences in perspective and terminology. Experience has shown that nearly every situation can be resolved in a meaningful way through integration techniques.

Schema diversity occurs when different users or user groups develop their own unique perspectives of the world or, at least, of the enterprise to be represented in the database. For instance, marketing tends to have the whole product as a basic unit for sales, but engineering may concentrate on the individual parts of the whole product. In another case, one user may view a project in terms of its goals and progress toward meeting those goals over time; another user may view a project in terms of the resources it needs and the personnel involved. Such differences cause the conceptual models to seem to have incompatible relationships and terminology. These differences show up in ER conceptual models as different levels of abstraction, connectivity of relationships (one-to-many, many-to-many, and so on), or as the same concept being modeled as an entity, attribute, or relationship, depending on the user's perspective.

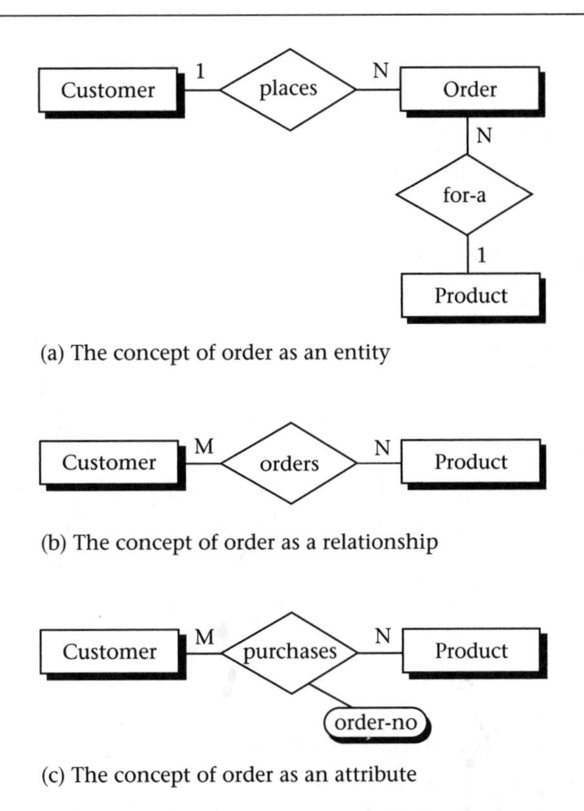

Figure 3.4 The concept of order as an entity, relationship, and attribute

As an example of the latter case, in Figure 3.4 we see three different perspectives of the same real-life situation—the placement of an order for a certain product. The result is a variety of schemas. The first schema (Figure 3.4a) depicts Customer, Order, and Product as entities and "places" and "for-a" as relationships. The second schema (Figure 3.4b), however, defines "orders" as a relationship between Customer and Product and omits Order as an entity altogether. Finally, in the third case (Figure 3.4c), the relationship "orders" has been replaced by another relationship "purchases"; "order-no," the identifier (key) of an order, is designated as an attribute of the relationship "purchases." In other words, the concept of order has been variously represented as an entity, a relationship, and an attribute, depending on perspective.

The resolution of different views is part of a view integration methodology defined by Batini, Lenzerini, and Navathe [BaLe84, BLN86]. They define four basic steps needed for conceptual schema integration:

1. preintegration analysis;
2. comparison of schemas;
3. conformation of schemas; and
4. merging and restructuring of schemas.

3.3.1 Preintegration Analysis

The first step, preintegration analysis, involves choosing an integration strategy. Typically, the choice is between a binary approach with two schemas merged at one time and an n-ary approach with n schemas merged at one time, where n is between 2 and the total number of schemas developed in the conceptual design. The binary approach is attractive because each merge involves a small number of ER constructs and is easier to conceptualize. The n-ary approach may require one grand merge only, but the number of constructs may be so large that it is not humanly possible to organize the transformations properly.

3.3.2 Comparison of Schemas

In the second step, comparison of schemas, the designer looks at how entities correspond and detects conflicts arising from schema diversity—that is, from user groups adopting different viewpoints in their respective schemas. Naming conflicts include synonyms and homonyms. Synonyms occur when different names are given for the same concept. These can be detected by scanning the data dictionary, if one has been established for the database. Homonyms occur when the same name is used for different concepts. These can only be detected by scanning the different schemas and looking for common names.

Structural conflicts occur in the schema structure itself. Type conflicts involve using different ER constructs to model the same concept. In Figure 3.4, for example, an entity, a relationship, or an attribute can be used to model the concept of order in a business database. Dependency conflicts result when users specify different levels of connectivity for similar or even the same concepts. One resolution of such conflicts might be to use only the most general connectivity—for example, many-to-many. If that is not semantically correct, change the names of entities so that each type of connectivity has a different set of entity names. Key conflicts occur when different keys are assigned to the same entity in different views. For example, a key conflict occurs if an employee's full name, employee id number, and social security number are all assigned as keys. Behavioral conflicts result from different integrity constraints, particularly on nulls and insert/delete rules.

3.3.3 Conformation of Schemas

The resolution of conflicts often requires user and designer interaction. The basic goal is to align or conform schemas to make them compatible for integration. The entities as well as the primary key attributes may need to be renamed. Conversion may be required so that concepts that are modeled as entities, attributes, or relationships are conformed to only one primitive data model type. Relationships with equal degree, roles, and connectivity constraints are easy to merge. Those with differing characteristics are more difficult and, in some cases, impossible to merge. In addition, relationships that are not consistent—for example, a relationship using generalization in one place and the exclusive OR in another—must be resolved. Finally, assertions may need to be modified so that integrity constraints are consistent.

Techniques used for view integration include abstraction, such as generalization and aggregation, to create new supertypes or subtypes, or even the introduction of new relationships. As an example, the generalization of Individual over different values of the descriptor attribute "job-title" could represent the consolidation of two views of the database—one based on an individual as the basic unit of personnel in the organization and another based on the classification of individuals by job titles and special characteristics within those classifications. An example of a special characteristic is the allocation of personal computers to reviewers.

3.3.4 Merging and Restructuring of Schemas

Step 4 consists of the merging and restructuring of schemas. This step is driven by the goals of completeness, minimality, and understandability. Completeness requires all component concepts to appear semantically intact in the global schema. Minimality requires the designer to remove all redundant concepts in the global schema. Examples of redundant concepts are overlapping entities, redundant hierarchies, and truly semantically redundant relationships. Understandability requires that the global schema make sense to the user.

Component schemas are first merged by superimposing the same concepts and then restructuring the resulting integrated schema for understandability. For instance, if a supertype/subtype combination is

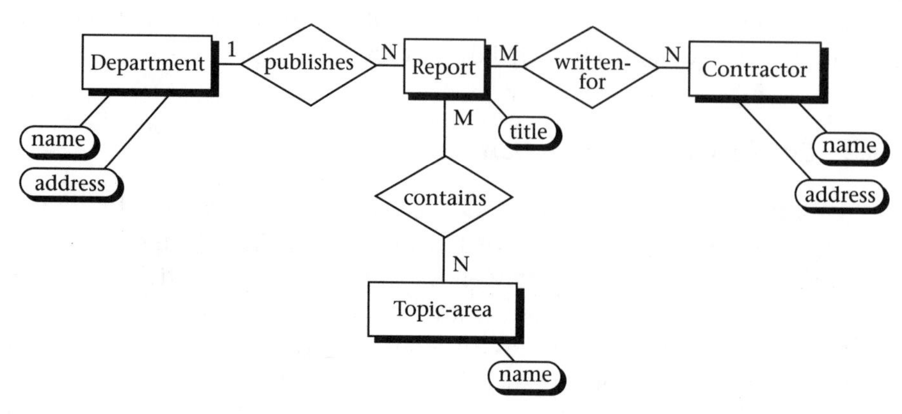

(a) Original schema 1, focused on reports

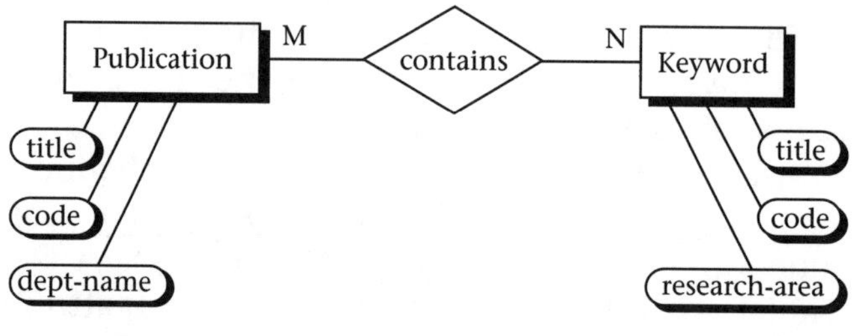

(b) Original schema 2, focused on publications

Figure 3.5 Example of two views and corresponding ER schemas

defined as a result of the merging operation, the properties of the subtype can be dropped from the schema because they are automatically provided by the supertype entity or object.

3.3.5 Example of View Integration

Let us look at two different views of overlapping data. The views are based on two separate interviews of end users. We adapt the interesting example cited by Batini, Lenzerini, and Navathe to a hypothetical situation related to our example. In Figure 3.5a we have a view that focuses on reports and includes data on departments that publish the reports, topic areas in reports, and contractors for whom the reports are written. Figure 3.5b shows another view, with publications as the central focus

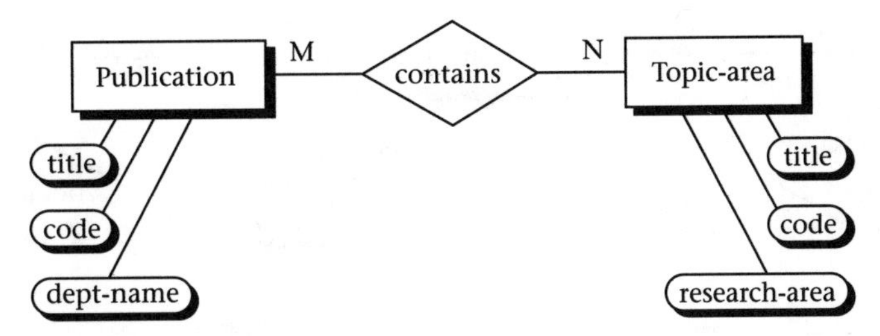

(a) Schema 2.1, in which Keyword has changed to Topic-area

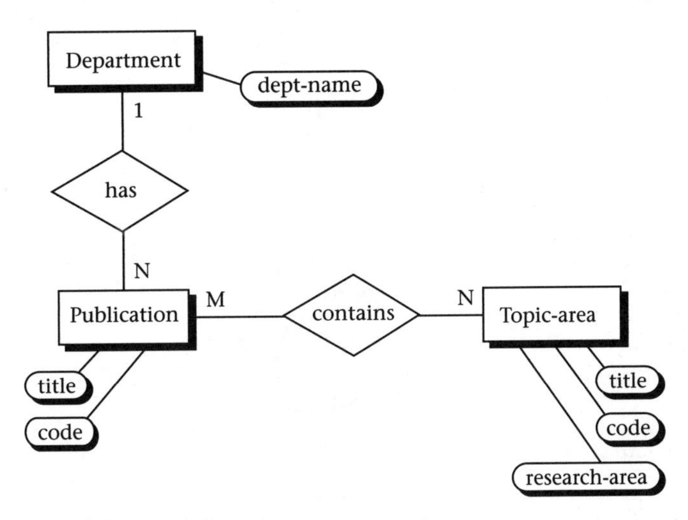

(b) Schema 2.2, in which the attribute "dept-name" has changed to an attribute and an entity

Figure 3.6 View integration: synonyms and structural conflicts

and keywords on publication as the secondary data. Our objective is to find meaningful ways to integrate the two views and maintain completeness, minimality, and understandability.

We first look for synonyms and homonyms, particularly among the entities. Note that a synonym exists between the entities Topic-area in schema 1 and Keyword in schema 2, even though the attributes do not match. However, we find that the attributes are compatible and can be consolidated. This is shown in Figure 3.6a, which presents a revised schema, schema 2.1. In schema 2.1 Keyword has been replaced by Topic-area.

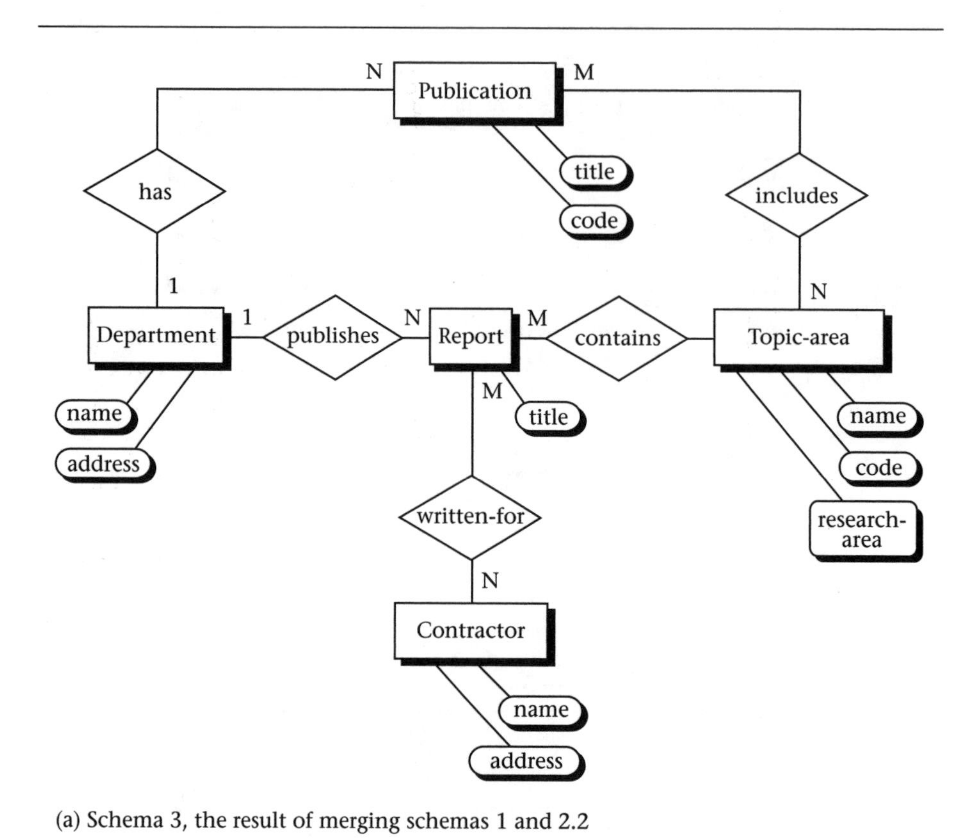

(a) Schema 3, the result of merging schemas 1 and 2.2

Figure 3.7 View integration: merging and restructuring of schemas

Next we look for structural conflicts between schemas. A type conflict is found to exist between the entity Department in schema 1 and the attribute "dept-name" in schema 2.1. The conflict is resolved by keeping the stronger entity type, Department, and moving the attribute type "dept-name" under Publication in schema 2 to the new entity, Department, in schema 2.2 (see Figure 3.6b).

At this point we have sufficient commonality between schemas to attempt a merge. In schemas 1 and 2.2 we have two sets of common entities, Department and Topic-area. Other entities do not overlap and must appear intact in the superimposed, or merged, schema. The merged schema, schema 3, is shown in Figure 3.7a. Because the common entities are truly equivalent, there are no bad side effects of the merge due to existing relationships involving those entities in one schema and not in the other. (Such a relationship that remains intact exists in schema 1

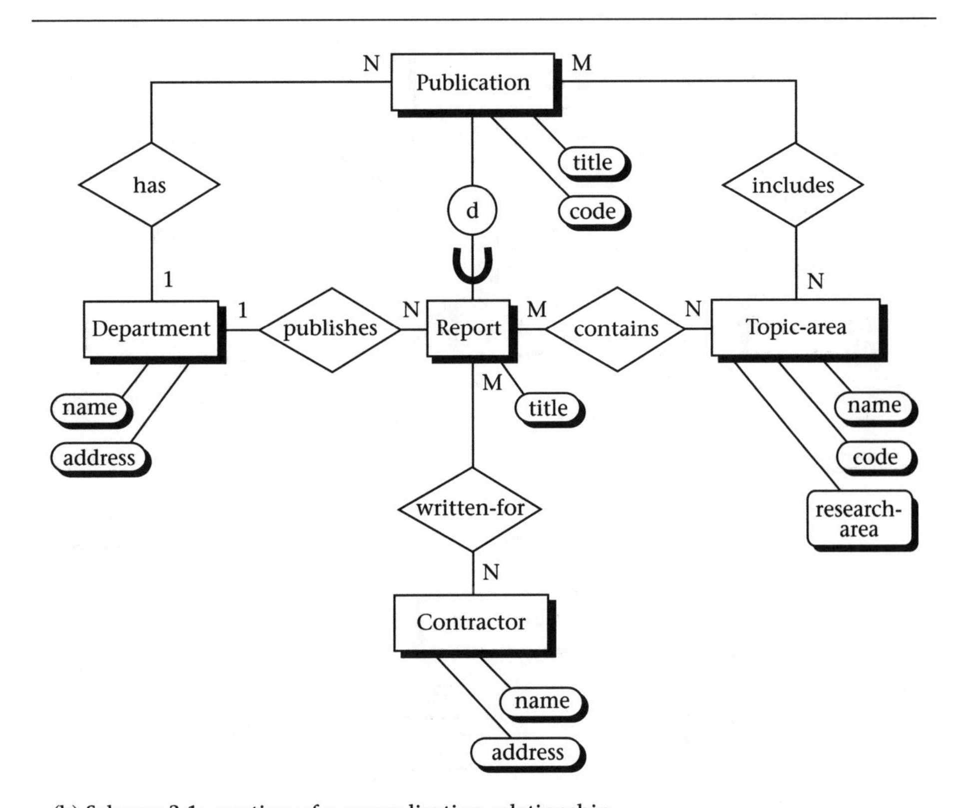

(b) Schema 3.1: creation of a generalization relationship

Figure 3.7 *Continued*

between Topic-area and Report, for example.) If true equivalence cannot be established, the merge may not be possible in the existing form.

In Figure 3.7, there is some redundancy between Publication and Report in terms of the relationships with Department and Topic-area. Such a redundancy can be eliminated if there is a supertype/subtype relationship between Publication and Report, which does in fact occur in this case because Publication is a generalization of Report. In schema 3.1 (Figure 3.7b) we see the introduction of this generalization from Report to Publication. Then in schema 3.2 (Figure 3.7c) we see that the redundant relationships between Report and Department and Topic-area have been dropped. The attribute "title" has been eliminated as an attribute of Report in Figure 3.7c because "title" already appears as an attribute of Publication at a higher level of abstraction; "title" is inherited by the subtype Report.

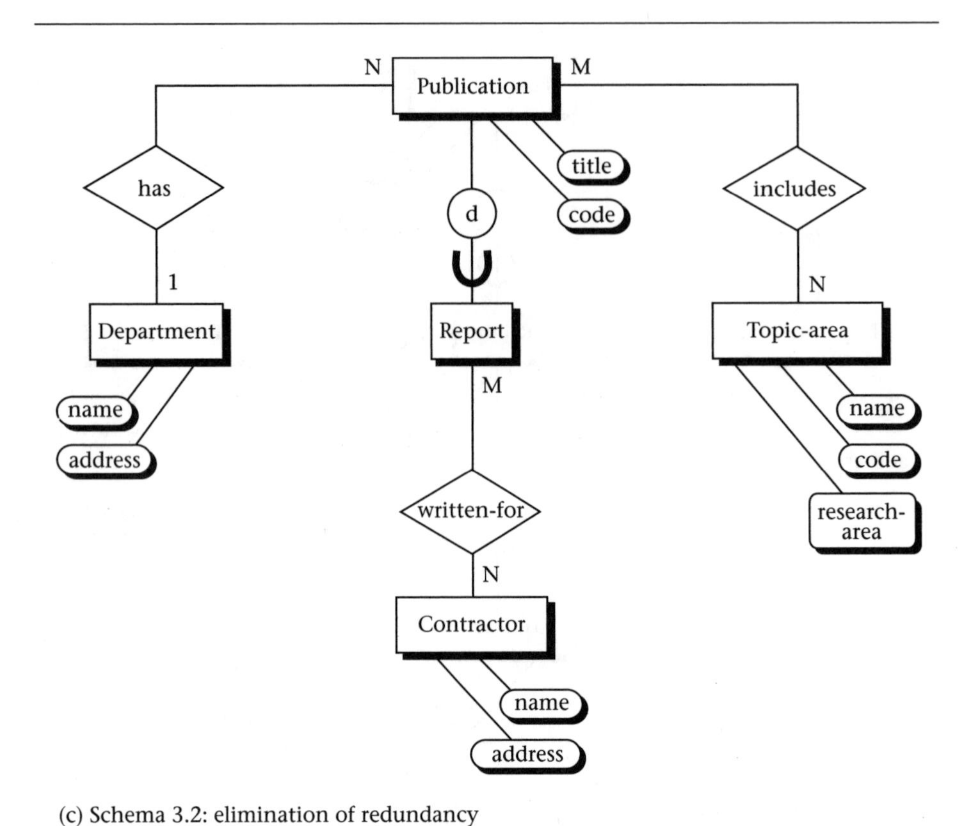

(c) Schema 3.2: elimination of redundancy

Figure 3.7 *Continued*

The final schema, in Figure 3.7c, expresses completeness because all the original concepts (report, publication, topic area, department, and contractor) are kept intact. It expresses minimality because of the transformation of "dept-name" from attribute in schema 1 to entity and attribute in schema 2.2, and the merger between schema 1 and schema 2.2 to form schema 3, and because of the elimination of "title" as an attribute of Report and of Report relationships with Topic-area and Department. Finally, it expresses understandability in that the final schema actually has more meaning than the individual original schemas.

The view integration process is one of continual refinement and reevaluation. It has therefore been difficult to automate, although some semiautomatic algorithms, with some designer interaction, can be used.

3.4 Entity Clustering

This section presents the concept of entity clustering, which abstracts the ER schema to such a degree that the entire schema can appear on a single sheet of paper or a single computer screen. This has happy consequences for the end user and database designer in terms of developing a mutual understanding of the database contents and formally documenting the conceptual model.

An entity cluster is the result of a grouping operation on a collection of entities and relationships. Clustering can be applied repeatedly, resulting in layered levels of abstraction with manager and end-user views at the top level, database designer views at middle levels, and both designer and programmer views at the bottom level.

Entity clustering is potentially useful for designing large databases. When the scale of a database or information structure is large and includes a large number of interconnections among its different components, it may be very difficult to understand the semantics of such a structure and to manage it, especially for the end users or managers. In an ER diagram with 1000 entities, the overall structure will probably not be very clear, even to a well-trained database analyst. Clustering is therefore important because it provides a method to organize a conceptual database schema into layers of abstraction, and it supports the different views of a variety of end users.

3.4.1 Clustering Concepts

The entity clustering technique integrates object clustering concepts with the traditional design of ER models to produce bottom-up abstraction of natural groupings of entities. Think of grouping as an operation that combines entities and their relationships to form a higher-level construct. The result of a grouping operation on purely elementary entities is called an *entity cluster*. A grouping operation on entity clusters or on combinations of elementary entities and entity clusters results in a higher-level entity cluster. The highest-level entity cluster, representing the entire database conceptual schema, is called the *root entity cluster*.

Figure 3.8a illustrates the concept of entity clustering in a simple case where (elementary) entities R-sec (report section), R-abbr (report abbreviation), and Author are naturally bound to (dominated by) the entity Report; and entities Department, Contractor, and Project are not dominated. (Note that to avoid unnecessary detail, we do not include the

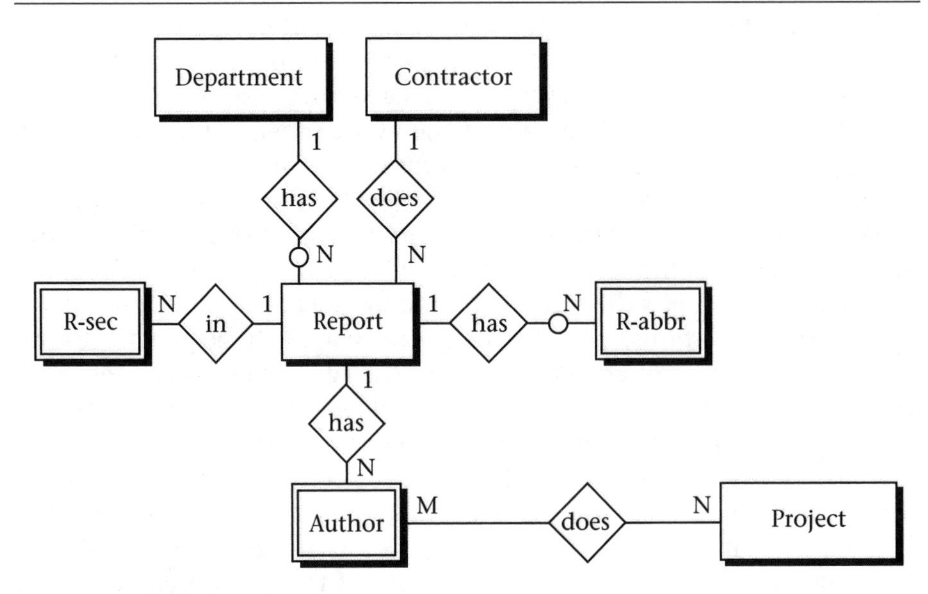

(a) ER model before clustering

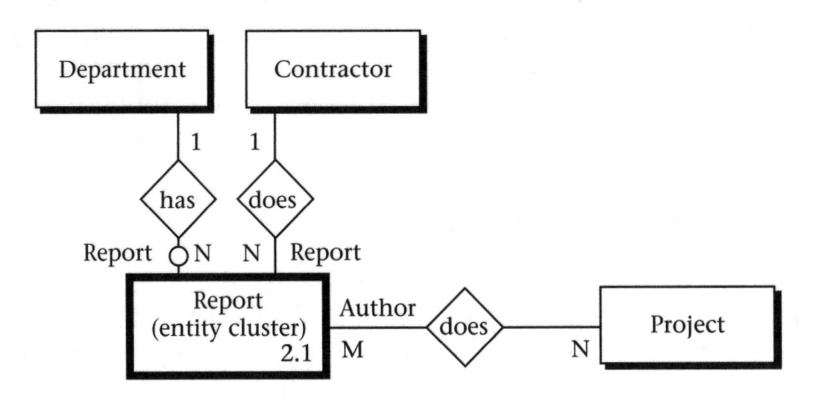

(b) ER model after clustering

Figure 3.8 Format of an entity cluster

attributes of entities in the diagrams.) In Figure 3.8b the dark-bordered box around the entity Report and the entities it dominates defines the entity cluster Report. The dark-bordered box is called the EC box to represent the idea of entity cluster. In general, the name of the entity cluster need not be the same as the name of any internal entity; however, when there is a single dominant entity, the names are often the same. The EC box number in the lower-right corner is a clustering-level number used to keep track of the sequence in which clustering is done. The number 2.1 signifies that the entity cluster Report is the first entity cluster at level 2. Note that all the original entities are considered to be at level 1.

The higher-level abstraction, the entity cluster, must maintain the same relationships between entities inside and outside the entity cluster as occur between the same entities in the lower-level diagram. Thus, the entity names inside the entity cluster should appear just outside the EC box along the path of their direct relationship to the appropriately related entities outside the box, maintaining consistent interfaces (relationships) as shown in Figure 3.8b. For simplicity, we modify this rule slightly: If the relationship is between an external entity and the dominant internal entity (for which the entity cluster is named), the entity cluster name need not be repeated outside the EC box. Thus, in Figure 3.8b, we could drop the name Report both places it occurs outside the Report box, but we must retain the name Author, which is not the name of the entity cluster.

Relationships in entity diagrams used here are not restricted to current ER model implementations and commercial tools, but they may include n-ary as well as binary degree relationships; optional/mandatory existence dependencies; abstractions; and, possibly, the role concept and integrity constraints of the NIAM model.

3.4.2 Grouping Operations

The grouping operations are the fundamental components of the entity clustering technique. They define what collections of entities and relationships comprise higher-level objects, the entity clusters. The operations are heuristic in nature and include

- dominance grouping
- abstraction grouping
- constraint grouping
- relationship grouping

These grouping operations can be applied recursively or used in a variety of combinations to produce higher-level entity clusters, that is, clusters at any level of abstraction. An entity or entity cluster may be an

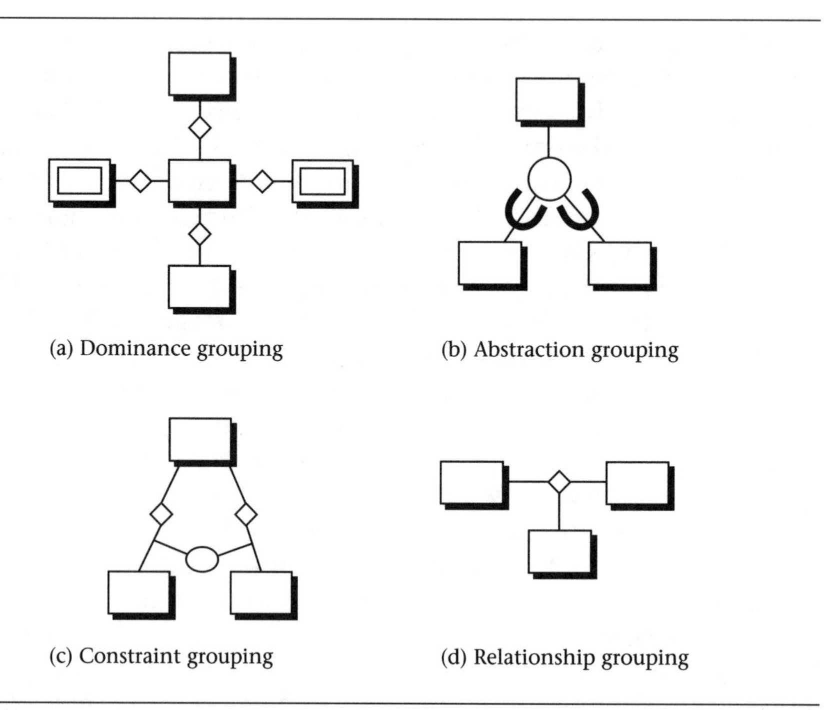

Figure 3.9 Grouping operations (generic forms)

object that is subject to combinations with other objects to form the next higher level. That is, entity clusters have the properties of entities and can have relationships with any other objects at any equal or lower level. The original relationships among entities are preserved after all grouping operations, as illustrated in Figure 3.8.

A cluster level number is given as x.y, where x is the next level above the highest level of entities and entity clusters being grouped. Elementary entities are considered to be at level 0. The y value represents a unique identification number given to each cluster at level x (see Figure 3.9 for the generic forms of grouping).

Dominant objects or entities normally become obvious from the ER diagram or the relationship definitions. Each dominant object is grouped with all its related nondominant objects to form a cluster. Weak entities can be attached to an entity to make a cluster.

Multilevel data objects using such abstractions as generalization, subset generalization, and aggregation can be grouped into an entity cluster. The supertype or aggregate entity name is used as the entity cluster name.

Constraint-related objects that extend the ER model to incorporate the integrity constraints of NIAM can be grouped into an entity cluster.

The n-ary relationships of degree 3 or more can potentially be grouped into an entity cluster. The cluster represents the relationship as a whole, such as the relationship table that would be defined when transforming the n-ary relationship into a set of equivalent normalized tables.

3.4.3 Clustering Technique

The grouping operations and their order of precedence determine the individual activities needed for clustering. We now learn how to build a root entity cluster from the elementary entities and relationships defined in the ER modeling process. This technique assumes that a top-down analysis has been performed as part of the database requirement analysis and that it has been documented so that the major functional areas and subareas are identified. Functional areas are often defined by an enterprise's important organizational units, business activities, or, possibly, by dominant applications for processing information. As an example, recall Figure 3.3 (reconstructed in Figure 3.10), which can be thought of as having three major functional areas: company organization (division, department), project management (project, skill, location, employee), and employee data (employee, manager, secretary, engineer, technician, prof-assoc, and desktop). Note that the functional areas are allowed to overlap. Using an ER diagram resulting from the database requirement analysis as shown in Figure 3.10, clustering involves a series of bottom-up steps using the basic grouping operations. The list that follows explains these steps.

1. *Define points of grouping within functional areas.* Locate the dominant entities in a functional area through the natural relationships, local n-ary relationships, integrity constraints, abstractions, or just the central focus of many simple relationships. If such points of grouping do not exist within an area, consider a functional grouping of a whole area.
2. *Form entity clusters.* Use the basic grouping operations on elementary entities and their relationships to form higher-level objects, or entity clusters. Because entities may belong to several potential clusters, we need to have a set of priorities for forming entity clusters. The following set of rules, listed in priority order, defines the set that is most likely to preserve the clarity of the conceptual model.

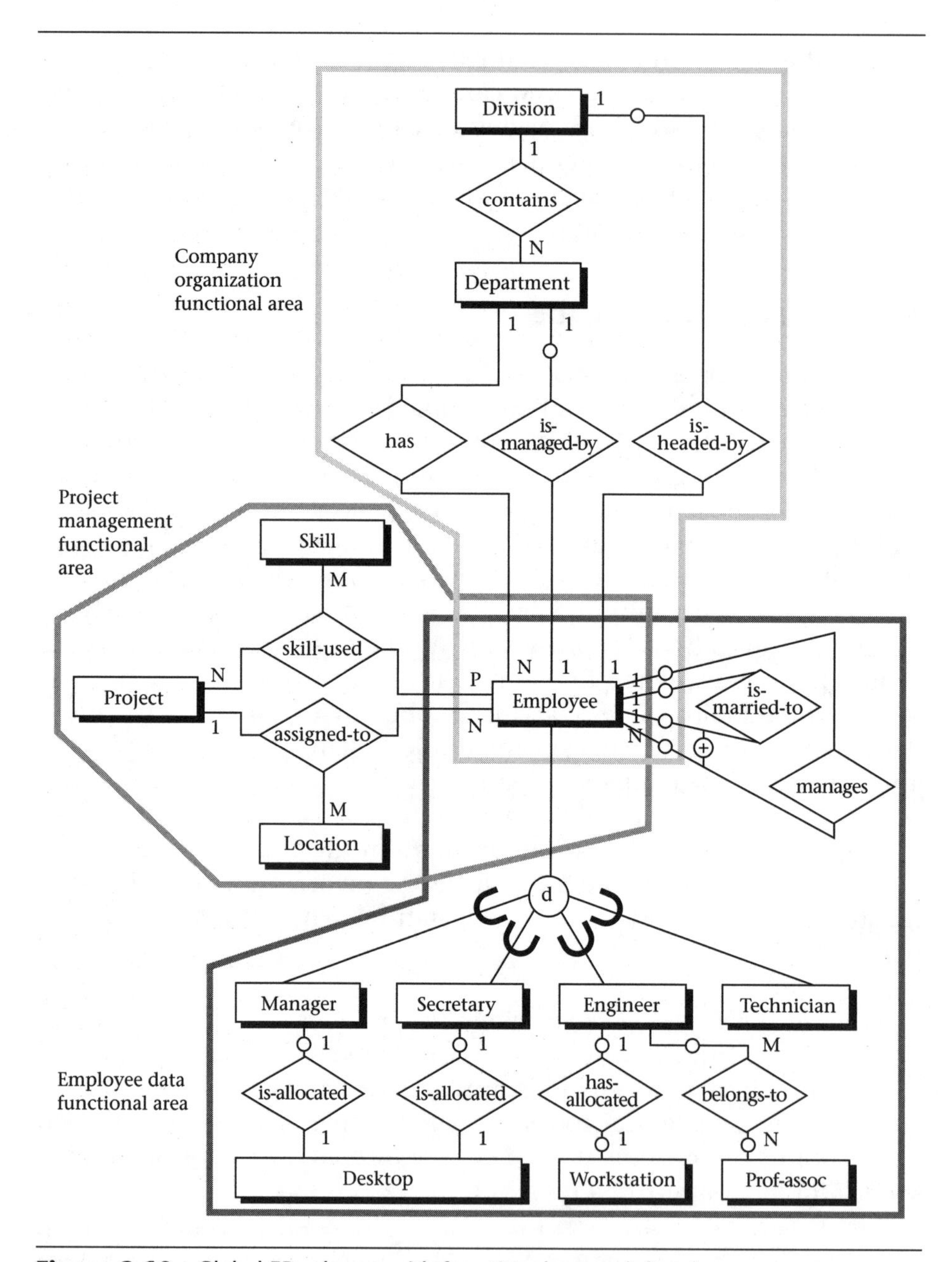

Figure 3.10 Global ER schema with functional areas defined

a. Entities to be grouped into an entity cluster should exist within the same functional area; that is, the entire entity cluster should occur within the boundary of a functional area. For example, in Figure 3.10, the relationship between Department and Employee should not be clustered unless Employee is included in the company organization functional area with Department and Division. In another example, the relationship between the supertype Employee and its subtypes could be clustered within the employee data functional area.

   b. If a conflict in choice between two or more potential entity clusters cannot be resolved (e.g., between two constraint groupings at the same level of precedence), leave these entity clusters ungrouped within their functional area. If that functional area remains cluttered with unresolved choices, define functional subareas in which to group unresolved entities, entity clusters, and their relationships.

3. *Form higher-level entity clusters.* Apply the grouping operations recursively to any combination of elementary entities and entity clusters to form new levels of entity clusters (higher-level objects). Resolve conflicts using the same set of priority rules given in step 2. Continue the grouping operations until all the entity representations fit on a single page without undue complexity. The root entity cluster is then defined.
4. *Validate the cluster diagram.* Check for consistency of the interfaces (relationships) between objects at each level of the diagram. Verify the meaning of each level with the end users.

The result of one round of clustering is shown in Figure 3.11, where each of the clusters is shown at level 2. The root entity cluster for this database would be a single box at level 3. This technique could feasibly be implemented with software whose diagrams are created and accessed with the simple open, close, group, and ungroup operations found in available object-oriented drawing packages.

3.5 Summary

The ER approach is particularly useful in the early steps of the database life cycle, which involve requirements analysis and logical design. These two steps are often done simultaneously, particularly when requirements are determined from end-user interviews and modeled in terms of data-to-data relationships and process-to-data relationships. The ER modeling step involves the classification of entities and attributes first, then

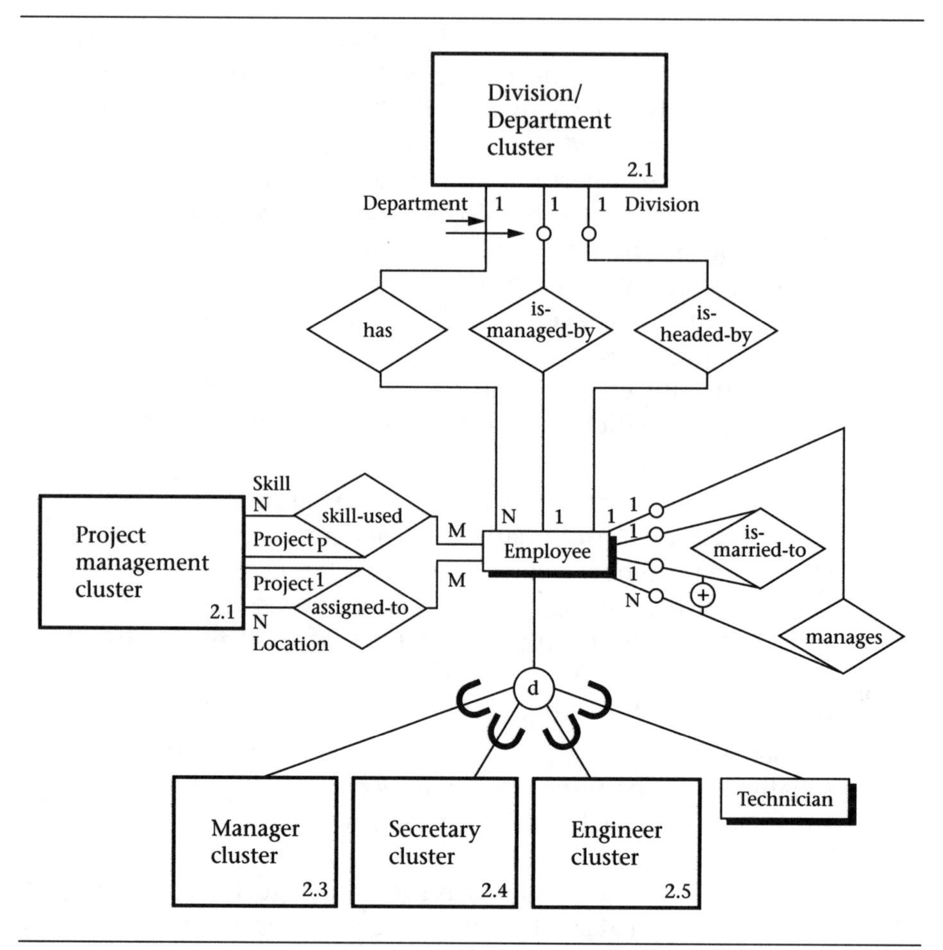

Figure 3.11 Entity clusters at the second (root) level

identification of generalization hierarchies and other abstractions, and finally the definition of all relationships among entities. Relationships may be binary (the most common), ternary, and higher-level n-ary.

ER modeling of individual requirements typically involves creating a different view for each end user's requirements. Then the designer must integrate those views into a global schema so that the entire database is pictured as an integrated whole. This helps to eliminate needless redundancy—such elimination is particularly important in logical design. Controlled redundancy can be created later, at the physical design level, to enhance database performance.

Finally, entity clustering promotes the simplicity that is vital for fast end-user comprehension, as well as the complexity at a more detailed level to satisfy the database designer's need for extended semantic expression in the conceptual model. An entity cluster is a grouping of entities and their corresponding relationships into a higher-level abstract object.

In the next chapter we take the global schema produced from the ER modeling and view integration steps and transform it into SQL tables. The SQL format is the end product of logical design, which is still independent of a database management system.

Literature Summary

Conceptual modeling is defined in [TsLo82, BMS84, NiHa89, BCN92]. At the theoretical level a top-down approach to database design is investigated with regard to the universal relation assumption [BBG78, Kent81] and the combined top-down and bottom-up approach is discussed in [Date95, Swee85]. Discussion of the requirements data collection process can be found in [Mart82, TeFr82, Yao85].

Recent research has advanced view integration from a representation tool [SmSm77] to heuristic algorithms [ElWi79, NaGa82, NSE84, BaLe84, EHW85, NEL86, BLN86]. These algorithms are typically interactive, allowing the database designer to make decisions based on suggested alternative integration actions. Adopting an ER extension called the entity-category-relationship model [EHW85], Navathe and others organized the different classes of objects and relationships into forms that are either compatible or incompatible for view integration [NEL86].

An entity cluster is also known in the literature as a complex object [Su83, DGL86, StRo86, PoKe86], molecular aggregation [BaBu84], or subject area [FeMi86]. The entity or object cluster concept can already be found in some database systems [BaBu84, MSOP86, Wied86]. Clustering models have been recently defined that provide a useful foundation for the proposed clustering technique [Ossh84, FeMi86, DGL86, TWBK89].

[BaBu84] Batory, D.S., and Buchmann, A.P. "Molecular Objects, Abstract Data Types, and Data Models: A Framework," *Proc. 10th Intl. Conf. on Very Large Data Bases,* Aug. 1984, IEEE, New York, pp. 172–184.

[BaLe84] Batini, C., and Lenzerini, M. "A Methodology for Data Schema Integration in the Entity Relationship Model," *IEEE Trans. on Software Eng.* SE-10, 6 (Nov. 1984), pp. 650–664.

[BBG78] Beeri, C., Bernstein, P., and Goodman, N. "A Sophisticated Introduction to Database Normalization Theory," *Proc. 4th Intl. Conf. on Very Large Data Bases,* Sept. 13–15, 1978, IEEE, New York, pp. 113–124.

[BCN92] Batini, C., Ceri, S., and Navathe, S. *Conceptual Database Design: An Entity-Relationship Approach,* Benjamin/Cummings, Redwood City, CA, 1992.

[BLN86] Batini, C., Lenzerini, M., and Navathe, S.B. "A Comparative Analysis of Methodologies for Database Schema Integration," *ACM Computing Surveys* 18, 4 (Dec. 1986), pp. 323–364.

[BMS84] Brodie, M.L., Mylopoulos, J., and Schmidt, J. (editors). *On Conceptual Modeling: Perspectives from Artificial Intelligence, Databases, and Programming Languages,* Springer-Verlag, New York, 1984.

[Date95] Date, C.J. *An Introduction to Database Systems, Vol. 1* (6th Ed.), Addison-Wesley, Reading, MA, 1995.

[DGL86] Dittrich, K.R., Gotthard, W., and Lockemann, P.C. "Complex Entities for Engineering Applications," *Proc. 5th ER Conf.,* North-Holland, Amsterdam, 1986.

[EHW85] Elmasri, R., Hevner, A., and Weeldreyer, J. "The Category Concept: An Extension to the Entity-Relationship Model," *Data and Knowledge Engineering* 1, 1 (1985), pp. 75–116.

[ElWi79] Elmasri, R., and Wiederhold, G. "Data Model Integration Using the Structural Model," *Proc. ACM SIGMOD Conf.,* Boston, 1979, ACM, New York, pp. 319–326.

[FeMi86] Feldman, P., and Miller, D. "Entity Model Clustering: Structuring a Data Model by Abstraction," *Computer Journal* 29, 4 (Aug. 1986), pp. 348–360.

[Kent81] Kent, W. "Consequences of Assuming a Universal Relation," *ACM Trans. Database Systems* 6, 4 (1981), pp. 539–556.

[Mart82] Martin, J. *Strategic Data-Planning Methodologies,* Prentice Hall, Englewood Cliffs, NJ, 1982.

[MSOP86] Maier, D., Stein, J., Otis, A., and Purdy, A. "Development of an Object-Oriented DBMS," *OOPSLA 1986 Proc.,* Sept. 1986, pp. 472–482.

[NaGa82] Navathe, S., and Gadgil, S. "A Methodology for View Integration in Logical Database Design," *Proc. 8th Intl. Conf. on Very Large Data Bases,* 1982, IEEE, New York, pp. 142–152.

[NEL86] Navathe, S., Elmasri, R., and Larson, J. "Integrating User Views in Database Design," *IEEE Computer* 19, 1 (1986), pp. 50–62.

[NiHa89] Nijssen, G.M., and Halpin, T.A. *Conceptual Schema and Relational Database Design: A Fact Oriented Approach,* Prentice Hall, New York, 1989.

[NSE84] Navathe, S., Sashidhar, T., and Elmasri, R. "Relationship Merging in Schema Integration," *Proc. 10th Intl. Conf. on Very Large Data Bases,* 1984, IEEE, New York, pp. 78–90.

[Ossh84] Ossher, H.L. "A New Program Structuring Mechanism Based on Layered Graphs," *Proc. 11th Annual ACM SIGACT-SIGPLAN POPL,* 1984, pp. 11–22.

[PoKe86] Potter, W.D., and Kerschberg, L. "A Unified Approach to Modeling Knowledge and Data," *IFIP WG 2.6 Working Conf. on Knowledge and Data,* Elsevier, North-Holland, Amsterdam, Sept. 1986.

[SmSm77] Smith, J., and Smith, D. "Database Abstractions: Aggregation and Generalization," *ACM Trans. Database Systems* 2, 2 (June 1977), pp. 105–133.

[StRo86] Stonebraker, M., and Rowe, L.A. "The Design of Postgres," *Proc. ACM-SIGMOD Intl. Conf. on Management of Data,* 1986, pp. 340–355.

[Su83] Su, S.Y.W. "SAM*: A Semantic Association Model for Corporate and Scientific Statistical Databases," *Inform. Sciences* 29, 2–3 (May–June 1983), pp. 151–199.

[Swee85] Sweet, F. "Process-Driven Data Design," *Datamation* (first of a series of 14 articles), 31, 16 (1985), pp. 84–85.

[TeFr82] Teorey, T., and Fry, J. *Design of Database Structures,* Prentice Hall, Upper Saddle River, NJ, 1982.

[TsLo82] Tsichritzis, D., and Lochovsky, F. *Data Models,* Prentice Hall, Englewood Cliffs, NJ, 1982.

[TWBK89] Teorey, T.J., Wei, G., Bolton, D.L., and Koenig, J.A. "ER Model Clustering as an Aid for User Communication and Documentation in Database Design," *Comm. ACM* 32, 8 (Aug. 1989), pp. 975–987.

[TYF86] Teorey, T.J., Yang, D., and Fry, J.P. "A Logical Design Methodology for Relational Databases Using the Extended Entity-Relationship Model," *ACM Computing Surveys* 18, 2 (June 1986), pp. 197–222.

[Wied86] Wiederhold, G. "Views, Objects, and Databases," *IEEE Computer* (Dec. 1986), pp. 37–44.

[Yao85] Yao, S.B. (editor). *Principles of Database Design,* Prentice Hall, Upper Saddle River, NJ, 1985.

Exercises

Problem 3-1

An ER diagram that satisfies the following assertions is shown below. For this diagram, fill in the missing relationship connectivities, optionalities, and entities (or weak entities).

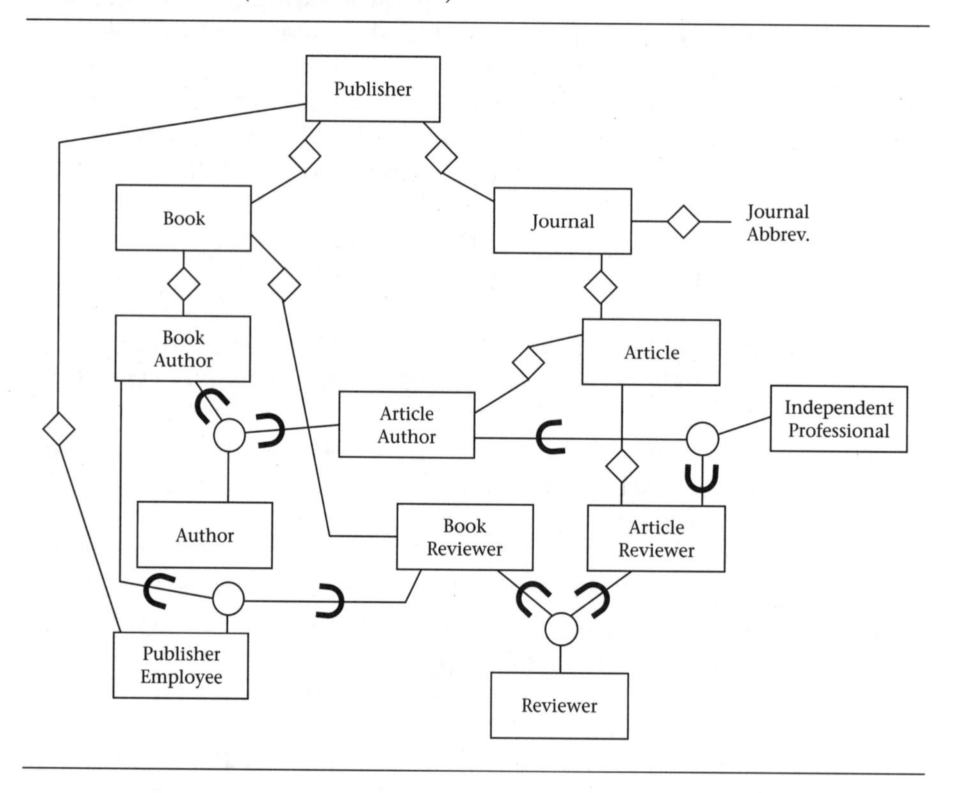

Publishers publish many different types of professional journals and books. Some publishers only publish books, some journals, and some both. No book or journal is published by more than one publisher. An author may write either books, journal articles, or both. A journal typically contains several articles, each one written by one or more authors. No article appears in more than one journal. Any journal may have one or more abbreviations, or none.

Every book and article is reviewed by several professionals in the field who may or may not be authors as well. Of course, an author never reviews his or her own book or article. Each book reviewer and author works for and is paid by a single publisher. Article authors and reviewers are not paid, however, and thus article reviewers are never book reviewers. Authors and reviewers who are not paid by a publisher are known as independent professionals.

Problem 3-2

Given the following assertions for a relational database that represents the current term enrollment at a large university, draw an ER diagram for this schema that takes into account *all* the assertions given. There are 2000 instructors, 4000 courses, and 30,000 students. Use as many ER constructs as you can to represent the true semantics of the problem.

Assertions:

a. An instructor may teach none, one, or more courses in a given term (average is 2.0 courses).

b. An instructor must direct the research of at least one student (average = 2.5 students).

c. A course may have none, one, or two prerequisites (average = 1.5 prerequisites).

d. A course may exist even if no students are currently enrolled.

e. All courses are taught by only one instructor.

f. The average enrollment in a course is 30 students.

g. A student must select at least one course per term (average = 4.0 course selections).

Please see page 348 for the solution to Problem 3-2.

Problem 3-3

Create an ER diagram for the database that satisfies the following assertions about a general-purpose community medical facility. What questions about this enterprise's environment do these assertions leave unanswered?

A person is represented as either a patient or a medical worker. A medical worker is either a doctor, nurse, paramedic, clerk, or administrator. Medical workers work in a medical facility that has a name, address, possibly a specialty area, and the name of an administrator.

A patient visits a medical facility for a diagnosis of a health problem and then may come for additional visits for treatment if so designated as a result of the diagnosis and if the facility has the expertise to treat the problem. Each visit is called an *encounter,* and it must involve a patient, a medical worker, and a service. The service could be a diagnosis, treatment, checkup, or payment. A patient may be eligible for company health benefits or must pay-as-you-go. Patients who are unable to pay are not turned away but are registered as indigent citizens and are given short-term care. Patient data includes name, id number (ssn), address (street, city, state, zip), phone (day and evenings), employer (company) name, employer address, type of benefits eligible for, and method of payment.

A medical worker must hold one or more credentials that are granted to work in a particular medical facility. Doctors are allowed to perform any kind of diagnosis and give treatment based on their specialty. Paramedics are allowed to give only emergency diagnoses and treatment, but for any type of life-threatening problem. Nurses do not do diagnoses but participate in treatment, particularly if the patient must be prepared for surgery or remain at the facility overnight.

The facility administrator is concerned with personnel needs and assignments. Each medical worker must have at least one and possibly more assignments at a facility. Each assignment partially or completely fills an authorized slot specified by the personnel needs; thus, an authorization may involve many assignments. Medical workers have certain skills that must be recorded and accessed for a new assignment.

4 Transformation of the ER Model to SQL

This chapter focuses on the database life cycle step that is of particular interest when designing relational databases: transformation of the ER model to candidate tables and their definition in SQL (step II(c)). We see a natural evolution from the ER model to a relational schema. The evolution is so natural, in fact, that it supports the contention that ER modeling is an effective early step in relational database development. This contention has been proven to some extent by the widespread commercialization and use of CASE tools that support not only ER modeling but also the automatic conversion of ER models to vendor-specific SQL table definitions and integrity constraints.

4.1 Transformation Rules and SQL Constructs

We now look at each ER modeling construct in detail to see how the rules about transforming the ER model to relational (SQL-92) schemas are defined and applied. Our example is drawn from the company personnel and project ER schemas illustrated in Figure 3.3.

The basic transformations can be described in terms of the three types of tables they produce:

- *An entity table with the same information content as the original entity.* This transformation always occurs for entities with binary relationships that are many-to-many, one-to-many on the "one" (parent) side, or one-to-one on one side; entities with binary recursive relationships that are many-to-many; and entities with any ternary or higher-degree relationship, or a generalization hierarchy.

- *An entity table with the embedded foreign key of the parent entity.* This transformation always occurs for entities with binary relationships that are one-to-many for the entity on the "many" (child) side, for one-to-one relationships for one of the entities, and for each entity with a binary recursive relationship that is one-to-one or one-to-many. This is one of the two most common ways CASE tools handle relationships, by prompting the user to define a foreign key in the child table that matches a primary key in the parent table.
- *A relationship table with the foreign keys of all the entities in the relationship.* This transformation always occurs for relationships that are binary and many-to-many, relationships that are binary recursive and many-to-many, and all relationships that are of ternary or higher degree. This is the other most common way CASE tools handle relationships in the ER model. A many-to-many relationship can only be defined in terms of a table that contains foreign keys that match the primary keys of the two associated entities. This new table may also contain attributes of the original relationship—for example, a relationship "enrolled-in" between two entities Student and Course might have the attributes "term" and "grade," which are associated with a particular student enrolled in a particular course.

The following rules apply to handling SQL null values in these transformations:

- Nulls are allowed in an entity table for foreign keys of associated (referenced) optional entities.
- Nulls are not allowed in an entity table for foreign keys of associated (referenced) mandatory entities.
- Nulls are not allowed for any key in a relationship table because only complete row entries are meaningful in the table.

In some relational systems, rules for nulls are different. These rules can be modified to be consistent with such systems. Figures 4.1 through 4.4 show standard SQL statements needed to define each type of ER model construct. Note that table names are shown in boldface for readability.

4.1.1 Binary Relationships

A one-to-one binary relationship between two entities is illustrated in Figure 4.1, parts a through c. When both entities are mandatory (Figure

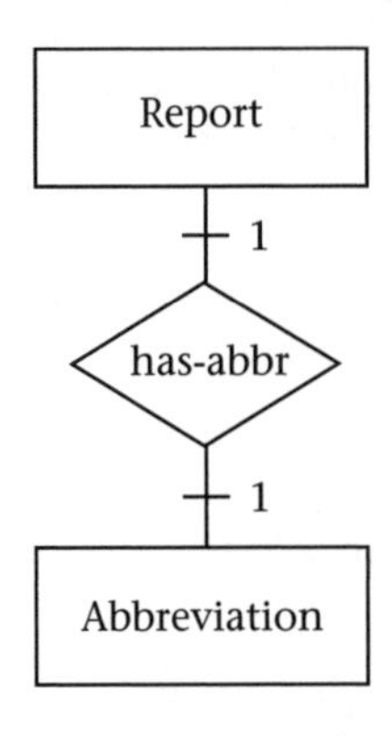

Every report has one abbreviation, and every abbreviation represents exactly one report.

```
create table report
        (report_no integer,
        report_name varchar(256),
        primary key(report_no);
create table abbreviation
        (abbr_no char(6),
        report_no integer not null unique,
        primary key (abbr_no),
        foreign key (report_no) references report
            on delete cascade on update cascade);
```

(a) One-to-one, both entities mandatory

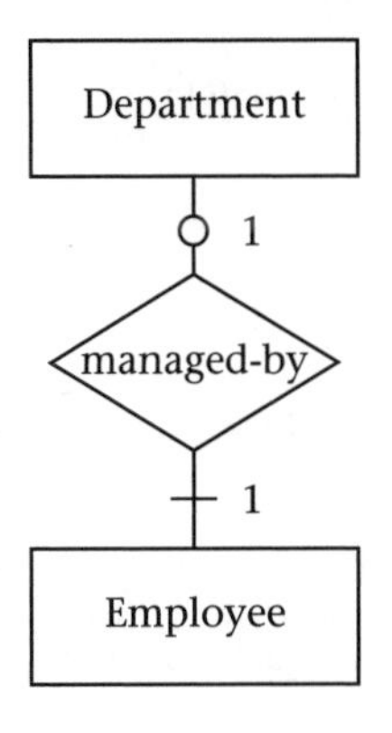

Every department must have a manager, but an employee can be a manager of at most one department.

```
create table department
        (dept_no integer,
        dept_name char(20),
        mgr_id char(10) not null unique,
        primary key (dept_no),
        foreign key (mgr_id) references employee
            on delete set default on update cascade);
create table employee
        (emp_id char(10),
        emp_name char(20),
        primary key (emp_id));
```

(b) One-to-one, one entity optional, one mandatory

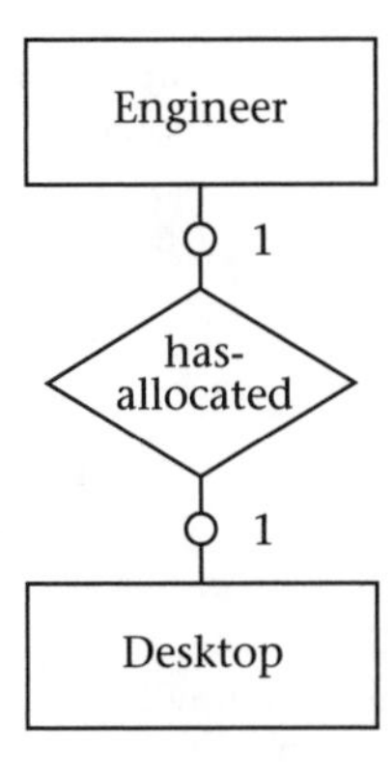

Some desktop computers are allocated to engineers but not necessarily to all engineers.

```
create table engineer
        (emp_id char(10),
        desktop_no integer,
        primary key (emp_id);
create table desktop
        (desktop_no integer,
        emp_id char(10),
        primary key (desktop_no),
        foreign key (emp_id) references engineer
            on delete set null on update cascade);
```

(c) One-to-one, both entities optional

Figure 4.1 Binary relationship transformation rules

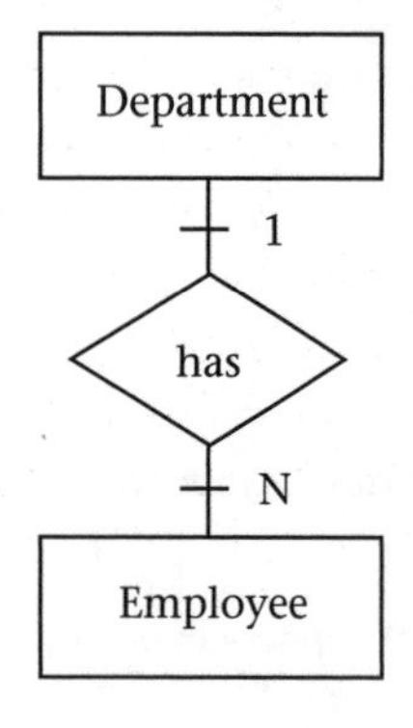

Every employee works in exactly one department, and each department has at least one employee.

```
create table department
        (dept_no integer,
        dept_name char(20),
        primary key (dept_no));
create table employee
        (emp_id char(10),
        emp_name char(20),
        dept_no integer not null,
        primary key (emp_id),
        foreign key (dept_no) references department
            on delete set default on update cascade);
```

(d) One-to-many, both entities mandatory

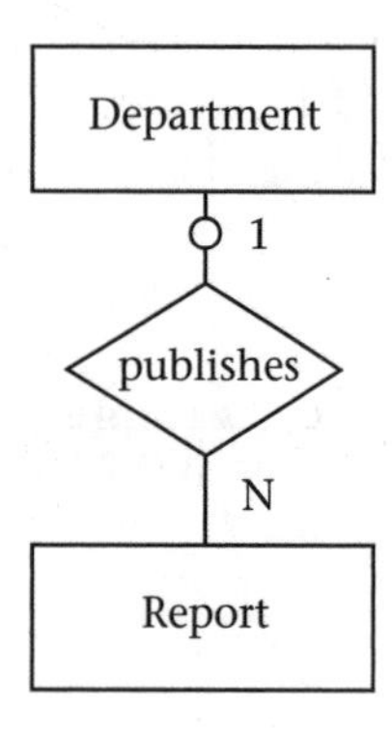

Each department publishes one or more reports. A given report may not necessarily be published by a department.

```
create table department
        (dept_no integer,
        dept_name char(20),
        primary key (dept_no));
create table report
        (report_no integer,
        dept_no integer,
        primary key (report_no),
        foreign key (dept_no) references department
            on delete set null on update cascade);
```

(e) One-to-many, one entity optional, one unknown

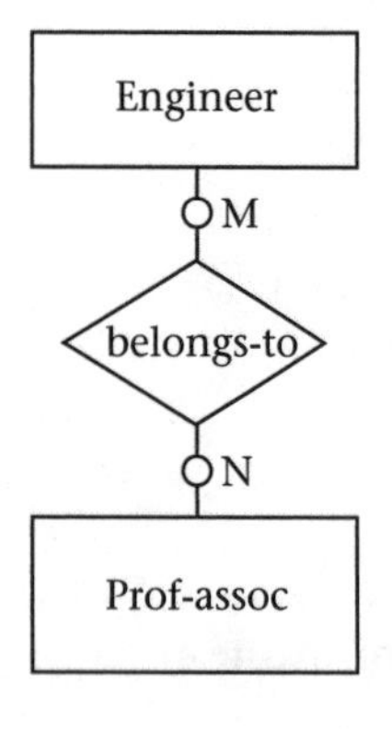

Every professional association could have none, one, or many engineer members. Each engineer could be a member of none, one, or many professional associations.

```
create table engineer
        (emp_id char(10),
        primary key (emp_id));
create table prof_assoc
        (assoc_name varchar(256),
        primary key (assoc_name));
create table belongs_to
        (emp_id char(10),
        assoc_name varchar(256),
        primary key (emp_id, assoc_name),
        foreign key (emp_id) references engineer
            on delete cascade on update cascade,
        foreign key (assoc_name) references prof_assoc
            on delete cascade on update cascade);
```

(f) Many-to-many, both entities optional

Figure 4.1 *Continued*

4.1a), each entity becomes a table and the key of either entity can appear in the other entity's table as a foreign key. One of the entities in an optional relationship (see Department in Figure 4.1b) should contain the foreign key of the other entity in its transformed table. Employee, the other entity in Figure 4.1b, could also contain a foreign key (dept_no) with nulls allowed, but this would require more storage space because of the much greater number of Employee entity instances than Department instances. When both entities are optional (Figure 4.1c), either entity can contain the embedded foreign key of the other entity, with nulls allowed in the foreign keys.

The one-to-many relationship can be shown as either mandatory or optional on the "many" side, without affecting the transformation. On the "one" side it may be either mandatory (Figure 4.1d) or optional (Figure 4.1e). In all cases the foreign key must appear on the "many" side, which represents the child entity, with nulls allowed for foreign keys only in the optional "one" case. Foreign key constraints are set according to the specific meaning of the relationship and may vary from one relationship to another.

The many-to-many relationship, shown in Figure 4.1f as completely optional, requires a relationship table with primary keys of both entities. The same transformation applies to either the optional or mandatory case, including the fact that the not null clause must appear for the foreign keys in both cases. Foreign key constraints on delete and update must always be *cascade* because each entry in the SQL table depends on the current value or existence of the referenced primary key.

4.1.2 Binary Recursive Relationships

A single entity with a one-to-one relationship implies some form of entity occurrence pairing, as indicated by the relationship name. This pairing may be completely optional, completely mandatory, or neither. In all of these cases (Figure 4.2a), the pairing entity key appears as a foreign key in the resulting table. The two key attributes are taken from the same domain but are given different names to designate their unique use. The one-to-many relationship requires a foreign key in the entity table (Figure 4.2b). The foreign key constraints can vary with the particular relationship.

The many-to-many relationship is shown as optional (Figure 4.2c) and uses a relationship table; it could also be defined as mandatory (using the word "must" instead of "may"); both cases have the foreign keys defined as "not null." In many-to-many relationships, foreign key

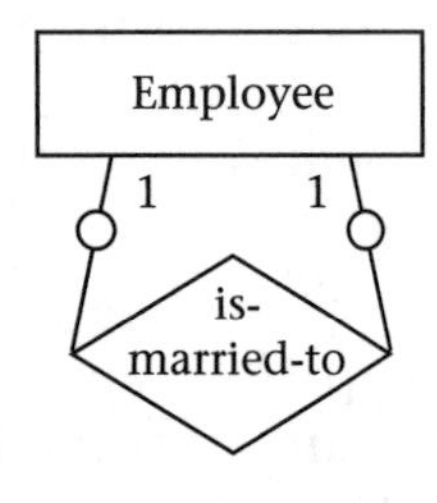

Any employee is allowed to be married to another employee in this company.

```
create table employee
    (emp_id char(10),
    emp_name char(20),
    spouse_id char(10),
    primary key (emp_id),
    foreign key (spouse_id) references employee
        on delete set null on update cascade);
```

(a) One-to-one, both sides optional

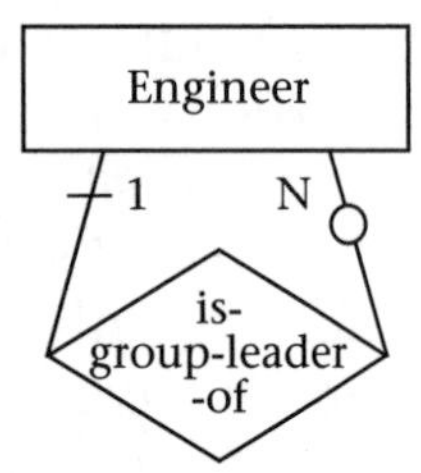

Engineers are divided into groups for certain projects. Each group has a leader.

```
create table engineer
    (emp_id char(10),
    leader_id char(10) not null,
    primary key (emp_id),
    foreign key (leader_id) references engineer
        on delete set default on update cascade);
```

(b) One-to-many, "one" side mandatory, "many" side optional

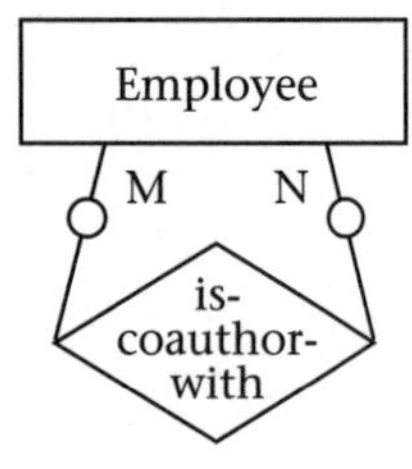

Each employee has the opportunity to coauthor a report with one or more other employees or to write the report alone.

```
create table employee
    (emp_id char(10),
    emp_name char(20),
    primary key (emp_id));

create table coauthor
    (author_id char(10),
    coauthor_id char(10),
    primary key (author_id, coauthor_id),
    foreign key (author_id) references employee
        on delete cascade on update cascade,
    foreign key (coauthor_id) references employee
        on delete cascade on update cascade);
```

(c) Many-to-many, both sides optional

Figure 4.2 Binary recursive relationship transformation rules

constraints on delete and update must always be cascade because each entry in the SQL table depends on the current value or existence of the referenced primary key.

4.1.3 Ternary and n-ary Relationships

An n-ary relationship has n + 1 possible variations of connectivity: all n sides with connectivity "one;" n – 1 sides with connectivity "one," and one side with connectivity "many;" n – 2 sides with connectivity "one" and two sides with "many;" and so on until all sides are "many."

The four possible varieties of a ternary relationship are shown in Figure 4.3. All variations are transformed by creating a relationship table containing the primary keys of all entities; however, in each case the meaning of the keys is different. When all relationships are "one" (Figure 4.3a), the relationship table consists of three possible distinct candidate keys. This represents the fact that there are three FDs needed to describe this relationship. The optionality constraint is not used here because all n entities must participate in every instance of the relationship to satisfy the FD (or multivalued dependency) constraints. (See Chapter 5 for more discussion of functional and multivalued dependencies.)

In general the number of entities with connectivity "one" determines the lower bound on the number of FDs. Thus, in Figure 4.3b, which is one-to-one-to-many, there are two FDs; in Figure 4.3c, which is one-to-many-to-many, there is only one FD. When all relationships are "many" (Figure 4.3d), the relationship table is all one composite key unless the relationship has its own attributes. In that case the key is the composite of all three keys from the three associated entities.

Foreign key constraints on delete and update for ternary relationships transformed to SQL tables must always be cascade because each entry in the SQL table depends on the current value of, or existence of, the referenced primary key.

4.1.4 Generalization and Aggregation

The transformation of a generalization abstraction produces a separate table for the generic or supertype entity and each of the subtypes (Figure 4.4). The supertype entity table contains the supertype entity key and all common attributes. Each subtype entity table contains the supertype entity key and only the attributes that are specific to that subtype. Update integrity is maintained by requiring all insertions and deletions to occur in both the supertype entity table and relevant subtype table—that is, the foreign key constraint cascade must be used. If the update is to the primary key of the supertype entity table, then all subtype tables as well as the supertype table must be updated. An update to a nonkey attribute affects either the supertype or one subtype table, but not both. The trans-

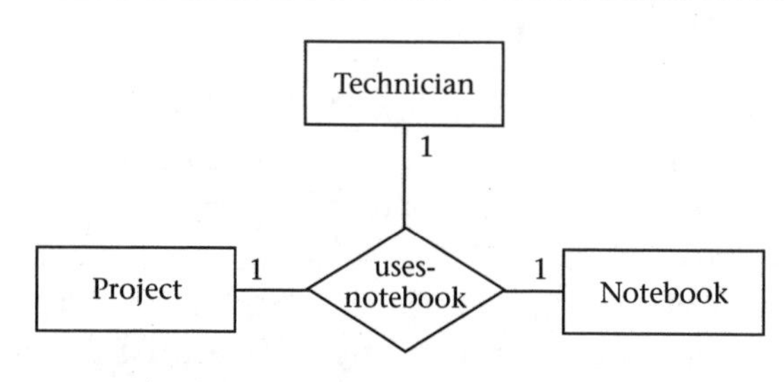

A technician uses exactly one notebook for each project. Each notebook belongs to one technician for each project. Note that a technician may still work on many projects and maintain different notebooks for different projects.

```
create table technician (emp_id char(10),
                         primary key (emp_id));
create table project (project_name char(20),
                      primary key (project_name));
create table notebook (notebook_no integer,
                       primary key (notebook_no));
create table uses_notebook (emp_id char(10),
                            project_name char(20),
                            notebook_no integer not null,
                            primary key (emp_id, project_name),
                            foreign key (emp_id) references technician
                              on delete cascade on update cascade,
                            foreign key (project_name) references project
                              on delete cascade on update cascade,
                            foreign key (notebook_no) references notebook
                              on delete cascade on update cascade,
                            unique (emp_id, notebook_no),
                            unique (project_name, notebook_no));
```

uses_notebook

emp_id	project_name	notebook_no
35	alpha	5001
35	gamma	2008
42	delta	1004
42	epsilon	3005
81	gamma	1007
93	alpha	1009
93	beta	5001

Functional dependencies

emp_id, project_name → notebook_no
emp_id, notebook_no → project_name
project_name, notebook_no → emp_id

(a) One-to-one-to-one ternary relationship

Figure 4.3 Ternary relationship transformation rules

formation rules (and integrity rules) are the same for both the disjoint and overlapping subtype generalizations.

Database practitioners often add a discriminator to the supertype when they implement generalization [BlPr98]. The discriminator is an attribute that has a separate value for each subtype and indicates which subtype to use to get further information.

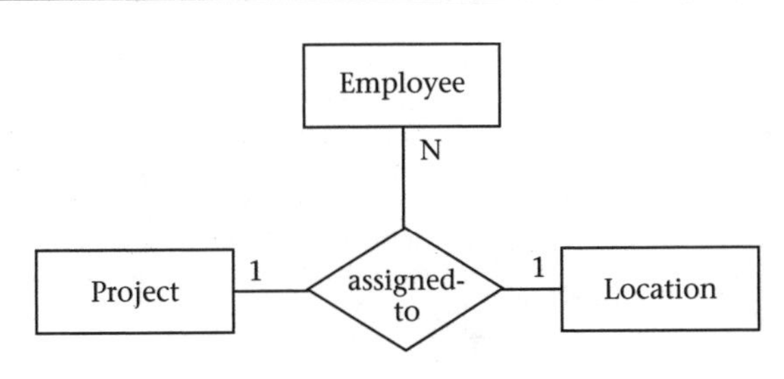

Each employee assigned to a project works at only one location for that project but can be at a different location for a different project. At a given location, an employee works on only one project. At a particular location, there can be many employees assigned to a given project.

```
create table employee (emp_id char(10),
                       emp_name char(20),
                       primary key (emp_id));
create table project (project_name char(20),
                      primary key (project_name));
create table location (loc_name char(15),
                       primary key (loc_name));
create table assigned_to (emp_id char(10),
                          project_name char(20),
                          loc_name char(15) not null,
                          primary key (emp_id, project_name),
                          foreign key (emp_id) references employee
                             on delete cascade on update cascade,
                          foreign key (project_name) references project
                             on delete cascade on update cascade,
                          foreign key (loc_name) references location
                             on delete cascade on update cascade,
                          unique (emp_id, loc_name));
```

assigned_to

emp_id	project_name	loc_name
48101	forest	B66
48101	ocean	E71
20702	ocean	A12
20702	river	D54
51266	river	G14
51266	ocean	A12
76323	hills	B66

Functional dependencies

emp_id, loc_name $\rightarrow$ project_name
emp_id, project_name $\rightarrow$ loc_name

(b) One-to-one-to-many ternary relationships

Figure 4.3 *Continued*

The transformation of an aggregation abstraction also produces a separate table for the supertype entity and each subtype entity. However, there are no common attributes and no integrity constraints to maintain. The main function of aggregation is to provide an abstraction to aid the view integration process during ER modeling.

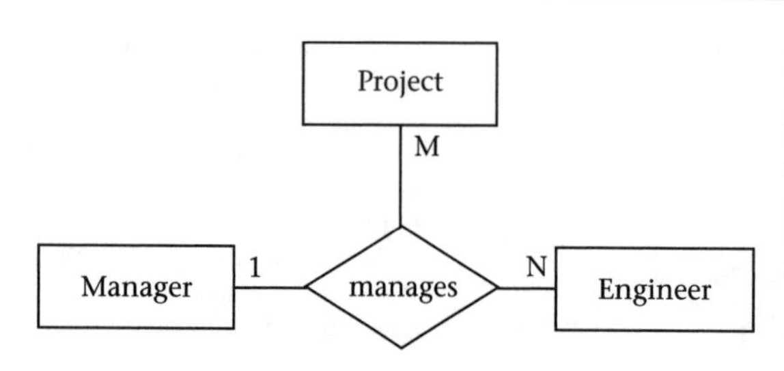

Each engineer working on a particular project has exactly one manager, but a project may have many managers and an engineer may have many managers and many projects. A manager may manage several projects.

```
create table project (project_name char(20),
                      primary key (project_name));
create table manager (mgr_id char(10),
                      primary key (mgr_id));
create table engineer (emp_id char(10),
                       primary key (emp_id));
create table manages (project_name char(20),
                      mgr_id char(10) not null,
                      emp_id char(10),
                      primary key (project_name, emp_id),
                      foreign key (project_name) references project
                         on delete cascade on update cascade,
                      foreign key (mgr_id) references manager
                         on delete cascade on update cascade,
                      foreign key (emp_id) references engineer
                         on delete cascade on update cascade);
```

manages

project_name	emp_id	mgr_id
alpha	4106	27
alpha	4200	27
beta	7033	32
beta	4200	14
gamma	4106	71
delta	7033	55
delta	4106	39
iota	4106	27

Functional dependencies

project_name, emp_id → mgr_id

(c) One-to-many-to-many ternary relationships

Figure 4.3 *Continued*

4.1.5 Multiple Relationships

Multiple relationships among n entities are always considered to be completely independent. One-to-one or one-to-many binary or binary recursive relationships that result in entity tables that are either equivalent or

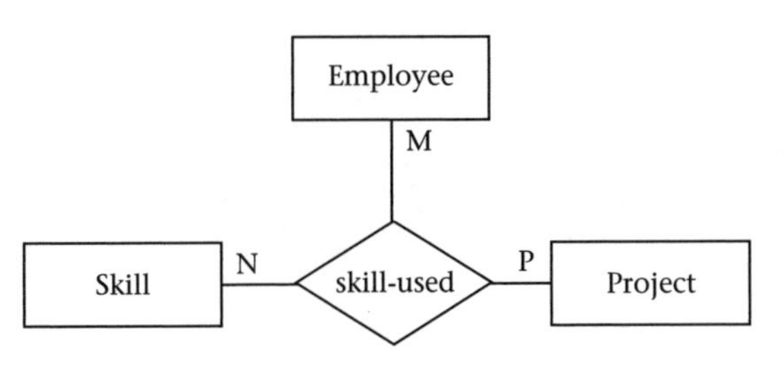

Employees can use different skills on any one of many projects, and each project has many employees with various skills.

```
create table employee (emp_id char(10),
                       emp_name char(20),
                       primary key (emp_id));
create table skill (skill_type char(15),
                    primary key (skill_type));
create table project (project_name char(20),
                      primary key (project_name));
create table skill_used (emp_id char(10),
                         skill_type char(15),
                         project_name char(20),
                         primary key (emp_id, skill_type, project_name),
                         foreign key (emp_id) references employee
                            on delete cascade on update cascade,
                         foreign key (skill_type) references skill
                            on delete cascade on update cascade,
                         foreign key (project_name) references project
                            on delete cascade on update cascade);
```

skill_used

emp_id	skill_type	project_name
101	algebra	electronics
101	calculus	electronics
101	algebra	mechanics
101	geometry	mechanics
102	algebra	electronics
102	set theory	electronics
102	geometry	mechanics
105	topology	mechanics

Functional dependencies

none

(d) Many-to-many-to-many ternary relationships

Figure 4.3 *Continued*

differ only in the addition of a foreign key can simply be merged into a single entity table containing all the foreign keys. Many-to-many or ternary relationships that result in relationship tables tend to be unique and cannot be merged.

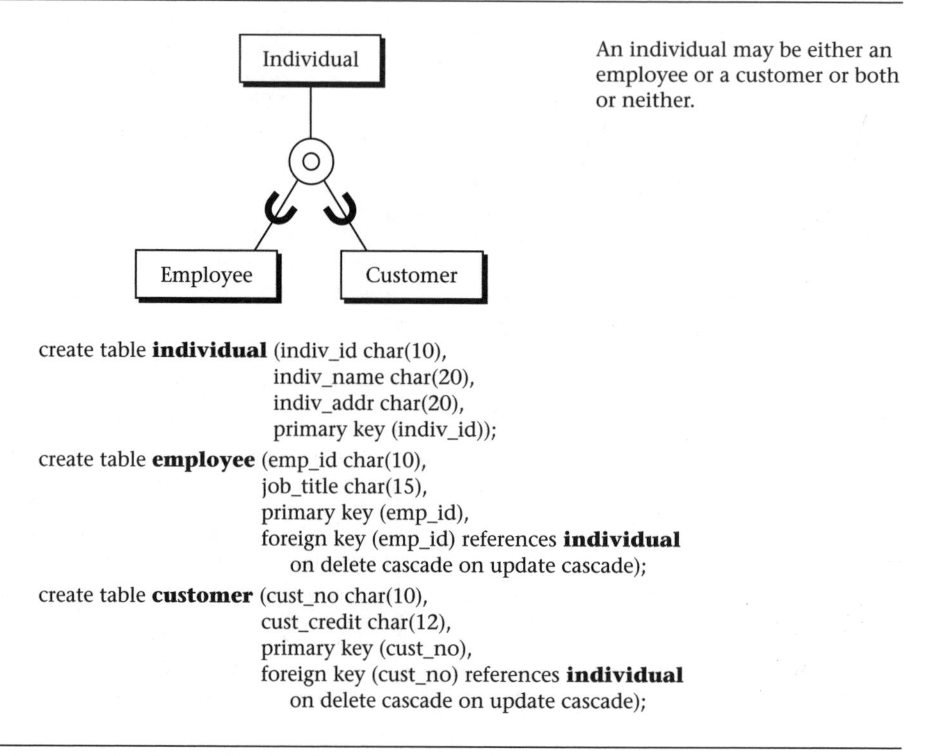

Individual
An individual may be either an employee or a customer or both or neither.
O
Employee
Customer
create table individual (indiv_id char(10),
indiv_name char(20),
indiv_addr char(20),
primary key (indiv_id));
create table employee (emp_id char(10),
job_title char(15),
primary key (emp_id),
foreign key (emp_id) references individual
on delete cascade on update cascade);
create table customer (cust_no char(10),
cust_credit char(12),
primary key (cust_no),
foreign key (cust_no) references individual
on delete cascade on update cascade);

Figure 4.4 Generalization abstraction transformation rules

4.1.6 Weak Entities

Weak entities differ from entities only in their need for keys from other entities to establish their uniqueness. Otherwise, they have the same transformation properties as entities, and no special rules are needed. When a weak entity is already derived from two or more entities in the ER diagram, it can be directly transformed into an entity table without further change.

4.2 Transformation Steps

The list that follows summarizes the basic transformation steps from an ER diagram to SQL.

- Transform each entity into a table containing the key and nonkey attributes of the entity.

- Transform every many-to-many binary or binary recursive relationship into a relationship table with the keys of the entities and the attributes of the relationship.
- Transform every ternary or higher-level n-ary relationship into a relationship table.

Now let us study each step in turn.

4.2.1 Entity Transformation

If there is a one-to-many relationship between two entities, add the key of the entity on the "one" side (the parent) into the child table as a foreign key. If there is a one-to-one relationship between one entity and another entity, add the key of one of the entities into the table for the other entity, thus changing it to a foreign key. The addition of a foreign key due to a one-to-one relationship can be made in either direction. One strategy is to maintain the most natural parent-child relationship by putting the parent key into the child table. Another strategy is based on efficiency: Add the foreign key to the table with fewer rows.

Every entity in a generalization hierarchy is transformed into a table. Each of these tables contains the key of the supertype entity; in reality, the subtype primary keys are foreign keys as well. The supertype entity table also contains nonkey values that are common to all the relevant entities; the other tables contain nonkey values specific to each subtype entity.

SQL constructs for these transformations may include constraints for not null, unique, and foreign key. A primary key must be specified for each table, either explicitly from among the candidate keys in the ER diagram or by taking the composite of all attributes as the default superkey. Note that the primary key designation implies that the attribute is not null unique. Check and default clauses are optional, depending on the narrative text associated with the ER diagram.

4.2.2 Many-to-Many Binary Relationship Transformation

In this step, every many-to-many binary (or binary recursive) relationship is transformed into a relationship table with the keys of the entities and the attributes of the relationship. A relationship table shows the correspondence between specific instances of one entity and those of another entity. Any attribute of this correspondence, such as the elected office an engineer has in a professional association (Figure 4.1f), is considered intersection data and is added to the relationship table as a nonkey attribute.

SQL constructs for this transformation may include constraints for not null. The unique constraint is not used here because all candidate keys are composites of the participating primary keys of the associated entities in the relationship. The constraints for primary key and foreign key are required because of the definition of a relationship table as a composite of the primary keys of the associated entities.

4.2.3 Ternary Relationship Transformation

In this step, every ternary (or higher n-ary) relationship is transformed into a relationship table. Ternary or higher n-ary relationships are defined as a collection of the n primary keys in the associated entities in that relationship, with possibly some nonkey attributes that are dependent on the superkey formed by the composite of those n primary keys.

SQL constructs for this transformation must include constraints for not null, since optionality is not allowed. The unique constraint is not used for individual attributes because all candidate keys are composites of the participating primary keys of the associated entities in the relationship. The constraints for primary key and foreign key are required because of the definition of a relationship table as a composite of the primary keys of the associated entities. The unique clause must also be used to define alternate candidate keys that often occur with ternary relationships. An n-ary relationship table has n foreign keys.

4.2.4 Example of ER-to-SQL Transformation

ER diagrams for the company personnel and project database (Figure 3.3) are transformed to candidate relational tables. A summary of the transformation of entities and relationships to candidate tables is illustrated in the list that follows.

SQL tables transformed directly from entities

division	**secretary**	**project**
department	**engineer**	**location**
employee	**technician**	**prof_assoc**
manager	**skill**	**desktop**

SQL tables transformed from many-to-many binary or binary recursive relationships

belongs_to

SQL tables transformed from ternary relationships

skill_used
assigned_to

4.3 Summary

Entities, attributes, and relationships can be transformed directly into SQL (SQL-92) relational table definitions with some simple rules. Entities are transformed into tables, with all attributes mapped one-to-one to table attributes. Tables representing entities that are the child ("many" side) of a parent-child (one-to-many or one-to-one) relationship must also include, as a foreign key, the primary key of the parent entity. A many-to-many relationship is transformed into a relationship table that contains the primary keys of the associated entities as its composite primary key; the components of that key are also designated as foreign keys in SQL.

A ternary or higher-level n-ary relationship is transformed into a relationship table that contains the primary keys of the associated entities; these keys are designated as foreign keys in SQL. A subset of those keys can be designated as the primary key, depending on the functional dependencies associated with the relationship.

Rules for generalization require the inheritance of the primary key from the supertype to the subtype entities when transformed into SQL tables. Optionality constraints in the ER diagram translate into nulls allowed in the relational model when applied to the "one" side of a relationship. In SQL the lack of an optionality constraint determines the not null designation in the create table definition.

Literature Summary

Definition of the basic transformations from the ER model to tables is covered in [McGe74, WoKa79, Saka83, Mart83, Hawr84, JaNg84]. The ISO and ANSI standard for SQL-92 is given in [MeSi92].

[BlPr98] Blaha, M., and Premerlani, W. *Object-Oriented Modeling and Design for Database Applications,* Prentice Hall, Englewood Cliffs, NJ, 1998.

[Hawr84] Hawryszkiewycz, I. *Database Analysis and Design,* SRA, Chicago, 1984.

[JaNg84] Jajodia, S., and Ng, P. "Translation of Entity-Relationship Diagrams into Relational Structures," *J. Systems and Software* 4, 2–3 (1984), pp. 123–133.

[Mart83] Martin, J. *Managing the Data-Base Environment,* Prentice Hall, Englewood Cliffs, NJ, 1983.

[McGe74] McGee, W. "A Contribution to the Study of Data Equivalence," *Data Base Management,* J.W. Klimbie and K.L. Koffeman (editors), North-Holland, Amsterdam, 1974, pp. 123–148.

[MeSi93] Melton, J., and Simon, A.R. *Understanding the New SQL: A Complete Guide,* Morgan Kaufmann, San Francisco, 1993.

[Saka83] Sakai, H. "Entity-Relationship Approach to Logical Database Design," *Entity-Relationship Approach to Software Engineering,* C.G. Davis, S. Jajodia, P.A. Ng, and R.T. Yeh (editors), Elsevier, North-Holland, New York, 1983, pp. 155–187.

[TYF86] Teorey, T.J., Yang, D., and Fry, J.P. "A Logical Design Methodology for Relational Databases Using the Extended Entity-Relationship Model," *ACM Computing Surveys* 18, 2 (June 1986), pp. 197–222.

[WoKa79] Wong, E., and Katz, R. "Logical Design and Schema Conversion for Relational and DBTG Databases," *Proc. Intl. Conf. on the Entity-Relationship Approach,* 1979, pp. 311–322.

EXERCISES

Problem 4-1

Define SQL tables for the ER diagram shown in Figure 3.7c.

Problem 4-2

Define SQL tables for the ER diagram you derived in Problem 3-2.

Please see page 348 for the solution to Problem 4-2.

Problem 4-3

Define SQL tables for the ER diagram you derived in Problem 3-3.

Problem 4-4

Given the following ER diagram, define the appropriate SQL tables.

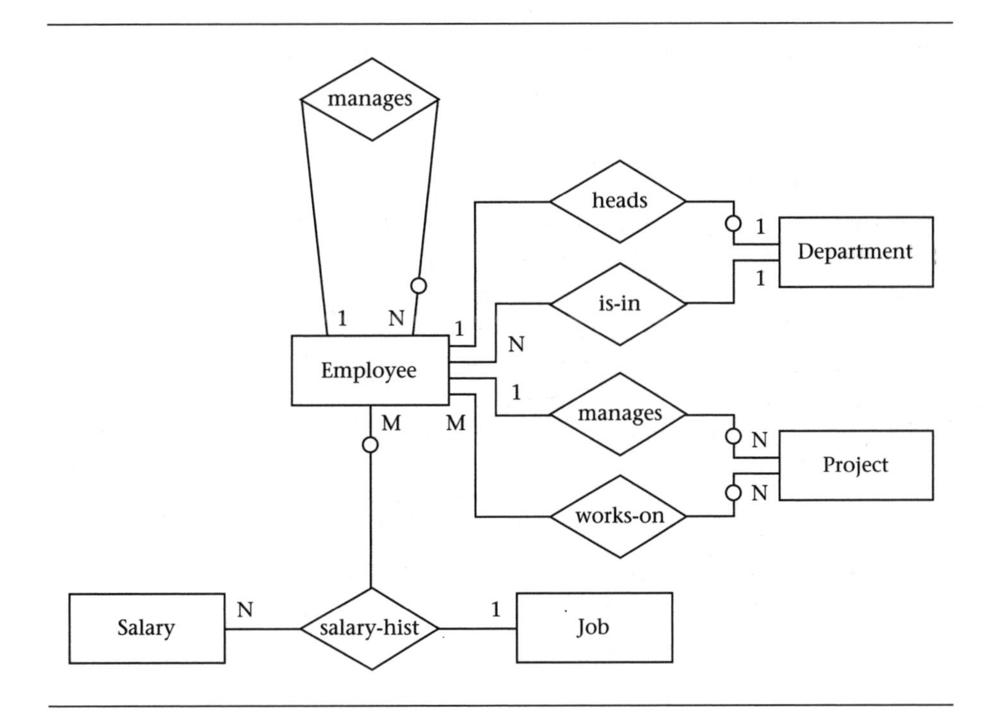

5 Normalization

This chapter focuses on the fundamentals of normal forms for relational databases and the database design step that normalizes the candidate tables (step II(d) of the database life cycle). It also investigates the equivalence between the ER model and normal forms for tables.

5.1 Fundamentals of Normalization

Relational database tables, whether they are derived from ER models or from some other design method, sometimes suffer from some rather serious problems in terms of performance, integrity, and maintainability. For example, when the entire database is defined as a single large table, it can result in a large amount of redundant data and lengthy searches for just a small number of target rows. It can also result in long and expensive updates, and deletions in particular can result in the elimination of useful data as an unwanted side effect.

Such a situation is shown in Figure 5.1, where products, salespersons, customers, and orders are all stored in a single table called **Sales**. In this table we see that certain product and customer information is stored redundantly, wasting storage space. Queries such as "Which customers ordered vacuum cleaners last month?" would require a search of the entire table. In addition, updates such as changing the address of the customer Dave Bachmann would require changing many rows. Finally, deleting the only outstanding order by a valued customer such as Elena Huang (who bought an expensive computer) also deletes the only copy

Sales

product-name	order-no	cust-name	cust-addr	credit	date	sales-name
vacuum cleaner	1458	Dave Bachmann	Austin	6	5-5-92	Carl Bloch
computer	2730	Elena Huang	Mt.View	10	5-6-92	Ted Hanss
refrigerator	2460	Mike Stolarchuck	Ann Arbor	8	7-3-92	Dick Phillips
television	519	Peter Honeyman	Detroit	3	9-5-92	Fred Remley
radio	1986	Charles Antonelli	Chicago	7	9-18-92	R. Metz
CD player	1817	C.V. Ravishankar	Bombay	8	1-3-93	Paul Basile
vacuum cleaner	1865	Charles Antonelli	Chicago	7	4-18-93	Carl Bloch
vacuum cleaner	1885	Betsy Blower	Detroit	8	5-13-93	Carl Bloch
refrigerator	1943	Dave Bachmann	Austin	6	6-19-93	Dick Phillips
television	2315	Dave Bachmann	Austin	6	7-15-93	Fred Remley

Figure 5.1 Example single table database

of her address and credit rating as a side effect. Such information may be difficult (or sometimes impossible) to recover. These problems also occur for situations in which the database has already been set up as a collection of many tables, but some of the tables are still too large.

If we had a method of breaking up such a large table into smaller tables so that these types of problems would be eliminated, the database would be much more efficient and reliable. Classes of relational database schemes or table definitions, called *normal forms,* are commonly used to accomplish this goal. The creation of a normal form database table is called *normalization.* It is accomplished by analyzing the interdependencies among individual attributes associated with those tables and taking projections (subsets of columns) of larger tables to form smaller ones.

Let us first review the basic normal forms that have been well established in the relational database literature and in practice.

5.1.1 First Normal Form

Relational database tables such as the **Sales** table illustrated in Figure 5.1 have no columns that repeat themselves—that is, each column appears exactly once in the table definition. Such tables are considered to be in first normal form, the most basic level of normalized tables. Obviously, a table in first normal form suffers from many problems (as we have seen in Figure 5.1) and must be further normalized to be useful in practice. However, there are other tables that are unnormalized to even this extent, and these must be avoided if we want to produce well-formatted business and personal databases. (On the other hand, there are some types of databases, particularly in scientific and engineering practice, where unnormalized data is actually good; we see this frequently in object-oriented databases.)

Before we give the definition for first normal form, we need to know the difference between a domain, an attribute, and a column. A *domain* is the set of all possible values for a particular type of attribute but may be used for more than one attribute. For example, the domain of people's names is the underlying set of all possible names that could be used for either customer-name or salesperson-name in the database table in Figure 5.1. Each column in a relational table represents a single attribute, but in some cases more than one column may refer to the same attribute. When this occurs, the table is said to have a repeating group (repeating column) and is therefore unnormalized.

> ***Definition:*** A table is in *first normal form* (1NF) if and only if all columns contain only atomic values; that is, there are no repeating groups (columns) within a row.

A repeating group occurs in a relational table when a multivalued attribute is allowed to have more than one value represented within a single row. When this happens, rows must either be defined as variable length or defined with enough attribute positions to accommodate the maximum possible set of values. For example, the ER diagram in Figure 5.2a would be transformed into an unnormalized table as shown in Figure 5.2b with multiple attribute positions (repeating groups) for author_id, author_name, and author_address. Figure 5.2c has the equivalent data defined in a normalized (1NF) table that puts each item of author information into a separate row.

The advantages of 1NF over unnormalized tables are its representational simplicity and the ease with which you can develop a query language for it. The disadvantage is the requirement of duplicate data. In this case, for instance, report_no appears in each row where there are multiple authors for a particular report.

5.1.2 Superkeys, Candidate Keys, and Primary Keys

A table in 1NF often suffers from data duplication, update performance, and update integrity problems. In order to understand these issues better, however, the concept of a key needs to be defined in the context of normalized tables. A *superkey* is a set of one or more attributes that, taken collectively, allows us to identify uniquely an entity or table. Any subset of the attributes of a superkey that is also a superkey and is not reducible

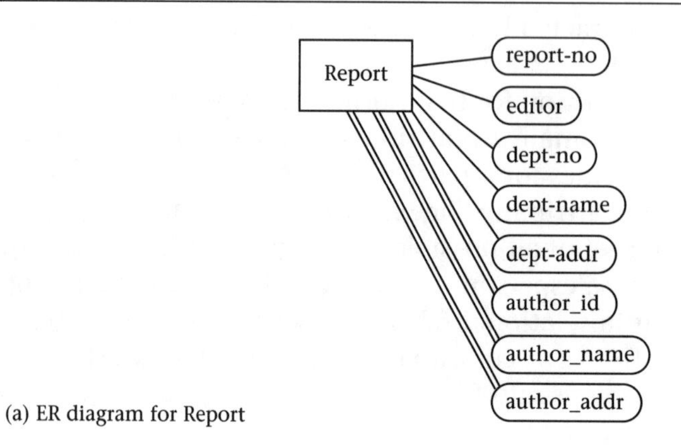

(a) ER diagram for Report

report_no	editor	dept_no	dept_name	dept_addr	author_id	author_name	author_addr	author_id	author_name	author_addr	author_id	author_name	. . .
4216	woolf	15	design	argus 1	53	mantei	cs-tor	44	bolton	mathrev	71	koenig	
5789	koenig	27	analysis	argus 2	26	fry	folkstone	38	umar	prise	71	koenig	

(b) Unnormalized table

Report

report_no	editor	dept_no	dept_name	dept_addr	author_id	author_name	author_addr
4216	woolf	15	design	argus 1	53	mantei	cs-tor
4216	woolf	15	design	argus 1	44	bolton	mathrev
4216	woolf	15	design	argus 1	71	koenig	mathrev
5789	koenig	27	analysis	argus 2	26	fry	folkstone
5789	koenig	27	analysis	argus 2	38	umar	prise
5789	koenig	27	analysis	argus 2	71	koenig	mathrev

(c) Normalized table (1NF)

Figure 5.2 ER diagram and transformation to unnormalized and normalize dtables

to another superkey is called a *candidate key*. A *primary key* is selected arbitrarily from the set of candidate keys to be used in an index for that table.

As an example, in Figure 5.2c a composite of all the attributes of the table forms a superkey because duplicate rows are not allowed in the relational model. Thus, a trivial superkey is formed from the composite of all attributes in a table. Assuming that each department address (dept_addr) in this table is single valued, we can conclude that the composite of all attributes except dept_addr is also a superkey. Looking at smaller and smaller composites of attributes and making realistic assumptions about which attributes are single valued, we find that the composite report_no, author_id uniquely determines all the other attributes in the table and is therefore a superkey. However, neither report_no nor author_id alone can determine a row uniquely, and the composite of these two attributes cannot be reduced and still be a superkey. Thus, the composite report_no, author_id becomes a candidate key. Since it is the only candidate key in this table, it also becomes the primary key.

A table can have more than one candidate key. If, for example, in Figure 5.2c we had an additional column for author_ssn, and the composite of report_no and author_ssn uniquely determines all the other attributes of the table, then both (report_no, author_id) and (report_no, author_ssn) would be candidate keys. The primary key would then be an arbitrary choice between these two candidate keys.

Other examples of multiple primary keys can be seen in Figure 4.3. In Figure 4.3a the table **uses_notebook** has three candidate keys: (emp_id, project_name), (emp_id, notebook_no), and (project_name, notebook_no); and in Figure 4.3b the table **assigned_to** has two candidate keys: (emp_id, loc_name), and (emp_id, project_name). Figures 4.3c and 4.3d each have only a single candidate key, (project_name, emp_id) and (emp_id, skill_type, project_name), respectively.

5.1.3 Second Normal Form

The goal of database normalization is to attain at least third normal form (3NF). Thus, first and second normal forms are merely intermediate stages to this goal. However, it helps to understand these stages as stepwise improvements of the database. In order to better understand the concept of second normal form and higher, we introduce the concept of functional dependency, which was briefly described in Chapter 2.

The property of one or more attributes that uniquely determines the value of one or more other attributes is called *functional dependency* (FD). Given a table (R), a set of attributes (B) is functionally dependent on another set of attributes (A) if, at each instant of time, each A value is associated with only one B value. Such a functional dependency is denoted by A→B. In the preceding example from Figure 5.2c, let us assume we are given the following functional dependencies for the table **report:**

report: report_no –> editor, dept_no
dept_no –> dept_name, dept_addr
author_id –> author_name, author_addr

Definition: A table is in *second normal form* (2NF) if and only if it is in 1NF and every nonkey attribute is fully dependent on the primary key. An attribute is fully dependent on the primary key if it is only on the right-hand side of FDs for which the left side is either the primary key itself or something that can be derived from the primary key using the transitivity of FDs.

An example of a transitive FD in **report** is the following:

report_no –> dept_no
dept_no –> dept_name

Therefore, we can derive the FD (report_no –> dept_name), since dept_name is transitively dependent on report_no.

Continuing our example, the composite key in Figure 5.2c, report_no, author_id, is the only candidate key and is therefore the primary key. However, there exists one FD (dept_no –> dept_name, dept_addr) that has no component of the primary key on the left side, and two FDs (report_no –> editor, dept_no and author_id–>author_name, author_addr) that contain one component of the primary key on the left side but not both components. As such, **report** does not satisfy the condition for 2NF for any of the FDs.

Consider the disadvantages of 1NF in the table **report**. Report_no, editor, and dept_no are duplicated for each author of the report. Therefore, if the editor of the report changes, for example, several rows must be updated. This is known as the *update anomaly*, and it represents a potential degradation of performance due to the redundant updating. If a new editor is to be added to the table, this can only be done if the new editor is editing a report (since both the report number and editor number must be known to add a row to the table) because you cannot have a primary key with a null value in most relational databases. This is known as the *insert anomaly*. Finally, if a report is withdrawn, all rows associated with that report must be deleted. This has the side effect of deleting the information that associates an author_id with author_name

Report 1

report_no	editor	dept_no	dept_name	dept_addr
4216	woolf	15	design	argus 1
5789	koenig	27	analysis	argus 2

Report 2

author_id	author_name	author_addr
53	mantei	cs-tor
44	bolton	mathrev
71	koenig	mathrev
26	fry	folkstone
38	umar	prise
71	koenig	mathrev

Report 3

report_no	author_id
4216	53
4216	44
4216	71
5789	26
5789	38
5789	71

Figure 5.3 2NF tables

and author_addr. Deletion side effects of this nature are known as *delete anomalies*. They represent a potential loss of integrity because the only way the data can be restored is to find the data somewhere outside the database and insert it back into the database. All three of these anomalies represent problems to database designers, but the delete anomaly is by far the most serious because you might lose data that cannot be recovered.

These disadvantages can be overcome by transforming the 1NF table into two or more 2NF tables by using the projection operator on the subset of the attributes of the 1NF table. In this example we project **report** over report_no, editor, dept_no, dept_name, and dept_addr to form **report1**; project **report** over author_id, author_name, and author_addr to form **report2**; and, finally, project **report** over report_no and author_id to form **report3**. The projection of **report** into three smaller tables preserves the FDs and the association between report_no and author_no that was important in the original table. Data for the three tables is shown in Figure 5.3. The FDs for these 2NF tables are

report1: report_no -> editor, dept_no
dept_no -> dept_name, dept_addr

report2: author_id -> author_name, author_addr

report3: report_no, author_id is a candidate key (no FDs)

We now have three tables that satisfy the conditions for 2NF, and we have eliminated the worst problems of 1NF, especially integrity (the delete anomaly). First, editor, dept_no, dept_name, and dept_addr are no longer duplicated for each author of a report. Second, an editor change results in only an update to one row for **report1**. Third, and most important, the deletion of the report does not have the side effect of deleting the author information.

Not all performance degradation is eliminated, however. Report_no is still duplicated for each author and deletion of a report requires updates to two tables (**report1** and **report3**) instead of one. However, these are minor problems compared to those in the 1NF table **report**.

Note that these three report tables in 2NF could have been generated directly from an ER diagram that equivalently modeled this situation with entities Author and Report and a many-to-many relationship between them.

5.1.4 Third Normal Form

The 2NF tables we established in the previous section represent a significant improvement over 1NF tables; however, they still suffer from the same types of anomalies as the 1NF tables but for different reasons associated with transitive dependencies. If a transitive (functional) dependency exists in a table, it means that two separate facts are represented in that table, one fact for each functional dependency involving a different left side. For example, if we delete a report from the database, which involves deleting the appropriate rows from **report1** and **report3** (see Figure 5.3), we have the side effect of deleting the association between dept_no, dept_name, and dept_addr as well. If we could project table **report1** over report_no, editor, and dept_no to form table **report11**, and project **report1** over dept_no, dept_name, and dept_addr to form table **report12**, we could eliminate this problem. Example tables for **report11** and **report12** are shown in Figure 5.4.

Report 11

report_no	editor	dept_no
4216	woolf	15
5789	koenig	27

Report 12

dept_no	dept_name	dept_addr
15	design	argus 1
27	analysis	argus 2

Report 2

author_id	author_name	author_addr
53	mantei	cs-tor
44	bolton	mathrev
71	koenig	mathrev
26	fry	folkstone
38	umar	prise
71	koenig	mathrev

Report 3

report_no	author_id
4216	53
4216	44
4216	71
5789	26
5789	38
5789	71

Figure 5.4 3NF tables

Definition: A table is in *third normal form* (3NF) if and only if for every nontrivial functional dependency X–>A, where X and A are either simple or composite attributes, one of two conditions must hold. Either attribute X is a superkey or attribute A is a member of a candidate key. If attribute A is a member of a candidate key, A is called a prime attribute. *Note:* A trivial FD is of the form YZ–>Z.

In the preceding example, after projecting **report1** into **report11** and **report12** to eliminate the transitive dependency report_no –> dept_no –> dept_name, dept_addr, we have the following 3NF tables and their functional dependencies (and example data in Figure 5.4):

report11: report_no –> editor, dept_no
report12: dept_no –> dept_name, dept_addr
report2: author_id –> author_name, author_addr
report3: report_no, author_id is a candidate key (no FDs)

5.1.5 Boyce-Codd Normal Form

Third normal form, which eliminates most of the anomalies known in databases today, is the most common standard for normalization in commercial databases and CASE tools. The few remaining anomalies can be eliminated by the Boyce-Codd normal form and higher normal forms defined here and in Section 5.5. Boyce-Codd normal form is considered to be a strong variation of 3NF.

> ***Definition:*** A table **R** is in *Boyce-Codd normal form* (BCNF) if for every nontrivial FD X–>A, X is a superkey.

BCNF is a stronger form of normalization than 3NF because it eliminates the second condition for 3NF, which allows the right side of the FD to be a prime attribute. Thus, every left side of an FD in a table must be a superkey. Every table that is BCNF is also 3NF, 2NF, and 1NF, by the previous definitions.

The following example shows a 3NF table that is not BCNF. Such tables have delete anomalies similar to those in the lower normal forms.

> ***Assertion 1:*** For a given team, each employee is directed by only one leader. A team may be directed by more than one leader.
>
> emp_name, team_name –> leader_name
>
> ***Assertion 2:*** Each leader directs only one team.
>
> leader_name –> team_name

This table is 3NF with a composite candidate key emp_name, team_name:

team:	emp_name	team_name	leader_name
	Sutton	Hawks	Wei
	Sutton	Condors	Bachmann
	Niven	Hawks	Wei
	Niven	Eagles	Makowski
	Wilson	Eagles	DeSmith

The **team** table has the following delete anomaly: If Sutton drops out of the Condors team, then we have no record of Bachmann leading the Condors team. As shown by Date [Date95], this type of anomaly cannot have a lossless decomposition and preserve all FDs. A lossless decomposition requires that when you decompose the table into two smaller tables by projecting the original table over two overlapping subsets of the scheme, the natural join of those subset tables must result in the original table without any extra unwanted rows. The simplest way to avoid the delete anomaly for this kind of situation is to create a separate table for each of the two assertions. These two tables are partially redundant, enough so as to avoid the delete anomaly. This decomposition is lossless (trivially) and preserves functional dependencies, but it also degrades update performance due to redundancy and necessitates additional storage space. The trade-off is often worth it because the delete anomaly is avoided.

5.2 The Design of Normalized Tables: A Simple Example

The example in this section is based on the ER diagram in Figure 5.5 and the FDs listed in the following. In general, FDs can be given explicitly, derived from the ER *diagram or from intuition (that is, from experience with the problem domain).*

1. emp_id, start_date -> job_title, end_date
2. emp_id -> emp_name, phone_no, office_no, proj_no, proj_name, dept_no
3. phone_no -> office_no
4. proj_no -> proj_name, proj_start_date, proj_end_date
5. dept_no -> dept_name, mgr_id
6. mgr_id -> dept_no

Our objective is to design a relational database schema that is normalized to at least 3NF and, if possible, to minimize the number of tables required. Our approach is to apply the definition of third normal form (3NF) in Section 5.1.4 to the preceding FDs, and to create tables that satisfy the definition.

If we try to put (1) through (6) into a single table with the composite candidate key (and primary key) emp_id, start_date, we violate the 3NF definition because FDs (2) through (6) involve left sides of FDs that are not superkeys. Consequently, we need to separate (1) from the rest of the FDs. If we then try to combine (2) through (6), we have many transitivities. Intuitively, we know that (2), (3), (4), and (5) must be separated into different tables because of transitive dependencies. We then must decide whether (5) and (6) can be combined without loss of 3NF; this can be done because mgr_id and dept_no are mutually dependent and both

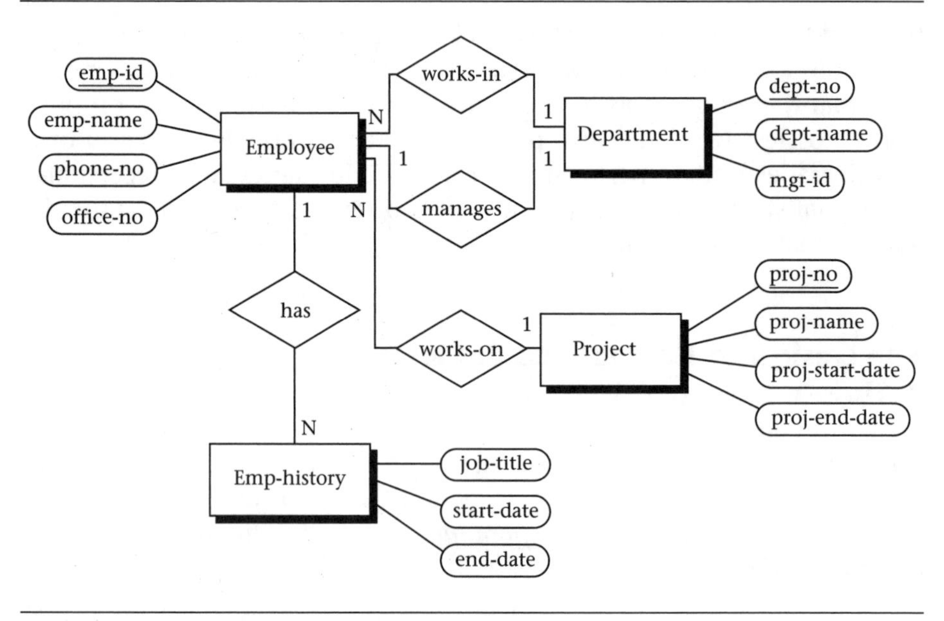

Figure 5.5 ER diagram for employee database example

attributes are superkeys in a combined table. Thus, we can define the following tables by appropriate projections from (1) through (6).

emp_hist:	emp_id, start_date –> job_title, end_date
employee:	emp_id –> emp_name, phone_no, proj_no, dept_no
phone:	phone_no –> office_no
project:	proj_no –> proj_name, proj_start_date, proj_end_date
department:	dept_no –> dept_name, mgr_id mgr_id –> dept_no

This solution, which is BCNF as well as 3NF, maintains all the original FDs. It is also a minimum set of normalized tables. In Section 5.4 we look at a formal method of determining a minimum set that we can apply to much more complex situations.

Alternative designs may involve splitting tables into partitions for volatile (frequently updated) and passive (rarely updated) data, consolidating tables to get better query performance, or duplicating data in different tables to get better query performance without losing integrity. In summary, the measures we use to assess the trade-offs in our design are

- query performance (time),
- update performance (time),
- storage performance (space), and
- integrity (avoidance of delete anomalies).

Analysis of these trade-offs is discussed in detail in Chapter 7.

5.3 Normalization of Candidate Tables Derived from ER Diagrams

Normalization of candidate tables (step II(d) in the database life cycle) is accomplished by analyzing the FDs associated with those tables: explicit FDs from the database requirements analysis (Section 5.2), FDs derived from the ER diagram, and FDs derived from intuition.

Primary FDs represent the dependencies among the data elements that are keys of entities—that is, the interentity dependencies. *Secondary FDs*, on the other hand, represent dependencies among data elements that comprise a single entity—that is, the intraentity dependencies. Typically, primary FDs are derived from the ER diagram and secondary FDs are obtained explicitly from the requirements analysis. If the ER constructs do not include nonkey attributes used in secondary FDs, the data requirements specification or data dictionary must be consulted. Table 5.1 shows the types of primary FDs derivable from each type of ER construct, consistent with the derivable candidate tables in Figures 4.1 through 4.4.

Each candidate table typically has several primary and secondary FDs uniquely associated with it, which determine the current degree of normalization of the table. Any of the well-known techniques for increasing the degree of normalization can be applied to each table, to the desired degree stated in the requirements specification. Integrity is maintained by requiring the normalized table schema to include all data dependencies existing in the candidate table schema.

Any table **B** that is subsumed by another table **A** can potentially be eliminated. Table **B** is subsumed by another table **A** when all the attributes in **B** are also contained in **A** and all data dependencies in **B** also occur in **A**. As a trivial case, any table containing only a composite key and no nonkey attributes is automatically subsumed by any other table containing the same key attributes because the composite key is the weakest form of data dependency. If, however, tables **A** and **B** represent the supertype and subtype cases, respectively, of entities defined by the generalization abstraction, and **A** subsumes **B** because **B** has no additional specific attributes, the designer must collect and analyze additional information to decide whether or not to eliminate **B**.

A table can also be subsumed by the construction of a join of two other tables (a "join" table). When this occurs, the elimination of a subsumed table may result in the loss of retrieval efficiency, although storage and update costs will tend to be decreased. This trade-off must be further analyzed during physical design with regard to processing requirements to determine whether elimination of the subsumed table is reasonable.

Table 5.1 Primary FDs derivable from ER relationship constructs

Degree	*Connectivity*	*Primary FD*
Binary or	one-to-one	2 ways: key(one side) –> key(one side)
Binary	one-to-many	key(many side) –> key(one side)
Recursive	many-to-many	none (composite key from both sides)
Ternary	one-to-one-to-one	3 ways: key(one), key(one) –> key(one)
	one-to-one-to-many	2 ways: key(one), key(many) –> key(one)
	one-to-many-to-many	1 way: key(many), key(many) –> key(one)
	many-to-many-to-many	none (composite key from all 3 sides)
Generalization	none	none (secondary FD only)

To continue our example company personnel and project database, we want to obtain the primary FDs by applying the rules in Table 5.1 to each relationship in the ER diagram in Figure 3.3. The results are shown in Table 5.2.

Table 5.2 Primary FDs derived from the ER diagram in Figure 3.3

dept_no -> div_no	in Department from relationship "contains"
emp_id -> dept_no	in Employee from relationship "has"
div_no -> emp_id	in Division from relationship "is-headed-by"
dept_no -> emp_id	from binary relationship "is-managed-by"
emp_id -> desktop_no	from binary relationship "has-allocated"
desktop_no -> emp_no	from binary relationship "has-allocated"
emp_id -> spouse_id	from binary recursive relationship "is-married-to"
spouse_id -> emp_id	from binary recursive relationship "is-married-to"
emp_id, loc_name -> project_name	from ternary relationship "assigned-to"

Next we want to determine the secondary FDs. Let us assume that the dependencies in Table 5.3 are derived from the requirements specification and intuition

Table 5.3 Secondary FDs derived from the requirements specification

div_no -> div_name, div_addr	from entity Division
dept_no -> dept_name, dept_addr, mgr_id	from entity Department
emp_id -> emp_name, emp_addr, office_no, phone_no	from entity Employee
skill_type -> skill_descrip	from entity Skill
project_name -> start_date, end_date, head_id	from entity Project
loc_name -> loc_county, loc_state, zip	from entity Location
mgr_id -> mgr_start_date	beeper_phone_no
assoc_name -> assoc_addr, phone_no, start_date	from entity Prof-assoc
desktop_no -> computer_type, serial_no	from entity Desktop

Normalization of the candidate tables is accomplished next. In Table 5.4 we bring together the primary and secondary FDs that apply to each candidate table. We note that for each table except **employee**, all attributes are functionally dependent on the primary key (denoted by the left side of the FDs) and are thus BCNF. In the case of table **employee** we note that spouse_id determines emp_id and emp_id is the primary key; thus, spouse_id can be shown to be a superkey (see Superkey Rule 2 in Section 5.4). Therefore, **employee** is found to be BCNF.

In general we observe that candidate tables, like the ones shown in Table 5.4, are fairly good indicators of the final schema and normally require very little refinement to get to 3NF or BCNF.

Table 5.4 Candidate tables (and FDs) from ER diagram transformation

division	div_no -> div_name, div_addr div_no -> emp_id
department	dept_no -> dept_name, dept_addr, mgr_id dept_no -> div_no dept_no -> emp_id
employee	emp_id -> emp_name, emp_addr, office_no, phone_no emp_id -> dept_no emp_id -> spouse_id spouse_id -> emp_id
manager	mgr_id -> mgr_start_date, beeper_phone_no
secretary	none
engineer	emp_id -> desktop_no
technician	none
skill	skill_type -> skill_descrip
project	project_name -> start_date, end_date, head_id
location	loc_name -> loc_county, loc_state, zip
prof_assoc	assoc_name -> assoc_addr, phone_no, start_date
desktop	desktop_no -> computer_type, serial_no desktop_no -> emp_no
assigned_to	emp_id, loc_name -> project_name
skill_used	none

5.4 Determining the Minimum Set of 3NF Tables

A minimum set of 3NF tables can be obtained from a given set of FDs by using the well-known synthesis algorithm developed by Bernstein [Bern76]. This process is particularly useful when you are confronted with a list of hundreds or thousands of FDs that describe the semantics of a database. In practice, the ER modeling process automatically decomposes this problem into smaller subproblems: The attributes and FDs of interest are restricted to those attributes within an entity (and its equivalent table) and any foreign keys that might be imposed upon that table. Thus, the database designer rarely has to deal with more than 10 or 20 attributes at a time, and in fact most entities are initially defined in 3NF already. For those tables that are not yet in 3NF, only minor adjustments are needed in most cases.

In the following we briefly describe the synthesis algorithm for those situations where the ER model is not useful for the decomposition. In order to apply the algorithm, we make use of the well-known Armstrong axioms, which define the basic relationships among FDs.

Inference rules (Armstrong axioms):

Reflexivity	If Y is a subset of the attributes of X, then X–>Y (i.e., if X is ABCD and Y is ABC, then X–>Y. Trivially, X–>X).
Augmentation	If X–>Y and Z is a subset of table **R** (i.e., Z is any attribute in **R**), then XZ–>YZ.
Transitivity	If X–>Y and Y–>Z, then X–>Z.
Pseudotransitivity	If X–>Y and YW–>Z, then XW–>Z.
	(Transitivity is a special case of pseudotransitivity when W = null.)
Union	If X–>Y and X–>Z, then X–>YZ (or equivalently, X–>Y,Z).
Decomposition	If X–>YZ, then X–>Y and X–>Z.

These axioms can be used to express two practical rules of thumb for deriving superkeys of tables, where at least one superkey is already known.

Superkey Rule 1: Any FD involving all attributes of a table defines a superkey as the left side of the FD.

Given: any FD containing all attributes in the table **R** (W,X,Y,Z), that is, XY–>WZ.

Proof:

1. XY–>WZ as given.
2. XY–>XY by applying the reflexivity axiom.
3. XY–>XYWZ by applying the union axiom.
4. XY uniquely determines every attribute in table **R**, as shown in (3).
5. XY uniquely defines table **R**, by the definition of a table as having no duplicate rows.
6. XY is therefore a superkey, by definition.

Superkey Rule 2: Any attribute that functionally determines a superkey of a table is also a superkey for that table.

Given: Attribute A is a superkey for table **R** (A,B,C,D,E), and E–>A.

Proof:

1. Attribute A uniquely defines each row in table **R**, by the definition of a superkey.
2. A–>ABCDE by applying the definition of a superkey and a relational table.
3. E–>A as given.
4. E–>ABCDE by applying the transitivity axiom.
5. E is a superkey for table **R**, by definition.

Before we can describe the synthesis algorithm, we must define some important concepts. Let H be a set of FDs that represents at least part of the known semantics of a database. The closure of H, specified by H^+, is the set of all FDs derivable from H using the Armstrong axioms or inference rules. For example, we can apply the transitivity rule to the following FDs in set H:

A–>B, B–>C, A–>C, and C–>D

to derive the FDs A–>D and B–>D. All six FDs constitute the closure H^+. A cover of H, called H′, is any set of FDs from which H^+ can be derived. Possible covers for this example are

1. A–>B, B–>C, C–>D, A–>C, A–>D, B–>D (trivial case where H′ and H^+ are equal)
2. A–>B, B–>C, C–>D, A–>C, A–>D
3. A–>B, B–>C, C–>D, A–>C (this is the original set H)
4. A–>B, B–>C, C–>D

A nonredundant cover of H is a cover of H that contains no proper subset of FDs that is also a cover. The synthesis algorithm requires nonredundant covers.

3NF Synthesis Algorithm

Given a set of FDs, H, we determine a minimum set of tables in 3NF.

H:		
	AB –> C	DM –> NP
	A –> DEFG	D –> M
	E –> G	L –> D
	F –> DJ	PQR –> ST
	G –> DI	PR –> S
	D –> KL	

From this point the process of arriving at the minimum set of 3NF tables consists of five steps:

1. elimination of extraneous attributes in the determinants of the FDs;
2. search for a nonredundant cover, G of H;
3. partitioning of G into groups so that all FDs with the same left side are in one group;
4. merge of equivalent keys; and
5. search for a nonredundant cover again and definition of tables.

Now we discuss each step in turn, in terms of the preceding set of FDs, H.

5.4.1 Elimination of Extraneous Attributes

The first task is to get rid of extraneous attributes in the determinants of the FDs.

The following two relationships (rules) among attributes on the left side (determinant) of an FD provide the means to reduce the left side to fewer attributes.

> ***Reduction Rule 1:*** XY –> Z and X –> Z => Y is extraneous on the left side (applying the reflexivity and transitivity axioms).

> ***Reduction Rule 2:*** XY –> Z and X –> Y => Y is extraneous; therefore, X –> Z (applying the pseudotransitivity axiom).

Applying these reduction rules to the set of FDs in H, we get

DM–>NP and D–>M => D–>NP

PQR–>ST and PR–>S => PQR–>T

5.4.2 Search for a Nonredundant Cover

We must eliminate any FD derivable from others in H using the inference rules. The transitive FDs to be eliminated are

A–>E and E–>G => eliminate A–>G

A–>F and F–>D => eliminate A–>D

5.4.3 Partitioning of the Nonredundant Cover

To partition the nonredundant cover into groups so that all FDs with the same left side are in one group, we must separate the non–fully functional dependencies and transitive dependencies into separate tables. At this point we have a feasible solution for 3NF tables, but it is not necessarily the minimum set.

These non–fully functional dependencies must be put into separate tables:

AB–>C

A–>EF

Groups with the same left side are

G1: AB–>C	G6: D–>KLMNP
G2: A–> EF	G7: L–>D
G3: E–>G	G8: PQR–>T
G4: G–>DI	G9: PR–>S
G5: F–>DJ	

5.4.4 Merge of Equivalent Keys

In this step we merge groups with determinants that are equivalent (e.g., X–>Y and Y–>X imply that X and Y are equivalent). This step produces a minimal set. Groups G6 and G7 have D–>L and L–>D. Therefore, merge these groups into a single group G67 with FDs D–>KLMNP and L–>D. We can also merge groups when the right-hand side of an FD is a prime attribute because this satisfies 3NF.

5.4.5 Definition of Tables

The minimum set has now been computed.

Tables and FDs:	**R1**: AB–>C	**R5**: F–>DJ
	R2: A–>EF	**R6**: D–>KLMNP and L–>D
	R3: E–>G	**R7**: PQR–>T
	R4: G–>DI	**R8**: PR–>S

Note that this result is not only 3NF but also BCNF, which is very frequently the case. This fact suggests a practical algorithm for a (near) minimum set of BCNF tables: Use Bernstein's algorithm to attain a minimum set of 3NF tables, then inspect each table for further decomposition (or partial replication, as shown in Section 5.1.5) to BCNF.

5.5 Fourth and Fifth Normal Forms

Normal forms up to BCNF have been defined solely on FDs, and for most database practitioners, either 3NF or BCNF is a sufficient level of normalization. However, there are in fact two more normal forms that are needed to eliminate the rest of the currently known anomalies. In this section we look at different types of constraints on tables: multivalued dependencies and join dependencies. If these constraints do not exist in a table, which is the most common situation, then any table in BCNF is automatically in fourth normal form (4NF) and fifth normal form (5NF) as well. However, when these constraints do exist, there may be further update (especially delete) anomalies that need to be corrected. First, we must define the concept of multivalued dependency.

5.5.1 Multivalued Dependencies

Definition: In a *multivalued dependency* (MVD), X–>>Y holds on table **R** with table scheme RS if, whenever a valid instance of table **R**(X,Y,Z) contains a pair of rows that contain duplicate values of X, then the instance also contains the pair of rows obtained by interchanging the Y values in the original pair. This includes situations where only pairs of rows exist. Note that X and Y may contain either single or composite attributes.

An MVD X –>> Y is trivial if Y is a subset of X or if X union Y = RS. Finally, an FD implies an MVD, which implies that a single row with a given value of X is also an MVD, albeit a trivial form.

The following examples show where an MVD does and does not exist in a table. In **R1**, the first four rows satisfy all conditions for the MVDs X–>>Y and X–>>Z. Note that MVDs appear in pairs because of the cross-product type of relationship between Y and Z = RS–Y as the two right sides of the two MVDs. The fifth and sixth rows of **R1** (when the X value is 2) satisfy the row interchange conditions in the preceding definition. In both rows the Y value is 2, so the interchanging of Y values is trivial. The seventh row (3,3,3) satisfies the definition trivially.

In table **R2**, however, the Y values in the fifth and sixth rows are different (1 and 2), and interchanging the 1 and 2 values for Y results in a row (2,2,2) that does not appear in the table. Thus, in **R2** there is no MVD between X and Y or between X and Z, even though the first four rows satisfy the MVD definition. Note that for the MVD to exist, all rows must satisfy the criterion for an MVD.

Table **R3** contains the first three rows that do not satisfy the criterion for an MVD, since changing Y from 1 to 2 in the second row results in a row that does not appear in the table. Similarly, changing Z from 1 to 2 in the third row results in a nonappearing row. Thus, **R3** does not have any MVDs between X and Y or between X and Z.

R1:

X	Y	Z
1	1	1
1	1	2
1	2	1
1	2	2
2	2	1
2	2	2
3	3	3

R2:

X	Y	Z
1	1	1
1	1	2
1	2	1
1	2	2
2	2	1
2	1	2

R3:

X	Y	Z
1	1	1
1	1	2
1	2	1
2	2	1
2	2	2

By the same argument, in table **R1** we have the MVDs Y–>> X and Y–>>Z but none with Z on the left side. Tables **R2** and **R3** have no MVDs at all.

The following inference rules for multivalued dependencies are somewhat analogous to the inference rules for functional dependencies given in Section 5.4 [BFH77]. They are quite useful in the analysis and decomposition of tables into 4NF.

Multivalued dependency inference rules:

Reflexivity	X —>> X.
Augmentation	If X —>> Y, then XZ —>> Y.
Transitivity	If X —>>Y and Y —>> Z, then X —>> (Z-Y).
Pseudotransitivity	If X —>> Y and YW —>> Z, then XW —>> (Z-YW). (Transitivity is a special case of pseudotransitivity when W is null.)
Union	If X —>> Y and X —>> Z, then X —>> YZ.
Decomposition	If X —>> Y and X —>> Z, then X —>> Y intersect Z and X —>> (Z–Y).
Complement	If X —>> Y and Z = R–X–Y, then X —>> Z.
FD implies MVD	If X –> Y, then X —>> Y.
FD, MVD mix	If X —>> Y and Z —>> W (where W is contained in Y and Y intersect Z is not empty), then X–>W.

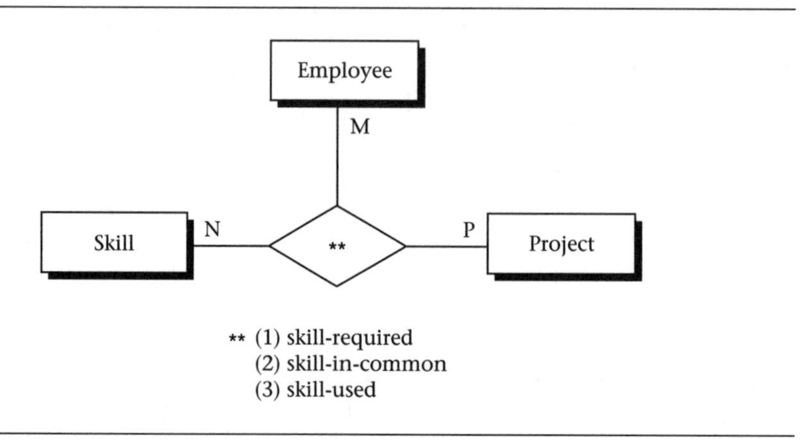

Figure 5.6 Many-to-many ternary relationship with multiple interpretations

5.5.2 Fourth Normal Form

The goal of fourth normal form is to eliminate nontrivial MVDs from a table by projecting them onto separate smaller tables, thus eliminating the update anomalies associated with the MVDs. This type of normal form is reasonably easy to attain if you know where the MVDs are. In general, MVDs must be defined from the semantics of the database; they cannot be determined from just looking at the data. The current set of data can only verify whether your assumption about an MVD is currently true or not, but this may change each time the data is updated.

> ***Definition:*** A table **R** is in *fourth normal form* (4NF) if and only if it is in BCNF and, whenever there exists an MVD in **R** (say, X –>> Y), at least one of the following holds: The MVD is trivial or X is a superkey for **R**.

Applying this definition to the three tables in the example in the previous section, we see that **R1** is not in 4NF because at least one nontrivial MVD exists and no single column is a superkey. In tables **R2** and **R3**, however, there are no MVDs. Thus, these two tables are at least 4NF.

As an example of the transformation of a table that is not in 4NF to two tables that are in 4NF, we observe the ternary relationship "skill-required" shown in Figure 5.6. The relationship "skill-required" is defined as, "An employee must have all the required skills needed for a project to work on that project." For example, in Table 5.5 the project with proj_no = 3 requires skill types A and B by all employees (see employees 101 and 102). The table **skill_required** has no FDs, but it does have several nontrivial MVDs and is therefore only in BCNF. In such a case it can have a lossless decomposition into two many-to-many binary relationships between the entities Employee and Project, and Project and Skill. Each of these two new relationships represents a table in 4NF. It can also have a lossless decomposition resulting in a binary many-to-many relationship between the entities Employee and Skill, and Project and Skill.

Table 5.5 The table **skill_required** and its three projections

skill_required	emp_id	proj_no	skill_type	*MVDs (nontrivial)*
	101	3	A	proj_no ->> skill_type
	101	3	B	proj_no ->> emp_id
	101	4	A	
	101	4	C	
	102	3	A	
	102	3	B	
	103	5	D	

emp_id	proj_no	emp_id	skill_type	proj_no	skill_type
101	3	101	A	3	A
101	4	101	B	3	B
102	3	101	C	4	A
103	5	102	A	4	C
		102	B	5	D
		103	D		

A two-way lossless decomposition occurs when **skill_required** is projected over {emp_id, proj_no} to form skill_req1 and projected over {proj_no, skill} to form skill_req3. Projection over {emp_id, proj_no} to form skill_req1 and over {emp_id, skill} to form skill_req2, however, is not lossless. A three-way lossless decomposition occurs when **skill_required** is projected over {emp_id, proj_no}, {emp_id, skill}, and {proj_no, skill}.

Tables in 4NF avoid certain update anomalies (or inefficiences). For instance, a delete anomaly exists when two independent facts get tied together unnaturally so there may be bad side effects of certain deletes.

For example, in **skill_required** the last row of a skill_type may be lost if an employee is temporarily not working on any projects. An update inefficiency may occur when adding a new project in **skill_required**, which requires insertions for many rows to include all the required skills for that new project. Likewise, loss of a project requires many deletions. These inefficiencies are avoided when skill_required is decomposed into skill_req1 and skill_req3. In general (but not always), decomposition of a table into 4NF tables results in less data redundancy.

5.5.3 Decomposing Tables to 4NF

Algorithms to decompose tables into 4NF are difficult to develop. We look at some straightforward approaches to 4NF from BCNF and lower normal forms. First, if a table is BCNF, it either has no FDs or each FD is characterized by its left side being a superkey. Thus, if the only MVDs in this table are derived from its FDs, they have only superkeys as their left sides, and the table is 4NF by definition. If, however, there are other nontrivial MVDs whose left sides are not superkeys, the table is only in BCNF and must be decomposed to achieve higher normalization.

The basic decomposition process from a BCNF table is defined by selecting the most important MVD (or, if that is not possible, by selecting one arbitrarily), defining its complement MVD, and decomposing the table into two tables containing the attributes on the left and right sides of that MVD and its complement. This type of decomposition is lossless because each new table is based on the same attribute, which is the left side of both MVDs. The same MVDs in these new tables are now trivial because they contain every attribute in the table. However, other MVDs may still be present, and more decompositions by MVDs and their complements may be necessary. This process of arbitrary selection of MVDs for decomposition is continued until only trivial MVDs exist, leaving the final tables in 4NF.

As an example, let **R**(A,B,C,D,E,F) with no FDs and with MVDs A –>> B and CD –>> EF. The first decomposition of **R** is into two tables **R1**(A,B) and **R2**(A,C,D,E,F) by applying the MVD A –>> B and its complement A –>> CDEF. Table **R1** is now 4NF because A –>> B is trivial and is the only MVD in the table. Table **R2**, however, is still only BCNF because of the nontrivial MVD CD –>> EF. We then decompose **R2** into **R21**(C,D,E,F) and **R2**(C,D,A) by applying the MVD CD –>> EF and its complement CD

–>> A. Both **R21** and **R22** are now 4NF. If we had applied the MVD complement rule in the opposite order, using CD –>> EF and its complement CD –>> AB first, the same three 4NF tables would result from this method. However, this does not occur in all cases but only in those tables where the MVDs have no intersecting attributes.

This method, in general, has the unfortunate side effect of potentially losing some or all of the FDs and MVDs. Therefore, any decision to transform tables from BCNF to 4NF must take into account the trade-off between normalization and the elimination of delete anomalies, and the preservation of FDs and possibly MVDs. It should also be noted that this approach derives a feasible, but not necessarily a minimum, set of 4NF tables.

A second approach to decomposing BCNF tables is to ignore the MVDs completely and split each BCNF table into a set of smaller tables in which the candidate key of each BCNF table is the candidate key of a new table, with the nonkey attributes distributed among the new tables in some semantically meaningful way. This form of decomposing by candidate key (that is, superkey) is lossless because the candidate keys uniquely join; it usually results in the simplest form of 5NF tables—those with a candidate key and one nonkey attribute, and no MVDs. However, if a table thus constructed has a composite key and there exists one or more MVDs still, further decomposition must be done with the MVD/MVD-complement approach given previously. The decomposition by candidate keys preserves FDs, but the MVD/MVD-complement approach does not preserve either FDs or MVDs.

Tables that are not yet in BCNF can also be directly decomposed into 4NF using the MVD/MVD-complement approach. Such tables can often be decomposed into smaller minimum sets than those derived from transforming into BCNF first and then 4NF, but with a greater cost of lost FDs. In most database design situations, it is preferable to develop BCNF tables first, then evaluate the need to normalize further while preserving the FDs.

5.5.4 Fifth Normal Form

Definition: A table **R** is in *fifth normal form* (5NF) or project-join normal form (PJ/NF) if and only if every join dependency in **R** is implied by the keys of **R**.

As we recall, a lossless decomposition of a table implies that it can be decomposed by two or more projections, followed by a natural join of those projections (in any order) that results in the original table, without any spurious or missing rows. The general lossless decomposition constraint, involving any number of projections, is also known as a *join dependency* (*JD*). A join dependency is illustrated by the following: In a table **R** with n arbitrary subsets of the set of attributes of **R**, then **R** satisfies a join dependency over these n subsets if and only if **R** is equal to the natural join of its projections on them. A JD is trivial if one of the subsets is **R** itself.

5NF or PJ/NF requires satisfaction of the membership algorithm [Fagi79], which determines whether a JD is a member of the set of logical consequences of (can be derived from) the set of key dependencies known for this table. In effect, for any 5NF table, every dependency (FD, MVD, JD) is determined by the keys. As a practical matter we note that because JDs are very difficult to determine in large databases with many attributes, 5NF tables are not easily derivable, and logical database design typically produces either BCNF or 4NF tables.

We should also note that by the preceding definitions, just because a table is decomposable, it does not necessarily mean it is not 5NF. For example, consider a simple table with four attributes (A,B,C,D), one FD (A->BCD), and no MVDs or JDs not implied by this FD. It could be decomposed into three tables A->B, A->C, and A->D all based on the same superkey A; however, it is already in 5NF without the decomposition. Thus, the decomposition is not required for normalization. On the other hand, decomposition could be a useful tool in some instances for performance improvement.

The following example demonstrates that a table representing a ternary relationship may not have any two-way lossless decompositions; however, it may have a three-way lossless decomposition, which is equivalent to three binary relationships, based on the three possible projections of this table. This situation occurs in the relationship "skill-in-common" (Figure 5.6), which is defined as, "The employee must apply the intersection of his or her available skills with the skills needed to work on certain projects." In this example skill-in-common is less restrictive than skill-required because it allows an employee to work on a project even if he or she does not have all the skills required for that project.

As Table 5.6 shows, the three projections of **skill_in_common** result in a three-way lossless decomposition. There are no two-way lossless decompositions and no MVDs; thus, the table **skill_in_common** is in 4NF.

Table 5.6 The table **skill_in_common** and its three projections

skill_in_common	emp_id	proj_no	skill_type
	101	3	A
	101	3	B
	101	4	A
	101	4	B
	102	3	A
	102	3	B
	103	3	A
	103	4	A
	103	5	A
	103	5	C

skill_in_com1		*skill_in_com2*		*skill_in_com3*	
emp_id	proj_no	emp_id	skill_type	emp_id	skill_type
101	3	101	A	3	A
101	4	101	B	3	B
102	3	102	A	4	A
103	3	102	B	4	B
103	4	103	A	5	A
103	5	103	C	5	C

The ternary relationship in Figure 5.6 can be interpreted yet another way. The meaning of the relationship "skill-used" is, "We can selectively record different skills that each employee applies to working on individual projects." It is equivalent to a table in 5NF that cannot be decomposed into either two or three binary tables. Note by studying Table 5.7 that the associated table, **skill_used**, has no MVDs or JDs.

Table 5.7 The table **skill_used**, its three projections, and natural joins of its projections

skill_used

emp_id	proj_no	skill_type
101	3	A
101	3	B
101	4	A
101	4	C
102	3	A
102	3	B
102	4	A
102	4	B

Three projections on **skill_used** result in:

skill_used1

emp_id	proj_no
101	3
101	4
102	3
102	4

skill_used2

proj_no	skill_type
3	A
3	B
4	A
4	B
4	C

skill_used3

emp_id	skill_type
101	A
101	B
101	C
102	A
102	B

join **skill_used1** with **skill_used2** to form:

skill_used_12

emp_id	proj_no	skill_type
101	3	A
101	3	B
101	4	A
101	4	B
101	4	C
102	3	A
102	3	B
102	4	A
102	4	B
102	4	C

join **skill_used12** with **skill_used3** to form:

skill_used_123

emp_id	proj_no	skill_type
101	3	A
101	3	B
101	4	A
101	4	B (spurious tuple)
101	4	C
102	3	A
102	3	B
102	4	A
102	4	B

A table may have constraints that are FDs, MVDs, and JDs. An MVD is a special case of a JD. In order to determine the level of normalization of the table, analyze the FDs first to determine normalization through BCNF; then analyze the MVDs to determine which BCNF tables are also 4NF; and, finally, analyze the JDs to determine which 4NF tables are also 5NF.

A many-to-many-to-many ternary relationship is

1. BCNF if it can be replaced by two binary relationships,
2. 4NF if it can only be replaced by three binary relationships, and
3. 5NF if it cannot be replaced in any way (and thus is a true ternary relationship).

We observe the equivalence between certain ternary relationships and the higher normal form tables transformed from those relationships. Ternary relationships that have at least one "one" entity cannot be decomposed (or broken down) into binary relationships because that would destroy the one or more functional dependencies required in the definition, as shown previously. A ternary relationship with all "many" entities, however, has no FDs, but in some cases may have MVDs and thus may have a lossless decomposition into equivalent binary relationships.

In summary, the three common cases that illustrate the correspondence between a lossless decomposition in a many-to-many-to-many ternary relationship table and higher normal forms in the relational model are shown in Table 5.8.

Table 5.8 Summary of higher normal forms

Table name	*Normal form*	*Two-way lossless decomp/ join?*	*Three-way lossless decomp/ join?*	*Nontrivial MVDs*
skill_required	BCNF	yes	yes	2
skill_in_common	4NF	no	yes	0
skill_used	5NF	no	no	0

5.6 Summary

In this chapter we define the constraints imposed on tables: FDs, MVDs, and JDs. Based on these constraints, normal forms for database tables are defined: 1NF, 2NF, 3NF, and BCNF. All are based on the types of FDs present. The 4NFs and 5NFs are dependent on the types of MVDs and JDs present. In this chapter a practical algorithm for finding the minimum set of 3NF tables is given.

The following statements summarize the functional equivalence between the ER model and normalized tables:

1. *within an entity*—the level of normalization is totally dependent upon the interrelationships among the key and nonkey attributes. It could be any form from unnormalized to BCNF or higher.
2. *binary (or binary recursive) one-to-one or one-to-many relationship*—within the "child" entity, the foreign key (a replication of the primary key of the "parent") is functionally dependent upon the child's primary key. This is at least BCNF, assuming the entity by itself without the foreign key is already BCNF.
3. *binary (or binary recursive) many-to-many relationship*—the intersection table has a composite key and possibly some nonkey attributes functionally dependent upon it. This is at least BCNF.
4. *ternary relationship*—
    a. one-to-one-to-one = three overlapping composite keys, at least BCNF;
    b. one-to-one-to-many = two overlapping composite keys, at least BCNF;
    c. one-to-many-to-many = one composite key, at least BCNF;
    d. many-to-many-to-many = one composite key with three attributes, at least BCNF. In some cases it can also be 4NF, or even 5NF.

In the next chapter we look at ways to refine the relational database for use by various applications. In order to make these refinements, the fundamentals of physical database design by using access methods are presented.

Literature Summary

Good summaries of normal forms can be found in [Date95, Kent83, DuHa89, Smit85]. Algorithms for normal form decomposition and synthesis techniques are given in [Bern76, Fagi77, Ullm88, Lien81, ZaMe81, Mart83, Maie83, Yao85]. Earlier work in normal forms was done by [Codd70, Codd74].

[Bern76] Bernstein, P. "Synthesizing 3NF Relations from Functional Dependencies," *ACM Trans. Database Systems* 1, 4 (1976), pp. 272–298.

[BFH77] Beeri, C., Fagin, R., and Howard, J.H. "A Complete Axiomization for Functional and Multivalued Dependencies in Database Relations," *Proc. 1977 ACM SIGMOD Int'l. Conf. on Management of Data, Toronto,* pp. 47–61.

[Codd70] Codd, E. "A Relational Model for Large Shared Data Banks," *Comm. ACM* 13, 6 (June 1970), pp. 377–387.

[Codd74] Codd, E. "Recent Investigations into Relational Data Base Systems," *Proc. IFIP Congress,* North-Holland, Amsterdam, 1974.

[Date95] Date, C.J. *An Introduction to Database Systems, Vol. 1* (6th Ed.), Addison-Wesley, Reading, MA, 1995.

[DuHa89] Dutka, A.F., and Hanson, H.H. *Fundamentals of Data Normalization,* Addison-Wesley, Reading, MA, 1989.

[Fagi77] Fagin, R. "Multivalued Dependencies and a New Normal Form for Relational Databases," *ACM Trans. Database Systems* 2, 3 (1977), pp. 262–278.

[Fagi79] Fagin, R. "Normal Forms and Relational Database Operators," *Proc. 1979 ACM SIGMOD Conf. on Mgmt. of Data,* pp. 153–160.

[Kent83] Kent, W. "A Simple Guide to Five Normal Forms in Relational Database Theory," *Comm. ACM* 26, 2 (Feb. 1983), pp. 120–125.

[Lien81] Lien, Y. "Hierarchical Schemata for Relational Databases," *ACM Trans. Database Systems* 6, 1 (1981), pp. 48–69.

[Maie83] Maier, D. *Theory of Relational Databases,* Computer Science Press, Rockville, MD, 1983.

[Mart83] Martin, J. *Managing the Data-Base Environment,* Prentice Hall, Englewood Cliffs, NJ, 1983.

[Smit85] Smith, H. "Database Design: Composing Fully Normalized Tables from a Rigorous Dependency Diagram," *Comm. ACM* 28, 8 (1985), pp. 826–838.

[Ullm88] Ullman, J. *Principles of Database and Knowledge-Base Systems, Vols. 1 and 2,* Computer Science Press, Rockville, MD, 1988.

[Yao 85] Yao, S.B. (editor). *Principles of Database Design,* Prentice Hall, Upper Saddle River, NJ, 1985.

[ZaMe81] Zaniolo, C.,s and Melkanoff, M. "On the Design of Relational Database Schemas," *ACM Trans. Database Systems* 6, 1 (1981), pp. 1–47.

Exercises

Problem 5-1

Answer each question "yes" or "no." Justify each answer. In each case you are given a relation R with a list of attributes without the candidate keys shown.

Given: R(A,B,C,D) and the functional dependencies A–>B, A–>C, and A–>D:

1. Is A a candidate key?
2. Is this relation, R, in 3NF?

Given: R(A,B,C,D) and the functional dependencies A–>B, B–>C, and C–>D:

3. Does A–>D?
4. Is A a candidate key?

Given: R(A,B) and the functional dependencies A–>B and B–>A:

5. Are both A and B candidate keys?
6. Is R in BCNF?

Given: R(A,B,C) and the functional dependencies A–>B, B–>C, and C–>A:

7. Is A the only candidate key?
8. Is R only in 2NF?

Given: R(A,B,C) and the functional dependencies AB–>C and C–>A:

9. Is AB a candidate key?
10. Is C a candidate key?
11. Is R in 3NF?
12. Is R in BCNF?

Given: R(A,B,C) and the functional dependency C–>A:

13. Is R in 3NF?
14. Is R in BCNF?

Given: R(A,B,C,D) and the functional dependencies A–>B and C–>D:

15. Is A a candidate key?
16. Is C a candidate key?
17. Is R in 3NF?

Given: R(A,B,C) and the functional dependencies AB–>C, AC–>B, and BC–>A:

18. Is A a candidate key?
19. Is BC a candidate key?
20. Is R in 3NF?

Given: R(A,B,C) and the functional dependencies AB–>C and AC–>B:

21. Is ABC a superkey?
22. Is AC a candidate key?
23. Is R in 3NF?
24. Is R in BCNF?

Given: R(A,B,C) with no functional dependencies:

25. Is AB a candidate key?
26. Is ABC a superkey?
27. Is R in BCNF?

Given: R(A,B,C,D) with the functional dependency A–>B:

28. Is A a candidate key?
29. Is ACD a superkey?
30. Is R in 3NF?

Problem 5-2

Answer each question "yes" or "no." Justify each answer. In each case you are given a relation R with a list of attributes, with one explicit candidate key (the candidate key may be either a single attribute or composite attribute key, shown underlined). Other candidate keys may be possible.

Given: R(A,B,C) and the functional dependencies A–>B and B–>C:

1. Is R in 3NF?

Given: R(A,B,C) and the functional dependency BC–>A:

2. Is R in 3NF?
3. Is R in BCNF?
4. Is BC a candidate key?

Given: R(A,B,C) and the functional dependency A–>C:

5. Is R in 3NF?
6. Does AB–>C?

Given: R(A,B,C,D) and the functional dependency C–>B:

7. Is R in 3NF?

Please see page 349 for the solution to Problem 5-2.

Problem 5-3

Given the assertions below for the current term enrollment at a large university, do the following:

1. List the obvious functional dependencies (FDs) from the given description.

Please see page 349 for the solution to Problem 5-3.

2. At what level of normalization is the database implemented as a single table with no repeating columns? Justify your answer.
3. If not in BCNF already, convert the database to BCNF.

Assertions:

a. An instructor may teach none, one, or more courses in a given term (average is 2.0 courses).
b. An instructor must direct the research of at least one student (average = 2.5 students).
c. A course may have none, one, or two prerequisites (average = 1.5 prerequisites).
d. A course may exist even if no students are currently enrolled.
e. All courses are taught by only one instructor.
f. The average enrollment in a course is 30 students.
g. A student must select at least one course per term (average = 4.0 course selections).

Problem 5-4

Answer each question as true or false.

When a relation R in 2NF with functional dependencies (FDs) A –> B and B –> CDEF (where A is the only candidate key), is decomposed into two relations R1 (with A –> B) and R2 (with B –> CDEF), the relations R1 and R2

1. are always a lossless decomposition of R.
2. usually have total combined storage space less than R.
3. have no delete anomalies.
4. will always be faster to execute a query than R.

When a relation S in 3NF with FDs GH –> I and I –> H is decomposed into two relations S1 (with GH –> null, i.e., all key) and S2 (with I –> H), the relations S1 and S2

5. are always a lossless decomposition of S.
6. are both dependency preserving.
7. are both in BCNF.

When a relation T in BCNF with FDs W –> XYZ (where W is the primary key) is decomposed into two relations T1 (with W –> X) and T2 (with W –> YZ), the resulting two relations T1 and T2

8. are always dependency preserving.
9. usually have total combined storage space less than T.
10. have no delete anomalies.

Note: A –> BC implies that A –> B and A –> C (an Armstrong axiom).

Problem 5-5

The following functional dependencies (FDs) represent a set of airline reservation system database constraints. Design a minimum set of 3NF relations, preserving all FDs, and express your solution in terms of the code letters that follow (a timesaving device for your analysis).

reservation_no –> agent_no, agent_name, airline_name, flight_no, passenger_name
reservation_no –> aircraft_type, departure_date, arrival_date, departure_time, arrival_time
reservation_no –> departure_city, arrival_city, type_of_payment, seating_class, seat_no
airline_name, flight_no –> aircraft_type, departure_time, arrival_time
airline_name, flight_no –> departure_city, arrival_city, meal_type
airline_name, flight_no, aircraft_type –> meal_type
passenger_name –> home_address, home_phone, company_name
aircraft_type, seat_no –> seating_class
company_name –> company_address, company_phone
company_phone –> company_name

A: reservation_no
B: agent_no
C: agent_name
D: airline_name
E: flight_no
L: departure_city
M: arrival_city
N: type_of_payment
P: seating_class
Q: seat_no

F:	passenger_name	R:	meal_type
G:	aircraft_type	S:	home_address
H:	departure_date	T:	home_phone
I:	arrival_date	U:	company_name
J:	departure_time	V:	company_address
K:	arrival_time	W:	company_phone

Problem 5-6

Given the following set of FDs, find the minimum set of 3NF relations. Designate the candidate key attributes of these relations. Is the set of relations you derived also BCNF?

1. A –> B
2. A –> C
3. B –> C
4. B –> D
5. D –> B
6. ABE –> F
7. E –> J
8. EG –> H
9. H –> G

Please see page 350 for the solution to Problem 5-6.

Problem 5-7

Given the following set of FDs, find the minimum set of 3NF relations. Designate the candidate key attributes of these relations. Is the set of relations you derived also BCNF?

1. J –> KLMNP
2. JKL –> MNP
3. K –> MQ
4. KL –> MNP
5. KM –> NP
6. N –> KP

Problem 5-8

Given the following set of FDs, find the minimum set of 3NF relations. Designate the candidate key attributes of these relations. Is the set of relations you derived also BCNF?

1. A –> BCDEF
2. AB –> CDEF
3. ABC –> DEF
4. ABCD –> EF
5. ABCDE –> F
6. B –> DG
7. BC –> DEF
8. BD –> EF
9. E –> BF

Please see page 350 for the solution to Problem 5-8.

Problem 5-9

Given the following functional dependencies, determine the minimum set of 3NF relations. Make sure that all functional dependencies are preserved. Specify the candidate keys of each relation. Note that each letter represents a separate data element (attribute). Is the set of relations you derived also BCNF?

1. A –> BGHJ
2. AG –> HK
3. B –> K
4. EA –> F
5. EB –> AF
6. EF –> A
7. H –> J
8. J –> AB

Problem 5-10

Given the following functional dependencies, determine the minimum set of 3NF relations. Make sure that all functional dependencies are preserved. Specify the candidate keys of each relation. Note that each letter represents a separate data element (attribute). Is the set of relations you derived also BCNF?

1. ABCD –> EFGHIJK
2. ACD –> JKLMN
3. A –> BH
4. B –> JKL
5. BH –> PQR
6. BL –> PS
7. EF –> ABCDH
8. JK –> B
9. MN –> ACD
10. L –> JK
11. PQ –> S
12. PS –> JKQ
13. PSR –> QT

Problem 5-11

Given the following functional dependencies, determine the minimum set of 3NF relations. Make sure that all functional dependencies are preserved. Specify the candidate keys of each relation. Note that each letter represents a separate data element (attribute).

1. A –> B
2. AB –> DE
3. ABCDET –> GHIJKW
4. ABDET –> CGHIJKW
5. CG –> KW
6. DT –> K

7. E –> ABCMNPQRT
8. GH –> AIJKT
9. HJR –> S
10. HJS –> R
11. HRS –> J
12. J –> BCKT
13. JRS –> H
14. KW –> M
15. KM –> W
16. M –> PQR
17. MN –> P
18. N –> T
19. T –> MN

If we add the functional dependency J –> A in the preceding list, what effect does this have on the solution?

Problem 5-12 (FDs and MVDs)

Answer each question "yes" or "no." Justify each answer. In most cases you are given a relation R with a list of attributes, with at most one candidate key (the candidate key may be either a single attribute or composite attribute key, shown underlined).

Given: R(A,B,C,D) and the functional dependency AB–>C:

1. Is R in 3NF?
2. Is R in BCNF?
3. Does the multivalued dependency AB –>>C hold?
4. Does the set {R1(A,B,C), R2(A,B,D)} satisfy the lossless join property?

Given: R(A,B,C) and the set {R1(A,B), R2(B,C)} satisfies the lossless decomposition property:

5. Does the multivalued dependency B–>>C hold?
6. Is B a candidate key?
7. Is R in 4NF?

Given: a relation "skills_available" with attributes empno, project, and skill. The semantics of "skills_available" state that every skill an employee has must be used on every project that employee works on.

8. Is the level of normalization of "skills_available" at least 4NF?

Given: relation R(A,B,C) with actual data as follows:

9. Does the multivalued dependency B–>>C hold?
10. Is R in 5NF?

R:	**A**	**B**	**C**
	w	x	p
	w	x	q
	z	x	p
	z	x	q
	w	y	q
	z	y	p

Problem 5-13 (MVDs and 4NF)

Given the minimum set of BCNF tables constructed from Problem 5-10, determine which tables are also 4NF from the following explicit MVDs:

1. B –>> H
2. K –>> B
3. LP –>> S
4. T –>> PSR

6 Access Methods

Physical database design normally commences after the logical design of the schema (SQL tables) has been completed. Generally, the physical database designer has the option to pick one normalized schema from the many schemas available; cluster two or more record types together (using the SQL "create cluster" command); specify primary keys for fast random access to individual records; define indexes on primary keys and secondary indexes to allow fast access by nonkey attributes (using the SQL "create index" command); and specify physical parameters such as block size, buffer pool size, lock granularity, and recovery protocol.

This chapter focuses on the various access methods available and the system parameters associated with them. In order to classify access methods, we define three broad categories of database applications in terms of generic data manipulation commands:

1. *sequential access*—select all records of a given type (or a large subset of those records);
2. *random access*—select one record of a given type; and
3. *Boolean query access*—select a group of records based on some Boolean search criterion.

Each type of application, which includes both query and update requirements, implies a class of efficient access methods. The algebra used to describe the performance of each access method is typical of what a query optimizer might calculate to determine good query plans.

The logical design of a database results in the schema definition of logical records. A *logical record* (or record) is a named collection of data items or attributes treated as a unit by an application program. In storage, a record includes the pointers and record overhead needed for identification and processing by the database management system. A *file* is a set of similarly constructed records of one or more types. For simplicity, in this chapter we assume that a file consists of records of a single type. A *physical database* (or database) is a collection of interrelated records of different types, possibly including a collection of interrelated files. Query and update transactions (or applications) to a database are made efficient by the implementation of certain access methods as part of the database management system.

An *access method* consists of two integrated components: data structure and search mechanism. The data structure defines the framework for storing index and data blocks in memory. The search mechanism defines the access path—that is, how the tables are searched. As an example, consider a sequential file. The data structure is simply a collection of contiguously stored records of a single type. The search mechanism, however, could be either a sequential search of all the records in storage order, a binary search, or some other type of random search mechanism; each combination of the one data structure with one of the several search mechanisms would be considered a different access method.

Let us now look at some simple models of database access methods. We shall see that we can capture the essence of database performance by defining and analyzing just a few important parameters.

6.1 Sequential Access Methods

A sequential file is a set of contiguously stored records on a physical device such as a disk, tape, or CD-ROM. Let us consider a sequential file of n records. To be stored on disk, these n records must be grouped into physical blocks as shown in Figure 6.1. A block is the basic unit of input/output from disk to RAM. It can range in size from a fraction of a record to hundreds or thousands of records. Typically, a block size ranges from 1 to 100 records. If a database has normalized records—that is, records of constant size—the number of records in a block is called the *blocking factor* (bf). For consistency and ease of programming, block sizes are usually constant for a whole system. On the other hand, almost all relational systems allow variable-size records; thus, we use average record size for simplicity in our performance analysis.

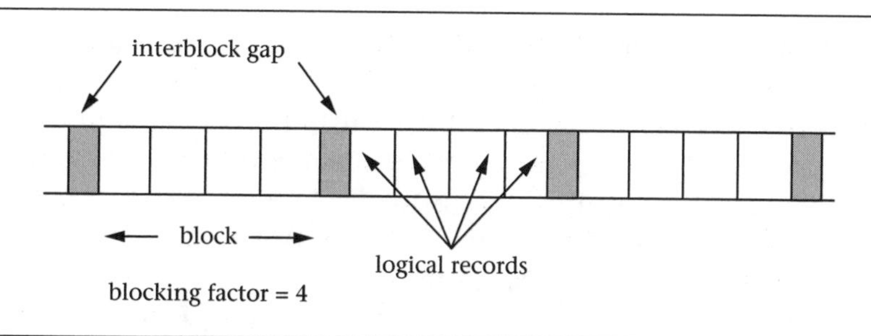

Figure 6.1 Sequential file parameters

6.1.1 Sequential Processing for an Entire File

If we have a file of n records and a blocking factor bf, the basic performance measures for a sequential search of the entire file are as follows.

lra = n	logical record accesses	(6.1)
sba = ceil(n/bf)	sequential block accesses	(6.2)
rba = 0	random block accesses	(6.3)
iotime = sba*Tsba + rba*Trba		
= ceil(n/bf)*Tsba	seconds	(6.4)

where Tsba is the average disk I/O service time for a sequential block access and Trba is the average disk I/O service time for a random block access. Note that the ceiling function, ceil, in Equation 6.2 is the next higher whole number (or integer) when the number of block accesses is a fraction instead of a whole number. Note that the second term in iotime drops out because rba = 0.

Obviously, sequential block accesses can be minimized when the blocking factor is maximized. However, block size is usually a function of some portion of a disk track. It is also limited by the size of buffers allowed in RAM since block size and buffer size must be the same for efficient data transfer from disk to RAM.

If we were to access the sequential file of n records in a completely random sequence, the performance measures would be

lra = n	logical record accesses	(6.5)
sba = 0	sequential block accesses	(6.6)
rba = n	random block accesses	(6.7)
iotime = sba*Tsba + rba*Trba		
= n*Trba	seconds	(6.8)

Note that the first term in iotime drops out because sba = 0.

These two situations, sequential and random access to a sequential file, show that a sequential search mechanism makes efficient use of the blocking factor, but a random search mechanism does not. Thus, when random searches are required of a sequential file, a blocking factor of 1 minimizes the search time (I/O service time), assuming that 1 is the lowest value we can use in a typical system.

Because time is a common unit for all databases, I/O service time is the most important performance measure. Response time as a performance measure is too difficult to control from the database designer perspective; that is, response time includes disk and CPU wait times, which are often dependent on the rest of the computing environment workload. Response time also includes CPU service time, which unfortunately is dependent on the amount of processing a database user does with the records retrieved, and it is not a function of the access method or database implementation.

The disk service time can be estimated from this simple model:

$$\text{Tsba} = \text{rot}/2 + \text{bks}/\text{tr} \tag{6.9}$$

where rot is the disk rotation time (for a full rotation), bks is the block size in bytes (bf*record size), and tr is the disk transfer rate in bytes per second.

In other words, the average sequential block I/O service time is the average time to access the next block on disk, which is a half rotation as the average rotational delay, plus the block transfer time. The average random block I/O service time is similarly computed:

$$\text{Trba} = \text{seek(file)} + \text{rot}/2 + \text{bks}/\text{tr} \tag{6.10}$$

where seek(file) is the average seek time over the extent of the file on disk.

The average random block I/O service time is the average seek time over the extent of the file plus the average rotational delay plus the block transfer time. The average seek time assumption depends on the type of disk and the workload environment, dedicated or shared. In a dedicated disk environment, the disk arm is confined to the extent of the file, which we assume is in contiguous storage. In a shared disk environment, the disk arm is moved an average seek distance for each block access to your file; this assumes that other users of this disk move the disk arm away from your file some random distance.

Consequently, in a shared disk environment, we have

$$\text{Tsba} = \text{Trba} = \text{seek(disk)} + \text{rot}/2 + \text{bks/tr} \quad (6.11)$$

where seek(disk) is the average seek time over the extent of the entire disk.

Equation 6.11 is the same as Equation 6.10 except that the seek component is potentially greater in size. In this chapter we assume that the disk environment is dedicated unless stated otherwise. Also, in the following analyses we compute only lra, sba, and rba and assume that the disk characteristics are known to compute the disk I/O service time, iotime.

The disk time analysis can sometimes be further simplified by noting that many systems do some sort of prefetching of multiple blocks (typically 64 KB per disk I/O, such as in DB2) to speed up the sequential processing activity. Under these conditions, dedicated disks have negligible seek times and rotational delay, while shared disks are dominated by seek times and data transfers.

6.1.2 Sequential Processing for a Single Record

If there are n records in a sequential file that is sorted by primary key, a sequential search for a single record, whether that record exists or not, requires approximately

lra = n/2	logical record accesses	(6.12)
sba = ceiling(lra/bf)	sequential block accesses	(6.13)

If the file is unsorted, a sequential search for the record is lra = n/2 if the record exists and lra = n when the record does not exist.

6.1.3 Batch Processing of k Records

One of the advantages of a sequential database or file is the efficiency of batch processing. Let us assume a batch system with a master file and a transaction file (Figure 6.2). Both files are sorted by primary key. The transaction file is assumed to have records of fixed size that specify what update action is to be taken on a record in the master file. Thus, each transaction record includes the primary key of a master file record, but the record size of the transaction file may be quite different from the

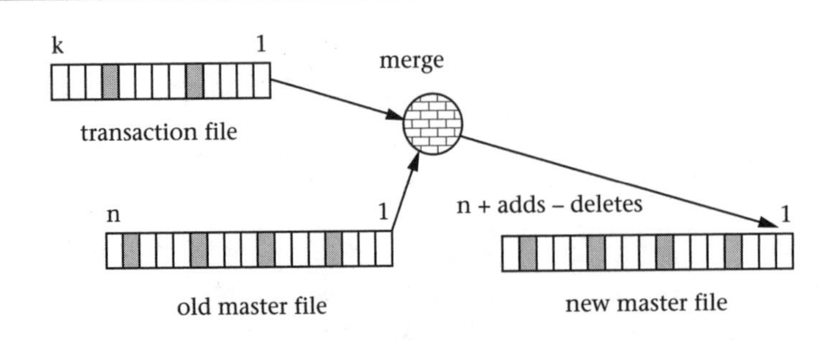

Figure 6.2 Batch processing of sequential files

record size in the master file. The I/O service time to execute the batch of update transactions is the sum of the time to read the entire transaction file, read the entire master file, and create a new master file. In other words:

read the transaction file

lra = k, where k = number of transaction records (6.14)

sba = ceil(k/tfbf), where tfbf is the transaction file blocking factor (6.15)

read the master file

lra = n (6.16)

sba = ceil(n/bf), where bf is the master file blocking factor (6.17)

write a new master file

lra = n + adds – deletes (6.18)

sba = ceil((n + adds – deletes)/bf) (6.19)

where adds is the number of records added or inserted and deletes is the number of records deleted.

6.2 Random Access Methods

Random files differ from sequential files in that the access to individual records is done much more directly, either through a hashing mechanism or an index instead of an exhaustive search. Physically, the data

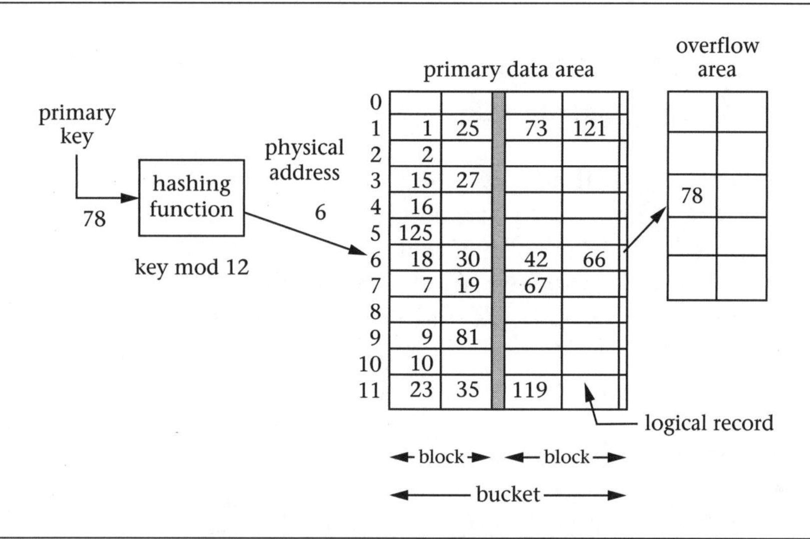

Figure 6.3 Hashing access method with separate chaining for overflow

structure of random files may be either similar or quite different from sequential files, depending on the access method used.

6.2.1 Hashing

Hashing is the most common form of purely random access to a file or database. It is also used to access columns that do not have an index as an optimization technique. The most popular form of hashing is division hashing with chained overflow, which is illustrated in Figure 6.3. The basic mechanism is the transformation of a primary key identifier directly to a physical address, called a *bucket*, or indirectly to a bucket by first transforming it to a logical address (an integer) and letting the database management system transform it again to a physical address.

Address transformation is done by the central processing unit. The actual access to the target database is done using the disk. The address transformation for division hashing is typically done by dividing the primary key into partitions and applying a simple arithmetic function (such as adding) to those partitions to get a single address value. For instance, given a primary key of a person's social security number, 527-45-6783, we can add the subset numbers: 527 + 45 + 6783 = 7355. Then we can transform this number into a physical disk address for a disk with 32 devices, 404 cylinders per disk, 20 tracks per cylinder, and 5 blocks per track:

device address = 7355 mod 32 = 27
cylinder address = 7355 mod 404 = 83
track address = 7355 mod 20 = 15 (6.20)

Access to this physical address allows us to either retrieve an existing record or store a new record in a block on that track.

Collisions occur when the database user attempts to insert a record into the target (bucket) address and the bucket is filled, causing overflow. *Collision resolution* is the process of deciding where to store (and later to find) the next record when a collision occurs. The *open addressing* approach involves a sequential search of the records until an open position is found [ElNa94].

Another approach, *chained overflow*, is typically handled by establishing a series of overflow blocks (on each track), tracks (on each cylinder), and cylinders (on each disk). Overflow records are chained in some order, usually either FIFO (first in, first out) or LIFO (last in, first out), and the length of overflow chains is a function of the density of the database and the type of overflow data structure and search mechanism [TeFr82].

A third approach, *multiple hashing* or *rehashing*, involves calculating a second hashing function when the first one results in a collision. If the second hashing function also results in a collision, then either open addressing or further rehashing is attempted until an open record position is reached.

For our simple model, we compute the performance for chained overflow as follows.

random access to a hashed file

lra = 1 + overflow(avg) (6.21)
rba = 1 + overflow(avg) (6.22)

insertion into a hashed file

lra = 1 + overflow(avg) + rewrite (6.23)
rba = 1 + overflow(avg) (6.24)
rba = 1 for the rewrite (6.25)

Note that a rewrite of a block accessed requires a single random block access (rba), assuming a dedicated disk. That is, a rewrite occurs after we have retrieved the block and processed the information in that block

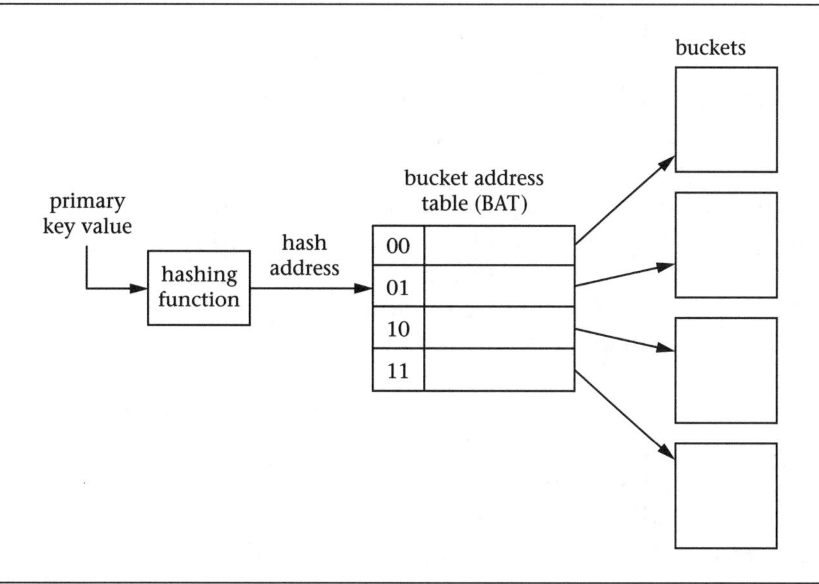

Figure 6.4 Extendible hashing architecture

(e.g., searched for the record position needed for a rewrite and then rewritten into the block in RAM). When we are ready to do the rewrite on disk, the disk physical position is at a random distance from the beginning of the block position where we want to write, so the average delay to get to that point is Trba. Thus, a rewrite is simply a single rba. In a shared disk environment, a rewrite is also a single rba.

Techniques that combine basic hashing with dynamic file expansion are also very popular today [ElNa94]. In *extendible hashing,* for example, the number of buckets grows or contracts, depending on the need. When a bucket becomes full, it splits into two buckets, and records in the bucket are reallocated to the two new buckets based on the first i bits of their hash value. Thus, collisions are resolved immediately and dynamically, and long sequential searches, long overflow chains, and multiple hashing computations are avoided.

The basic structure or architecture of extendible hashing is illustrated in Figure 6.4. The primary key is sent to a hash function that produces a hash address pointing to an entry in the bucket address table (BAT), which normally resides in RAM. The BAT contains pointers to the respective physical (disk) buckets that hold the actual data records. The BAT is initialized with space for one entry and expands as the database records are inserted and more differentiation is needed to allocate records to the buckets. If i high-order bits of the hash address are used to determine the bucket to store to or retrieve from, the BAT contains 2^i entries. Thus, if the 8 high-order bits are needed to allocate records to buckets, the BAT contains 256 entries, and therefore up to 256 buckets can be defined and pointed to from these BAT entries. In Figure 6.5 we take the same data shown in Figure 6.3 and apply it with a slightly different hash function to illustrate how the BAT and buckets are allocated for a database with eight entries, requiring 3 higher-order bits to differentiate the records. The buckets split when saturated, and the existing entries are balanced as closely as possible between the two split buckets (blocks). Note that only seven buckets are required at this state of the database.

The cost to retrieve a single record using extendible hashing is 1 access to the BAT in RAM plus 1 disk access (1 rba) to the bucket that contains the record desired. The analysis of the I/O cost for bucket updates, inserts, and deletes, with the possible occasional splitting of buckets, is the same as for B^+-trees and is covered in the next section.

6.2.2 B-trees and B^+-trees

The *B-tree* is the access method supported by DB2, SQL/DS, Oracle, and NonStop/SQL and is the dominant access method used by other relational database management systems such as Ingres and Sybase. It features not only fast random and sequential access but also the dynamic maintenance that virtually eliminates the overflow problems that occur in the older hashing and indexed sequential methods (although we noted previously that the more recent dynamic hashing methods make use of the dynamic maintenance capability as well).

The data structure of a B-tree has evolved considerably since its inception in 1972 [BaMc72, ElNa94]. Originally, each node in the tree consisted of p – 1 records and p tree pointers to the next level in the tree, consisting of p nodes (see Figure 6.6a). The value p is known as the *order* of the B-tree. More recently, the structure of each node has been modified to become p pointers and p – 1 sets of pairs: a search key value for a data record and a pointer to that data record, called a data pointer (Figure 6.6b). The actual record is stored elsewhere, not in the path of the B-tree search. Because the search key value/data pointer pair is usually much smaller than the entire logical record, the order of a B-tree is potentially much larger than originally defined, given a physical limit on node size (similar to the limit on block size). Thus, the search time to a random record in the file or database can be greatly decreased.

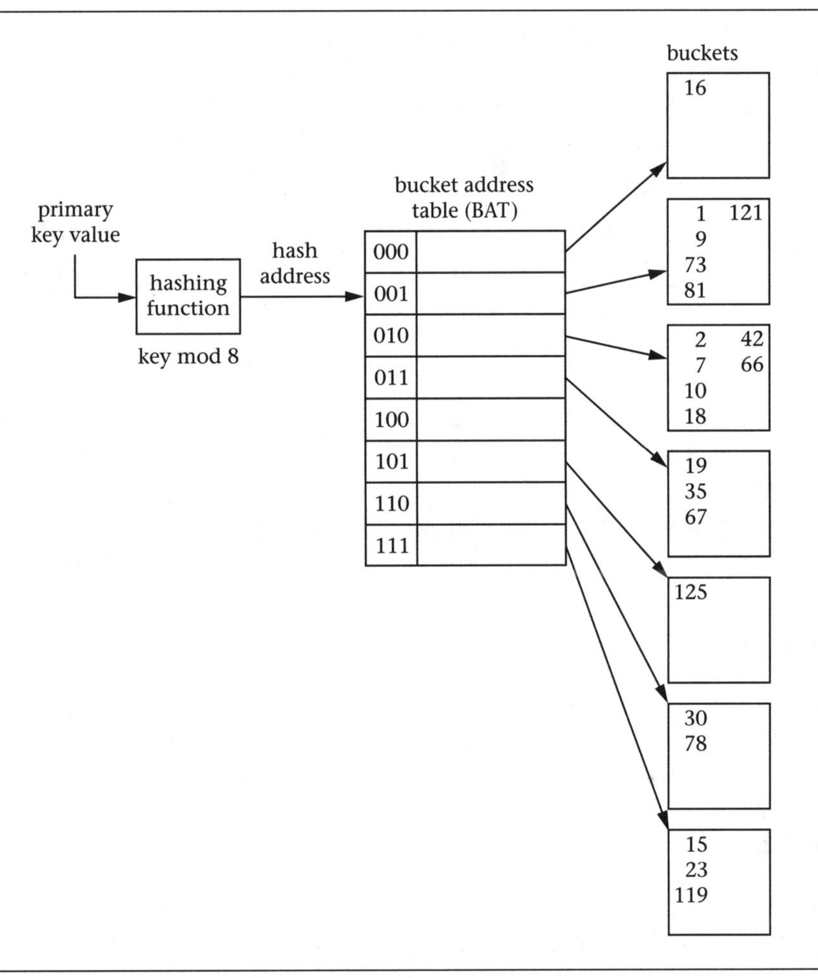

Figure 6.5 Extendible hashing table for example in Figure 6.3

The most often used implementation of the B-tree is the B+-tree (or B*-tree). This variation eliminates the data pointers from all nodes but the leaf nodes in the B+-tree index (see Figure 6.7). Therefore, the tree index search is very efficient. Each nonleaf index node consists of p tree pointers and p – 1 key values. The key values denote where to search to find records that have either smaller key values (by taking the tree pointer to the left of the key) or greater or equal key values (by taking the tree pointer to the right of the key). Each leaf index node consists of a series of key and data pointer combinations that point to each record. The leaf index nodes (and the associated data blocks) are connected logically by

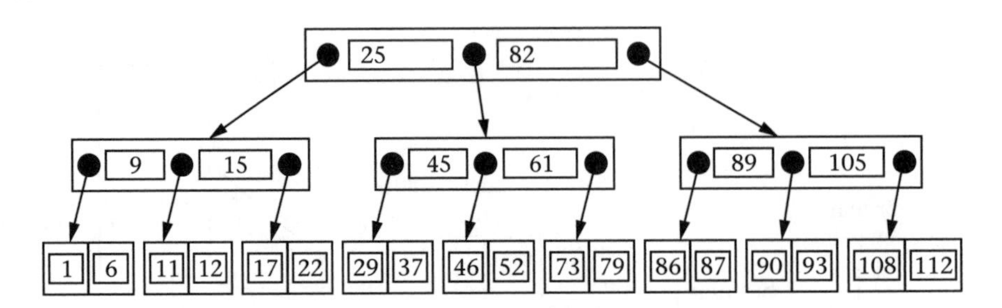

(a) B-tree with embedded records at each node

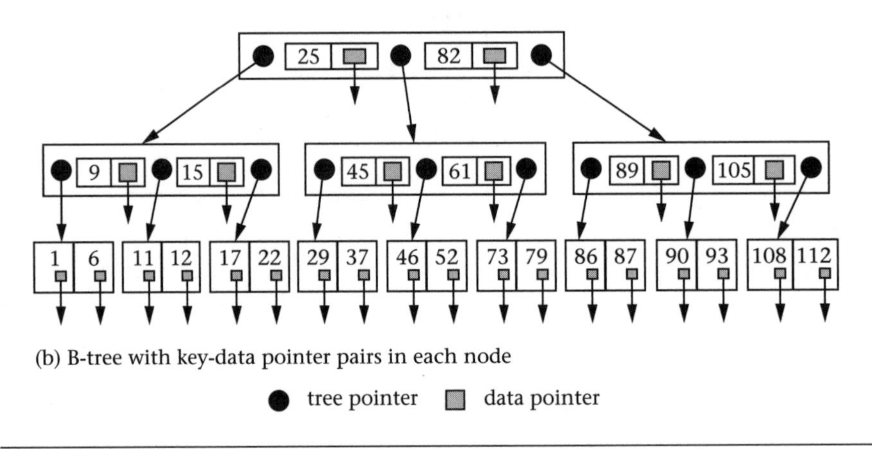

(b) B-tree with key-data pointer pairs in each node

tree pointer   data pointer

Figure 6.6 B-tree configurations with order 3 (p = 3)

block pointers so that an ordered sequence of records can be found quickly.

Example: B+-tree

To determine the order of a B+-tree, let us assume that the database has 500,000 records of 200 bytes each, the search key is 15 bytes, the tree and data pointers are 5 bytes, and the index node (and data block size) is 1024 bytes. For this configuration we have

$$\text{nonleaf index node size} = 1024 \text{ bytes} = p*5 + (p - 1)*15 \text{ bytes}$$

$$p = \text{floor}((1024 + 15)/20) = \text{floor}(51.95) = 51 \quad (6.26)$$

where the floor function is the next lower whole number, found by truncating the actual value to the next lower integer. Therefore, we can have

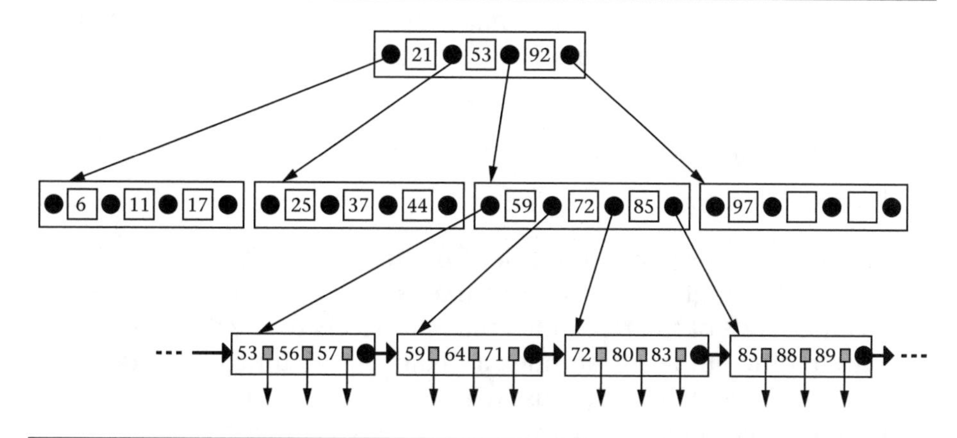

Figure 6.7 B⁺-tree configuration with order 4 and height 3

up to p – 1 or 50 search key values in each nonleaf index node. In the leaf index nodes there are 15 bytes for the search key value and 5 bytes for the data pointer. Each leaf index node typically has a single pointer to the next leaf index node to make a sequential search of the data records possible without going through the index-level nodes. In this example the number of search key values in the leaf nodes is floor ((1024 – 5)/(15 + 5)) = 50.

The height h of the B⁺-tree is the number of index levels, including the leaf nodes. It is computed by noting that the root index node (ith level) has p pointers, the i-1st level has p2 tree pointers, the i-2nd level has p3 tree pointers, and so on. At the leaf level the number of key entries and pointers are p – 1 per index node; the total number of pointers over all nodes at that level must be greater than or equal to the number of records in the database, n. Therefore,

$$p^{h-1}(p-1) > n$$
$$(h-1)\log p + \log(p-1) > \log n$$
$$(h-1)\log p > \log n - \log(p-1)$$
$$h > 1 + (\log n - \log(p-1))/\log p \qquad (6.27)$$

In this example, therefore,

$$h > 1 + (\log 500{,}000 - \log 49)/\log 50 = 3.34$$
$$h = 4$$

A good approximation can be made by assuming that the leaf index nodes are implemented with p pointers and p key values:

$$p^h > n$$
$$h \log p > \log n$$
$$h > \log n / \log p \qquad (6.28)$$

In this case, the preceding result becomes h > 3.35 or h = 4.

Query of a single record in a B^+-tree is simply the time required to access all h levels of the tree index plus the access to the data record. All accesses to different levels of index and data are assumed to be random, whereas a rewrite of a record just read is sequential in a dedicated disk environment and random in a shared disk environment.

$$\text{read a single record } (B^+\text{-tree}) = (h + 1) \text{ rba} \qquad (6.29)$$

Updates of records in a B^+-tree can be accomplished with a simple query and rewrite unless the update involves an insertion that overflows a data or index node or a deletion that empties a data or index node. For the simple case of updating data values in a record, assuming that each index node is implemented as a block:

$$\begin{aligned}\text{update a single record } (B^+\text{-tree}) &= \text{search cost} + \text{rewrite data block} \\ &= (h + 1) \text{ rba} + 1 \text{ rba} \qquad (6.30)\end{aligned}$$

If the update is an insertion and the insertion causes overflow of a data or leaf index node, additional accesses are needed to split the saturated node into two nodes that are half-filled (using the basic splitting algorithm) and to rewrite the next higher index node with a new pointer to the new index node (see Figure 6.8). The need for a split is recognized after the initial search for the record has been done. A split of a leaf index node requires a rewrite of the saturated leaf index node, half-filled with data, plus a random write of a new leaf index node also half-filled, plus a rewrite of the nonleaf index node with a new pointer value to the new leaf index node. When multiple rewrites are required, only the rewrite of the data block is typically sequential since it can be done immediately after it has been read; all other rewrites are random.

Occasionally, the split operation of a leaf index node necessitates a split of the next higher index node as well, and in the worst case the split operations may cascade all the way up to the index root node. The probability of additional splits depends on the type of splitting algorithm and the dynamics of insertions and deletions in the workload, and is beyond

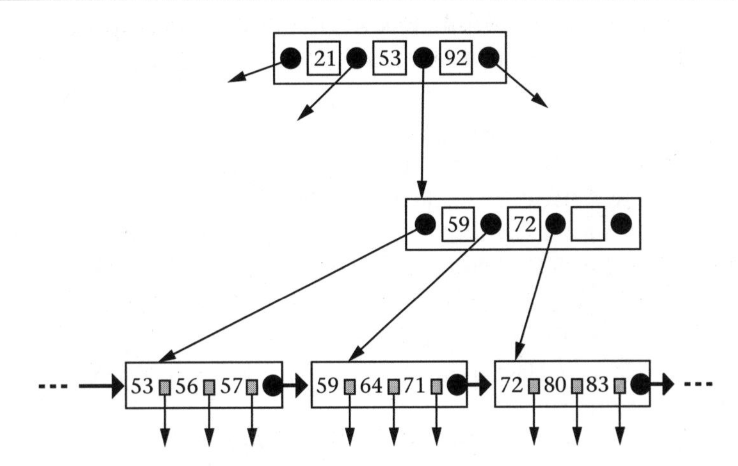

(a) B^+-tree before the insertion of record with key value 77

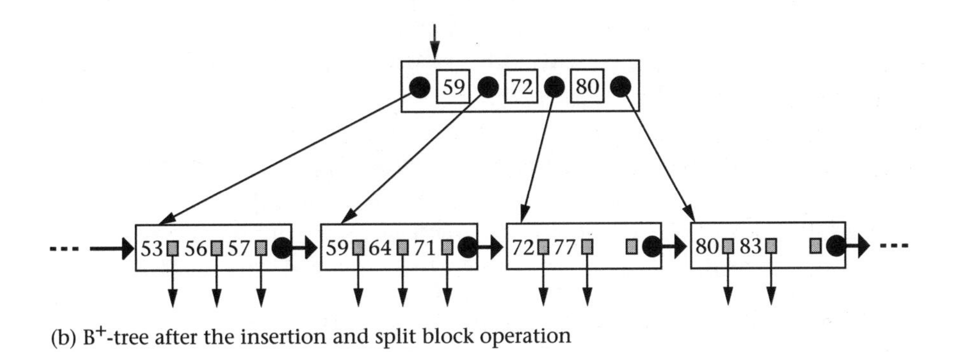

(b) B^+-tree after the insertion and split block operation

Figure 6.8 Dynamic maintenance in a B^+-tree for record insertion

the scope of this text. However, we can estimate the cost of each additional split in terms of block accesses required, as follows.

general update cost for insertion (B^+-tree)
= search cost (i.e., h + 1 reads)
+ simple rewrite of data block and leaf index node pointing to the data block (i.e., 2 rewrites)
+ nos*(write of new split index node
+ rewrite of the index node pointer to the new index node)
+ nosb*(write of new split data block)
= (h + 1) rba + 2 rba + nos*(2 rba) + nosb*(1 rba) (6.31)

where nos is the number of index split node operations required and nosb is the number of data split block operations required. Note that nosb is either 0 or 1. A more detailed treatment of B^+-tree splitting can be found in [ElNa94].

Deletions may result in emptying a data block or index node, which necessitates the consolidation of two nodes into one. This may require a rewrite of the leaf index node to reset its pointers. The empty data node can be either left alone or rewritten with nulls, depending on the implementation. We will assume that the node where data is deleted need not be rewritten. Occasionally, the leaf or nonleaf nodes become empty and need consolidation as well. Thus, we obtain the cost of deletion:

general update cost for deletion (B^+-tree)
= search cost (i.e., h + 1 reads)
+ simple rewrite of data block and leaf index node pointing to the data block (i.e., 2 rewrites)
+ noc*(rewrite of the node pointer to the remaining node)
= (h + 1) rba + 2 rba + noc*(1 rba) (6.32)

where noc is the number of consolidations of index nodes required.

As an example, consider the insertion of a node (with key value 77) to the B^+-tree shown in Figure 6.8. This insertion requires a search (query) phase and an insertion phase with one split node. The total insertion cost for height 3 is

insertion cost = (3 + 1) rba search cost + 2 rba rewrite cost
+ 1 split *(2 rba rewrite cost)
= 8 rba (6.33)

6.3 Secondary Indexes

A secondary index is an access method that efficiently searches a base (database) table, given a Boolean search criterion. Secondary indexes are tables that replicate secondary key data from the base table to allow quick lookup of the primary key, given secondary key values. Boolean search criteria such as "find all employee records where the job title is 'database administrator' and location is 'chicago'" result in the access to a set of target records that is typically a small subset of the entire population of records but usually significantly more than a single record. Using access methods based on the primary key will not work here, and

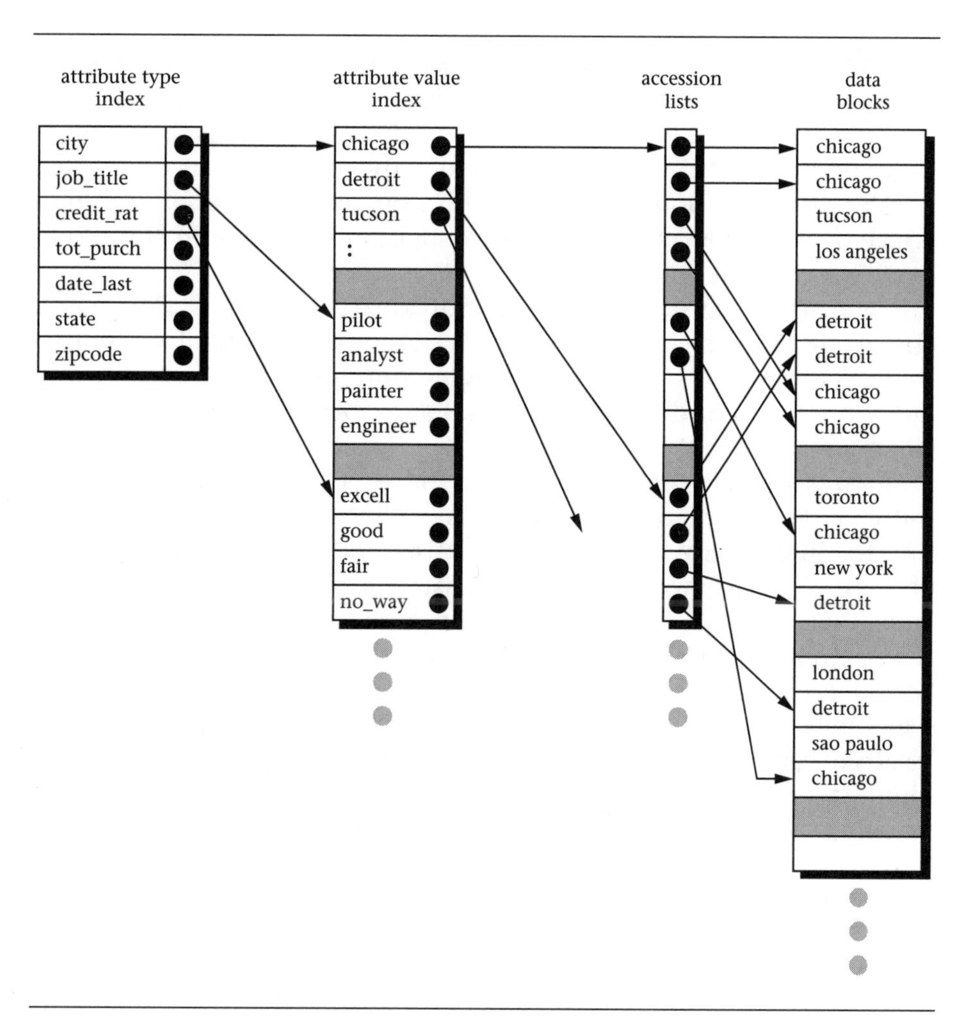

Figure 6.9 Secondary index structure

frequent exhaustive scans of the entire base table is usually prohibitively expensive.

Conceptually, the basic components of a secondary index (Figure 6.9) are the attribute type index, attribute value index, an accession list, and the data blocks that house the base table. The attribute type index is a simple index that lists all the attributes you wish to build secondary indexes on; each entry consists of the attribute name and a pointer to the appropriate attribute value index for that name. The attribute value index, in turn, has entries for each possible attribute value for each attribute type, and a pointer to an accession list for that value. Attribute type and value indexes are usually quite small and are usually permanently stored in RAM while the database is active.

An accession list is an ordered list of pointers to records that contain the appropriate attribute value specified in the attribute value index that points to the accession list. Each pointer consists of a block address plus a record offset that ensures that each pointer is unique in the file or database.

Each attribute value has its own individual accession list. The pointers are ordered by record address (block address and record offset) so that multiple accession lists representing a complex AND condition in a query can be merged in a single pass. For example, in our query, "Find all employee records where the job title is 'database administrator' and location is 'chicago'," an accession list for job_title = 'database administrator' and an accession list for location = 'chicago' must be searched to find the intersection of records that satisfy both conditions. The result of this merge is a new target accession list, held in a buffer in RAM unless larger than the block size. This list points to the target records that satisfy the conjunctive AND (condition AND condition AND condition AND . . .) query. A query that contains disjunctive OR conditions involves searching target records for each condition separately and appending the results to each other at the completion of each search. Queries that combine AND and OR conditions use a combination of the individual approaches, with the AND conditions within each OR condition executed first.

Assuming that the attribute type and attribute value indexes are stored in RAM, no disk access analysis is needed. However, we do need to analyze the access cost to the accession list and the target data blocks. The accession lists can be assumed to be linked sequential files, and the merge operation is similar to the merge required for a sequential file batch processing operation. Access to the data blocks is assumed to be strictly random via hashing or B-tree search. Each record pointer is treated as a random access since the data is rarely ordered by secondary key value.

Boolean query cost (secondary index)
= search attribute type index + search attribute value index
+ search and merge m accession lists + access t target records
= (0 + 0 + sum of m accession list accesses) rba + t rba (6.34)

where m is the number of accession lists to be merged and t is the number of target records to be accessed after the merge operation.

accession list cost (for accession list j) = ceil(pj/bfac) rba (6.35)

where pj is the number of pointer entries in the jth accession list and bfac is the blocking factor for all accession lists

bfac = block_size/pointer_size (6.36)

We assume that all block accesses to the accession list are random because physical sequentiality usually cannot be guaranteed. In practice it is usually random. Generally, we ignore errors of 1% or less in this type of analysis because of the simplifying assumptions we often make.

Example: Mail-Order Business

Assume we have a file of 10,000,000 records of mail-order customers for a large commercial business. Customer records have attributes for customer name, customer number, street address, city, state, zip code, phone number, employer, job title, credit rating, date of last purchase, and total amount of purchases. Assume that the record size is 250 bytes; block size is 5000 bytes (bf = 20); and pointer size, including record offset, is 5 bytes (bfac = 1000). The query to be analyzed is "Find all customers whose job title is 'engineer', city is 'chicago', and total amount of purchases is greater than $1000." For each AND condition we have the following hit rates—that is, records that satisfy each condition:

job title is 'engineer': 84,000 records
city is 'chicago': 210,000 records
total amount of purchases > $1000: 350,000 records
total number of target records that satisfy all three conditions = 750

Applying Equations 6.34 through 6.36, we estimate the query access cost to be

query cost (inverted file)
= merge of 3 accession lists + access 750 target records
= [ceil(n1/bfac) + ceil(n2/bfac) + ceil(n3/bfac)] rba + 750 rba
= [ceil(84,000/1000) + ceil(210,000/1000) + ceil(350,000/1000] rba
+ 750 rba
= (84 + 210 + 350) rba + 750 rba
= 1394 rba (6.37)

If we assume Tsba is 10 milliseconds and Trba is 25 milliseconds, we obtain

query iotime (secondary index)
= 1394 rba*25 ms
= 34,850 ms
= 34.85 sec (6.38)

query iotime (sequential scan)
= ceil(n/bf) sba *Tsba
= ceil(10,000,000/20)*10 ms
= 5,000,000 ms
= 5000 sec (6.39)

Thus, we see that the secondary index time reduces the exhaustive scan time by a factor of almost 150. In Figure 6.10 we see that at approximately 200,000 target records, sequential becomes the more efficient method.

There is an inherent inefficiency in secondary indexes with large numbers of target records in that each target record in a given data block has a separate (redundant) pointer to it from each accession list and from the target accession list. Variants of secondary indexes exist in which these redundant pointers are eliminated so that each accession list pointer references a data block that contains at least one target record for that Boolean condition, and it has a target accession list pointer that references a data block that contains at least one target record for all the Boolean conditions in the query. This reduces the lengths of the accession lists as well as the number of accesses to the target records, since an access to a data block containing at least one target record will result in accesses to all target records in that block.

Secondary Indexes Using B^+-trees

As an example of secondary indexes in practice, we extend the generic B^+-tree method to handle Boolean queries. This is the type of method used by Oracle and others for nonunique indexes (see Appendix B). In Section 6.2.2 we used B^+-trees to implement the concept of a unique index based on a primary key and for accessing a single record. Now we wish to use the same general structure to implement a nonunique index capable of accessing a set of records that satisfies a Boolean query. In a

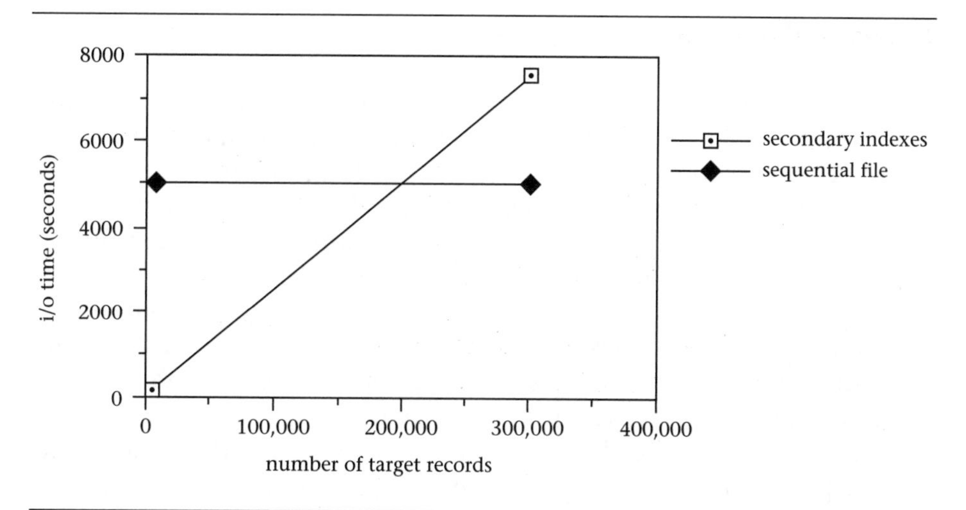

Figure 6.10 Secondary indexes versus sequential

unique index, the nonleaf nodes contain key-pointer pairs in which the key is the primary key of the table you want to access. In a nonunique index, the key field is a concatenation of all the secondary keys you want to set up to access the set of records desired. Taking another look at the preceding example, we form a nonunique index key by concatenating the secondary keys for job title, city, and total amount of purchases, as shown in Figure 6.11. The leaf nodes for unique indexes contain the complete set of primary key values, with each key value paired with a pointer to the block containing the record with the given primary key value. For the nonunique leaf nodes, we also have key-pointer pairs, but the key values are the complete set of all combinations of the concatenated secondary keys that actually occur in existing records. If a concatenated key value occurs in t records, then there are t key-pointer pairs required to point to those records, with the given key value repeated t times.

The analysis of a B^+-tree secondary (nonunique) index proceeds in the same way as for a primary key (unique) index, with the new definition of key fields accounting for the concatenation of secondary keys. It is also possible not to have concatenation; that is, the key can just be a single secondary key. In either case, the computations of query time and update times use the same equations as in Section 6.2.2.

6.4 Denormalization

Database designers for network systems (CODASYL, for example) and hierarchical systems often used processing requirements to refine the DBMS schema before or during the physical design phase, if there were obvious efficiency gains to be made. If it produced more efficient database schemas without loss of data integrity, a similar technique could be applied to relational databases, and it would be relatively easy to implement. Let us look at a relational schema refinement (denormalization) algorithm based on a process-oriented, or usage, view that increases database efficiency for current processing requirements and yet retains all the information content of the natural view of data.

The application of a denormalization algorithm is the logical next step in practical database design methodologies. Denormalization is often used to suggest alternative logical structures during physical design and thus provide the designers with other feasible solutions to choose from. More efficient databases are the likely outcome of evaluating alternative structures.

This process is referred to as denormalization because the schema transformation can cause the degree of normalization in the resulting table to be less than the degree of at least one of the original tables. Five basic types of denormalization are defined as follows:

1. ***Two entities in a many-to-many relationship.*** The relationship table resulting from this construct is composed of the primary keys of each of the associated entities. If we implement the join of this table with one of the entity tables as a single table instead of the original tables, we can avoid certain frequent joins that are based on both keys, but only the nonkey data from one of the original entities. This is similar to the so-called semi-join operation [CePe84]. This type is illustrated in the examples to follow.

2. ***Two entities in a one-to-one relationship.*** The tables for these entities could be implemented as a single table, thus avoiding frequent joins required by certain applications.

3. ***Reference data in a one-to-many relationship.*** When artificial primary keys are introduced to tables that either have no primary keys or have keys that are very large composites, they can be added to the child

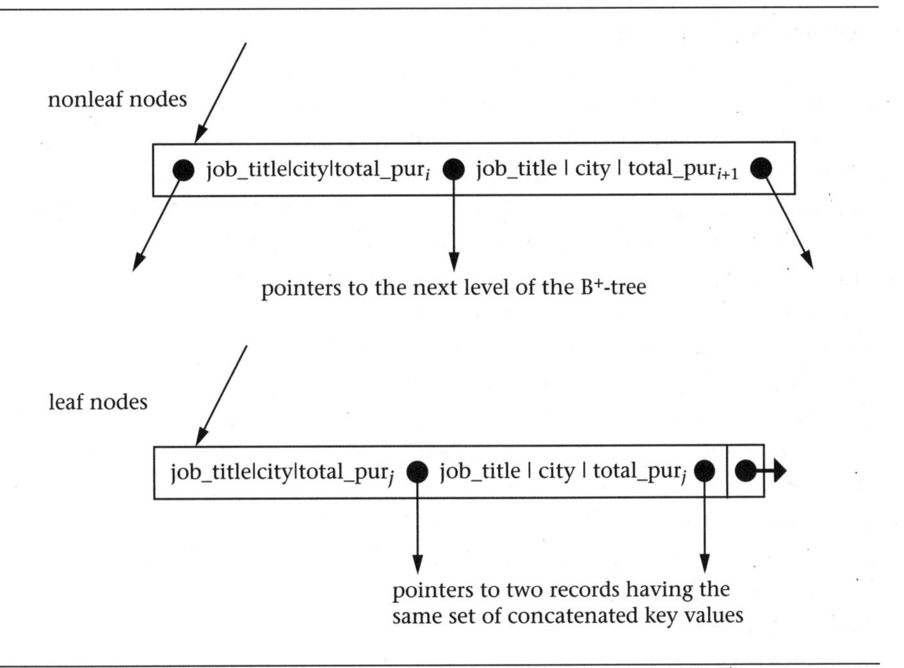

Figure 6.11 Using a B+-tree for a secondary index

entity in a one-to-many relationship as a foreign key and avoid certain joins in current applications.

4. ***Entities with the most detailed data***. Multivalued attributes (such as dependents or months in a year) are usually implemented as entities and are thus represented as separate records in a table. Sometimes it is more efficient to implement them as individually named columns as an extension of the parent entity (table) when the number of replications is a small fixed number for all instances of the parent entity.

5. ***Derived attributes***. If one attribute is derived from another at execution time, then in some cases it is more efficient to store both the original value and the derived value directly in the database. This adds at least one extra column to the original table and avoids repetitive computation.

Let us look at the first type of denormalization in the preceding list. We assume that all attributes are initially assigned to tables based on FDs and that the tables are at least 3NF. This establishes the requirement of an accurate representation of reality and of the flexibility of the design for future processing requirements. Efficiency of the current query requirements can be increased by redundantly adding attributes, used together in a query, to an existing table so that all attributes needed for that query reside in a new table, called a join table. Access time is now greatly reduced because fewer joins are needed. However, the side effects of this redundant extension include an increase in required storage space, an increase in the update cost, potential denormalization and loss of integrity, and the necessity for program transformations for all relevant queries. These effects require careful consideration.

To illustrate some of these effects, let us assume that the table **review** is associated with the tables **employee** and **manager** as the table that follows shows. The extension of the **review** table, **review-ext**, is shown as a means of reducing the number of joins required in the query shown below. This extension results in a real denormalization, that is,

review_no –> emp_id –> emp_name, emp_address

with the side effects of add and update anomalies. However, the delete anomaly cannot occur because the original data is redundant in the extended schema.

Original tables and process (query)

Table	*Primary key*	*Nonkeys*
employee	emp_id	emp_name, emp_address, mgr_id
manager	mgr_id	emp_name, emp_address
review	review_no	emp_id, mgr_id

Query: For a given review number, display the employee name and address.

```
select e.emp_name, e.emp_addr
    from employee as e, review as r
    where r.review_no = 'xxxx'
    and e.emp_id = r.emp_id;
```

Extended table **review_ext** in 2NF (using an SQL construct that produces a permanent table as the result of a query, not a standard SQL-92 construct, but available in other versions of SQL):

```
create table review_ext as
    select r.review_no, e.emp_id, e.emp_name, e.emp_addr, e.mgr_id
        from employee as e, review as r
        where e.emp_id = r.emp_id;
```

The storage and processing cost of a logical relational database is to be computed for both the existing and new join tables. The formula for the computation follows.

total cost = [iotime(q) + iotime(u)]*cost(q) + volume(s)*cost(s) (6.40)

where

cost(q) = unit cost per I/O second for query or update processes
cost(s) = unit cost per byte for stored data
iotime(q) = I/O service time (sec) for query processes
iotime(u) = I/O service time (sec) for update processes
volume(s) = total volume in bytes for stored data

Unit costs are selected based on the computing environment defined in the requirements specification. The I/O service time for query and update can be determined from the processing operations, their frequencies, and the hardware device characteristics; stored data volume can be obtained from the size of the tables defined. Each query process must be expressed in terms of basic relational algebra—operations such as selection, projection, and join. At this point some initial assumptions must be made about sequential and random accesses needed to efficiently accomplish the query or update, but the actual use of indexes, sorting, and the like is deferred to physical design when the final configuration decisions are made.

Table Denormalization Algorithm

A practical strategy for table denormalization is to select only the most dominant processes to determine those modifications that will most likely improve performance. The basic modification is to add attributes to existing tables to reduce join operations. The steps of the strategy follow.

1. Select the dominant processes based on such criteria as high frequency of execution, high volume of data accessed, response time constraints, or explicit high priority. Remember this rule of thumb: Any process whose frequency of execution or data volume accessed is 10 times that of another process is considered to be dominant.
2. Define join tables, when appropriate, for the dominant processes.
3. Evaluate total cost for storage, query, and update for the database schema, with and without the extended table, and determine which configuration minimizes total cost.
4. Consider also the possibility of denormalization due to a join table and its side effects. If a join table schema appears to have lower storage and processing cost and insignificant side effects, then consider using that schema for physical design in addition to the original candidate table schema. Otherwise, use only the original schema.

In general, avoid joins based on nonkeys. They are likely to produce very large tables, thus greatly increasing storage and update costs. For example, if two tables have 100 and 200 records, respectively, a join based on the key of either one results in a maximum of 200 records, but a join based on a nonkey of either one can result in a maximum of 100*200, or 20,000 records. Null values are also restricted to nonkey attributes so that they will not be used inadvertently in join operations.

6.5 Join Strategies

We now apply our knowledge of access methods to a comparison of join processing strategies. Our basic parameters are the number of rows, m and n, in the two tables to be joined; the blocking factor for each table, bfm and bfn; and the physical order of rows in each table. The basic join strategies we consider are

- nested loop: complexity O(mn)
- merge-join: complexity O(n $\log_2$ n)
- indexed join: complexity O(2m)
- hash-join: complexity O(m + n)

where the complexities are based on the assumption that if the join is between a table whose foreign key matches another table's primary key, then m represents the number of rows in the table with the primary key and n represents the number of rows in the table with the foreign key. If the join is not between two such tables, then the designations of which table has m rows and which one has n rows is arbitrary.

The nested loop strategy is the basic method of join. The outer loop is a sequential scan of the first table, and for each row in the first table scanned, the inner loop is executed, a sequential scan of the second table. The complexity is O(mn) because of the double loop. We assume that each table is stored in physically contiguous disk space; otherwise, each disk access becomes a random access (rba) instead of a sequential access (sba). The time cost of executing this strategy also depends on which table we select for the outer and inner loops. Continuing the example we defined in Chapters 2 through 4, let us assume that the **assigned_to** table has 50,000 rows and the **project** table has 250 rows. Let the blocking factors for the **assigned_to** and **project** tables be 100 and 50, respectively, and the block size be equal for the two tables. The common join column is project_name. We omit the time required to display the results of the join since it is constant for all the strategies and depends heavily on the display medium.

```
select project_name, emp_id
   from project as p, assigned_to as a
   where p.project_name = a.project_name;
```

Nested Loop Case 1: **assigned_to** is the outer loop table.

join cost = scan **assigned_to** once, scan **project** n times
= 50,000/100 + 50,000*250/50
= 500 + 250,000
= 250,500 sequential block accesses (sba's)

If a sequential block access requires an average of 10 ms, the total time required is 2505 seconds.

Nested Loop Case 2: **project** is the outer loop table.

join cost = scan **project** once, scan **assigned_to** m times
= 250/50 + 250*50,000/100
= 5 + 125,000
= 125,005 sequential block accesses (or 1250 seconds)

The nested loop strategy can obviously improve its performance by a proper selection of outer and inner loop tables, but for this example both cases result in a prohibitively long query (approximately 20 to 40 minutes). Note that this strategy does not take advantage of row order for these tables.

The merge-join strategy, unlike the nested loop strategy, takes advantage of row order in the same way that batch processing does (see Section 6.1). If the tables are both sorted on the join columns, then only a single sequential scan of each table is required to complete the join. If one or both tables are not sorted on the join column, then each unsorted table is sorted before the merge is executed. Even with the overhead of a sort operation, this algorithm is faster than nested loop. We assume the complexity of the sort of n rows is $O(n*\log_2*n)$.

Merge-Join Case 1: Both **project** and **assigned_to** are already ordered by project_name.

join cost = merge time (to scan both tables)
= 50,000/100 + 250/50
= 505 sequential block accesses (or 5 seconds)

Merge-Join Case 2: Only **project** is ordered by project_name.

join cost = sort time for **assigned_to** + merge time (to scan both sorted tables)
= $(50{,}000*\log_2 50{,}000)/100$ + 50,000/100 + 250/50
= (50,000*16)/100 + 500 + 5
= 8505 sequential block accesses (or 85 seconds)

Merge-Join Case 3: Neither **project** nor **assigned_to** is ordered by project_name.

join cost = sort time for both tables + merge time for both tables
= $(50{,}000 * \log_2 50{,}000)/100 + (250 * \log_2 250)/50$
$+ 50{,}000/100 + 250/50$
= 8000 + 40 + 500 + 5
= 8545 sequential block accesses (or 85 seconds)

We see that the sort phase of the merge-join strategy is the costliest component, but it still significantly improves performance compared to the nested loop strategy.

The indexed join is most useful when one of the common join columns is a primary key and has an index already available and the join selectivity (percentage of rows actually participating in the join) is very low. It can also be effectively used with nonunique (secondary) indexes as long as the join selectivity is low. The strategy is to do a full scan of the first table and, for each qualifying join attribute value, locate the corresponding row in the second table via the index. If there are mt qualifying rows in the first table, and nt qualifying rows in the second table, there will be m/bfm sequential block accesses for the first table and mt random block accesses to the second table, one rba for each qualifying row found in the first table. Let mt = 100 qualifying rows for the first table (**assigned_to**) and let nt = 5 qualifying rows for the second table (**project**) in the following example.

```
select project_name, emp_id
   from project as p, assigned_to as a
   where p.project_name = a.project_name
   and p.project_name = 'financial analysis';
```

Indexed join basic algorithm:

join cost = scan entire first table (**assigned_to**)
+ access second table (**project**) qualifying rows
= 50,000/100 sba + 100 rba
= 500 sba + 100 rba

If Tsba = 10 ms and Trba = 40 ms, then the total iotime is 9 seconds.

The hash-join strategy is also effective for low selectivity joins. The basic strategy is to scan each table once and hash the qualifying join column attribute value to a hash file in RAM. Each entry in the hash file contains the attribute value and a pointer to the table row containing that value. The second phase of the algorithm is to access the actual qualifying rows from each of the two tables, that is, those rows from the tables with matching attribute values in the hash file. As in the preceding indexed join example, let mt = 100 and nt = 5 qualifying rows for the first and second tables, respectively.

Hash-join basic algorithm:

join cost = scan first table (**assigned_to**) + scan second table (**project**) + access qualifying rows in the two tables
= 50,000/100 sba + 250/50 sba + 100 rba + 5 rba
= 505 sba + 105 rba

Thus, we get iotime of 9.25 seconds for this case when Tsba = 10 ms and Trba = 40 ms.

6.6 Summary

This chapter discusses the basic principles of physical database design in terms of the types of processing of data typically done in database applications and the access methods needed to do each type of processing efficiently. Database performance is defined at three levels of detail: logical record access, sequential and random block access, and disk I/O service time. The I/O time computation applies to a dedicated or shared disk environment.

Sequential processing uses sequential data structures and search mechanisms that range from sequential scans to binary searches. Random processing of individual records is best done by hashing. The B-tree, and in particular the B^+-tree, is the dominant sequential and random access method used today, and it has the added advantage of dynamically maintaining the database and avoiding the severe performance degradation that results from long overflow chains, such as in indexed sequential files. Hashing methods, such as extendible hashing, that use the dynamic maintenance facilities found in B-trees are rapidly replacing the older implementations.

Database applications involving complex Boolean queries are used effectively only with systems that have some form of secondary index capability. Secondary indexes are implemented using accession lists of pointers to target records and can be merged easily for complex query conditions. Cellular secondary indexes are variants of secondary indexes that enhance performance, particularly when target records are clustered in data blocks.

Denormalization of relational databases is seen as a method to decrease query time for certain queries requiring multiple table joins. Analysis of the effectiveness of a pre-join strategy is done using the block access and I/O time approach defined earlier in this chapter and illustrated in the example in Chapter 7.

Literature Summary

The idea for extending a table for usage efficiency came from [ScSo80], and practical advice on denormalization is given in [Rodg89]. Comprehensive surveys of access methods can be found in [Harb88, Gros86, Loom83, TeFr82, Wied87], and brief surveys are given in [Card85, ElNa94].

[BaMc72] Bayer, R., and McCreight, E. "Organization and Maintenance of Large Ordered Indexes," *Acta. Inf.* 1, 3 (1972), pp. 173–189.

[Card85] Cardenas, A.F. *Data Base Management Systems* (2nd Ed.), Allyn & Bacon, Boston, 1985.

[ElNa94] Elmasri, R., and Navathe, S.B. *Fundamentals of Database Systems* (2nd Ed.), Benjamin/Cummings, Redwood City, CA, 1994.

[Gros86] Grosshans, D. *File Systems Design and Implementation,* Prentice Hall, Englewood Cliffs, NJ, 1986.

[GrRe93] Gray, J., and Reuter, A. *Transaction Processing: Concepts and Techniques,* Morgan Kaufmann, San Francisco, 1993.

[Harb88] Harbron, T.R. *File Systems Structures and Algorithms,* Prentice Hall, Englewood Cliffs, NJ, 1988.

[Loom83] Loomis, M.E.S. *Data Management and File Processing,* Prentice Hall, Englewood Cliffs, NJ, 1983.

[Rodg89] Rodgers, U. "Denormalization: Why, What, and How?" *Database Prog. & Design* 2, 12 (Dec. 1989), pp. 46–53.

[ScSo80] Schkolnick, M., and Sorenson, P. "Denormalization: A Performance Oriented Database Design Technique," *Proc. AICA 1980 Congress,* AICA, Brussels, pp. 363–377.

[TeFr82] Teorey, T., and Fry, J. *Design of Database Structures,* Prentice Hall, Upper Saddle River, NJ, 1982.

[Wied87] Wiederhold, G. *File Organization for Database Design,* McGraw-Hill, New York, 1987.

Exercises

Problem 6-1

In this problem set you are given disk and data volume statistics for a simple customer database. Answer each question with the appropriate numerical value. Assume KB => 1000 bytes and MB => 1,000,000 bytes. Assume a *dedicated disk* unless specified otherwise. Also assume the 1% error rule, that is, ignore parameters that affect the performance by <1%.

Disk minimum seek time (to the next adjacent cylinder) = 10 milliseconds (ms)

Disk average seek time (over all cylinders) = 20 ms

Disk (full) rotational time = 20 ms

Disk data transfer rate = 3 MB/second

Data block size = 15 KB

CUSTOMER record size = 650 bytes

Pointer size = 4 bytes

Primary key size = 12 bytes

Block size for the transaction file = 15 KB (avg. of 20 transactions per block)

1. What is the average elapsed I/O service time for a sequential block access (Tsba)?
2. What is the average elapsed I/O service time for a random block access (Trba) over the whole disk?
3. What is the average elapsed I/O service time for a random block access (Trba) for a table (file) that fills up exactly two contiguous (adjacent) dedicated disk cylinders?
4. What is the cost (in sba's) to sequentially search 2,000,000 CUSTOMER records?
5. How much elapsed I/O service time does this represent, in *seconds*?
6. If the blocking factor is doubled, what is the elapsed time, in *seconds*?
7. Design a B^+-tree for 2,000,000 CUSTOMER records that has minimum "order" and no more than 4 index levels (plus a data level). Assume that each data node is a block of 15 KB. Note that "order" is the number of tree pointer values in each index node. In sum-

mary, find the minimum order p, assuming the approximation p^h >>= n, where h is the height and n is the total number of records.

Given a database with the following characteristics:

a. One record type
b. 2,000,000 records with record size of 200 bytes each
c. 11 attributes (primary key and ten nonkeys)
d. Nonkey attributes can have anywhere from 2 values to 50,000 values
e. 40,000 blocks (i.e., bf = 50) for data, with block size of 10 KB
f. Blocking factor for accession lists = 2000 (each pointer is assumed to be 5 bytes)
g. Attribute name and attribute value indexes are always in main memory

A particular query for this *inverted file* requires the merge of accession lists of 10,000, 20,000, and 50,000 entries, respectively, and 300 target records that satisfy all three query conditions.

8. What is the total cost in rba's, sba's, and elapsed I/O service time for this query (assuming that access to the first block in the accession list is a sequential access and assuming a dedicated disk environment)?
9. What is the total cost in rba's, sba's, and elapsed I/O service time for this query (assuming that access to the first block in the accession list is a sequential access and assuming a dedicated disk environment), if we use a *cellular inverted file* instead of just an inverted file?

Problem 6-2

A single record-type database (i.e., a file) stored on disk and typical queries on that database are described in the following. Attribute sizes are given in bytes (B):

Database:

Number of employees = 150,000 (*id-no =1 0 B (key)*, name = 25 B, addr = 30 B)

Number of departments = 80 (dept-no = 2 B, dept-name = 12 B)

Number of degree types = 6 (degree = 3 B)

Number of job titles = 150 (job-title = 18 B)

Other attributes total 300 B (*Note:* total of 20 attributes)

Total logical records (tuples) = 150,000 (size of each record is 400 B)

Block size (data and index blocks) is 6000 B

Pointer size is 5 B

Average I/O time for a sequential block access = 15 ms

Average I/O time for a random block access = 30 ms over the file or disk

We also assume the following:

a. The database is new and has no overflow or other degradation.

b. Dedicated disk environment.

c. The pointers in B^+-tree data blocks can be ignored.

d. Any level of an index that fits into a single index block can be considered to reside in RAM and does not need a disk access.

Queries:

Q1. List all employee information in id-no order.

Q2. Display all employee data for id-no = zzzzzzzzzz.

Q3. Display the name and department name of employees with job title x and holding degree y. Average number of target records = 600.

1. Given that a B^+-tree is to be used for some of these queries, how many levels of indexing would be required for an order-14 B^+-tree index? How many index nodes could fit into a single index block?
2. Compute the time for sequential access for query Q1.
3. Compute the I/O service time for sequential and B^+-tree access for query Q2.
4. Analyze the trade-offs between sequential access and secondary index for query Q3, given that the number of target records is 600.

Problem 6-3

Given the relational schema and physical characteristics as follows, evaluate the total I/O time for the following access methods to obtain "all students whose research is directed by John Smith." State all the assumptions that you must make.

1. Sequential search of the student records (rows), testing for the foreign key for the research instructor.
2. Secondary index access to student records (rows).

Each instructor directs the research of an average of 10 students. Not all students conduct research, only seniors and graduate students.

Each instructor teaches an average of three course sections per term.

Each student takes an average of five courses per term.

Courses contain an average of 25 students.

Relational schema (SQL):

```
create table instructor  (instr_id char(9),
                          instr_name char(20),
                          instr_room_no char(6),
                          primary key (instr_id));
create table course      (course_no char(6),
                          course_name char(15),
                          course_instr_name char(20),
                          day char(5),
                          hour char(2),
                          primary key (course_no),
                          foreign key (course_instr_name) references
                              instructor);
create table student         (student_id char(10),
                          student_name char(20),
                          student_addr char(25),
                          research_instr_id char(9),
                          primary key (student_id),
                          foreign key (research_instr_id) references
                              instructor);
create table enrollment  (student_id char(10),
                          course_no char(6)
                          primary key (student_id, course_no),
                          foreign key (student_id) references student,
                          foreign key (course_no) references course);
```

Number of instructor records = 2500

Number of course records = 4000

Number of student records = 20,000

Number of enrollment records = 100,000

Block size = 1000 B

Disk seek time = 40 ms (avg.)

Disk full rotation time = 20 ms

Disk transfer rate = 200 KB/second

Please see page 350 for the solution to Problem 6-3.

Problem 6-4

Given the tables and applications (queries with equal frequency) specified as follows, state one argument in favor of and one argument against each of the two proposed schema refinements, taking into consideration usage and integrity:

Table	*Primary key*	*Foreign key(s)*	*Other attributes*
employee	emp_no	dept_no; proj_no; office_no	emp_name
emp_job	emp_no	start_date	emp_no
department	dept_no	–	dept_name
office	office_no	–	office_size
project	proj_no	–	proj_name

Proposal 1: Split relation **employee** into two tables with only the employee's name and address in one table, and the other table containing everything except the address.

Proposal 2: Add the foreign key dept_no to table **office**.

Queries:

Q1. Which office numbers are associated with each department?

Q2. List all employee names and their addresses.

Q3. Which employees currently work on the "clean air" project?

7 An Example of Relational Database Design

The following example illustrates how to proceed through the database life cycle, in a practical way, for a centralized relational database. We see how physical design for denormalization and index selection extends a logical design methodology to attain significant improvements in performance, given that the available access methods are known.

7.1 Requirements Specification

The management of a large retail store would like a database to keep track of sales activities. The requirements for this database lead to the following six entities and their unique identifiers:

Entity	*Entity id*	*Id length(avg) in characters*	*Cardinality*
Customer	cust-no	6	80,000
Job	job-title	24	80
Order	order-no	9	200,000
Salesperson	sales-name	20	150
Department	dept-no	2	10
Item	item-no	6	5000

The following assertions describe the data relationships:

- Each customer has one job title, but different customers may have the same job title.
- Each customer may place many orders, but only one customer may place a particular order.
- Each department has many salespeople, but each salesperson must work in only one department.
- Each department has many items for sale, but each item is sold in only one department. (Item means item type, like IBM PC.)
- For each order, items ordered in different departments must involve different salespeople, but all items ordered within one department must be handled by exactly one salesperson. In other words, for each order, each item has exactly one salesperson; and for each order, each department has exactly one salesperson.

Design Problems

1. Using the information given and, in particular, the five assertions, derive an ER diagram and a set of FDs that represent all the data relationships.
2. Transform the ER diagram into a set of candidate tables. List the tables, their primary keys, and other attributes.
3. Find the minimum set of 3NF tables that are functionally equivalent to the candidate tables. Analyze performance and integrity trade-offs resulting from the definition of this minimum set.
4. Given the transactions "Select all order numbers assigned to customers who are computer engineers" and "Add a new customer and the customers order to the database," analyze the performance and data integrity trade-offs for strategies to execute these transactions by using both the minimum set 3NF schema and a refined schema designed to reduce the number of joins needed for data retrieval.

7.2 Logical Design

Our first step is to develop an ER diagram and a set of FDs to correspond to each of the assertions given. Figure 7.1 presents the diagram. Nor-

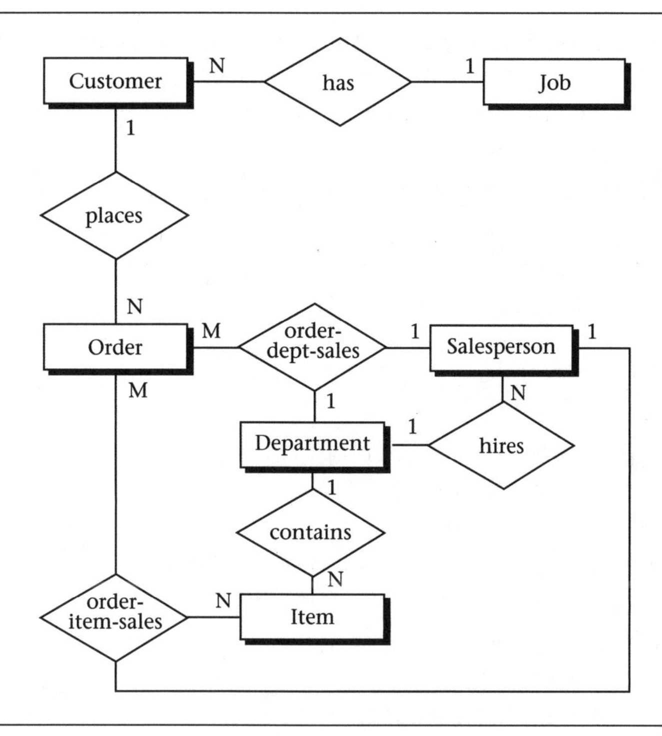

Figure 7.1 ER diagram for the retail store database example

mally, the ER diagram is developed without knowing all the FDs, but in this example the nonkey attributes are omitted so that the entire database can be represented with only a few statements and FDs. The result of this analysis, relative to each of the assertions given, follows.

ER construct	*FDs*
Customer(many): Job(one)	cust-no –> job-title
Order(many): Customer(one)	order-no –> cust-no
Salesperson(many): Department(one)	sales-name –> dept-no
Item(many): Department(one)	item-no –> dept-no
Order(many): Item(many): Salesperson(one)	order-no,item-no–> sales-name
Order(many): Department(many): Salesperson(one)	order-no,dept-no–> sales-name

The candidate tables needed to represent the semantics of this problem can be easily derived from the constructs for entities and relationships. Primary keys and foreign keys are explicitly defined.

```
create table customer (cust_no char(6),
        job_title varchar(256),
        primary key (cust_no),
        foreign key (job_title) references job
            on delete set null on update cascade);

create table job (job_title varchar(256),
        primary key (job_title));

create table order (order_no char(9),
        cust_no char(6) not null,
        primary key (order_no),
        foreign key (cust_no) references customer
            on delete cascade on update cascade);

create table salesperson (sales_name varchar(256),
        dept_no char(2),
        primary key (sales_name),
        foreign key (dept_no) references department
            on delete set null on update cascade);

create table department (dept_no char(2),
        primary key (dept_no));

create table item (item_no char(6),
        dept_no char(2),
        primary key (item_no),
        foreign key (dept_no) references department
            on delete set null on update cascade);

create table order_item_sales (order_no char(9),
        item_no char(6),
        sales_name varchar(256) not null,
        primary key (order_no, item_no),
        foreign key (order_no) references order
            on delete cascade on update cascade,
        foreign key (item_no) references item
            on delete cascade on update cascade,
        foreign key (sales_name) references salesperson
            on delete cascade on update cascade);
```

```
create table order_dept_sales (order_no char(9),
        dept_no char(2),
        sales_name varchar(256) not null,
        primary key (order_no, dept_no),
        foreign key (order_no) references order
            on delete cascade on update cascade,
        foreign key (dept_no) references department
            on delete cascade on update cascade,
        foreign key (sales_name) references salesperson
            on delete cascade on update cascade);
```

This process of decomposition and reduction of tables moves us closer to a minimum set of 3NF tables. Additionally, we must consider the tables **job** and **department**. Because we have not defined other attributes in these tables, **job** and **department** are simple tables consisting of a single key attribute. When this occurs and the key attribute appears in other tables as a nonkey, we can consider the elimination of the simple table. The trade-off is between the decrease in storage space and update cost when we eliminate a table and the possible loss of data integrity as a side effect of deletions on another table in which the key of the eliminated table has become a nonkey. In our example, if we can justify this trade-off and eliminate the simple tables, we have the following minimum set of 3NF tables:

Table	*Primary key*	*Nonkey*
customer	cust_no	job_title
order	order_no	cust_no
salesperson	sales_name	dept_no
item	item_no	dept_no
order_item_sales	order_no,item_no	sales_name
order_dept_sales	order_no,dept_no	sales_name

In summary, the reductions shown in this section have decreased storage space and update cost and have maintained the normalization at a minimum of 3NF. But we have potentially higher retrieval cost—given the transaction "list all job_titles," for example—and have increased the potential for loss of integrity because we have eliminated simple tables with only key attributes.

7.3 Physical Design

7.3.1 Schema Refinement (Denormalization) Based on Usage

Let us now look at the quantitative trade-offs of further refinement of tables to improve processing efficiency. Assume that each of the following transactions are to be executed once per fixed time unit.

Query: Select all order numbers assigned to customers who are computer engineers.

```
select o.order_no, c.cust_no, c.job_title
       from order as o, customer as c
       where c.cust_no = o.cust_no
       and c.job_title = computer engineer;
```

Update: Add a new customer, a painter, with number 423378 and the customer's order number, 763521601, to the database.

```
insert into customer (cust_no, job_title)
       values ('423378','painter');
insert into order (order_no, cust_no)
       values ('763521601','423378');
```

Using the minimum set 3NF schema, the system query optimizer can choose from a number of different ways to execute the transaction. Let us first assume that the tables are all ordered physically by their primary keys. We use the sort/merge-join strategy for the first transaction: Sort the **order** table by cust_no, then join tables **order** and **customer** with a single scan of each, and select only rows that have job_title of computer engineer. We then project on order_no to answer the query. To simplify the analysis, we assume that a sort of n rows takes n $\log_2$ n row accesses (logical record, lra) and that computer engineers make up 5% of the customers and orders in the database.

lra = sort **order** + scan **order** + scan **customer** + create **order_cust**
  + scan **order_cust** + create **comp_engr** + project **comp_engr**
 = (200,000 $\log_2$ 200,000) + 200,000 + 80,000
  + 200,000 + 200,000 + 200,000*.05 + 200,000*.05
 = 200,000*(17.61 + 3.10) + 80,000
 = 4,222,000 row accesses

All row accesses are sequential in this strategy. We also assume 30 ms for a sequential block access, 60 ms for a random block access, a block size of 4 KB (4096 bytes), and a prefetch buffer size of 64 KB (as done in DB2). We can estimate the I/O service time by first computing the effective prefetch blocking factors for the tables **order**, **customer**, **order_cust**, and **comp_engr**: 4368, 2176, 1680, and 1680, respectively. We compute the sequential block accesses as follows.

sba = ceiling(200,000*(17.61 + 1)/4368) + ceiling(80,000/2176)
+ ceiling(420,000/1680)
= 1140

iotime = 1140*30 ms = 34.2 sec

The strategy to execute the second transaction, using the same schema, is to scan each table (**order** and **customer**) and rewrite both tables in the new order.

sba = ceiling(200,000/4368)*2 + ceiling(80,000/2176)*2
= 166

iotime = 166*30 ms = 5.0 sec

If we refine the minimum set 3NF schema to avoid the join in the first transaction, the resulting schema will have a single table **order_cust**, with primary key order_no and nonkey attributes cust_no and job_title, instead of separate tables **order** and **customer**. This avoids not only the join but also the sort needed to get both tables ordered by cust_no. The strategy for the first transaction is now to scan **order_cust** once to find the computer engineers, write the resulting data on disk, and then read back from disk to project the resulting temporary table, **comp_engr**, to answer the query.

sba = ceiling(200,000/1680) + [ceiling(200,000*.05/1680)]*2 = 132

iotime = 132*30 ms = 4.0 sec

The strategy for the second transaction, using this refined schema, is to scan **order_cust** once to find the point of insertion and then to scan again to reorder the table.

sba = ceiling(200,000/1680)*2 = 240

iotime = 240*30 ms = 7.2 sec

Common to both strategies is the addition of an order record to the tables **order_item_sales** and **order_dept_sales**. For the sake of simplicity, we assume these tables are unsorted, so the addition of a new order requires only one record access at the end of the table and, thus, negligible I/O time.

The basic performance and normalization data for these two schemas and the two transactions given previously are summarized in Table 7.1.

The refined schema dramatically reduces the I/O time for the query transaction, but the cost is the loss of performance for the update, more storage space, and significant reduction in the degree of normalization. The normalization is reduced because we now have a transitive FD: order_no –> cust_no –> job_title in table **order_cust**. The implication of this is, of course, that there is a delete anomaly for job_title when a customer deletes an order or the order is filled.

The significance of these performance and data integrity differences depends upon the overall objectives as well as the computing environment for the database, and it must be analyzed in that context. For instance, the performance differences must be evaluated for all relevant transactions, present and projected. Storage space differences may or may not be significant in the computing environment. Integrity problems with the deletion commands need to be evaluated on a case-by-case basis to determine whether the side effects of certain record deletions are destructive to the objectives of the database. In summary, the database designer now has the ability to evaluate the trade-offs among query and update requirements, storage space, and integrity associated with normalization. This knowledge can be applied to a variety of database design problems.

Table 7.1. Comparison of performance and integrity of original tables and join table

	Minimum set 3NF schema (order and customer)	*Denormalized schema (order_cust)*
Query	34.2 sec	4.0 sec
Update	5.0 sec	7.2 sec
Storage space (relevant tables)	5.4 MB	7.8 MB
Normalization	3NF	2NF

7.3.2 Index Selection Problem

The denormalization solution can be further improved by a careful selection of indexes. If we create a secondary index to access the **order_cust** table for the 5% of customers with orders who are computer engineers, we then will have 5% of 200,000 records, or 10,000 records, to randomly access at 60 ms each. This will take 600 seconds, which is clearly unacceptable compared to the previously mentioned solutions (Table 7.1). Building a secondary index on job_title to the **customer** table is similarly poor in performance.

On the other hand, the performance of the update to **customer** and **order** would significantly improve with a primary index to each table. In each case, access via hashing is typically one random block access to each table plus a sequential rewrite, while access via B^+-tree is one to two random block accesses plus a sequential rewrite. In either case, the total time to perform the update is well under 1 second. Similarly, with the join table **order_cust**, a primary index can be built for the composite key order_no, cust_no, which results in less than 1 second update time. Thus, creation of two primary indexes clearly improves update performance and hence improves overall performance.

In general, picking an optimal index is known to be NP-complete, so we usually use heuristic approaches such as the one illustrated above. It should also be noted that adding an index can sometimes fool a query optimizer and actually degrade performance instead of improving it. To avoid this type of problem, you should always investigate the side effects of implementing an index by testing the dominant transactions for the database.

7.4 Summary

In this chapter we developed a global (logical) schema for a centralized relational database, given the requirements specification for a retail store database. The example illustrates the life cycle steps of ER modeling, global schema design, normalization, and schema refinement based on processing efficiency. It summarizes the techniques presented in Chapters 1 through 6. Now we turn to distributed databases as the next part of our analysis of database design.

8 Distributed Data Allocation

Distributed and multidatabase design is an integral part of the database life cycle. Design components that apply to both homogeneous distributed and heterogeneous multidatabases include data fragmentation, data distribution methods, and data allocation strategies. In this chapter we look at each of these components briefly and then examine two data allocation methods in detail, one in which no data redundancy is allowed and another with data redundancy. These methods are easily computable by hand for small to medium configurations or implementable in software for large configurations.

8.1 Introduction

Advances in the computer and communications technologies have led to distributed computer systems, which interconnect mainframes, minicomputers, and workstations through various communications media. This was accompanied by the development of distributed operating systems, distributed languages, and distributed database management systems. A distributed database management system (DDBMS) is a software system that supports the transparent creation, access, and manipulation of interrelated data located at the different sites of a computer network. Each site of the network has autonomous processing capability and can perform local applications. Each site also participates in the execution of at least one global application, which requires network communication [Chu84, CePe84]. The goal of a DDBMS is to improve the accessibility, sharability, and performance of a DBMS while preserving the appearance of a centralized DBMS.

Because of the nature of the loosely coupled network of computers, the database design issues encountered in distributed database systems differ from those encountered in centralized database systems [Heba77, FHS80]. In centralized databases, access efficiency is achieved through local optimization by using complex physical structures. In distributed databases, the global optimization of processing, including cost of network communication and local processing, is of major concern. Total cost is a function of the network configuration, the user workload, the data allocation strategy, and the query optimization algorithm.

DDBMSs may be homogeneous or heterogeneous, semiautonomous (federated) or autonomous (multidatabase). We first look at the basic data allocation problem common to the variety of DDBMSs and then illustrate two easily computable methods, or strategies, for allocating data (files, tables, or fragments of tables) in a distributed database system.

8.2 Distributed and Multidatabase Design

Once a DDBMS has been developed or purchased, the database designers or administrators need to know how to design and allocate the distributed database. This is significantly influenced by the architecture and the facilities of the DDBMS; it, in turn, significantly impacts the query processing, concurrency control, and availability of the database.

The three most common objectives of distributed database design are

- separation of data fragmentation from data allocation,
- control of data redundancy, and
- independence from local DBMSs.

The distinction between designing the fragmentation and allocation schema is conceptually relevant: The first is a logical mapping but the second is a physical mapping. In general, it is not possible to determine the optimal fragmentation and allocation by solving the two problems independently; they are interrelated.

8.2.1 Fragmentation

A table **r** is fragmented by partitioning it into a minimal number of disjoint subtables (fragments) r1,r2, . . . ,rn. These fragments contain sufficient information to reconstruct the original table **r**. Basically, there are two different schemes for fragmenting a table: horizontal and vertical.

Horizontal fragmentation partitions the records of a global table into subsets. A fragment, ri, is a selection on the global table **r** using a predicate Pi, its qualification. The reconstruction of **r** is obtained by taking the union of all fragments.

Vertical fragmentation subdivides the attributes of the global table into groups. The simplest form of vertical fragmentation is decomposition. A unique record id may be included in each fragment to guarantee that reconstruction through a join operation is possible. Note that mixed fragmentation is the result of the successive application of both fragmentation techniques.

Rules for Fragmentation

- Fragments are formed by the select predicates associated with dominant database transactions. The predicates specify attribute values used in the conjunctive (AND) and disjunctive (OR) form of select commands.
- Fragments must be disjoint and their union must become the whole table. Overlapping fragments are too difficult to analyze and implement.
- The largest fragment is the whole table. The smallest fragment is a single record. Fragments should be designed to maintain a balance between these extremes. The whole table as a fragment disallows the potential efficiency of partitioning the table across local sites by usage. Single records as fragments, on the other hand, introduce undue complexity into the data allocation problem, extreme sensitivity to changing applications, and potentially too much overhead to execute joins between tables.

8.2.2 Data Allocation

The constraints under which data allocation strategies may operate are determined by the system architecture and the available network database management software. The four basic approaches are

- centralized,
- partitioned,
- replicated data, and
- selective replication.

In the centralized approach, all the data is located at a single site. The implementation of this approach is simple. However, the size of the database is limited by the availability of the secondary storage at the central site. Furthermore, the database may become unavailable from any of the remote sites when communication failures occur, and the database system fails totally when the central site fails.

In the partitioned approach, the database is partitioned into disjoint fragments, and each fragment is assigned to a particular site. This strategy is particularly appropriate where local secondary storage is limited compared to the database size, the reliability of the centralized database is not sufficient, or operating efficiencies can be gained through the exploitation of the locality of references in database accesses.

The completely replicated data approach allocates a full copy of the database to each site in the network. This completely redundant distributed data strategy is only appropriate when reliability is critical, the database is small, and update inefficiency can be tolerated. It is much less commonly used than selective replication.

The selective replication approach partitions the database into critical and noncritical fragments. Noncritical fragments need only be stored once, whereas critical fragments are replicated as desired to meet the required level of availability and performance. This is the most commonly used strategy because of its great flexibility; some fragments may be small, while others can be quite large—possibly entire tables.

The cost/benefit of the replicated database allocation strategy can be estimated in terms of storage cost, communication costs (query and update time), and data availability. Figure 8.1 briefly illustrates the trade-off by showing the data replication on the horizontal axis and costs on the vertical axis. It can be seen from Figure 8.1 that

- the query communication cost decreases as the number of copies increases because most data can be found at local sites, thus eliminating the need for communication calls.
- the update communication cost increases with the number of copies because duplicated data will need to be updated.
- the storage cost and local processing cost increase as the number of copies increases.
- the read availability increases with the number of copies in the system, while the write availability generally decreases; a write requires most or all copies to be available.

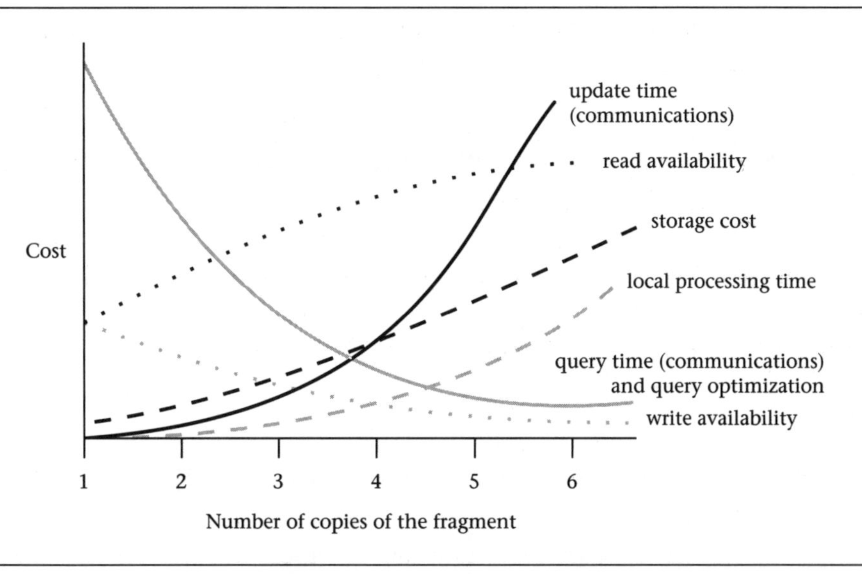

Figure 8.1 Trade-offs in database distribution due to data replication

An optimal data allocation can be theoretically determined to minimize the total cost (storage + communication + local processing) subject to some response time and availability constraints. This problem, traditionally referred to as the file allocation problem (FAP) in computing networks, was first addressed by Wesley Chu [Chu69]. Since then, many different file allocation algorithms have appeared in the literature [Case72, MaRi76, MoLe77, CGP80, FiHo80]. Earlier allocation resolutions were simple, but more recent methods are actual design methodologies that utilize the allocation techniques for one of the decisions [CPW87]. Application of the FAP problem depends on the nature of the problem, the availability of information needed to reach an exact solution, and the need to determine optimal versus approximate solutions in real life. It has often been found that, for real-life situations, sophisticated FAP solutions are rarely needed. In most cases, data allocation decisions can be made by exercising judgment and using real-life constraints of security and management. However, it is preferable to use simple analytical models to support the decisions and improve insights.

8.3 The General Data Allocation Problem

Assume knowledge of application system specifications and distributed system configuration as outlined in the list that follows.

- *Application system specifications:*

  A database global schema and fragmentation schema

  A set of user transactions and their frequencies

  Security: data ownership (who can update) and access authorization (who can query) for each transaction

  Recovery: estimated frequency and volume of backup operations

  Integrity: referential integrity, boundary value integrity rules, journaling overhead

- *Distributed or multidatabase system configuration and software:*

  The network topology, network channel capacities, and network control mechanism

  The site locations and their processing capacity (CPU and I/O processing)

  Sources of data (where data can be located) and sinks of data (where user transactions can be initiated and data transferred)

  The transaction processing options and synchronization algorithms

  The unit costs for data storage, local site processing, and communications

Find the allocation of programs and database fragments to sites that minimizes C, the total cost. Keep in mind that

$$C = C_{comm} + C_{proc} + C_{stor}$$

where

C_{comm} = communications cost for message and data

C_{proc} = site processing cost (CPU and I/O)

C_{stor} = storage cost for data and programs at sites

are subject to possible additional constraints on

- transaction response time, which is the sum of communication delays, local processing, and all resource queuing delays, and
- transaction availability, which is the percentage of time the transaction executes with all components available.

In some cases, the total cost (possibly including equipment cost) could be considered a constraint and minimum response time the objective. In other cases, the network topology and/or local site processing capacity is to be analyzed as well as the data distribution.

8.4 Data Allocation Strategies

A general rule for data allocation states that data should be placed as close as possible to where it will be used, and load balancing should be used to find a global optimization of system performance. In the following sections we describe two methods originally defined by Ceri and Pelagatti [CePe84] and extend the discussion by adding illustrative examples and practical interpretation of the important parameters.

8.4.1 The Nonredundant Best Fit Method

The nonredundant *best fit* method determines the single site most likely to allocate a fragment (which may be a file, table, or subset of a table) based on maximum benefit, where benefit is interpreted to mean total query and update references. In particular, place fragment ri at the site s*, where the number of local query and update references by all the user transactions is maximized.

Let us illustrate the application of this method with a simple example of a global schema and its processing characteristics. In this example each fragment to be allocated is an entire table. The average disk I/O service times are given for a query or update originating from the same site in the network (local) or combined disk and network service times from different sites (remote).

System Parameters

	Table size	*Avg local query (update) time (milliseconds)*	*Avg remote query (update) time (milliseconds)*
R1	300 KB	100 (150)	500 (600)
R2	500 KB	150 (200)	650 (700)
R3	1.0 MB	200 (250)	1000 (1100)

User transactions are described in terms of their frequency of occurrence, which tables they access, and whether the accesses are reads or writes.

Transaction	*Site(s)*	*Frequency*	*Table accesses (reads, writes)*
T1	S1, S4, S5	1	Four to **R1** (3 reads, 1 write), two to **R2** (2 reads)
T2	S2, S4	2	Two to **R1** (2 reads), four to **R3** (3 reads, 1 write)
T3	S3, S5	3	Four to **R2** (3 reads, 1 write), two to **R3** (2 reads)

Security: User transactions T1, T2, and T3 can either query or update (no restrictions)

Sources of data: All sites—S1, S2, S3, S4, S5

Sinks of data (possible locations of transactions): All sites—S1, S2, S3, S4, S5

Local Reference Computations

Our goal is to compute the number of local references to each table residing at each site, one by one. The site that maximizes the local references to a given table is chosen as the site where that table should reside.

The preceding tables tell us that table **R1** has the following local references: At site S1 it has only transaction T1 with four references at a frequency of one, and thus four total references; at site S2 it has transaction T2 with two references at a frequency of two, and thus four total references; at site S3 it has no transaction references; at site S4 it has both transactions T1 and T2 for a total of eight references; and at site S5 it has transaction T1 for a total of four references. A maximum of eight local references to table **R1** occurs at site S4 (see Table 8.1).

Table **R2** has the following local references: at site S1 it has only transaction T1 for a total of 2 references; at site S2 it has no references by any transaction; at site S3 it has 4 references by transaction T3 and a frequency of three, thus 12 total references; at site S4 it has only transaction T1 for a total of 2 references; at site S5 it has transactions T1 and

T3 for a total of 14 references. A maximum of 14 local references to table **R2** occur at site S5 (see Table 8.1).

Table **R3** local references are computed in a similar fashion: At sites S2 and S4 there are a maximum of eight references.

Table 8.1 Local references for each table at each of five possible sites

Table	*Site*	*Transactions T1 (frequency)*	*T2 (frequency)*	*T3 (frequency)*	*Total local references*
R1	S1	3 read, 1 write (1)	0	0	4
	S2	0	2 read (2)	0	4
	S3	0	0	0	0
	S4	3 read, 1 write (1)	2 read (2)	0	8 (max.)
	S5	3 read, 1 write (1)	0	0	4
R2	S1	2 read (1)	0	0	2
	S2	0	0	0	0
	S3	0	0	3 read, 1 write (3)	12
	S4	2 read (1)	0	0	2
	S5	2 read (1)	0	3 read, 1 write (3)	14 (max.)
R3	S1	0	0	0	0
	S2	0	3 read, 1 write (2)	0	8 (max.)
	S3	0	0	2 read (3)	6
	S4	0	3 read, 1 write (2)	0	8 (max.)
	S5	0	0	2 read (3)	6

Allocation Decision

Figure 8.2 presents the allocation decision. Allocate table **R1** at site S4 and table **R2** at site S5. At these sites the number of local references to these tables is clearly maximized. However, table **R3** is maximized at both sites S2 and S4, so additional information is needed to choose the

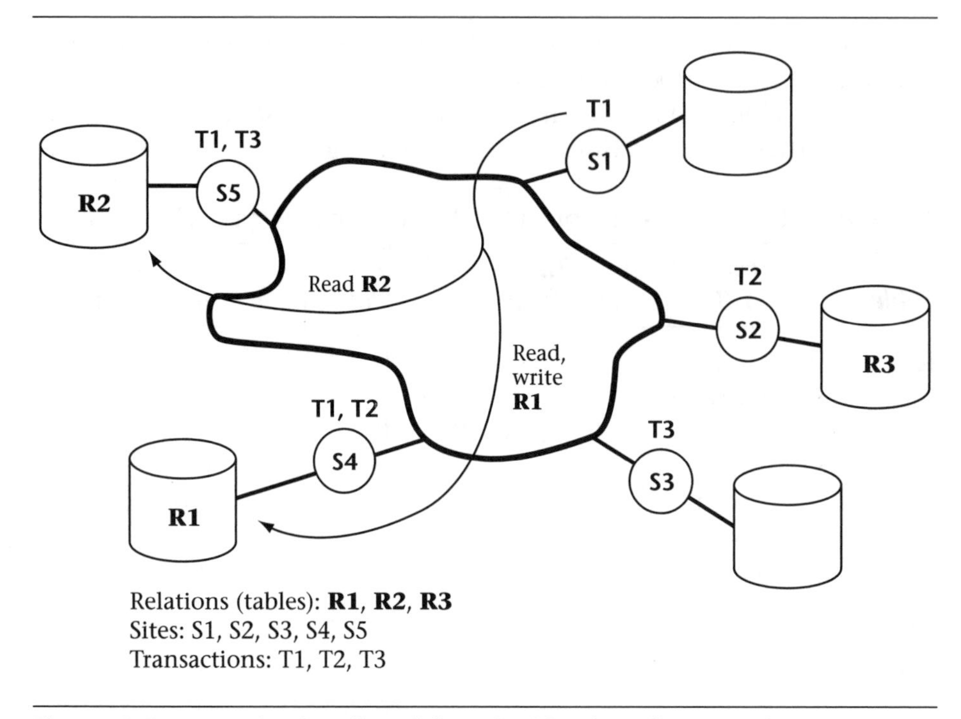

Figure 8.2 Nonredundant "best fit" method for data allocation, showing remote query and update for transaction T1 originating at site S1

allocation. For instance, if maximum availability of data is a major consideration, choose site S2 for table **R3** because site S4 already has table **R1** allocated to it; putting **R3** there as well would decrease the potential availability of data should site S4 crash. The final allocation under these assumptions: S1 is empty, S2 has table **R3**, S3 is empty, S4 has table **R1**, and S5 has table **R2**.

The advantage of the best fit method is its computational simplicity. The main disadvantage is in accuracy: Computing the number of local references does not accurately characterize disk service time or response time. Furthermore, it does not give any insights regarding data replication. A better approach is to compute total block accesses or total I/O time.

8.4.2 The Redundant "All Beneficial Sites" Method

The redundant *all beneficial sites* method (ABS) can be used for either the redundant or nonredundant case. It selects all sites for a fragment allocation where the benefit is greater than the cost for one additional copy of that fragment. You are assumed to start with no copy or one copy of each table or fragment of a table.

The benefit for an additional copy of a given fragment F at site S is measured by the difference in elapsed time between a remote query (i.e., no replicated copy) and a local query (i.e., replicated copy available), multiplied by the frequency of queries to fragment F originating from site S.

The cost for an additional copy of a given fragment F at site S is the total elapsed time for all the local updates for fragment F from transactions originating at site S, plus the total elapsed time for all the remote updates of fragment F at site S from transactions originating at other sites.

Cost/Benefit Computations

The cost/benefit computations described in this section are summarized in Table 8.2.

Table R1

Table **R1** at site S1 has the following cost: two remote updates (writes) by transaction T1 (frequency of one), one each from sites S4 and S5, multiplied by 600 ms per write, totaling 1200 ms; plus one local update by T1 at site S1 at 150 ms for a grand total of 1350 ms. The benefit is from three queries (reads) by transaction T1 at site S1, multiplied by the difference between a remote and local query (500 – 100 = 400 ms), totaling 1200 ms.

Table **R1** at site S2 has the cost of three remote updates by transaction T1 (frequency of one)—one each from sites S1, S4, and S5—multiplied by 600 ms per write, totaling 1800 ms. The benefit is from two queries (reads) by transaction T2 at site S2 (frequency of two), multiplied by the difference between a remote and local query (400 ms), totaling 1600 ms.

Table **R1** at site S3 has the cost of three remote updates by transaction T1 (frequency of one)—one each from sites S1, S4, and S5—multiplied by 600 ms per write, totaling 1800 ms. There is no benefit because no transaction accesses table **R1** locally at site S3.

Table **R1** at site S4 has the cost of two remote updates by transaction T1 from sites S1 and S5 (frequency of one), multiplied by 600 ms per write, totaling 1200 ms; plus one local update by T1 at site S4 at 150 ms, for a grand total of 1350 ms. The benefit is three queries by transaction

Table 8.2 Cost and benefit for each table located at five possible sites

Table	*Site*	*Remote update (local update) transactions*	*No. of writes* freq*time (ms)*	*Cost (ms)*
R1	S1	T1 from S4 and S5 (T1 from S1)	2*1*600 + 1*1*150	1350
	S2	T1 from S1, S4, S5	3*1*600	1800
	S3	T1 from S1, S4, S5	3*1*600	1800
	S4	T1 from S1 and S5 (T1 from S4)	2*1*600 + 1*1*150	1350
	S5	T1 from S1 and S4 (T1 from S5)	2*1*600 + 1*1*150	1350
R2	S1	T3 from S3 and S5	2*3*700	4200
	S2	T3 from S3 and S5	2*3*700	4200
	S3	T3 from S5 (T3 from S3)	1*3*700 + 1*3*200	2700
	S4	T3 from S3 and S5	2*3*700	4200
	S5	T3 from S3 (T3 from S5)	1*3*700 + 1*3*200	2700
R3	S1	T2 from S2 and S4	2*2*1100	4400
	S2	T2 from S4 (T2 from S2)	1*2*1100 +1*2*250	2700
	S3	T2 from S2 and S4	2*2*1100	4400
	S4	T2 from S2 (T2 from S4)	1*2*1100 +1*2*250	2700
	S5	T2 from S2 and S4	2*2*1100	4400

T1 (frequency of one) and two queries by transaction T2 (frequency of two), multiplied by 400 ms, totaling 2800 ms.

Table **R1** at site S5 has the cost of two remote updates by transaction T1 from sites S1 and S4 (frequency of one), multiplied by 600 ms per write, totaling 1200 ms; plus one local update by T1 at site S5 at 150 ms, for a grand total of 1350 ms. The benefit is three queries by transaction T1 (frequency of one), multiplied by 400 ms, totaling 1200 ms.

In summary, for table **R1** benefit exceeds cost only at site S4; thus, only one copy of **R1** is allocated to this network.

Table 8.2 Continued

Table	*Site*	*Query (read) sources*	*No. of reads*frequency *(remote–local time)*	*Benefit (ms)*
R1	S1	T1 at S1	3*1*(500 – 100)	1200
	S2	T2 at S2	2*2*(500 – 100)	1600
	S3	None	0	0
	S4	T1 and T2 at S4	(3*1 + 2*2)*(500 – 100)	2800
	S5	T1 at S5	3*1*(500 – 100)	1200
R2	S1	T1 at S1	2*1*(650 – 150)	1000
	S2	None	0	0
	S3	T3 at S3	3*3*(650 – 150)	4500
	S4	T1 at S4	2*1*(650 – 150)	1000
	S5	T1 and T3 at S5	(2*1 + 3*3)*(650 – 150)	5500
R3	S1	None	0	0
	S2	T2 at S2	3*2*(1000 – 200)	4800
	S3	T3 at S3	2*3*(1000 – 200)	4800
	S4	T2 at S4	3*2*(1000 – 200)	4800
	S5	T3 at S5	2*3*(1000 – 200)	4800

Tables R2 and R3

With similar computations we obtain the results for tables **R2** and **R3** as shown in Table 8.2.

In summary, for table **R2**, benefit exceeds cost at sites S3 and S5. For table **R3**, benefit exceeds cost at all sites except S1.

Allocation Decision

Figure 8.3 presents the allocation decision. Allocate table **R1** to site S4. Allocate table **R2** to sites S3 and S5. Allocate table **R3** to sites S2, S3, S4, and S5.

In the cases where benefit and cost are equal, consider whether either cost or benefit (or both) is likely to change in the near future or if greater availability is important. Adjust the allocation accordingly. If cost exceeds benefit at all sites for a given fragment, then pick the site for a single allocation where the difference between cost and benefit is minimized.

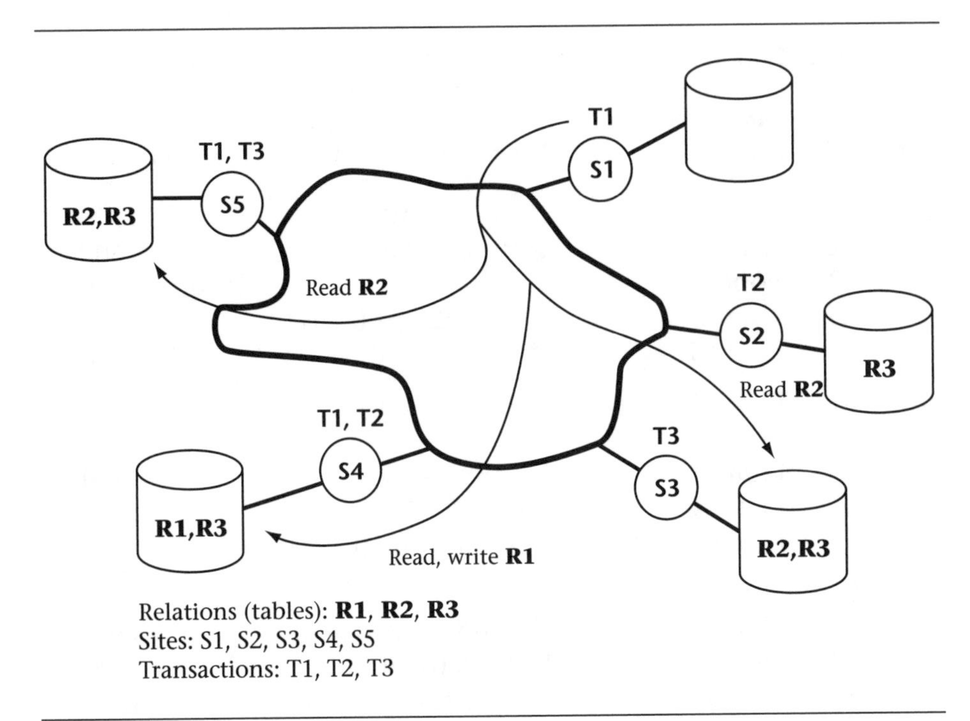

Figure 8.3 Redundant "all beneficial sites" method for data allocation, showing remote query and update for transaction T1 originating at site S1

Note that there exist many more elaborate fragmentation and data allocation strategies than are covered here; however, this text highlights the major issues to provide a simple method when quick analysis is needed.

The all beneficial sites method can be derived from exhaustive enumeration of total cost for the initial allocation configuration and the total cost for a new allocation configuration after the replication of a fragment (or table) at a given site. The decision is made to replicate the fragment (or table) if the total cost after replication is lower than total cost before replication.

For example, let fragment F1 be initially allocated to site S1. We need to decide whether to replicate F1 at site S2. Let query Q1 and update U1, both originating at site S1, access F1; and let query Q2 and update U2, both originating at site S2, also access F1.

$$\text{Total-cost}_1\text{(initial allocation of F1 to S1)} = \text{Q1(local)} + \text{U1(local)} + \text{Q2(remote)} + \text{U2(remote)}$$

$$\text{Total-cost}_2\text{(after replication of F1 at S2)} = \text{Q1(local)} + \text{U1(local)} + \text{U1(remote)} + \text{Q2(local)} + \text{U2(local)} + \text{U2(remote)}$$

where queries Q1 and Q2 are made to the closest copy of F1 and updates U1 and U2 must be made to both copies of F1. We allow F1 to be replicated at S2 if the following condition holds:

$$\text{Total-cost}_2 < \text{Total-cost}_1$$

$$\text{Q1(local)} + \text{U1(local)} + \text{U1(remote)} + \text{Q2(local)} + \text{U2(local)} + \text{U2(remote)} < \text{Q1(local)} + \text{U1(local)} + \text{Q2(remote)} + \text{U2(remote)}$$

$$\text{U1(remote)} + \text{Q2(local)} + \text{U2(local)} < \text{Q2(remote)}$$

$$\text{Q2(remote)} - \text{Q2(local)} > \text{U1(remote)} + \text{U2(local)}$$

which is the relationship that defines the all beneficial sites method—that is, the benefit is the difference between a remote and local query time to F1, and the cost is the sum of the local and remote update times for the new copy of F1.

8.4.3 Progressive Fragment Allocation

A practical extension of the all beneficial sites method, called the *progressive fragment allocation method* [JWBT91], allocates the first copy of each fragment on the basis of maximum value of benefit minus cost. It remembers where that copy is and bases the next allocation decision on the location of that first copy and the maximum value of benefit minus cost for the remaining sites. This procedure is continued, one allocation at a time, until benefit no longer exceeds cost for any of the remaining sites. Note that for this method, cost stays constant for each decision because the update for an additional fragment is independent of previous allocations. However, benefit does not stay constant; it decreases each time a new copy is allocated that is closer to a given site than the previous set of allocations. The decrease in the benefit at a given site, which must have at least one query to this fragment, is measured by the decrease in propagation delay between the former closest copy and the proposed new copy of the fragment, relative to that given site. In the worst case, when a new copy is no closer than any previous copies, the benefit stays the same but does not increase.

This approach gives a more realistic allocation based on a progressive set of allocations rather than a set of independent allocation decisions.

It is also a fast method because sites where benefit is less than cost need no longer be evaluated in future iterations.

As an example, let us assume that two fragments, F1 and F2, are to be allocated to either or both sites S1 and S2. The costs and benefits are computed to be

F1	S1	cost = 150	benefit = 200
	S2	cost = 170	benefit = 175
F2	S1	cost = 60	benefit = 30
	S2	cost = 50	benefit = 45

Using the all beneficial sites method, F1 is allocated to both S1 and S2 because benefits exceed costs at both sites. F2 is allocated to S2 because it minimizes the amount by which cost exceeds benefit.

Using the progressive fragment allocation method, F1 is initially allocated to site S1 where benefit exceeds cost by the greatest amount; and F2 is initially allocated to site S2 where the differential between benefit and cost is minimized, although cost exceeds benefit at all sites. After this initial allocation, let us assume the benefit of F1 at S2 is decreased due to the presence of a copy of F1 at S1:

F1	S2	cost = 170	benefit = 165

At this point no further allocations can be made for F1 (beyond site S1) because cost now exceeds benefit. This decision is based on more precise data than the all beneficial sites method and is therefore more accurate.

8.4.4 Practical Considerations

One of the disadvantages of the data allocation methods presented in this chapter is the use of averages for query times and update times. This does not take into account the possibility of dominant transactions whose I/O specifications are known or an environment where the network configuration and network protocol details are given. Under such circumstances, the actual I/O times and network delay times can be estimated for individual dominant transactions instead of averages across all transactions. A dominant transaction is defined by criteria such as high frequency of execution, high volume of data accessed, tight response time constraints, and explicit priority. The following list of assumptions is typical of those used to estimate the components of transaction response time in a detailed analysis. A detailed example using this approach is given in [Teor89].

1. The generic packet-switched network has a known data transmission rate (e.g., T3 links at 45 mb/s or fast Ethernet at 100 mb/s). Pick the shortest distance between two sites and assume a simple protocol with no overhead: Send a one-packet query or update and receive a result of one packet or more with no processing overhead, only disk and transmission delays. Packet size is assumed to be the same as block size unless known to be otherwise. Typical packet sizes are well known for various protocols (e.g., ATM cells are 53 bytes and can be consolidated into larger packets; maximum Ethernet packets are 1512 bytes).
2. The ideal network propagation delay is the speed of light, approximately 300,000 kilometers per second. We assume a lower speed of 200,000 kilometers per second (200 km/millisecond), which is commonly used to take cable degradation into account. We also assume that station latency overhead is negligible.
3. Network contention is ignored because database design decisions are normally independent of total network load.
4. Local query and update: Compute access times based on disk I/O for read and rewrite.
5. Remote query and update: Compute access times based on disk I/O for read and rewrite, plus network propagation and transmission delays for the query/update, including the actual data being transferred to answer the query/update. Pick an intelligent (near-optimal) query processing strategy for each query and update; absolute optimality is not necessary for estimation at this level.
6. Assume that all tables are initially sorted by the primary key. Also assume that the local database systems contain sufficient indexing so that all searches for individual records (rows), based on the key value, take one random block access; if a rewrite is necessary for an update, it takes one random block access. When joins of tables are required, do appropriate selections and projections first to reduce the cost of a join. If necessary, one or both tables may need to be sorted on the attribute used in the join.

8.5 Summary

We have seen that distributed database design requires much more analysis than centralized databases; but there exists a set of basic principles we can use for everyday design decisions. We have also seen that both nonredundant and redundant data allocation methods can be simply expressed and implemented to minimize the time needed to execute a collection of transactions on a distributed database. These methods take into account the execution times of remote and local database transactions for query and update and the frequencies of these transactions.

The advantages of the all beneficial sites method, compared to the best fit method, are its computational simplicity, its greater attention to the relative weights of service time for reads and writes, and its applicability to either the nonredundant or redundant data alternatives. It has no disadvantages relative to best fit, but it does have some general limitations regarding the difficulty of obtaining the average query and update times over all applications and the fact that it ignores the details of network topology and protocols. Better estimating techniques for average I/O time and network delay costs would improve these methods.

Literature Summary

[ACM90] *ACM Computing Surveys Special Issue on Heterogeneous Databases,* 22, 3 (Sept. 1990), pp. 173–293.

[BeGr92] Bell, D., and Grimson, J. *Distributed Database Systems,* McGraw-Hill, New York, 1992.

[Case72] Casey, R.G. "Allocation of Copies of a File in an Information Network," *Spring Joint Computer Conf., 1972,* AFIPS Press, Washington D.C., Vol. 40.

[CePe84] Ceri, S., and Pelagatti, G. *Distributed Databases: Principles and Systems,* McGraw-Hill, New York, 1984.

[CGP80] Coffman, E.G., Gelenbe, E., and Plateua, B. "Optimization of the Number of Copies in Distributed Databases," *Proc. of the 7th IFIP Symposium on Computer Performance Modelling, Measurement and Evaluation,* Springer-Verlag, New York, 1980, pp. 257–263.

[Chu69] Chu, W.W. "Optimal File Allocation in a Multiple Computer System," *IEEE Trans. on Computers,* C-18, 10 (Oct. 1969), pp. 885–889.

[Chu84] Chu, W.W. *Distributed Data Bases, Handbook of Software Engineering,* C.R. Vick and C.V. Ramamoorthy (editors), Van Nostrand Reinhold, New York, 1984.

[CNP82] Ceri, S., Negri, M., and Pelagatti, G. "Horizontal Data Partitioning in Database Design," *Proc. ACM-SIGMOD Int'l. Conf. on Management of Data,* 1982, pp. 128–136.

[CPW87] Ceri, S., Pernici, B., and Wiederhold, G. "Distributed Database Design Methodologies," *Proc. of the IEEE,* May 1987, pp. 533–546.

[FHS80] Fisher, P., Hollist, P., and Slonim, J. "A Design Methodology for Distributed Databases," *Proc. IEEE Conf. Distributed Computing,* 1980, IEEE, pp. 199–202.

[FiHo80] Fisher, M.L., and Hochbaum, D. "Database Location in Computer Networks," *J. ACM* 27, 4 (Oct. 1980), pp. 718–735.

[Heba77] Hebalkar, P.G. "Logical Design Considerations for Distributed Database Systems," *IEEE COMPSAC,* Nov. 1977, pp. 562–580.

[HsKa89] Hsiao, D.K., and Kamel, M.N. "Heterogeneous Databases: Proliferations, Issues, and Solutions," *IEEE Trans. on Knowledge and Data Engineering* 1, 1 (March 1989), pp. 45–62.

[JWBT91] Janakiraman, J., Warack, C., Bhal, G., and Teorey, T.J. "Progressive Fragment Allocation," *Proc. 10th Int'l. Conf. on the Entity Relationship Approach,* ER Institute, San Mateo, CA, 1991, pp. 543–560.

[MaRi76] Mahmood, S., and Riordan, J . "Optimal Allocation of Resources in Distributed Information Networks," *ACM Trans. Database Systems* 1, 1(March 1976), pp. 66–78.

[MoLe77] Morgan, H.L., and Levin, K.D. "Optimal Program and Data Allocation in Computer Networks," *Comm. ACM* 32, 5 (May 1977), pp. 345–353.

[OzVa91] Ozsu, M.T., and Valduriez, P. *Principles of Distributed Database Systems,* Prentice Hall, Upper Saddle River, NJ, 1991.

[TCOU89] Teorey, T.J., Chaar, J., Olukotun, K., and Umar, A. "Distributed Database Design: Some Basic Concepts and Strategies," *Database Prog. & Design* 2, 4 (April 1989), pp. 34–42.

[Teor89] Teorey, T.J. "Distributed Database Design: A Practical Approach and Example," *SIGMOD Record* 18, 4 (Dec. 1989), pp. 23–39.

Exercises

Problem 8-1

First use the best fit method based on frequency of applications to determine a feasible nonredundant allocation for the three unfragmented tables (**R1**, **R2**, **R3**) among the three equidistant sites (S1, S2, S3). Then use the all beneficial sites approach to determine where to replicate the tables, using the following workload and configuration parameters. Assume that each site has adequate sequential and random (hashing) access methods for disk files.

Workload (applications)

Query 1: requires a three-way join (single full scan, no sort required) of tables **R1**, **R2**, and **R3**.

Query 2: requires a random access to one record in **R2**.

Update 1: requires a random access to one record in **R1** and a rewrite of that record.

Update 2: requires a sequential scan of table **R2** and a rewrite of every record.

Type of application	*Origin of application*	*Application frequency*
Query 1	(on **R1**	**R2**
Query 2	(on **R2** only)	Sites S1
Update 1	(on **R1** only)	Site S2
Update 2	(on **R2** only)	Site S3

Tables

R1 fits exactly into 100 blocks. Blocking factor = 20.
R2 fits exactly into 100 blocks. Blocking factor = 10.
R3 fits exactly into 100 blocks. Blocking factor = 50.

Critical disk and network times

Trba = 40 ms at all sites (disk I/O time for a random block access)

Tsba = 10 ms at all sites (disk I/O time for a sequential block access)

network propagation delay = 10 ms; transmission delay for one packet (or block) = 100 ms

Please see page 351 for the solution to Problem 8-1.

Problem 8-2

Repeat Problem 8-1 using the best fit method based on total block accesses for each application (block accesses per application execution times frequency) instead of just frequency of the application. Why does this give a different result from Problem 8-1?

Problem 8-3

Apply the all beneficial sites approach to determine an optimal redundant allocation for the three fragments (F1, F2, F3) across the four sites given in the following figure. Assume that each allocation decision can be made independently of the other decisions. To determine where to replicate the fragments, use the following workload and configuration parameters. Assume that each site has adequate sequential and random (hashing) access methods for disk files.

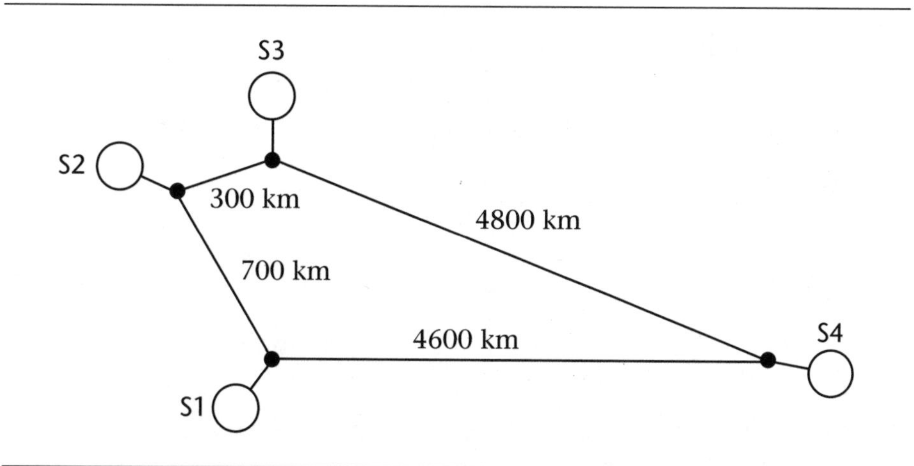

Workload (transactions)

Query 1: requires a three-way join (single full scan, no sort required) of fragments F1, F2, and F3.

Query 2: requires a random access to one record in F2, then to one record in F1.

Query 3: requires a random access to one record in F3.

Update 1: requires a random access to one record in F1 and a rewrite of that record.

Update 2: requires a sequential scan of fragment F2 and a rewrite of each record updated.

Type of transaction	*Origin of transaction*	*Transaction frequency*	*Size of reply*
Query 1 (on F1	F2	F3)	Site S1
Query 2 (on F2	F1)	Sites S2	S3
Query 3 (on F3)	Site S3	5	1 packet
Update 1 (on F1 only)	Site S2	50	1 packet
Update 2 (on F2 only)	Sites S1	S3	S4

Fragments

F1 has 20,000 records, blocking factor = 20.
F2 has 10,000 records, blocking factor = 100.
F3 has 50,000 records, blocking factor = 25.
Block size = 10,000 bytes.
Packet size = 1000 bytes.

Critical disk and network times

Trba = 40 ms at all sites (disk I/O time for a random block access)
Tsba = 10 ms at all sites (disk I/O time for a sequential block access)
network propagation delay is based on degraded speed of light estimate (200 km/ms)
network transmission rate is based on T1 speed (1.544 Mbps)

Problem 8-4

Redo Problem 8-3 with a variation of ABS called *progressive fragment allocation* that first allocates an initial copy of each fragment as the one that has the maximum value of benefit minus cost, then remembers where that copy is (e.g., has memory), and successively determines where each of the next copies should go on the basis of maximum value of benefit minus cost, one at a time, so long as benefit exceeds cost. Note that after each specific fragment allocation, the benefit decreases because additional copies make the query times decrease, and it is assumed that the benefit is a function of a closer copy, not just a local copy being created.

Problem 8-5

Consider how your allocation strategy in Problem 8-3 would change under the two extremes of network configuration:

a. Every link is 56 Kbps so that packet transmission is dominant.
b. Every link uses a future technology of Gbps so that packet transmission delays are minimal.

9 Data Warehousing, OLAP, and Data Mining

A *data warehouse* is a large repository of historical data that can be integrated for decision support. The vast size of data warehouses can run up to hundreds of gigabytes or even terabytes. The essential elements of decision support are considered to be data warehousing capability and on-line analytical processing (OLAP). Many commercial products are now available to provide data warehousing and OLAP, and most of the DBMS vendors provide tools for these technologies.

The three primary uses of data warehouses are for standard reports and graphical data similar to that provided by relational database systems today, for dimensional analysis such as OLAP, and for data mining. OLAP is a sophisticated form of query methodology used to aggregate and summarize data in a data warehouse. Data mining is an even more complex query methodology used to discover nonobvious relationships or trends in the data. All three uses are related to the way data in a data warehouse is logically and physically organized, and performance is highly sensitive to the database design techniques used [BaEd97].

In this chapter we take a close look at the requirements for a data warehouse, its basic components and principles of operation, the critical issues in the design of a data warehouse, and the important logical and physical database design elements in a data warehouse environment. We then investigate the basic elements of OLAP and data mining as special query techniques applied to data warehousing.

9.1 Overview of Data Warehousing

A data warehouse contains a collection of tools for decision support associated with very large historical databases that enable the end user to make quick and sound decisions. It grew out of the technology for decision support systems (DSS) and executive information systems (EIS) that have been available to some degree for the past decade or more. DSSs are used to analyze data from commonly available databases with multiple sources and to create reports. The report data is not time critical in the sense of real-time systems but must be timely for decision making. EISs are like DSSs but more powerful, easier to use, and more business specific. These systems were designed to provide an alternative to the classical on-line transaction processing (OLTP) systems common to most database systems commercially available. OLTP systems are often used to create common applications, including those with mission-critical deadlines or response times. They typically require a great deal of custom programming effort and are not particularly user friendly [OHE96]. Table 9.1 summarizes the basic differences between OLTP and data warehouse systems.

Table 9.1 Comparison between OLTP and data warehouse databases

OLTP	*Data warehouse*
Transaction oriented	Subject oriented
Thousands of users	Few users (typically under 100)
Small (MB up to several GB)	Large (hundreds of GB up to several TB)
Current data	Historical data
Normalized data (many tables, few columns per table)	Denormalized data (few tables, many columns per table)
Continuous updates	Batch updates
Simple to complex queries	Usually very complex queries

The basic architecture for a data warehouse environment is shown in Figure 9.1. Here we see that the data warehouse is stocked by a variety of source databases from possibly different geographical locations. Each source database serves its own applications, and the data warehouse serves a DSS/EIS with its informational requests. Each feeder system database must be reconciled with the data warehouse data model; this is accomplished in the processing that takes place for the extraction of the required data from the feeder database system, the transformation of data from the feeder system to the data warehouse, and the actual loading of the data into the data warehouse [Cata97].

In a two-tier architecture, Figure 9.2a, tier 1 is a collection of backend servers for specific applications, all connected to a backbone net-

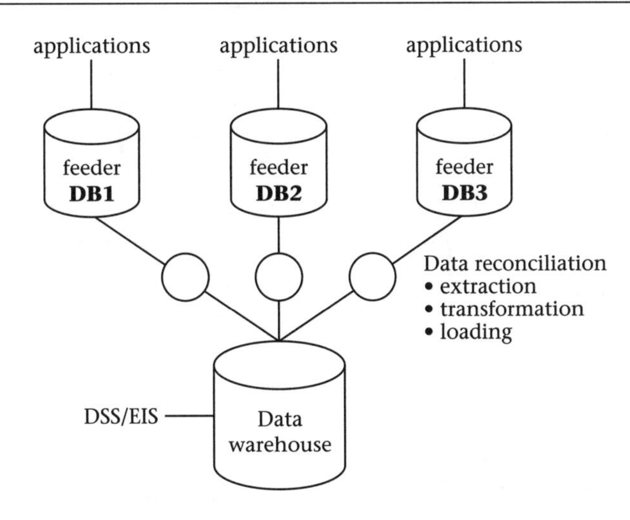

Figure 9.1 Basic data warehouse architecture

work, and tier 2 is a collection of mainframe clients with their own databases and access to the same backbone network. The mainframe clients (legacy systems) are left alone but have special front-end systems to provide transparent access to the legacy systems. This approach does not scale well to more systems or to large numbers of on-line users.

A three-tier architecture, Figure 9.2b, works better than the two-tier systems by putting the clients at tier 3, the local servers and graphically oriented user interfaces at tier 1, and the high-speed database and application servers at tier 2, which handle business rules and data that are shared across the organization. The tier 2 servers provide high-speed access to the shared data in the data warehouse. Typical middleware used to realize tier 2 are CORBA, Microsoft's DCOM, Sun's RMI, and Java Beans [PDH97]. The choice of the best architecture depends on the size of the data warehouse and the expected traffic. The three-tiered architecture tends to be more expensive but more easily scalable for the larger systems.

Sometimes enterprises do not have the capability to develop a data warehouse immediately after the need is determined but develop smaller-entity data marts first. A *data mart* is a departmental subset of data from the data warehouse; ideally, it is created after the data warehouse is set up but is not always done in practice because of the extreme cost to set up. This bottom-up approach of developing a series of data marts and integrating them into one large data warehouse can be done only if careful attention is paid to common definitions and data types.

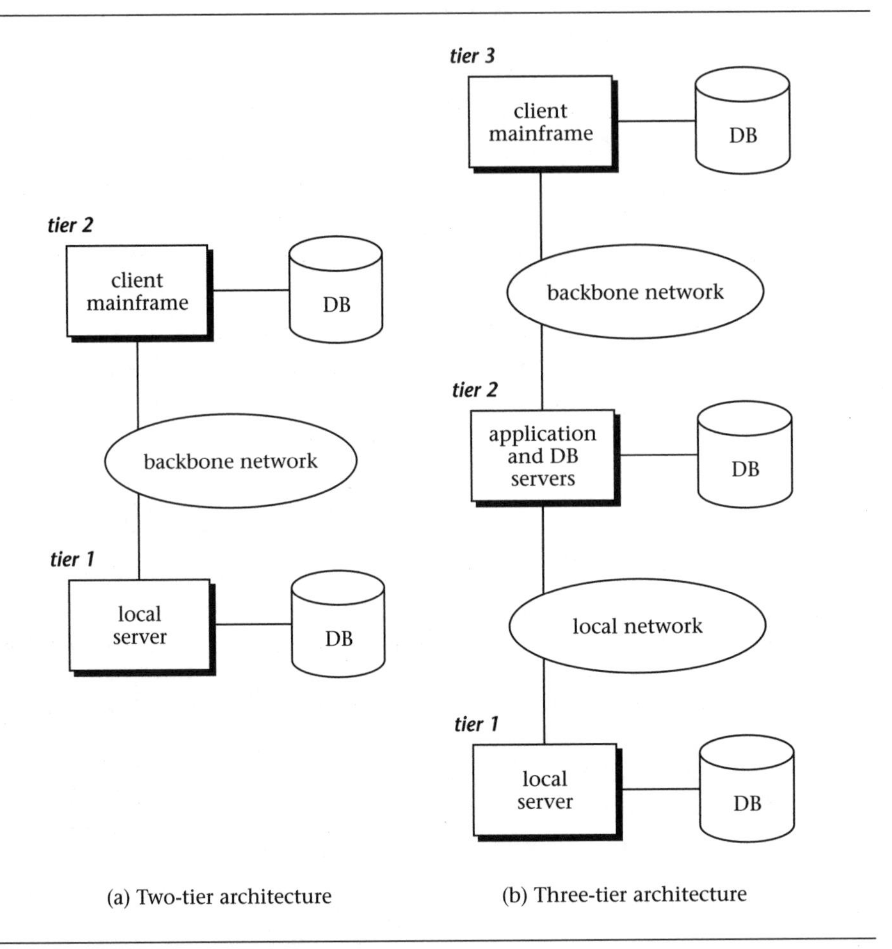

Figure 9.2 Data warehouse architecture

9.1.1 Core Requirements for Data Warehousing

Let us now take a look at the core requirements and principles that guide the design of data warehouses (DWs) [Simo95, BaEd97, ChDa97, GrWa98]:

1. *DWs are organized around subject areas.* Subject areas are analogous to the concept of functional areas such as sales, project management, or employees as discussed in the context of ER diagram clustering in Section 3.4. Each subject area has its own conceptual schema and can be represented using one or more entities in the ER data model or by one or more object classes in the object-oriented data model. Subject areas are typically independent of

individual transactions involving data creation or manipulation. Metadata repositories are needed to describe source databases, DW objects, and how to transform data from the sources to the DW.

2. *DWs should have some integration capability.* A common data representation should be designed so that all the different individual representations can be mapped to it. This is particularly useful if the warehouse is implemented as a multidatabase or federated database.
3. *The data is considered to be nonvolatile and should be mass loaded.* Data extraction from current databases to the DW requires that a decision should be made whether to extract the data using standard relational database (RDB) techniques at the row or column level or specialized techniques for mass extraction. Data cleaning tools are required to maintain data quality, for example, to detect missing data, inconsistent data, homonyms, synonyms, and data with different units. Data migration, data scrubbing, and data auditing tools handle specialized problems in data cleaning and transformation. Such tools are similar to those used for conventional relational database schema (view) integration. Load utilities take cleaned data and load it into the DW, using batch processing techniques. Refresh techniques propagate updates on the source data to base data and derived data in the DW. The decision of when and how to refresh is made by the DW administrator and depends on user needs (e.g., OLAP needs) and existing traffic to the DW.
4. *Data tends to exist at multiple levels of granularity.* Most important, the data tends to be of a historical nature, with potentially high time variance. In general, however, granularity can vary according to many different dimensions, not only by time frame but also by geographic region, type of product manufactured or sold, type of store, and so on. The sheer size of the databases are a major problem in the design and implementation of DWs, especially for certain queries and updates and sequential backups. This necessitates a critical decision between using a relational database (RDB) or a multidimensional database (MDD) for the implementation of a DW.
5. *The DW should be flexible enough to meet changing requirements rapidly.* This involves making the data definitions (schemas) broad enough to anticipate the addition of new types of data. For rapidly changing data retrieval requirements, the types of data and levels of granularity actually implemented must be chosen carefully.

6. *The DW should have a capability for rewriting history, that is, allowing for "what-if" analysis.* The DW should allow the administrator to update historical data temporarily for the purpose of "what-if" analysis. Once the analysis is completed, the data must be correctly rolled back. This assumes that the data must be at the proper level of granularity in the first place.
7. *A usable DW user interface should be selected.* The leading choices today are SQL, multidimensional views of relational data, or a special-purpose user interface. Tools are needed within the user interface language for retrieving, formatting, and analyzing data.
8. *Data should be either centralized or distributed physically.* The DW should have the capability to handle distributed data over a network. This requirement will become more critical as the use of DWs grows and the sources of data expand.

9.1.2 The Life Cycle for Data Warehouses

The actual design and implementation of a data warehouse is a long and complex process, consisting of the following basic activities [Kimb96, ChDa97]. We can organize these activities in terms of the database design life cycle described in Chapter 1.

I. ***Requirements analysis and specification.***
   a. Analyze the end-user requirements and develop a requirements specification. This step follows the practice used by conventional relational databases (see Chapter 1).
   b. Define the DW architecture and do some initial capacity planning for servers and tools. Integrate the servers, storage elements, and client tools.

II. ***Logical database design.*** Design the enterprise DW schema and views.

III. ***Physical database design.*** Define the physical DW organization and access methods.

IV. ***Data distribution.*** Define data placement, partitioning, and replication.

V. ***Database implementation, monitoring, and modification.***
   a. Connect the data sources (using gateways, ODBC drivers, etc.).

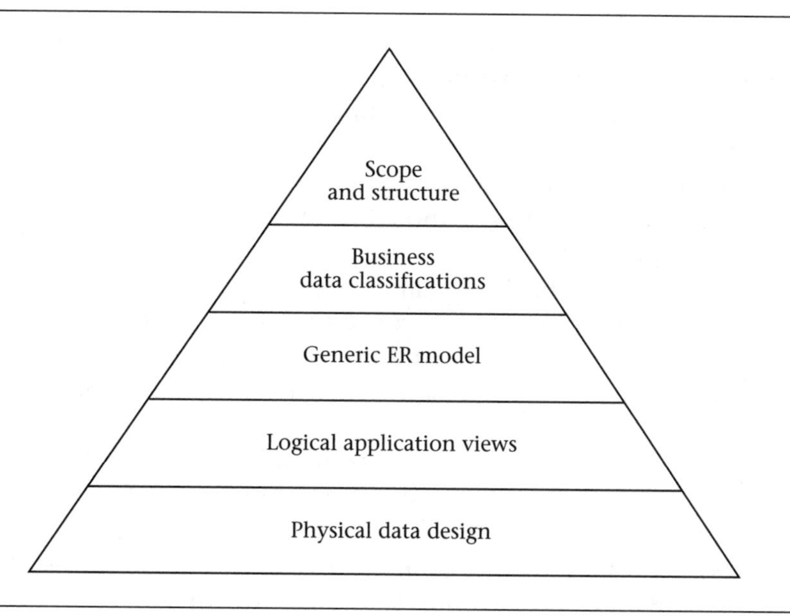

Figure 9.3 The layered enterprise data model [IBM94]

b. Design and implement scripts for data extraction, cleaning, transformation, load, and refresh.
c. Populate the repository with the schema and view definitions, scripts, and other metadata.
d. Design and implement end-user applications. Roll out the DW and applications.

9.2 Logical Design

This section describes the concept of enterprise data modeling as applied to the data warehouse. We see that the star schema is recommended as the basic logical data model. Many variations of the star schema are implemented today, and we explore several of these alternatives.

9.2.1 Enterprise Data Modeling

The layered enterprise data model, the triangular structure shown in Figure 9.3 [Devl97, IBM94], grew out of information engineering and various proposals for an architecture for data modeling in the DW. It represents the data model for the whole company or enterprise. At the top of the structure, the least detailed part, is the scope and architecture layer. This layer describes the basic business concepts or subject areas about which the enterprise must store information. It is written completely in business terminology and presents a comprehensive view of the enterprise that stands as a model to which the lower-level detailed descriptions can relate.

The second layer, business data classifications, further defines the subject areas into categories according to existing business rules. This results in a comprehensive starting point for the customization of the data model to the particular business. For instance, an order can be unfilled or filled; an employee can be temporary or permanent, which can be further broken down as hourly or salaried.

The third layer is the generic entity-relationship (ER) model, which is a structured ER diagram of the enterprise-wide data as described in the top two layers. It may consist of up to several hundred entities. The ER model also describes the attributes and relationships used in the business, in detail, using a data dictionary format.

The fourth layer, logical application views, clusters a number of entities from the layer above into views for specific applications. It is often the case that applications overlap in terms of data used, so the entities that appear in the views are allowed to be redundant if necessary.

The fifth layer is physical data design (see Section 9.3). This design must meet the constraints identified in the requirements analysis for the DW for physical implementation, such as performance constraints and physical data distribution needs.

Devlin defines a three-level architecture for data that helps to clarify the purposes of the various layers in the enterprise data model [Devl97]:

Derived data
|
Reconciled data
|
Real-time data

The bottom level, the real-time data, is the raw data that appears in a database and is used by operational applications for query and update. The top level, the derived data, is data that has been derived or transformed by some computation on the real-time data, including possibly the null computation. In some contexts only the top and bottom levels are needed to describe the whole situation; in many contexts, however, we need a middle level to describe reconciled data, or data needed to rationalize data between two existing applications or views, much as we would need to reconcile data between views in schema integration in a relational database (see Chapter 3). Examples of reconciled data are the use of ssn for employee id in many contexts or transforming units among data for consistency. Examples of derived data are averages of data over different time frames or computation of total sales volume over a specific time period.

We apply the different levels of data in the enterprise data model as follows. Real-time data, which is used by operational applications, is modeled in the logical application layer. Reconciled data, which spans the entire enterprise, is modeled in the generic ER layer. Derived data, which is intended to meet the needs of a single user or group of users, is modeled at the logical application layer along with the real-time data. All three levels of data can be represented at the physical design layer in some fashion, depending on the implementation constraints. For a more detailed and thorough account of how to build and use the enterprise data model for the business data warehouse and business information warehouse, see [Devl97].

9.2.2 The Star Schema

The dominating conceptual data model for data warehouses is the multidimensional view, based on two factors: a set of mostly numeric measures that define the objects associated with the subject areas (e.g., sales-total, customer-id, order-no) and a set of dimensions (represented by entities) that provide the context for the measures (e.g., products, orders, regions, customers). A collection of dimensions uniquely defines each measure, and each dimension is described by either a set of flat attributes or a hierarchy of attributes. The multidimensional data model grew out of the spreadsheet structure and programs popular in PCs and used by business analysts. It can be implemented with specialized multidimensional databases or mapped into existing relational databases. If we choose to use existing relational technology, we can implement the multidimensional view using the star schema. This is the choice of the majority of DW vendors today that base the technology on the relational database model [ChDa97, Devl97, BaEd97].

The *star schema* consists of a single fact table and a set of dimension tables. The *fact table* contains the numeric or nonnumeric measures described in the preceding and is the basic transaction-level data for the

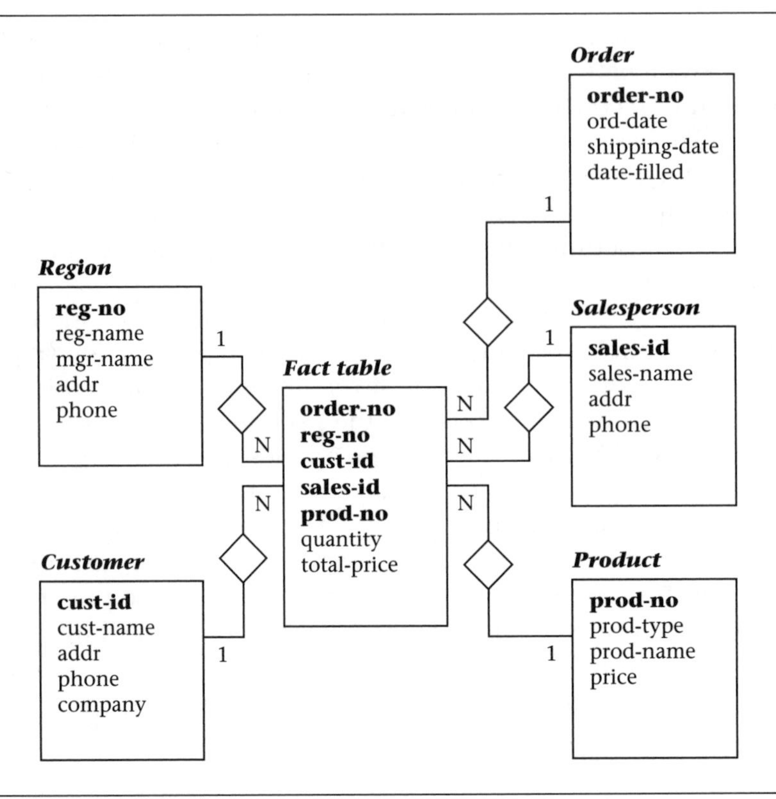

Figure 9.4 Star scheme for the "order" data warehouse

business. The fact table is usually extremely large; it has numerous rows due to the many possible combinations of dimension values and a number of columns equal to the number of dimensions it represents simultaneously. The combination of rows and columns results in an extremely large volume of data. The *dimension tables* are usually much smaller, containing the largely nonnumeric data associated with the attributes of the dimensions (or entities). The fact table acts like an intersection table for a many-to-many relationship or ternary relationship for the pure ER model, in that it tends to contain only the keys of the related entities (dimension tables) as its foreign keys. In effect the fact table is the "many" side of a one-to-many relationship with each of the dimension tables (see Figure 9.4). The connection of a primary key in the dimension table and its corresponding foreign key in the fact table allows this approach to provide referential integrity to the data.

The major advantages of the star schema are performance and ease of use. The star schema allows a variety of queries to be efficiently processed, and it is intuitive for most end users to visualize. These characteristics meet the basic goals of a DW to have an intuitive, simple schema for easy querying and end-user communication, flexibility to accommodate the needs of all end-user groups, and efficiency for queries and updates and for data loading. The example star schema in Figure 9.4 applies to a typical "order" database. The fact table is created to connect the dimension tables through the concept of an order. The dimension tables are created for the dimensions order, product, salesperson, customer, and region.

As an example of the performance benefit of the star schema, consider the query, "Rank the regions in terms of number of units of product x sold" using Figure 9.4. First we can look up product x in the product dimension table to get the prod-no value. Then we effectively join the product table with the fact table for product x, using a fast (bit-map) indexing technique to avoid a full table scan of the fact table. For each record found in the fact table, we add the quantity of product x sold to the subtotal for the region number in that record. If there are 500 products, we only need to access 1/500th of the fact table on the average to answer the query. In another example, shown in Figure 9.5, the star schema with the time dimension added allows us to answer queries with time constraints quickly without having to scan all the data over all the time periods.

Note that the dimension tables may be unnormalized. For instance, if the salesperson's address determined the phone number, or the actual address included street number, city, state, and zip code where the zip code is dependent on the other components, then that table could be considered unnormalized.

9.2.3 Alternative Logical Structures

Real databases sometimes need more functionality than simple star schemas can provide. In such cases minor variations of the star schema may be required. One of these alternative structures is the so-called snowflake schema, a refinement of the star schema to provide attribute hierarchies by normalizing the dimension tables [ChDa97]. This makes maintaining the dimension tables easier but is less efficient for browsing because of the extra joins required. An example snowflake schema for our "order" DW is shown in Figure 9.6. Note that it differs from the star schema in

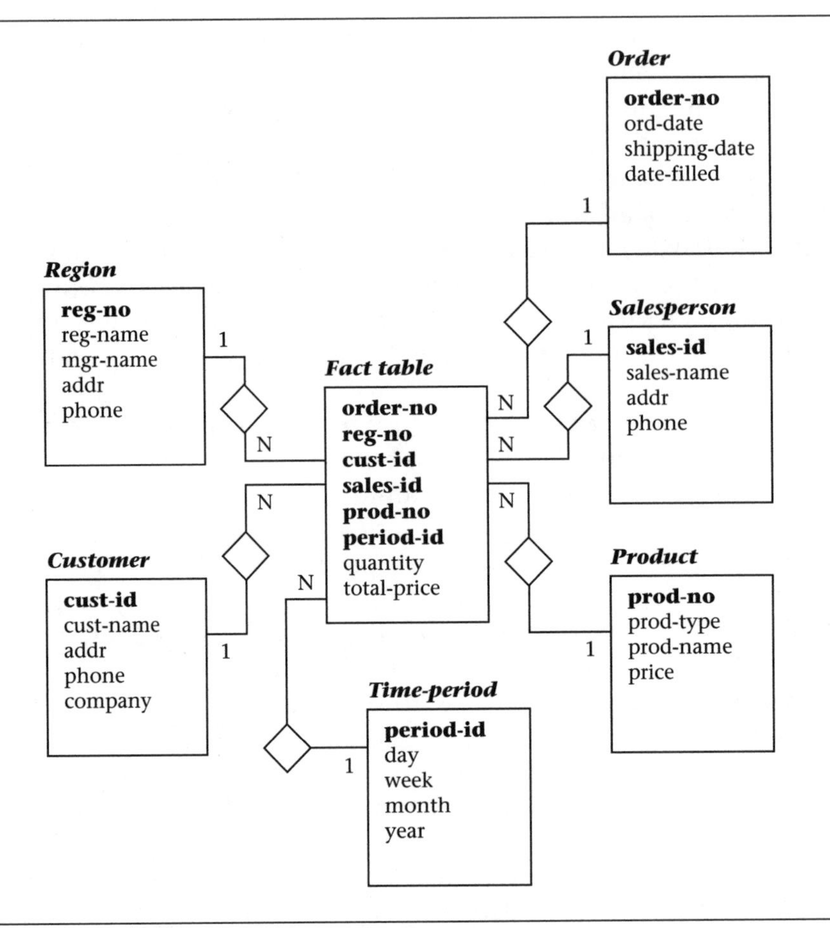

Figure 9.5 Star schema with time dimension added

that the dimension tables "Salesperson" and "Customer" are normalized and two new dimension tables, "Company" and "Sales-addr", are created. An *outboard table* is a variation of a snowflake schema table; it is created for data that is used much less frequently than other data; this allows you to attain better performance for the highly used data.

Another useful variation of the star schema that falls into the gray area between logical and physical design is the *fact table family* or *fact constellation,* in which multiple fact tables are allowed to share dimension tables. This typically occurs when the fact tables represent different aggregations of data—daily, weekly, monthly, quarterly, or annual summaries of sales data. These fact tables are really summary tables with preaggregated data. You can imagine such a configuration by visualizing

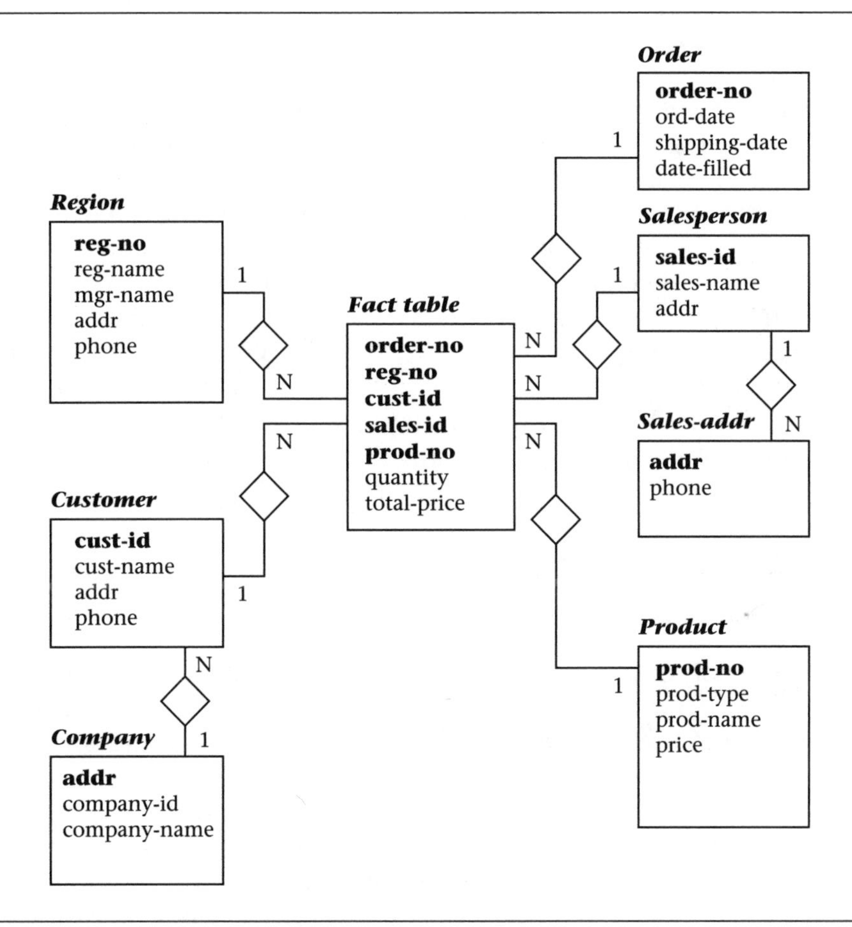

Figure 9.6 Snowflake schema for the "order" data warehouse

the fact table in Figure 9.4 as a family of tables, one for each time frame. For each summary fact table, there is a separate shrunken dimension table that contains only the attributes associated with that particular time frame.

Alternatively, the same correspondence between fact time frame and dimension time frame can be achieved without adding new tables of any kind, by encoding data in the existing fact and dimension tables as follows. The fact table contains separate sets of rows for each aggregate desired. The dimension table contains attributes that flag daily, weekly, monthly, or other time frames that can be joined with the fact table rows. This alternative format saves space at the expense of complexity and potential errors in the operational software [ChDa97].

9.3 Physical Design

Data warehouses are very large, and applications tend to emphasize query processing more and updates less. Thus, physical design needs to be concerned with the physical database structures and query optimization techniques that enhance query performance for very large DWs. The basic structures used by DWs for this purpose are indexes and materialized views. Therefore, the design of these structures—which types of indexes to build and which views to materialize—is of utmost importance. The most common type of matrialized views are created by aggregation, which is described later. Horizontal and vertical table partitioning are other techniques by which we can improve performance with physical reallocation of data. Still other techniques, such as the use of parallel database hardware and disk striping, can be very effective but are beyond the scope of this book.

9.3.1 Indexing

One of the most basic rules of thumb for index design in DWs is to create indexes on each column of each of the dimension tables and on all the corresponding foreign keys in the fact table. This facilitates any joins required between the fact table and the corresponding dimension tables, including multiple joins. Join indexes that map an attribute value (or a concatenation of several attribute values) of a dimension table to one or more rows in a fact table are just variations on the secondary indexes we discussed in Chapter 6. Thus, a join index is really a binary precomputed join, and multikey join indexes are really n-way precomputed joins. These techniques can greatly enhance performance of a DW.

Highly analytical queries that are weakly selective can make use of bitmap (or bit vector) indexes [Fren95, ONGr95]. *Bitmap indexes* are particularly useful for low-selectivity queries, such as those that search based on few alternative values, like male/female attributes or salaried/hourly employee attributes. Bitmap indexes speed up special index operations such as intersection or union. In a typical B^+-tree secondary index, for instance, leaf nodes have a pointer array of physical row addresses for all rows that meet a given criterion defined by the index.

In a bitmap, however, the structure is different. Each row of the DW table is represented by a single bit in a bit vector, and each row satisfying the criterion (e.g., reg-name = "southwest" or sales-id = 412) has its bit set in that bit vector, as shown in Figure 9.7. Here we see that each attribute value has a separate bit vector. Those rows satisfying all criteria are

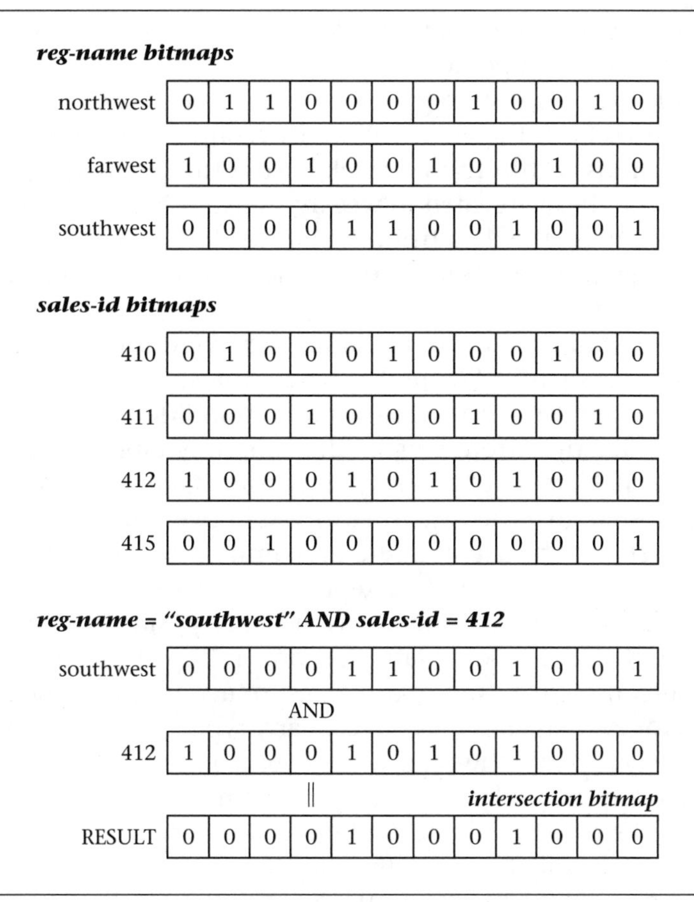

Figure 9.7 Bitmaps and query processing

found by taking the AND of the bit vectors, as shown in Figure 9.7 for the intersection of reg-name = "southwest" and sales-id = 412. Bitmap indexes are now quite common in commercial systems, for example, IBM's DB2, Oracle, Red Brick Warehouse, and Sybase IQ.

9.3.2 View Materialization

View materialization is closely associated with the aggregation of data by one or more particular dimensions, such as time or location. A view is created by joining the fact table with a subset of dimension tables, and the aggregation is set up by a group of attributes from the dimension tables. The selection of which views to materialize is highly dependent on factors such as the type of workload, storage constraints, and the cost to do an incremental update.

A simple but useful strategy for materializing a view for aggregation is to select rows from the view (rollup) by grouping and aggregating additional columns within the same table. For example, daily statistics on total orders can be aggregated to weekly statistics by applying the selection and rolling up the data from days to weeks [ChDa97]. It should be noted that aggregations should only be done when the data is numeric and can be summed.

Another useful strategy for materializing a view for aggregation with a new table is shown in Figure 9.5, where the star schema example in Figure 9.4 is extended with the time dimension [MeKh96]. This schema is then modified by introducing a sales summary table for each month (see Figure 9.8). Note that "quantity" is not moved to the summary table because it would give the total quantity sold over all products for that month, which is not a useful figure to maintain. However, the quantity for a particular product could be kept in the sales summary table if the summary table were also connected as the "many" side in a one-to-many relationship with the product table (or some rollup of the product table).

We could also create summary tables for every other time unit (and in general for every hierarchical level of any type of dimension), but this would quickly increase the total storage space immensely and would seriously increase the update overhead to maintain all the aggregates in addition to the finest granularity of data. However, a practical compromise is often possible by carefully selecting which levels to aggregate, then deriving a new level by summing over the totals at the previous level. For example, a yearly summary could be obtained by summing the results over each of the 12 monthly summaries instead of over hundreds of daily summaries or thousands of hourly sales.

9.3.3 Partitioning

Horizontal table partitioning is common to many commercial systems (e.g., Red Brick Systems, Informix) and allows you to store a large table in meaningful pieces, depending on the dimensions you want to partition. The most common dimension for partitioning is time, but other dimensions can also be good candidates for partitioning, depending on the query processing required. For the time dimension, you could divide data by month over n years and have 12*n partitions, and the union of these tables would form the whole table.

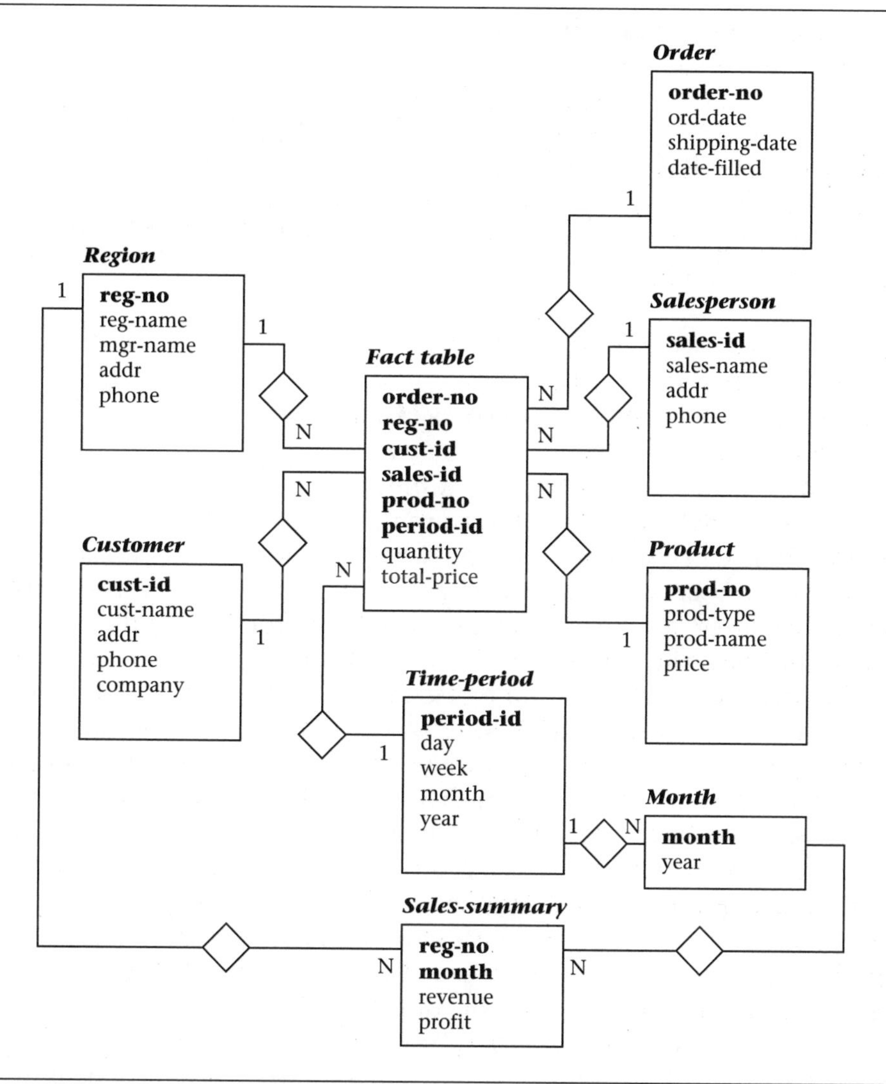

Figure 9.8 Sales summary as an example of aggregation

Vertical table partitioning allows you to separate tables physically by groups of columns. This has the advantage of putting rarely used columns out of the mainstream of query processing, and in general it helps match up the processing requirements with the available columns. Some overhead is incurred because the table key must be replicated in each partition. In the extreme, an entire table could be stored column-wise instead of row-wise, but the designer is cautioned that this should only be done if the query processing is clearly benefited by such a transformation.

9.3.4 Query Processing

Query processing techniques make use of indexing strategies, especially for handling intersection joins, and view materialization techniques to improve performance. Some useful approaches used in systems today include unnesting (flattening) complex nested subqueries, making use of parallel hardware, extending SQL in existing relational systems, and using special SQL server architectures. Many of these techniques are used to accommodate OLAP.

9.4 On-Line Analytical Processing (OLAP)

OLAP is the process of creating and summarizing historical, multidimensional data to help users understand the data better and make informed decisions. The key points about the data are that the summarization or aggregation process creates derived data, which is the level that the user wants visualized, and the fact that the base data from which the summaries are taken can be constantly changing. The terms *OLAP* and *data warehousing* are often confused, but a case can be made to distinguish them from each other. Data warehousing is the process of setting up a large repository of historical data with reasonably clean data and then maintaining that data as it evolves over time. OLAP is more concerned with getting data out of a data warehouse in a summary form that is useful for management decision making. The basic goals of OLAP are to produce information that is accurate, timely, and understandable [Thom97c, ChDa97].

The basic conceptual model that drives OLAP tools and techniques is the multidimensional view of data, illustrated by the star schema. The fact table contains mostly numeric measures that are the basic elements used for analysis. The dimension tables represent a set of dimensions or perspectives (entities) about the system you want to study. The dimensions, in turn, are described by a set of attributes. The multidimensional view contains measures that are values in multidimensional space, and they are most commonly implemented as either extensions to relational databases (RDBs) with records and tables or as multidimensional databases (MDDs), which store data in arrays. MDD products vary widely in terms of the actual multidimensional model, access methods, application programming interfaces (APIs), and level of decision support using multidimensional OLAP (MOLAP). Relational OLAP (ROLAP) servers, on the other hand, tend to be more consistent in terms of SQL extensions, access methods, and efficient methods to implement multidimensional data.

One of the earliest and most successful users of this technology is Wal-Mart, but many other medium to large companies have already become users as well. There are approximately 15 to 20 major players in the OLAP software business. Excellent surveys of available ROLAP and MOLAP tools and vendors can be found in an article by Neil Raden [BaEd97] and, more recently, by Erik Thomsen [Thom97c], as well as recent surveys on the World Wide Web [Grov98]. Raden suggests the following selection criteria when comparing different tools: range of functionality, fit with your current environment, performance, scalability, and future potential. Both surveys make a clear distinction between ROLAP and MOLAP tools.

9.4.1 Common Features of MDD Software

The most common features of multidimensional databases are dimensions, hypercubes, hierarchies, formulas, and links. Let us look at each of these in more detail.

Dimensions

Dimensions, as described previously, are perspectives or entities about the real-world system you want to model. In the extended star schema example of a sales data warehouse in Figure 9.5, the major dimensions are "Region," "Customer," "Order," "Salesperson," "Product," and "Time-period." Any MDD must be able to handle multiple dimensions.

Hypercubes

The simplest structure for multidimensional data is a two-dimensional table. A three-dimensional structure is called a *cube,* and any structure above three dimensions is called a *hypercube.* Hypercubes are difficult to visualize directly but are commonly displayed on a two-dimensional medium in various ways. Examples of multidimensional views of the sales data are shown in Figure 9.9. The first view (9.9a) shows a linear sequence of the four dimensions: "Time-period," "Region," "Product," and "Variable," listing sample dimension members. The second view (9.9b) shows an actual two-dimensional layout of the multidimensional data values. Note that each table represents a separate region, and within each table we represent the other three dimensions: "Time-period," "Product," and "Variable." Many other representations are possible for the same data, and the designer tries to choose a representation that is most likely to be aesthetically pleasing to the user.

Time-period	*Region*	*Product*	*Variable*
January 1998	Southwest	Ford Mustang	quantity sold
February 1998	Northwest	Chrysler Eagle	total revenue
March 1998	North central	GM Camaro	
April 1998	South central	Toyota Camry	
May 1998	Northeast		
June 1998	Midwest		
1st quarter 1998	Southeast		
2nd quarter 1998			
3rd quarter 1998			
year 1997			
year 1998			

(a) Linear sequence of sample members from each of four dimensions

Region: Southwest		*Quantity sold*	*Total revenue*
January 1998	Ford Mustang	426	6317
	Chrysler Eagle	179	3004
	GM Camaro	318	5261
	Toyota Camry	299	4783
February 1998	Ford Mustang	451	6542
	Chrysler Eagle	192	3119
	GM Camaro	356	6007
	Toyota Camry	301	4936

(b) Two-dimensional layout of four dimensions of data

Figure 9.9 Display of multidimensional sales data

Hierarchies

Certain dimensions are hierarchical in nature, and the hierarchies present natural boundaries for aggregating or summarizing data. Examples of a strict hierarchy are time period (day, month, year) and geographic locations (city, state, region, country). Broader types of hierarchies include dimensions like product (appliances—refrigerators, stoves, washers, with subtypes; entertainment systems—TV, radio, CD players, with subtypes; etc.). Hierarchies are not necessarily unique to dimensions; that is, a dimension may have multiple hierarchies. For example, products can be arranged by pricing as well as by functionality. The OLAP operation of going from a more detailed lower level to a less detailed higher (aggregate) level is called *rollup*, and the process of navigating the

Report for January 1998

	Southwest	*Northwest*	*Total of regions*
Ford Mustang	426	457	883
Chrysler Eagle	179	216	395
GM Camaro	318	245	563
Toyota Camry	299	322	621
Total of products	1222	1240	2462

(a) Pure operations computed the same in any order (sums)

Report for January 1998, Southwest region

	Quota	*Quantity sold*	*Quantity sold/quota*
Ford Mustang	400	426	1.065
Chrysler Eagle	200	179	0.895
GM Camaro	300	318	1.060
Toyota Camry	300	299	0.997
Total of products	1200	1222	Ratio of sums = 1.018 Sum of ratios = 4.017

(b) Mixed sums and ratios give inconsistent results

Figure 9.10 Examples of mixing formulas for derived data values

data from a higher level to a lower level is called *drill-down*. Other OLAP operations include *slice* (vertical partitioning or projection), *dice* (horizontal partitioning or selection), and *pivot* (switching dimensions on a grid).

Formulas

Derived data values are defined by formulas such as sum, difference, average, variance, product, ratio, and so on. In spreadsheets derived data is determined by using a formula that pertains to a given cell. In SQL derived data results from creating a view whose columns are explicitly defined by a formula. In MDDs formulas are attached to nonleaf members of each dimension that is not a variable and leaf members of dimensions that represent variables. Formulas combine when the dimensions intersect to form cells that contain the derived data. Figure 9.10a illustrates how certain formula combinations can be calculated in either the horizontal or vertical direction first and still maintain the same result over the two dimensions. In general we get the same results for combinations of sums and sums, differences and differences, ratios and ratios, and products and ratios in either order. In Figure 9.10b we see that certain combinations (e.g., the sums and ratios) give inconsistent results when computed in different order, and therefore a precedence order must be established. When sums and ratios are combined, it is generally preferable to take the sums first and then take the ratio of the sums as the last step. Other inconsistent combinations besides sums and ratios are combinations of differences and ratios and combinations of differences and products.

Links

Links are needed to connect hypercubes and their data sources, which are constantly being modified. As soon as the external data is changed, the changes must be automatically propagated to the hypercube. Because the hypercube often contains aggregate data, the propagation function must be quite sophisticated. Both dimension modifications and data calculations need to be propagated quickly and accurately.

9.4.2 Functional Requirements for OLAP

The functional requirements for an OLAP system with the preceding components are rapid access; powerful analytical capabilities; flexibility in terms of visualization, interfaces, and analysis; and multiuser support in collaborative work environments [Thom97c]. These requirements are easily satisfied with MDDs, but a number of successful implementations have also been done with extensions to relational systems, overcoming some inherent limitations of SQL and the ability to do interrow analysis. Spreadsheets were the earliest implementation of OLAP concepts, but they remain limited in that formulas are confined to individual cells in a two-dimensional grid. While useful for taking totals and averages of a list of data, a huge number of separate spreadsheets would be required for the enormous combinations of dimension member values you would want to calculate.

Although OLAP is a concept that has been around for almost 30 years, the actual term was coined in 1993 in a white paper by E.F. Codd, the originator of the concept of relational databases, and later published in *Computerworld* [Codd95]. Despite the furor that erupted about the motivation for the paper [Thom97c, BaEd97], the original 12 rules for OLAP were expanded to 18 and are considered the standard starting point for discussions about OLAP functionality. Table 9.2 lists the basic 18 rules or features.

Table 9.2 Codd's 18 Rules for OLAP

Basic Features

1.Multidimensional conceptual view
2.Intuitive data manipulation (including drill-down and rollup)
3.Accessibility (single logical view to the user)
4.Batch extraction versus interpretive
5.OLAP analysis models (four types of analysis models)
6.Client/server architecture
7.Transparency (user's front-end should not be aware of the OLAP tool—this is difficult to do!)
8.Multi-user support (with concurrent read/write operations)

Special Features

9.Treatment of nonnormalized data (calculations should not affect the external data)
10.Storing OLAP results
11.Extraction of missing values (missing values versus zeros or meaningless values)
12.Treatment of missing values

Reporting Features

13.Flexible reporting (of a cube's dimensions)
14.Consistent reporting performance
15.Automatic adjustment of physical level (when the data changes)

Dimension Control

16.Generic dimensionality
17.Unlimited dimensions and aggregation levels
18.Unrestricted cross-dimensional operations

9.4.3 OLAP Logical Design

Some practical steps for defining an OLAP logical model are discussed in Erik Thomsen's book on OLAP solutions [Thom97c].

The discussion that follows fits Thomsen's steps into our extension of database design steps for data warehousing and OLAP. Let us look at each of these steps in detail, using the sales data example defined previously. This is essentially a top-down approach, starting at the highest level of abstraction and working down to the lowest level.

Step 1. Analyze the end-user requirements and environment. This step is similar to the first step in any database design process (see Chapter 1), except that the special problems and environment are particular to data warehouses. The designer needs to understand the data flow in the current system and the specific problems that are associated with current users and their applications. Logical problems include any difficulty in defining multidimensional calculations, drilling down from summaries to lower-level details, changing views, or running applications. Physical problems include lack of sufficient speed (i.e., poor performance) or obvious bottlenecks at the client, server, or network. Finally, constraints need to be identified, such as the hardware/software environment being used, network protocols and client tools available, system use levels, and data volume.

Step 2. Define cubes, dimensions, hierarchies, and links (high level). Step 2 is the high-level logical multidimensional modeling, starting with the logical cube and dimension structure. The concepts for these are taken from the requirements analysis and specification in step 1. Dimensions are much like entities in the ER model, and cubes (or hypercubes) are created in a similar way to the fact table in the star schema. One dimension needs to be allocated to the variables that result from the formulas such as mean, total, variance, or ratio of certain data. Variables that share the same dimensions should be considered for the same cube, but only if it makes sense logically. If you have multiple tables defined, check to see whether you should merge their key structures, and if so, merge them into a single cube. Otherwise, you should maintain separate cubes.

Dimensions can be added to or subtracted from the cube, depending on how they are used. Dimensions are usually added when they act independently of each other, like time and location. Dimensions can be subtracted when their cardinalities are small and their intersections are not meaningful.

Hierarchies are gleaned from the requirements analysis and personal experience. Symmetric hierarchies, such as those for time period and geographical location, can be represented in linear fashion as levels. Asymmetric hierarchies, like products or customers, have a broad structure where levels do not easily apply. Both general types of hierarchies are common in OLAP logical structures.

At this point it is useful to define the links between the external source data and the leaf nodes of the dimension hierarchies associated with the cubes. Bringing in some data at this stage gives you a chance to test some of the variable formulas in step 4 (and make adjustments) before the whole design is set in concrete.

Step 3. Define dimension members (low level). Step 3 starts the low-level logical model by defining the actual members of each dimension, striking a balance between too much abstraction and too much detail. Most cubes should have a fairly low cardinality of levels, thus keeping the model reasonably simple. Variables need to be analyzed individually to determine which to keep in the model and at what level of detail. You also need to look at the relationships between members of different dimensions, whether their intersections have meaning, and whether ordering of dimensions must be done (i.e., when the variables must be correlated).

Step 4. Define aggregations and other formulas (derived data). Aggregation is the function of summarizing data over a particular dimension, such as time or geographic location, and applying one or more formulas to the raw (input) data, thus creating new (derived) data. For instance, assume the sales of Nike shoes of a particular type is recorded by individual sale by all stores. A typical aggregate needed for a report might be to obtain the total sales per month for the past three years, listed by store. Once that data has been collected and analyzed, you might want to look at total sales per year by region. This second report can be obtained from either the input data or a materialization of the aggregate data created for the first report. Obviously, the second method should be faster if the aggregate data is stored properly, but it also incurs the overhead of calculating the aggregate the first time and the storage space required to hold it.

This step is concerned with issues such as which data to aggregate, how to store the aggregate data, and when to preaggregate (precalculate) the derived data. Each of these issues requires an analysis of the inherent trade-offs in the potential implementations.

Which Data to Aggregate

The question of which data to aggregate depends on the dimension structure of the model and the current and future processing requirements of the end users. Dimensions that are hierarchical (e.g., products, time period, customers, location) create obvious points of aggregation from the dimension members. For instance, products can be aggregated by product type (automobile), product manufacturer (Ford), product name (Mustang), or product subgroup (specific Mustang model). Thus, dimension members form a natural set of aggregation points regardless of the end-user needs. Specific user needs can then be superimposed on the potential aggregation points for a set of priority aggregation points.

The basic trade-offs that need to be considered are time and space. Time is required to create reports from either input data or derived (aggregate) data, to create and store the aggregate data in advance, and to update both the input and derived data. Frequency of known and anticipated queries and updates needs to be considered here. Space is also important, in fact critical, to store any precalculated aggregates [Kimb96, Thom97c].

A sample calculation of space requirements illustrates the problem of space inflation. In the preceding Nike shoe example, given that each record attribute (field) has a length of 5 bytes, we have

Time dimension: monthly data over 3 years

Location dimension: 4,000 stores

Product dimension: 20 types of shoes

Number of line items per month for shoe sales: $4000 \times 20 = 80{,}000$

Number of base fact records: $80{,}000 \times 36$ months
$= 2{,}880{,}000$ records

Number of key fields + fact fields = 6

Base fact table size = $2{,}880{,}000 \times 6 = 17{,}280{,}000$ bytes (16.48 MB)

This by itself is not large, but with new dimensions it can explode quickly. For instance, if we want to keep track of all types of all products (20,000 products), the base table size increases to 16.48 GB. If we then start looking at different levels of time and location, the table size continues to increase rapidly to the terabyte level and beyond. Thus we have a major problem of having to decide which tables to pre-aggregate and how to store the data. In general, data inflation depends on the quantity of derived data needed, which is a function of the number of dimensions and dimension members.

Data inflation also depends on the degree of sparsity of the input data. It is well known that the ratio of derived data to input data increases dramatically as the degree of sparsity increases. Therefore, even though input data that is 80% sparse is only half the density of data that is 40% sparse, the derived data from the 80% sparse input data is typically considerably more than half of the derived data from the 40% sparse input data [Kimb96, Thom97c].

How to Store Aggregate Data

There are two basic ways to store aggregate data. One is to have a separate derived fact table for each aggregate (as shown in the preceding example). The other is to build new level fields within the original fact and dimension tables, thus expanding those tables considerably. The argument in favor of separate derived fact tables is to keep the data organization simple with more tables, which are kept transparent from the end user. The second approach has fewer tables but is more complex and has approximately the same amount of total data [Kimb96]. It should also be noted that the creation of aggregate fact table records requires the creation of artificial keys (foreign keys) in each referenced dimension. The second approach works well for a small number of aggregates and users.

When to Preaggregate the Derived Data

The use of prestored summaries or aggregates is possibly the single most effective tool for the data warehouse designer to control performance. The following options illustrate the wide spectrum of possible approaches being used today [Bulo96, Kimb96, Thom97]:

1. *Preaggregate nothing.* This strategy implies that all aggregations are to be computed at run time as needed. The main advantage is that this approach incurs no overhead to preaggregate but has the disadvantage of slow queries for aggregate reports in many cases. This would be a proper strategy only when very little querying is going on.

2. *Preaggregate nothing, but save the materialized view.* This is a variation of strategy 1 that allows you to save the materialized view (aggregate data) after it is used to answer a specific query on the input data. This has the advantage of making future queries for this derived data, or for further aggregations built on top of this derived data, much faster. In other words, for queries with a high degree of locality, this approach works well.
3. *Preaggregate everything.* This strategy is only feasible for an environment with a small number of dimensions and dimension members. Otherwise, the overhead to set up the derived fact tables, storage space, and updating of derived data would be prohibitive. The main advantage of this approach is very fast query time for aggregate reports.
4. *Preaggregate selectively, based on known statistics.* Experience with working data warehouses has shown that preaggregation improves performance for aggregates that are most often used as inputs to other calculations and those that depend on the greatest number of inputs, that is, those aggregates that are the most active. Similarly, aggregates that should be delayed for calculation until request time are those that are least requested by end users, those that are least used by other calculations, and those that are least costly to compute.

It is very difficult, if not impossible, to anticipate all the aggregate (formula-based) queries that end users may want to use. The most flexible systems allow the user to iteratively formulate queries based on previous results. Based on detailed data collection of an operating OLAP environment and/or studies of end-user habits, a more scientific approach to determining which data to preaggregate can be made. Analysis of preaggregation is still an active research topic.

9.4.4 OLAP Physical Design

OLAP physical design is not a well-structured discipline as yet, but we can gain some insight by observing the basic trade-offs and performance tuning methods used today. Most of our knowledge of physical database design techniques can be applied here (see Chapter 6).

Much of the physical design aspect of OLAP is associated with using RAM and disk to support the aggregation and preaggregation of data. The basic issue between RAM and disk is when to use each one. If the amount of data is small, up to several hundred megabytes, RAM alone may suffice since current large systems are known to have up to 1 GB of RAM and even desktop computers have 32 MB or more. However, disk is needed for persistent storage and must always be used as backup for RAM. Disk availability can be measured in terms of hundreds of gigabytes or several terabytes for some of the large systems today. As disks get larger, the designer is able to preaggregate more data and devote more space to indexes.

Sparse data is common to OLAP applications. Therefore, it is important to use good data compression and sparse data indexing techniques whenever possible. These techniques usually degrade query time to preserve space, so this trade-off needs to be looked at closely in terms of available resources.

The star schema uses a single fact table to store data. In large applications it may be more appropriate to partition the fact table into smaller tables for different groups of variables, depending on their sparsity, which dimensions they represent, and where the data originates.

OLAP products sometimes improve performance by determining the minimum amount of data needed to fill the user's screen and then querying only that amount of data initially. If the user chooses to scroll data as part of an iterative approach of analysis, the next window of data must be requested quickly to overlap the use of available resources.

9.5 Data Mining

Data mining is the activity of sifting through large files and databases to discover useful, nonobvious, and often unexpected trends and relationships. It helps the interactive user to find patterns among the data, using predictive methods such as classification, clustering, or regression analysis. The goals of data mining can be summarized in terms of two types of activities: discovery of new patterns and verification of a user's hypothesis about patterns.

Data mining is closely related to data warehousing and in fact is highly dependent on the use of the data warehouse to organize, clean, and integrate the data before the search process can begin. After the user has made a "discovery" from the mining process, further queries are usually necessary to confirm the results and explore further. Data warehouses are set up to support this type of inquiry.

Typical applications of data mining include searches for credit card fraud, determination of which loan applications are most likely to succeed (or fail), and unforeseen marketing trends that will boost sales (e.g., which items people tend to purchase together and whether it would make sense to put those items in close proximity in the store). Uses have also been found in health care prediction, sales and profitability analysis, investment analysis, customer profiling, forecasting, space exploration, biosequence patterns, and earthquake analysis [Bran96, FHS96]. Data mining requires a higher degree of intelligence than purely SQL or OLAP queries because of the unknown nature of the patterns and trends. However, there is now a significant trend toward integrating OLAP and data mining because of the usefulness of OLAP aggregate data in the mining process [Pars97, Thom97b, Fayy98].

It is useful to distinguish between data mining and knowledge discovery, although there is still considerable overlap among their definitions from different sources [OHE96, FPS96, WeIn98]. *Knowledge discovery* can be thought of as the process of discovering useful information, whereas data mining can be viewed as the set of techniques or algorithms for carrying out that discovery. A data mining tool is often referred to as an intelligent agent. A relatively new discipline, *knowledge discovery in databases* (KDD), commonly represents the overall process of selecting and preparing the data as well as searching it and interpreting the results. Data mining is considered to be a very critical step in the KDD process—the enumeration of trends and patterns from the data on the basis of some model of classification and/or clustering.

A major issue in data mining is to figure out which patterns are "interesting" and need to be pursued further and to discard the many uninteresting patterns that show up. Some patterns are extremely obvious and uninteresting while others show up from purely random data and need to be discarded. Generic and domain-specific tools to support discovery tasks are summarized in [Bran96].

In this section we look at each of the steps of the KDD process, including data mining, in more detail. Then we look at some of the more common approaches and methodologies for the predictive functions of data mining. A list of current vendors of KDD and data mining technology is given in Appendix D.

9.5.1 The Knowledge Discovery in Databases (KDD) Process

KDD brings together methodologies from disciplines such as database theory, statistics, pattern recognition, machine learning, data visualization, and high-performance computing. The basic steps of KDD, illustrated in Figure 9.11, are data selection and cleaning, data transformation and

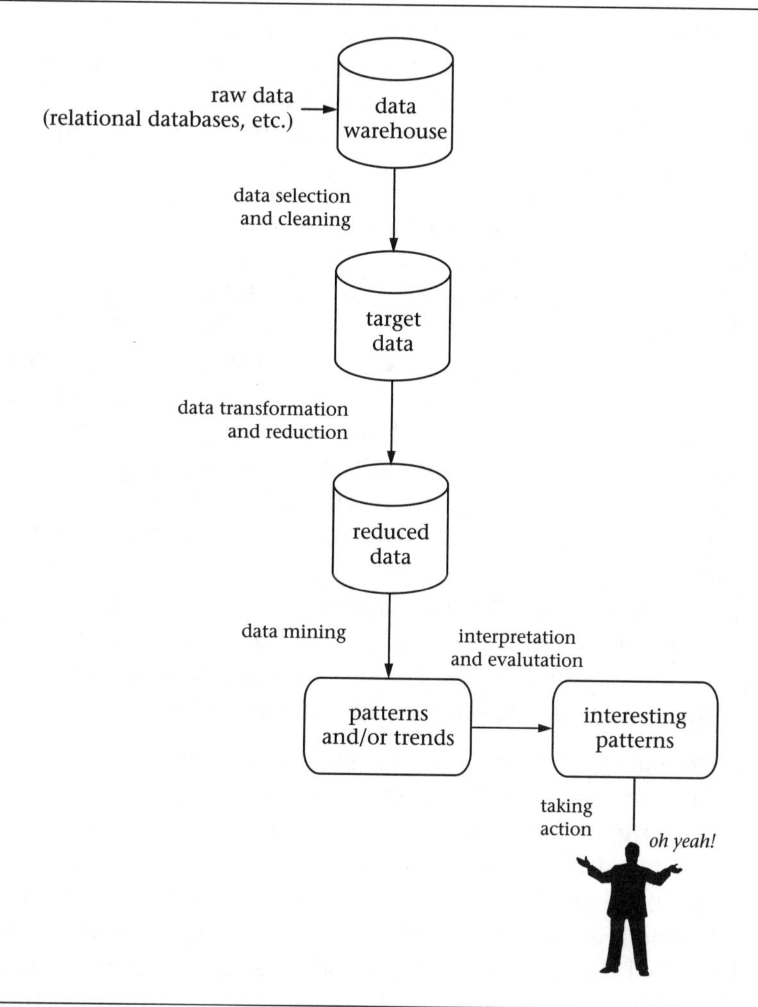

Figure 9.11 The KDD Process

reduction, data mining (the predictive model), interpretation and evaluation of the mined data, and taking action based on each new discovery [Fayy98, WeIn98]. Let us take a look at each of these steps in more detail.

1. *Data selection and cleaning.* We assume that the raw data has been organized with a unified logical view and has been implemented in a data warehouse (DW). Basic operations of data extraction, cleaning, transformation, and loading already should have been accomplished as part of the DW setup. However, additional data selection and cleaning needs to be done specifically for the data

mining task. This includes handling missing data fields, detecting and removing noisy data and outliers if required, and enforcing any other constraints specified in the requirements. The result of this step should be in some standard form such as a spreadsheet or relational database.

2. *Data transformation and reduction.* The cleaned data must now be transformed into a form that is compatible with the data mining (prediction) software. Typical transformations include steps to reduce the dimensionality by replacing several fields with a derived field or by summarizing several rows into an aggregate row (data reduction as a form of rollup). Other transformations actually do the opposite—adding new fields that are judged relevant to the data mining problem. Most often, however, the goal is to reduce the number of dimensions (variables). Time-oriented data often needs to be transformed into a more manageable format. Finally, some transformations are associated with statistical measures and involve data smoothing associated with regression techniques, or data normalization operations such as scaling of decimal numbers, or standard deviation normalization that makes the data compatible with the program format expectations.

3. *Data mining.* Data mining has several aspects: choosing the function of the data mining model (e.g., summarization, classification, clustering, or regression, as described in Section 9.5.2), choosing the data mining search algorithm (or algorithms) to look for patterns in the data, and executing the algorithm. A pattern could be a predictive model, a data summary, a data segmentation, or a model of dependencies or links in the data. The main issues addressed by data mining are how to minimize or avoid having to scan the entire database; how to automate the process more and reduce the workload on the user, making the mined data more understandable to the user; and how to find patterns that are "interesting" to the user.

4. *Interpretation and evaluation.* The selected patterns are evaluated to see which ones are interesting and subject to further analysis. They must then be interpreted into a form that is understandable by the user or application that uses them. Key criteria for evaluation include validity, utility, novelty, and understandability.

5. *Taking action on the discovery.* Once some discovery has been made, it should be used to take action in the real world. If the user is an

application, the process of interpretation and evaluation may be integrated with software to do the prediction or control.

9.5.2 Data Mining Methods

In this section we look at the methods used in data mining to get a clearer picture of the breadth of this discipline. First, however, we need to understand the two basic components of data used in data mining—cases and features. A *case* is a specific entity or event commonly represented as a record, for instance, a particular loan to a small business. A *feature*, on the other hand, is a particular measurement on the data, for example, recent profit, outstanding debt, or the applicant's credit rating. A feature is usually represented as an attribute. The volume of features is typically in the tens or hundreds, while the volume of cases is typically in the thousands or millions. A typical mission of data mining is to observe certain features for a variety of cases and come up with a decision criteria for new (unlabeled) cases. For instance, it looks at outstanding debt and credit rating for an applicant to see if their loan is too big a risk or not, then labels their case as desirable or undesirable in terms of risk of default on the loan.

The methods of data mining fall roughly into the following categories [Fayy98, FPS96, WeIn98]:

1. *Predictive modeling.* This involves using one or more fields (features) in the data to predict the rest of the fields. This is called *classification* when the field (variable) being predicted is categorical for the many cases considered. For example, a categorical (discrete) variable would be whether credit card fraud is likely or unlikely or whether a loan is desirable or not desirable. When the variable is continuous, the result is a number such as total sales, and this is called *regression*. Popular techniques used to support predictive modeling include linear regression, neural networks (nonlinear regression), decision trees, and association rules.
2. *Database segmentation.* Database segmentation (or clustering) looks for groups or clusters of records or rows (cases) that have certain similarities, usually according to the values of their attributes. Thus, a large problem is segmented into several smaller problems that form natural clusters. An example would be the collection of customers of a certain type of income or education. The clustering is not predefined but determined only from the

current data. Popular techniques used to support segmentation include k-means clustering and the Estimation-Maximization (EM) algorithm.

3. *Data summarization and link analysis. Summarization* provides a simple, compact description for a subset of data, typically across fields (columns) rather than records (rows). Examples include the sum, mean, or standard deviation across fields of data, commonly for but not limited to repeating groups; and they are commonly used for interactive exploratory analysis, report generation, or visualization. Closely associated with summarization is *link analysis,* which determines associations between fields. For example, link analysis is used to determine which products tend to be purchased together.
4. *Dependency analysis or modeling. Dependency modeling* tries to find the most significant dependencies among two or more variables. In some cases you must actually compute the joint probability density of the variables. This can be extremely difficult in high-dimensional databases. Dependency modeling tends to focus on continuous data, whereas link analysis focuses on discrete or categorical data. Another form of dependency analysis, called *sequence analysis,* looks for sequential patterns or trends over time and is used mostly for time-dependent data (i.e., time series analysis).
5. *Change and deviation analysis.* This method focuses on determining the most significant changes in data from one set of data to the next, whether over time or some other measure. It must account for the sequence in which the data sets appear [FPSU96].
6. *Optimization searching.* Data mining search algorithms tend to fall into two categories: Parameter search within a model and search among models. In the former category, well-known optimization search algorithms are used, for example, gradient methods for nonlinear optimization. In the latter category, greedy heuristic algorithms are usually used.

In summary, data mining is still an emerging technology area, and many changes will continue to occur over the next several years as the database, machine learning, and statistical communities learn to come together better.

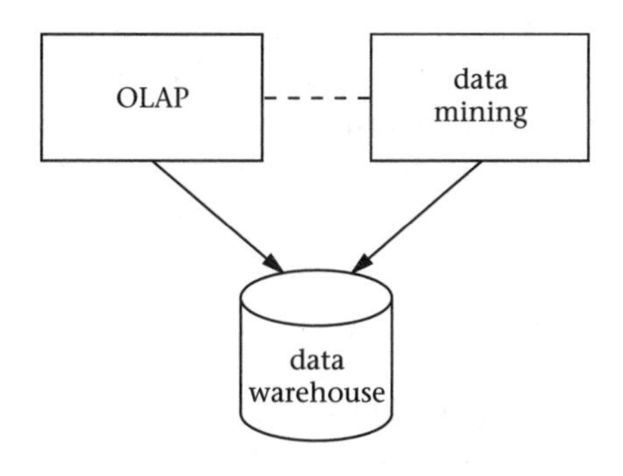

Figure 9.12 Data warehouse and analysis tools

9.6 Summary

The fundamentals of data warehousing, OLAP, and data mining are described in this chapter. The data warehouse is defined as a large repository of historical data that can be integrated for decision support. The major disciplines for decision support are on-line analytical processing (OLAP) and data mining (see Figure 9.12). The text first defines the requirements for data warehousing and then describes a variety of data warehouse architectures that try to meet those requirements. Next, we look at the logical and physical design aspects of data warehouses and denote the differences between a data warehouse and a typical relational database. The star schema is recommended as the basic logical data model, with its large fact table and smaller independent dimension tables. Variations of the star schema are used to satisfy particular requirements such as time-dependent data analysis. On the physical design side, we look at advances in indexing using bitmap indexes and methods for view materialization.

OLAP is a major decision support tool applied to data warehouses and has common features such as dimensions, hypercubes, hierarchies, formulas, and links. We investigate the details of each feature and how to design them for each step in the logical design process. Logical design also involves the selection of aggregations, the storage of aggregate data, and the analysis of trade-offs between when to preaggregate the derived data used for decision analysis and when to aggregate dynamically.

Data mining is also a very sophisticated discipline for searching and analyzing data in a data warehouse and is used to look for unknown patterns and trends in the data. As such, it has the unique requirement of predictive modeling and is closely associated with statistical and machine learning techniques. We look at the overall knowledge discovery in database (KDD) process and how data mining methods are used to enhance that process. Current research is focusing on how to combine OLAP and data mining tools most effectively.

Literature Summary

Much of the original work on data warehousing was done by Inmon [Inmo92a]. Some recent books of significant interest are by Kimball [Kimb96], Barquin and Edelstein [BaEd97], Devlin [Devl97], Mattison [Matt96], and Watson and Gray [WaGr97]. An excellent book on OLAP that is very easy to read is by Thomsen [Thom97c]. Another OLAP book of note is by Pendse and Creeth [PeCr95]; the original list of OLAP rules by Codd is in [Codd95]. Major recent data mining books are by Fayyad et al. [FPSU96], Lin and Cercone [LiCe96], and Weiss and Indurkhya [WeIn96]. Fayyad is also the main contributor and editor of a special "Communications of the ACM" issue on data mining [CACM96].

[AdZa96] Adriaans, P., and Zantinge, D. *Data Mining*, Addison-Wesley Longman, Reading, MA, 1996.

[BaEd97] Barquin, R., and Edelstein, H. (editors). *Planning and Designing the Data Warehouse*, Prentice Hall, Upper Saddle River, NJ, 1997, Chapter 10 (OLAP).

[BaSu97] Barbara, D., and Sullivan, M. "Quasi-Cubes: Exploiting approximations in multidimensional databases," *SIGMOD Record* 26, 3 (Sept. 1997), pp. 12–17.

[BeSm97] Berson, A., and Smith, S.J. *Data Warehousing, Data Mining, & OLAP*, McGraw-Hill, New York, 1997.

[Bran96] Branchman, R.J., Khabaza, T., Kloesgen, W., Piatetsky-Shapiro, G., and Simoudis, E. "Mining Business Databases," *Comm. ACM* 39, 11 (Nov. 1996), pp. 42–48.

[Bulo96] Bulos, D. "OLAP Database Design: A New Dimension," *Database Prog. & Design* 9, 6 (June 1996), pp. 33–37.

[CACM96] *Comm. ACM* (Special Issue: *Data Mining and Knowledge Discovery in Databases*), Fayyad, U., and Uthurusamy, R. (editors), 39, 11 (Nov. 1996), 24–68.

[Cata97] Cataldo, J. "Care and Feeding of the Data Warehouse," *Database Prog. & Design* 10, 12 (Dec. 1997), pp. 36–42.

[ChDa97] Chaudhuri, S., and Dayal, U. "An Overview of Data Warehousing and OLAP Technology," *SIGMOD Record* 26, 1 (March 1997), pp. 65–74.

[Codd95] Codd, E.F. "Twelve Rules for On Line Analytical Processing," *Computerworld*, April 13, 1995.

[Coll96] Colliat, G. "OLAP, Relational, and Multidimensional Database Systems," *SIGMOD Record* 25, 3 (Sept. 1996), pp. 64–69.

[Devl97] Devlin, B. *Data Warehouses: From Architecture to Implementation*, Addison-Wesley, Reading, MA, 1997.

[Ever96] Evernden, R. "The Information FrameWork," *IBM Syst. J.* 35, 1 (1996), pp. 16–27.

[Fayy98] Fayyad, U. "Diving into Databases," *Database Prog. & Design* 11, 3 (March 1998), pp. 24–31.

[FHS96] Fayyad, U., Haussler, D., and Stolorz, P. "Mining Scientific Data," *Comm. ACM* 39, 11 (Nov. 1996), pp. 51–57.

[FPS96] Fayyad, U., Piatetsky-Shapiro, G., and Smyth, P. "The KDD Process for Extracting Useful Knowledge from Volumes of Data," *Comm. ACM* 39, 11 (Nov. 1996), pp. 27–34.

[FPSU96] Fayyad, U.M., Piatetsky-Shapiro, G., Smyth, P., and Uthurusamy, R. (editors). *Advances in Knowledge Discovery and Data Mining,* MIT Press, Cambridge, MA, 1996.

[Fren95] French, C.D. "'One Size Fits All' Database Architectures Do Not Work for DSS," *Proc. 1995 ACM SIGMOD Intl. Conf. on Management of Data,* M. Carey and D. Schneider, (editors), *SIGMOD Record* 24, 2 (1995), pp. 449–450.

[GBJP97] Gray, J., Bosworth, A., Jayman, A., and Pirahesh, H. "Data Cube: A Relational Aggregation Operator Generalizing Group-by, Cross-Tab and Sub Totals," *Data Mining and Knowledge Discovery* 1, 1 (1997), pp. 29–53.

[Grim98] Grimes, S. "The New Face of Data Access," *Database Prog. & Design* 11, 2 (Feb. 1998), pp. 35–40.

[Grov98] Groves, S. "Business Intelligence Products," Savant, *http://www.sgroves.demon.co.uk/bi_products.html.*

[GrWa98] Gray, P., and Watson, H.J. *Decision Support in the Data Warehouse,* Prentice Hall, Upper Saddle River, NJ, 1998.

[HHW97] Hellerstein, J.M., Haas, P.J., and Wang, H.J. "Online Aggregation," *Proc. 1997 ACM SIGMOD Conf. on Mgt. of Data,* Tucson, AZ, pp. 171–182.

[HRU96] Harinarayan, V., Rajaraman, A., and Ullman, J. "Implementing Data Cubes Efficiently," *Proc. 1996 ACM SIGMOD Conf. on Mgt. of Data,* Montreal, pp. 205–216.

[IBM94] IBM. "IFW Financial Services Data Model Description," IFW 03101, IBM Corporation, San Jose, CA, 1994.

[Inmo92a] Inmon, W.H. *Building the Data Warehouse*, Wiley-QED Publishing, Somerset, NJ, 1992.

[Inmo92b] Inmon, W.H. "Should We Rewrite History?" *Database Prog. & Design* 5, 3 (March 1992), pp. 70–71.

[Kimb96] Kimball, R. *The Data Warehouse Toolkit*, John Wiley & Sons, New York, 1996.

[LiCe96] Lin, T.Y., and Cercone, N. *Rough Sets and Data Mining*, Kluwer, Norwell, MA, 1996.

[LiWa96] Li, C., and Wang, X.S. "A Data Model for Supporting On-Line Analytical Processing," *Proc. CIKM Conf.*, 1996.

[Matt96] Mattison, R. *Data Warehousing: Strategies, Technologies, and Techniques*, McGraw-Hill, New York, 1996.

[MeKh96] Meredith, M.E., and Khader, A. "Divide and Aggregate: Designing Large Warehouses," *Database Prog. & Design* 9, 6 (June 1996), pp. 24–30.

[MQM97] Mumick, I.S., Quass, D., and Mumick, B.S. "Maintenance of Data Cubes and Summary Tables in a Warehouse," *Proc. 1997 ACM SIGMOD Intl. Conf. on Mgt. of Data*, pp. 100–111.

[OHE96] Orfali, R., Harkey, D., and Edwards, J. *The Essential Client/Server Survival Guide* (2nd Ed.), John Wiley & Sons, New York, 1996.

[ONGr95] O'Neil, P., and Graefe, G. "Multi-Table Joins through Bitmapped Join Indices," *SIGMOD Record* 24, 3 (Sept. 1995).

[Pars97] Parsaye, K. "OLAP and Data Mining: Bridging the Gap," *Database Prog. & Design* 10, 2 (Feb. 1997), pp. 30–37.

[PDH97] Papiani, M., Dunlop, A.N., and Hey, A.J.G. "Automatic Web Interfaces and Browsing for Object-Relational Databases," *Advances in Databases: Proc. 15th British National Conf. on Databases, BNCOD15*, 1997, pp. 131–132.

[PeCr95] Pendse, N., and Creeth, R. *The OLAP Report: Succeeding with On-Line Analytical Processing*, Business Intelligence Ltd., London, 1995.

[Poe96] Poe, V. *Building a Data Warehouse for Decision Support*, Prentice Hall, Upper Saddle River, NJ, 1996.

[RKR97] Roussopoulos, N., Kotidis, Y., and Roussopoulos, M. "Cubetree: Organization of and Bulk Incremental Updates on the Data Cube," *Proc. 1997 ACM SIGMOD Intl. Conf. on Mgt. of Data*, pp. 89–99.

[Simo95] Simon, A.R. *Strategic Database Technology: Management for the Year 2000*, Morgan Kaufmann, San Francisco, 1995.

[Stod97] Stoddard, D. "The Database Dozen," *Database Prog. & Design* 10, 13 (Dec. 1997), pp. 8–24.

[Thom97a] Thomsen, E. "Dimensional Modeling: An Analytical Approach," *Database Prog. & Design* 10, 3 (March 1997), pp. 29–35.

[Thom97b] Thomsen, E. "Mining Your Way to OLAP," *Database Prog. & Design* 10, 9 (Sept. 1997), pp. 101–103.

[Thom97c] Thomsen, E. *OLAP Solutions*, John Wiley & Sons, New York, 1997.

[WaGr97] Watson, H.J., and Gray, P. *Decision Support in the Data Warehouse*, Prentice Hall, Upper Saddle River, NJ, 1997.

[WeIn98] Weiss, S.M., and Indurkhya, N. *Predictive Data Mining*, Morgan Kaufmann, San Francisco, 1998.

[ZDN97] Zhao, Y., Deshpande, P.M., and Naughton, J.F. "An Array-Based Algorithm for Simultaneous Multidimensional Aggregates," *Proc. 1997 ACM SIGMOD Conf. on Mgt. of Data*, pp. 159–170.

10 Advanced Database Technologies

Companies that own large and complex databases normally assign the task of managing them to a database administrator (DBA), who organizes teams of programmers and analysts according to the existing applications and software systems being used to drive those applications. The DBA and the database teams must constantly be watching for the advance of new technologies in database systems so they can evolve efficiently from legacy relational systems to those systems that improve functionality and performance.

This chapter focuses on the changes needed for database design methodologies as we progress from relational databases to advanced technologies such as object-oriented, object-relational, spatial, multimedia, temporal, text, active, and real-time database systems. The technologies are ordered starting with those that are real now with stand-alone systems available and those making the greatest impact today. They are followed by those technologies with narrower focus and less maturity. Similarly, the database design techniques for the more mature systems are better tested, whereas those for the less mature systems tend to be still experimental in nature.

10.1 Architecture for Advanced Technologies

A simplistic and useful way to view the wide spectrum of advanced database technologies is with the architecture and taxonomy shown in Figure 10.1. The architecture has three parts: the general classes of database

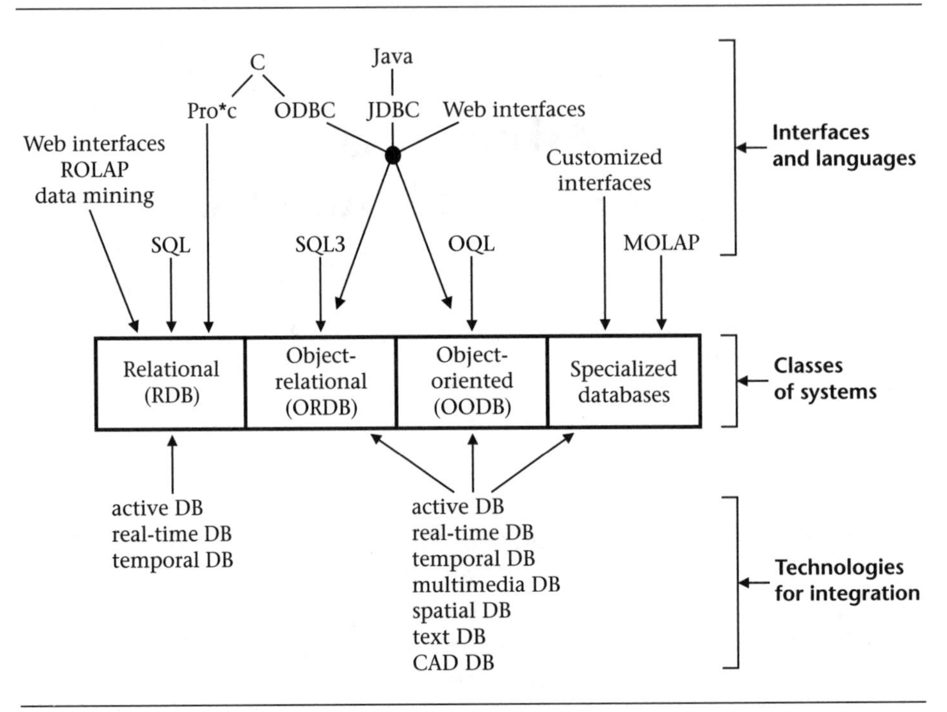

Figure 10.1 Advanced database architecture

systems, the new technologies that can be integrated into those systems, and the interfaces and languages with which the systems are compatible.

10.1.1 General Classes of Database Systems

Individual database system implementations can be classified as relational, object-relational, object-oriented, or specialized. Relational databases (RDBs) have been in existence since the 1970s and are the most commercially available systems in the world. Some older types of systems (e.g., CODASYL and IMS) are still in use today but are not usually applied to new applications.

In the late 1980s object-oriented database (OODB) systems were proposed, and many variations have been implemented over the past 10 years. They initially filled a niche left open by relational databases for nontext data types and are now trying to compete with relational databases in terms of user interfaces and performance. An object-oriented database stores and retrieves data as objects and as such has a much broader range of applications (scientific and engineering databases) than the relational model. OODBs have their own unique data structures and query languages, and they support abstract data types (ADTs). Examples of OODBs include Gemstone, Itasca, Jasmin, O_2, Objectivity, ObjectStore, ORION, and Versant.

An object-relational database (ORDB) is an extension of a relational database that supports the object concept to some degree (new data types, encapsulation, inheritance, etc.). ORDBs have, for the most part (with the exception of CA-Ingres in 1988), only been commercially available since the mid-1990s: DB2/6000 C/S, Illustra, ODB II, Odapter, Omniscience, and UniSQL [StMo96]. While there is considerable debate between the OODB and ORDB communities as to which technology is superior, it is clear that both will continue to thrive over the next five years. They will also converge as query languages such as SQL3 [Beec93, MeMa95, SQL3] and open access languages such as the Java Database Connectivity (JDBC) specification [Java96, HaCa97] or Microsoft's Open Database Connectivity (ODBC) become more standardized and commonplace for object-relational systems. OODB vendors are incorporating these languages to stay competitive [Papi97]. JDBC is being supported by the major database vendors and allows open database connectivity from within Java. ODBC allows a C application to connect to data in any one of many DBMSs (e.g., Oracle, DB2, NonStop SQL).

The decision as to which technology to buy, OODB or ORDB, depends largely on the extent of legacy relational databases you have and the new types of applications you need that cannot be represented by relational databases alone. If you have extensive legacy relational systems and few new applications, for instance, then ORDB would be preferred as the near-future technology shift. For more specialized engineering and multimedia applications, a clear break to OODB may be the better choice.

Finally, in some cases specialized databases have been required because new technology could not be immediately integrated into one of the existing database system types. For example, many multidimensional databases used with OLAP have their own unique implementations, and some multimedia databases do not fit well into OODBs. The most common criteria cited for the use of specialized databases are scalability and performance.

10.1.2 New Database Technologies for System Integration

Time-oriented databases such as temporal, active, and real-time have been successfully integrated into relational, OODB, and ORDB systems [Rama96, Papi97, Zani97, SQL3]. Abstract data-oriented databases such as computer-aided design (CAD), spatial, and text have been integrated into OODBs or ORDBs or, more frequently, as in the case of multimedia, implemented as a specialized database [CMCL95, Zani97].

10.1.3 Database Interfaces and Languages

Typical user interfaces for relational databases include SQL, embedded SQL in a host language like C (as in Oracle's Pro*C), and forms (such as Microsoft Access, Visual Basic, or Oracle Forms). On-line analytical processing (OLAP) techniques, when applied to relational databases or data warehouses of relational databases, are referred to as ROLAP. More sophisticated techniques to search data for unforeseen trends and insights are part of data mining. World Wide Web interfaces are available to relational and object databases today and continue to evolve [Papi97]. Active database features, such as triggers, have become part of mainstream relational systems and the SQL3 standard. Some of the temporal extensions to SQL include TempSQL, HSQL for the historical data model, and TSQL2, which might eventually be incorporated into the evolving SQL3 standard [SQL3, Zani97].

The new SQL3 standard will include many object concepts and will eventually be used by relational, OODB, and ORDB systems. The object-oriented part of SQL3 falls under the development of MOOSE—Major Object-Oriented SQL Extensions [Simo95]. Similarly, the Object Database Management Group (ODMG) is a standardization effort that began in 1991 to provide portability for database schemas, data manipulation languages, and query languages [Catt95]. Its goal is to integrate database capabilities with object programming methods. Its basic components are an object definition language (ODL), similar to a standard data definition language, an object manipulation language (OML), and an object query language (OQL), which was a missing and sorely needed element in the earlier OODB systems.

Finally, specialized databases will likely need unique interfaces until they can be integrated into mainstream systems. For example, multidimensional OLAP (MOLAP) is the term applied to interfaces to special multidimensional databases.

10.2 Object-Oriented and Object-Relational Databases

Both object-oriented databases (OODBs) and object-relational databases (ORDBs) are undergoing wide acceptance as the basis of the next generation of databases. All the major vendors of relational DBMSs are developing object-relational versions of their current systems. As discussed in Section 10.1, OODBs and ORDBs are providing the foundation for advanced technologies such as CAD, spatial, temporal, and (to some degree) multimedia databases. Consequently, there is a need for new database design techniques to handle the wide variety of data types prevalent in the industry today.

In terms of logical database design, we have already discussed the object modeling technique (OMT) for conceptual modeling of object databases in Section 2.3, a methodology that will in all likelihood continue to be the dominant one in the logical design of object databases for the next several years [BlPr98]. However, in terms of object modeling, the OMT notation is being superceded by the unified modeling language (UML) notation, and the OMT authors are upgrading the OMT process to work with the UML notation [FoSc97, TeWi97, BRJ98, BlPr98].

In this section we focus our attention on the physical design aspects of object databases and, in particular, on the various proposed (and, in some cases, implemented) indexing methods. Other physical design techniques, such as caching and pointer swizzling, can be found in [KeMo94].

Indexing for object databases is heavily influenced by certain features that do not appear in relational databases: nested predicates, inheritance, and methods [Bert97]. Objects often have nested structures (i.e., unnormalized), and most object query languages allow objects to be restricted by predicates on both nested and nonnested attributes of objects. Nested predicates are often written as path expressions. To illustrate we continue the employee example in Chapter 2 (see Figure 2.2). The query, "Find the projects assigned to employees in the marketing department," can be represented by a path expression:

project.employee.department.deptname = "marketing"

Regarding inheritance, a query may refer to a class by itself or to a class and all its subclasses in the hierarchy. Methods can return derived attributes or logical constants (true or false) that can be used to determine whether or not the query is satisfied.

Object databases are oriented along two dimensions—aggregation and inheritance [Bert97]. The aggregation dimension treats classes as individual entities, and the index methods used to access them are referred to as *single-class* (SC) *indexes*. The inheritance dimension considers the entire hierarchy of classes and subclasses to be accessed, and the index methods used to access them are referred to as *class hierarchy* (CH) *indexes*. Traversal strategies can be either forward or reverse. *Forward traversal* visits the target class of the query first (the root of the query graph), and the remaining classes are traversed starting from the target class in any depth-first search order. *Reverse traversal* visits the target class of the query last, that is, it starts at the leaf nodes of the query graph and works toward the target class. The forward traversal strategy for the preceding query has the path expression project.employee.department; the reverse traversal strategy has the path expression department.employee.project.

10.2.1 Indexes for the Aggregation Dimension (Aggregation Graphs)

The basic indexing techniques for aggregation (aggregation graphs) are based on extensions of the B^+-tree concept commonly used in relational databases. The critical features of these techniques are summarized as follows [Bert97]:

1. *Multi-index*. The multi-index is really a set of n simple B^+-tree indexes for n classes specified in the path expression for a query. It is limited to reverse traversal only, working its way to the target class at the end of the chain of accesses. In the preceding example with the reverse traversal path expression department.employee.project, the multi-index consists of B^+-tree indexes for department names pointing to department numbers, department numbers pointing to employee numbers, and employee numbers pointing to project names. Note that scanning of each index could result in multiple "hits," so an inverted file format for the B^+-tree indexes might be required in many cases.
2. *Join index*. The join index is an extension of the multi-index to provide two-way traversal, forward or reverse, to handle more complex queries. It is a set of equijoin B^+-tree indexes that can easily be used in either direction. It is more suitable for high-selectivity queries that involve two or more classes.
3. *Nested index*. The nested index is a single B^+-tree index that acts like an inverted file and operates in the reverse traversal only. It is particularly useful for getting from the class at the start of the query path to the target class quickly when the query path is quite long, normally requiring a large value n for the multi-indexes. Retrieval time is very low for such queries, but there is a trade-off

with high update cost. In our example the index would have an entry for each department that points to a list of projects for the employees of that department.

4. *Path index*. The path index, like the nested index, is a single B^+-tree index, but instead of each entry pointing to a list of projects, it points to all instantiations of objects in the path of the query, including department numbers, employee numbers, and project names. This index is useful for complex queries involving select conditions that need to be applied to the intermediate path objects. Like the nested index, it pays a high price for update costs, but queries are very fast.
5. *Access support relation (ASR)*. The ASR is similar to the path index except that two B^+-tree indexes are allocated—one to the first class in the path and the other to the target class in the path—allowing bidirectional access to the full path instantiations. Queries are very fast, but once again, the update cost is high.

Relative performance results for these indexes are given in [BeKi89, Bert97] as well as descriptions of advanced index techniques such as path splitting, ASR decomposition, and join index hierarchy.

10.2.2 Indexes for the Inheritance Dimension (Inheritance Hierarchies)

In some cases object-oriented queries apply to both a class and all its subclasses in the hierarchy. These are called *class hierarchy* (CH) queries. For CH queries the single-class indexes associated with the aggregation dimension are inadequate.

1. *SC index*. The single-class index, or SC index, uses a B^+-tree index in the indexed attribute for each class in the inheritance hierarchy. This is efficient for a single-class query (SC query), but requires many index accesses for a CH query.
2. *CH-tree*. The class hierarchy tree, or CH-tree, uses a single B^+-tree index for the entire inheritance hierarchy and is very fast for queries to multiple classes in the hierarchy. Each entry consists of indexed attribute values for the root node of the hierarchy. The entry also has pointers to target attribute values associated with each class in the hierarchy. It can be used very efficiently for CH

queries and somewhat less efficiently for SC queries and has a high update cost.

3. *H-tree.* The H-tree attempts to combine the best features of the SC index and the CH-tree to handle both SC queries and CH queries efficiently. It uses a B+-tree index for each class in the inheritance hierarchy like the SC index, but the difference occurs because the B+-trees between a class and its subclasses are linked by pointers to speed up the access to the indexed attributes. The trade-off cost is higher storage space allocation and higher update costs. Enhancements of the H-tree, such as the CG-tree and the hcC-tree, show some improvements but still have serious trade-offs [Bert97].
4. *x-tree.* The x-tree is a two-dimensional approach that tries to combine the effects of indexed attribute indexing and class indexing [CGO97]. As such, it has similarities to the multidimensional indexing techniques R-tree and R*-tree, described in Section 10.3. The performance of the x-tree is better than the CH-tree for some situations and not as good in others.

For a more detailed comparative analysis of these techniques, see [Bert97]. A newly proposed index, the nested inheritance index, is a combination of the concepts from the nested index, join index, and CH-tree techniques, with a format similar to B+-tree indexes. Preliminary results show it has excellent query and good update performance.

10.3 Spatial and Geographic Databases

Spatial databases deal with geometric points and links as found in CAD systems or geographic information systems (GISs). *Geographic databases* are a subset of spatial databases that store geographic information such as maps. Properties of geometrical relationships that are preserved in spatial databases include connectivity, adjacency, order, and metric relations [ASS93]. Connectivity refers to being able to move from one road to another along a map; adjacency implies that two objects are separated by a clear boundary; order is illustrated by a series of landmarks along a given road; and metric relations refer to generic distance measures such as "near" and "far away."

Spatial database requirements are much more complex than conventional databases. They must handle complex data types and relationships, vast amounts of data, possible real-time access and query processing, and varying levels of granularity for the same type of data. Pattern recognition techniques are required, and the database system, rather than the application system, must determine the characteristics of an image through analysis of the image bit streams.

Spatial databases, such as CAD databases, are most often called upon to handle geometric information in the form of line segments and closed polygons in which the representation used is commonly the x,y coordinates of its endpoints. In the case of two-dimensional figures, like closed polygons, the vertices can also be represented by the x,y coordinates. Complex polygons can be reduced to simpler ones by triangulation—the process of dividing a more complex polygon into simple triangles. For curved figures, the curves can often be approximated by polygons. This process can be generalized to higher dimensions, 3D being the most common [KSS97]. Geographic data, as found in maps and satellite images, require pixel maps, orbit maps (raster data), or vector data obtained from basic geometric shapes or objects.

In classical relational databases, the most common queries are *exact match queries*, in which all attributes are specified and must match. *Partial match queries* are used when a subset of the attributes are specified. A *range query* is used when a single attribute range of values is specified. Finally, a *Boolean query* is used when attribute values are specified with Boolean operators such as AND, OR, and NOT.

Spatial queries extend the notion of queries as follows. First, *nearness queries* look for objects that lie near a given location. *Region queries* (range queries) look for objects that lie inside or partially inside a specified region. As an example, a query to locate all the auto repair shops in a given square-mile area of a large city would be a form of region query, whereas a query to find the nearest auto repair shop would be a form of nearness query, called the *nearest-neighbor query*. Queries that involve the intersection of two types of regions, for example, one involving air temperature maximums and the other the type of soil, can be determined using a *spatial join* [LoRa94, LoRa96, Zani97].

Indexing for spatial data includes the k-D tree (or the k-D-B tree, an extension to allow multiple child nodes just as a B-tree extends a binary tree for multiple child nodes), the quadtree, and the R-tree. In each of these methods, n-dimensional space is subdivided into smaller spaces to create greater isolation for the individual points that lie in the space given. Examples of these indexing methods are shown in Figure 10.2.

A *k-D tree* is a main memory (RAM) access method used to partition multidimensional space into disjoint subspaces. In Figure 10.2a various

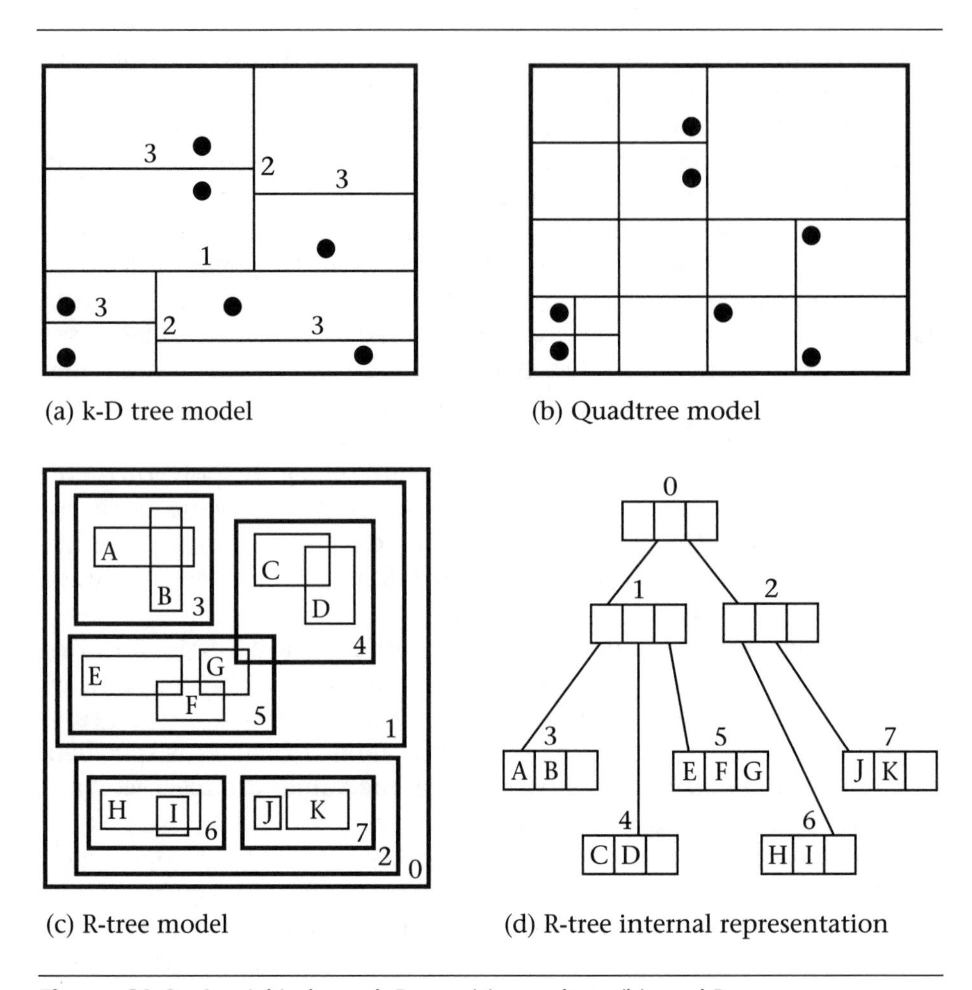

(a) k-D tree model

(b) Quadtree model

(c) R-tree model

(d) R-tree internal representation

Figure 10.2 Spatial indexes: k-D tree (a), quadtree (b), and R-tree (c) and (d) models

geometric points (dots) are shown in two-dimensional space representing the root of the tree. The tree (implemented as a binary tree) is partitioned by a single line (1) such that those points that lie in the upper partition go into the left subtree and those points that lie in the lower partition go into the right subtree. The next level of subtree is shown in the figure by a partition in the opposite direction (dimension or attribute), and the dimensions are rotated through the levels of subtrees in a consistent round-robin order with a different discriminator used at each step to separate subtrees. In a two-dimensional space the dimensions are simply alternated. Partitioning terminates when a subtree (node) has fewer than two points since the k-D tree is a binary tree.

A variation of the k-D tree, also a main memory access method, is the *quadtree* or *point quadtree*, as shown in Figure 10.2b. The quadtree starts at the same root as the k-D tree but then divides the space into equal-sized quadrants (quads) as long as the number of points (dots) in any given quadrant is greater than a specified threshold number. When all the quadrants have fewer numbers of points than or equal numbers of points to the threshold, the process terminates. (The threshold is 1 in the figure.) A variation of the quadtree, called the *MX quadtree* , is more balanced due to the emphasis on having the height of the tree independent of the number of nodes in the tree or of the order of insertion of those nodes [Subr98].

The *R-tree* is the dominant structure used today for indexing of geometric figures such as polygons, including rectangles, as shown in Figure 10.2c [Gutt84]. Polygons are stored only in leaf nodes, and tree nodes are defined by the minimum bounding rectangle (MBR) that encompass one or more geometric objects or other bounding boxes. Higher-level bounding boxes, for example, those that encompass other bounding boxes, form the intermediate nodes. The root node encompasses all the objects in the database. The bounding boxes are defined by the objects they encompass and may overlap other bounding boxes in geometric space. The R-tree is a balanced tree structure (see Figure 10.2d), as is a B-tree. When objects are inserted into the R-tree, a node is selected to hold the new object. If the node is full, it is split in the same manner as a B^+-tree, with equal splitting and split propagation up to the root if necessary. R-trees are storage efficient because polygons only need to be stored once, but sometimes at the cost of query time due to overlapped bounding boxes and multiple path searches. Variations such as the R^*-tree [BKSS90, Bert97] and the R^+-tree [SRF87] have been proposed and used to overcome some of these deficiencies.

10.4 Multimedia Databases

A *multimedia database* is a general term for a database that consists of unstructured (abstract) data such as image, video, audio, graphics, animation, hypertext, and hypermedia. *Hypertext* is a nonsequential (nonlinear) manner of looking at text-based information, including the capability to return to the point from which a given traversed path began; it maintains an infrastructure of information nodes and links, with pointers used to facilitate browsing and navigation among objects rather than user-induced operations [Simo95].

Hypermedia, on the other hand, involves the organization of multimedia information into nonlinear structures, with data organized into discrete chunks or objects. Hypermedia extends the hypertext paradigm into multimedia: instead of navigating among text objects only, hypermedia offers links among text, video, images, and voice [Simo95]. Hypermedia is rapidly becoming the primary user interface for multimedia applications; the World Wide Web is the best-known example of a hypermedia system. The basic modeling construct for hypermedia is the hypermedia link between arbitrary nodes, where a node can be a text document, image, video clip, and so on. Links can be directional or nondirectional, start from a node or some point within a node, and may or may not have other information associated with them. All these options could be supplied by the link generation facility [ElNa94].

Multimedia databases are very complex and must deal with a large number of complex issues. A data modeling approach must encompass the spectrum of numeric, text, graphic, animation, audio stream, and video sequences. Very little research has been done on logical design of multimedia databases. Data storage is another major issue. Multimedia databases must also support large objects (BLOBs) since video data can use many gigabytes of storage. Furthermore, there are problems of representation of multimedia data on disk, compression, and archiving of data. Fast access via special indexing techniques is the core of the performance issue, especially for the special problems of video playback and audio/video synchronization.

Multimedia data models are often based on the conceptual separation of the multimedia data and their presentation. Multimedia presentations involve complex specifications of layout, rate, color, user interface components, and quality of service (QoS). An interesting approach that provides clear separation is the layered multimedia data model (LMDM), illustrated in Figure 10.3 [ScWy95]. The lowest layer above the raw multimedia data is the data definition layer, which defines a multimedia data object class to provide the abstraction of data objects needed for the higher layers. The next higher layer is the data manipulation layer, providing services for grouping data objects into multimedia events. The third layer is the data presentation layer, which provides a description of how data is to be communicated to the user. The top layer, the control layer, describes how a multimedia composition is built up from individual presentations. It describes signals that the multimedia composition can accept from the user or I/O devices and what actions to take.

On the physical design side, most common multimedia formats use compression techniques to efficiently store and retrieve the data. The

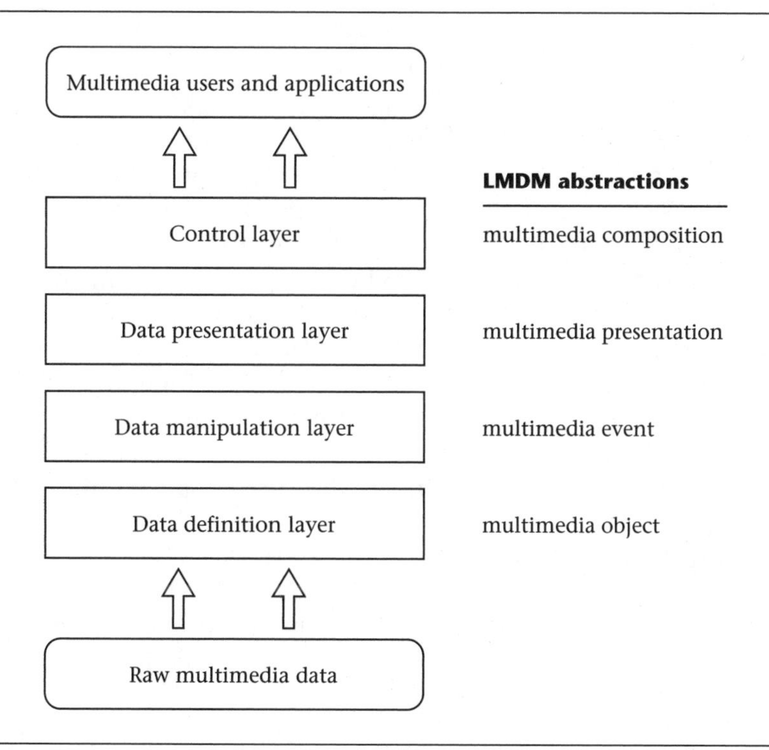

Figure 10.3 Layered multimedia data model (LMDM) [ScWy95]

Joint Picture Experts Group (JPEG) standard is most efficient for image data, whereas the Motion Picture Experts Group (MPEG-1) standard is better for video and audio data, storing a minute of 30 frame/second video in about 12.5 MB, compared to 75 MB for JPEG of the data video. The MPEG-2 standard is designed for digital broadcast systems and digital video disks and can put a one-minute video and audio in approximately 17 MB of disk storage [KSS97]. Other specialized performance-enhancing techniques such as disk striping, RAID architectures, scheduling, and buffer management are discussed in [Kuni95, ORS97].

Similarity-based retrieval is a common requirement, for example, fingerprint analysis, handwriting analysis, or image scanning for common shapes or shadings. Special indexes are required for such applications, beyond the B-tree or R-tree indexes used in spatial databases. The indexing of images can make use of either well-known image processing techniques or manual indexing techniques applied to images. The major issues are accuracy, performance, and scalability to more complex images.

A good introduction to content-based multimedia indexing is given by Faloutsos, based on the GEMINI method, in [Falo96, Zani97]. The GEMINI approach combines two ideas: first, a quick-and-dirty test to eliminate nonqualifying objects by extracting some k numerical features from each object tested; second, a further acceleration of the search by organizing the k-dimensional points using spatial access methods such as R*-trees, which group neighboring points together as a form of pruning the address space. This method has been applied successfully to time sequence data and two-dimensional color images. A survey and analysis of content-based image indexing techniques are given in [Bert97, GJM97]. In addition to using variations of classical indexing methods (e.g., inverted files, two-level B^+-trees) and methods from other database technologies (e.g., signature files, R-trees), several new structures are proposed, such as the three-tier color index and the sequenced multiattribute tree (SMAT).

Video and audio indexing techniques are discussed in detail in [Subr98]. Subrahmanian also compares the different multimedia architectures possible from the extremes of totally autonomous indexes for each type of media (video, image, text, etc.) to a unified index across all media.

10.5 Temporal Databases

A *temporal* database is one that includes the time property in all underlying data and that normally has validity intervals associated with each data element. It is also common to see active and temporal features in data warehouses because of their historical nature. A conventional database can be considered to be a *snapshot database*, that is, capturing the current state of the database in a single instant in time. On the other hand, a temporal database keeps track of previous states (versions) of the database after important (or all) updates.

There are two types of time in temporal databases. First, there is *valid time*—the time in which a certain fact about the enterprise becomes true in the real world. Valid time is often represented by a time interval, with a start (t_s) and end (t_e) time. Second, there is *transaction time*—the time when a change to the database is made during a transaction and that transaction is committed. Transaction-time databases support easy rollback to previous database states. A *valid-time database* is a form of temporal database that supports valid time and allows retroactive changes to the different versions of the database. A *bitemporal database* is a form of temporal database that supports both valid time and transaction time.

An example of a simple bitemporal database for project assignment and completion times is shown in Table 10.1, with columns for start_valid and end_valid times, and separate columns for start_trans and end_trans times. An end_valid time of NULL indicates that the end_valid time has not been fixed yet and is considered "now." The table shows transaction times for which those changes were recorded (and committed) into the database; that is, the time at which the new project assignment was actually stored in the database (start_trans) and the time an update to project completion (p1) was made or an erroneous project assignment (p3) was (logically) deleted from the database (end_trans). An end_trans time of NULL denotes that the associated fact is still true and logically in the database.

Table 10.1 Example bitemporal database: Project assignments

empid	*project*	*start_valid*	*end_valid*	*start_trans*	*end_trans*
e1	p1	01-JAN-98	NULL	05-JAN-98	03-JUL-98
e1	p1	01-JAN-98	30-JUN-98	03-JUL-98	NULL
e1	p2	30-JUN-98	15-SEP-98	10-JUL-98	NULL
e1	p3	01-JAN-98	NULL	05-JAN-98	14-FEB-98

In this example employee e1 starts working on project p1 on 01-JAN-98 with no known completion date. The first record is entered (created) on 05-JAN-98 with a NULL value for end_trans. However, it is updated on 03-JUL-98 as a logical deletion when we find out that employee e1 finished the project on 30-JUN-98. The second record is created to indicate the true project start and completion times, whereas the first record's end_valid time of NULL is no longer true and the record is logically deleted by specifying end_trans = 03-JUL-98.

The third record is created on 10-JUL-98 when we find out that employee e1 is scheduled to start project p2 on 30-JUN-98 with a fixed completion date of 15-SEP-98. The fourth record is created on 05-JAN-98 when we learn that employee e1 was supposed to be working on project p3 as well as p1 (compare first and fourth records). However, on 14-FEB-98 we find out this is not true; in fact, employee e1 never worked on project p3, so we logically delete the fourth record by entering end_trans = 14-FEB-98, the current date. At this point only the second and third records represent the current database.

From this table we can summarize the transactions as taking place on 05-JAN-98 (e1 starts working on p1 and p3), 14-FEB-98 (delete e1 working on p3), 03-JUL-98 (update e1 working on p1 with a known completion date), and 10-JUL-98 (e1 starts working on p2). We can also determine which records exist at certain rollback times (see Table 10.2).

Table 10.2 Bitemporal database rollback states

Rollback to:	*empid*	*project*	*start_valid*	*end_valid*	
01-JAN-98					no records
01-FEB-98	e1	p1	01-JAN-98	NULL	(first record)
	e1	p3	01-JAN-98	NULL	(fourth record)
01-MAR-98	e1	p1	01-JAN-98	NULL	(first record)
01-JUL-98	e1	p1	01-JAN-98	NULL	(first record)
15-JUL-98	e1	p1	01-JAN-98	30-JUN-98	(second record)
	e1	p2	30-JUN-98	15-SEP-98	(third record)

In terms of standards for SQL, temporal extensions were discussed but not implemented in SQL-92, but they are being considered for inclusion in SQL3. In addition, specialized temporal extensions to SQL, called TempSQL, HSQL for historical databases, and TSQL2, have been proposed and implemented [Simo95, Zani97]. For instance, in TSQL2, the data types include DATE, TIME, TIMESTAMP, INTERVAL, and PERIOD; temporal comparison operators include BEFORE, AFTER, DURING, EQUIVALENT, ADJACENT, OVERLAP, FOLLOWS, and PRECEDES. These greatly enhance the ease of coding queries and transactions. The command

```
CREATE TABLE salaryhist
   name  char(25),
   salary number
   AS VALID DAY AND TRANSACTION;
```

includes AS VALID DAY to denote valid time having a granularity of one day, and AND TRANSACTION to denote that transaction commit times will be noted in the database. The command

```
SELECT SNAPSHOT name, salary
from salaryhist;
```

from a temporally defined table retrieves all present and previous salaries for each person listed in the salaryhist table.

10.5.1 Types of Temporal Queries

The physical design of temporal databases involves the selection of indexing and clustering methods associated with variations of the B+-tree index and R-tree spatial index. To clarify the need for many types of indexes, we need to understand the types of queries typically found in OODBs but also often made in temporal databases [Bert97, SaTs98].

1. *Time slice query*—find all valid versions of the data during the given time interval T = $[t_s, t_e]$. For a valid-time database, list rows whose valid time falls within the query time interval. For a transaction-time database, list snapshots that occur within the query time interval.
   - *Intersection query*—given a time interval T, list all rows whose time intervals intersect it.
   - *Inclusion query*—given a time interval T, list all rows whose time intervals are wholly included with it.
   - *Containment query*—given a time interval T, list all rows whose time intervals contain it.
   - *Point query* (or *pure time-slice query*)—given a specific time point T (when $t_s = t_e$), list all rows whose time intervals intersect it. This is a special case of intersection queries when T is a single point.
2. *Key query*—list all historical versions for rows whose time invariant attribute (key) is within a given key range K = $[k_s, k_e]$.
3. *Key range time slice query*—list all rows within a given key range K that are valid within a time interval T, where K and T are as defined above. This type of query is an exact match if K and T are both reduced to a single point.
4. *Bitemporal time slice query*—list all versions that are valid during the time interval T as of a given transaction time T_r. As a variation of this type of query, a bitemporal key range time slice query is a bitemporal time slice query where the rows must be in the key range K.

10.5.2 Temporal Database Design

Many data models have been proposed for temporal databases [OzSn95]. A comprehensive summary of the basic concepts and taxonomy of temporal data models is given by Jensen and Snodgrass [JeSn96]. Temporal specialization is based on the different interactions between valid time and transaction time in temporal tables. Temporal specialization adds constraints on the interaction, and temporal generalization removes constraints from the interaction. One of the basic interactions is whether the facts stored in temporal rows are valid after the data is entered into the database *(predictively bounded)* or valid before the data is entered into the database *(retroactively bounded)*. If the valid times and transaction times are tightly coupled, they are described as degenerate. A typical constraint that specializes the temporal data model is when the temporal table is retroactively bounded and there is a bound on the time between when the fact is valid and when it was stored in the database; in this case it is called *delayed retroactive*. This taxonomy allows us to classify the many data models proposed.

The design of indexes for temporal queries is much more complex than for conventional database queries. Inverted indexes are usually avoided because data is multidimensional, based on key values and time, and hard to cluster efficiently for both dimensions. Most temporal indexes so far proposed have been based on variations of the B^+-tree or spatial indexes such as the R-tree [Gutt84], which can support both transaction time and valid time to some degree on two separate axes in a multidimensional index. There are no single optimal methods for all types of queries, but there exist those that work well for each special case. An excellent qualitative comparison of index methods for temporal databases is given in [Bert97], and a comprehensive quantitative performance analysis is given in [SaTs98]. Table 10.3 summarizes some of the leading index methods as a function of the type of query.

Time slice queries require indexes that are able to support retrieval based on time. The key range time slice queries require the support of both key and time line segments. The support of valid time requires more than the support of transaction time since valid time is normally expressed as an interval and allows dynamic insertion, deletion, and update of data. Bitemporal queries need the additional support of both transaction and valid time, and indexes are typically implemented as variations of spatial indexes.

As an example of a pure time slice query index, an Append-only tree is shown in Figure 10.4 as a variation of an ISAM index and B^+-tree. The index is built on valid start time (t_s) values in the database, with leaf nodes consisting of start time values and pointers to a bucket containing start times greater than the largest start time in the previous bucket and

Table 10.3 Temporal queries and appropriate indexes

Type of query	*Type of index*
1. Time slice query	
(transaction time)	Time-split B-tree (TSB tree) [LoSa93]
(valid time)	Append-only tree (AP tree) [GuSe93]
(valid time interval)	Time index [EWK90]
	Interval B-tree [AnTa95]
	B^+-tree with linear order represented in two-dimensional space and linearized [GLOT96]
	R-tree [Gutt84]
	Time polygon index (TP index) [SOL94]
	Checkpoint index [LeMu92]
	Snapshot index [TGH94]
2. Key query	Same access methods for historical data (time slice with valid time interval) with extensions to support both key and time dimensions
	Reverse chaining [BenZ82]—previous versions of a given key are linked together in chronological order; separate data stores for current and past data
	Time sequence arrays (TSAs)—array with a row for each key ever created and a column for a time instant
3. Key range time slice query	Same access methods as for time slice queries with extensions to support both key and time dimensions
	ST-tree [GuSe93]
4. Bitemporal time slice query	Dual R-tree [KTF95]

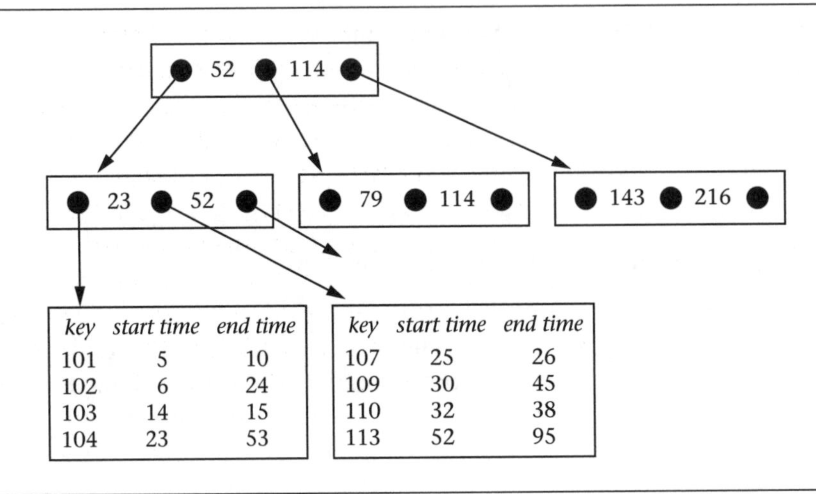

Figure 10.4 Append-only tree based on valid start times

less than or equal to t_s associated with this bucket pointer. Note that end times could be quite long and in fact overlap start times in the same or different nodes.

10.6 Text Databases

Traditional text retrieval systems use standard file indexes to locate a variety of documents containing certain keywords or text strings [Simo95]. Textbases (or component document managers) organize documents into individual user-defined units (e.g., chapters or sections) and manage those units as objects. Document management systems encompass all the functions of text retrieval systems and textbases, including the use of hypertext. Typical types of media used to store text data include CD-ROMs, optical disks, and magnetic disks.

There are several basic methods for text-based retrieval: full text scanning, indexing using inverted lists, TV-trees, and signature files [Zani97, Subr98]. In full text scanning there is no space overhead for indexing or preprocessing, but it obviously becomes very slow for large databases. It is typically used in small databases of a few megabytes or less.

Text-based systems typically use inverted list data structures in which selected keyword values are used as the index entries, which point to an accession list (pointer list) of documents that contain the keyword. Inverted lists are typically organized as B^+-trees, hashing, or variations of these. An important design decision is the selection of keywords to use for the indexes. Too few keywords result in fewer or no documents found, whereas too many keywords, especially words like "the," "a," and "and," do not filter the documents at all and are of no use to the person making the queries. The more recent document management systems also automate the loading of indexes as new documents are loaded into the system and eliminate time-consuming human intervention.

A signature file is a form of quick-and-dirty filter that separates qualifying and nonqualifying documents for the query [Falo92]. Each document has a single coded signature that is a function of the keywords for that document (sometimes the OR function of the individual bit-coded signatures for the keywords). A keyword given in a query is then converted to its signature and compared to the document signatures for all the documents in the database. Those that match the keyword signature are then investigated more closely to make sure there are no false matches. The advantages of this method are ease of implementation and efficiency of insertions. The disadvantage is the potential retrieval time for large databases unless a better method than sequential scan is used for the document signatures [Zani97].

A text indexing method that has generated considerable interest is called *latent semantic indexing* or LSI. This method tries to overcome the problem of exact matching of query words with words that exist in documents in a world where many keywords have multiple meanings and other words have multiple synonyms. The LSI method applies singular value decomposition to analyze the higher-order "semantic" structure of documents in terms of the correlation of words in documents. Retrieval is accomplished by using the words in a query to identify a point in space; for example, large term document matrices and documents in its neighborhood are marked for retrieval [Deer90, FoDu92].

10.7 Active Databases

Active databases are typically implemented as extensions to relational (e.g., Oracle, DB2) or object-oriented databases that support special mechanisms like triggers and alerters for time-constrained applications. An active database environment supports the initiation and control of these actions from within the database environment according to preset rules, without the need for further guidance from the applications or from other outside sources [ElNa94, Simo95].

Active databases contain a set of active rules that consider events that represent database state changes, look for TRUE or FALSE conditions as the result of a database predicate or query, and take an action via a data manipulation program embedded in the system. Applications for active databases include integrity management (e.g., referential integrity or data value range limits in the CHECK function), derived data management or views, replication data management for updates, version maintenance, security, or logging of transactions.

The design of an active database focuses on the properties of active rule execution, such as termination conditions, rule modularization, and rule debugging and monitoring [CBFP95, CeFr92, Zani97]. Since the focus is on the processing of code and not on database structure, the database design requirements are approximately the same as the host relational or object-oriented database, and new techniques are not required.

10.8 Real-Time Databases

Real-time databases (RTDBs) support transactions that must be answered in a real-time manner. RTDBs can be implemented as an extension to either a stand-alone relational or object-oriented database system, as a specialized active database [Rama96], or as an embedded component in a multidatabase system. The real-time part is a timing constraint that must be satisfied when transactions are executed and is in addition to the logical or concurrency control constraints normally imposed on transactions to insure consistency of the data [OzSn95]. Concurrency control mechanisms must often be modified to allow for urgent transactions to commit sooner. Other necessary interactions that need to be addressed are between the RTDB system and the OS in terms of resource management (including I/O scheduling) and security [Best96]. The most important database design issues center around granularity (logical design) and data density (physical design), which must be factored into the retrieval performance of the system [Simo95].

10.9 Summary

This chapter describes the several advanced database technologies making a major impact on the computer community today and challenging the limitations of the relational model. First, it shows that for the next decade or so the relational databases will still be in use, but they will share the stage with object-oriented databases and some specialized databases that cannot be made to fit in either the relational or object-oriented mold. In addition, the rise of object-relational databases is seen as a life-preserving measure for relational vendors to survive in a world of many data types.

The major advanced technologies we investigate include object-oriented and object-relational databases currently available today, temporal databases, multimedia databases, spatial and geographic databases, and text, active, and real-time databases. For each of these technologies we look at the advances in logical and physical database design. In many cases logical design techniques merely borrow from the relational technology, and there is a need to improve these models. In physical design, the most common improvements have occurred in the methods of indexing for complex data types.

Literature Summary

A good overview of all advanced database technologies is the book by Simon [Simo95]. A more technical textbook that summarizes active, temporal, spatial, text, and multimedia database systems is by Zaniolo and colleagues [Zani97]. A large number of books on multimedia and related database systems have come out recently. A comprehensive book on physical design of multimedia databases is by Subrahmanian [Subr98]; the leading textbook on spatial database structures is by Samet [Same90]; and an excellent technical survey of indexing techniques for object-oriented, temporal, spatial, and image databases is by Bertino and colleagues [Bert97].

[Adal96] Adali, S., Candan, K.S., Chen, S.-S., Erol, K., and Subrahmanian, V.S. "The Advanced Video Information System: Data Structures and Query Processing," *Multimedia Systems* 4 (1996), pp.172–186.

[AnTa95] Ang, C., and Tan, K. "The Interval B-Tree," *Information Processing Letters* 53, 2 (1995), pp. 85–89.

[ASS93] Al-Taha, K., Snodgrass, R.T., and Soo, M.D. "Bibliography on Spatiotemporal Databases," *SIGMOD Record* 22, 1 (March 1993).

[Banc96] Bancilhon, F. "Object Databases," *ACM Computing Surveys* 28, 1 (1996), pp. 137–140.

[Beec93] Beech, D. "Collections of Objects in SQL3," *Proc. 19th Intl. Conf. on VLDB*, 1993, pp. 244–255.

[BEGL95] Bukres, O.A., Elmagarmid, A.K., Gherfal, F.F., and Liu, X. "The Integration of Database Systems," *Object-Oriented Multibase Systems*, O.A. Bukhres and A.K. Elmagarmid (editors), Prentice Hall, Upper Saddle River, NJ, 1995.

[BeKi89] Bertino, E., and Kim, W. "Indexing Techniques for Queries on Nested Objects," *IEEE Trans. on Knowledge and Data Engineering* 1, 2 (1989), pp. 196–214.

[BenZ82] Ben-Zvi, J. "The Time Relational Model," Ph.D. dissertation, UCLA, 1982.

[Bert97] Bertino, E., Ooi, B.C., Sacks-Davis, R., Tan, K.-L., Zobel, J., Shidlovsky, B., and Catania, B. *Indexing Techniques for Advanced Database Systems*, Kluwer, Norwell, MA, 1997.

[Best96] Bestavros, A. "Advances in Real-Time Database Systems Research," *SIGMOD Record* 25, 1 (March 1996), pp. 3–7.

[BKSS90] Beckman, N., Kriegel, H.-P., Schneider, R., and Seeger, B. "The R*-Tree: An Efficient and Robust Access Method for Points and Rectangles," *Proc. ACM SIGMOD Intl. Conf. on Mgt. of Data*, 1990, pp. 322–331.

[BlPr98] Blaha, M., and Premerlani, W. *Object-Oriented Modeling and Design for Database Applications*, Prentice Hall, Englewood Cliffs, NJ, 1998.

[BRJ98] Booch, G., Rumbaugh, J., and Jacobson, I. *UML User's Guide*, Addison-Wesley, Reading, MA, 1998.

[Catt95] Cattell, R.G.G. (editor). *The Object Database Standard: ODMG–93*, Morgan Kaufmann, San Francisco, 1995.

[CBFP91] Ceri, S., Baralis, E., Fraternali, P., and Paraboschi, S. "Design of Active Rule Applications: Issues and Approaches," *Proc. Intl. Conf. on Deductive and OO Databases*, 1995, pp. 1–18.

[CeFr92] Ceri, S., and Fraternali, P. *Designing Database Applications with Objects and Rules: The IDEA Metholology, Series on Database Systems and Applications*, Addison-Wesley, Reading, MA, 1997.

[CGO97] Chan, C., Goh, C., and Ooi, B.C. "Indexing OODB Instances Based on Access Proximity," *Proc. 13th Intl. Conf. on Data Engineering*, 1997, pp. 14–21.

[Cham96] Chamberlin, D. *Using the New DB2*, Morgan Kaufmann, San Francisco, 1996.

[CMCL95] Chen, C.Y.R., Meliksetian, D.S., Chang, M.C.-S., and Liu, L.J. "Design of a Multimedia Object-Oriented DBMS," *Multimedia Systems* 3 (1995), pp. 217–227.

[Cole94] Coleman, D., Arnold, P., Bodoff, S., Dollin, C., and Gilchrist, H. *Object-Oriented Development: The Fusion Method*, Prentice Hall, Upper Saddle River, NJ, 1994.

[Conk87] Conklin, J. "Hypertext: An Introduction and Survey," *Computer* 20, 9 (1987), pp. 17–41.

[Deer90] Deerwester, S., Dumais, S.T., Furnas, G.W., Kandauer, T.K., and Harshman, R. "Indexing by Latent Semantic Analysis," *J. American Society for Information Science* 41, 6 (1990), pp. 391–407.

[DKS92] Du, W., Krishnamurthy, R., and Shan, M.-C. "Query Optimization in Heterogeneous DBMS," *Proc. 18th Intl. Conf. on VLDB*, 1992, pp. 277–291.

[DPH96] Dunlop, A.N., Papiani, M., and Hey, A.J.G. "Providing Access to a Multimedia Archive Using the World-Wide Web and an Object-Relational Database Management System," *IEE Computing and Control Engineering Journal* 7, 5 (Oct. 1996), pp. 221–226.

[ElNa94] Elmasri, R., and Navathe, S.B. *Fundamentals of Database Systems*, (2nd Ed., Chap. 25), Benjamin/Cummings, Redwood City, CA, 1994.

[EWK90] Elmasri, R., Wuu, G.T., and Kouramajian, V. "The Time Index: An Access Structure for Temporal Data," *Proc. 16th Intl. Conf. on VLDB*, 1990, pp. 1–12.

[Falo92] Faloutsos, C. "Signature Files," *Information Retrieval: Data Structures and Algorithms*, W.B. Frakes and R. Baeza-Yates (editors), Prentice Hall, Upper Saddle River, NJ, 1992.

[Falo96] Faloutsos, C. *Searching Multimedia Databases by Content*, Kluwer, Norwell, MA, 1996.

[FoDu92] Foltz, P.W., and Dumais, S.T. "Personalized Information Delivery: An Analysis of Information Filtering Methods," *Comm. ACM* 35, 12 (Dec. 1992), pp. 51–60.

[FoSc97] Fowler, M., with Scott, K. *UML Distilled: Applying the Standard Modeling Language*, Addison-Wesley, Reading, MA, 1997.

[GJM97] Grosky, W.I., Jain, R., and Mehrotra, R. *The Handbook of Multimedia Information Management*, Prentice Hall, Upper Saddle River, NJ, 1997.

[GLOT96] Goh, C.H., Lu, H., Ooi, B.C., and Tan, K.L. "Indexing Temporal Data Using B+-Tree," *Data and Knowledge Engineering* 18 (1996), pp. 147–165.

[GST96] Gardarin, G., Sha, F., and Tang, Z.-H. "Calibrating the Query Optimizer Cost Model of IOR-DB, an Object-Oriented Federated Database System," *Proc. 22nd Intl. Conf. on VLDB,* 1996, pp. 378–389.

[GuSe93] Gunadhi, O. and Segev, A. "Efficient Indexing Methods for Temporal Relation," *IEEE Trans. on Knowledge and Data Engineering* 5, 3 (1993), pp. 496–509.

[Gutt84] Guttman, A. "R-trees: A Dynamic Index Structure for Spatial Searching," *Proc. ACM SIGMOD Intl. Conf. on Mgt. of Data,* B. Yormack (editor), 1984, pp. 47–57.

[HaCa97] Hamilton, G., and Cattell, R. "JDBC: A JAVA SQL API," Version 1.20, JavaSoft Inc., January 10, 1997.

[HuBr95] Hurson, A.R. and Bright, M.W. "Object-Oriented Multidatabase Systems," *Object-Oriented Multibase Systems,* O.A. Bukres and A.K. Elmagarmid (editors), Prentice Hall, Upper Saddle River, NJ, 1995.

[Java96] Java database access, Sun Microsystems Inc., 1996, *http://splash.javasoft.com/jdbc/jdbc.databases.html.*

[Jens94] Jenson, C.S., Clifford, J., Elmasri, R., Gadia, S.K., Hayes, P., and Jajodia, S. (editors). "A Glossary of Temporal Database Concepts," *SIGMOD Record* 23, 1 (March 1994), pp. 52–64.

[JeSn96] Jensen, C.S., and Snodgrass, R.T. "Semantics of Time-Varying Information," *Information Systems* 21, 4 (1996), pp. 311–352.

[KeMo94] Kemper, A., and Moerkotte, G. *Object-Oriented Database Management,* Prentice Hall, Upper Saddle River, NJ, 1994.

[KhBa96] Khoshafian, S., and Baker, A.B. *Multimedia and Imaging Databases,* Morgan Kaufmann, San Francisco, 1996.

[KiLo89] Kim, W., and Lochovsky, F. *Object-Oriented Concepts, Databases, and Applications,* Addison-Wesley, Reading, MA, 1989.

[Kolo93] Kolovson, C. "Indexing Techniques for Historical Databases," *Temporal Databases: Theory, Design, and Implementation,* A. Tansel (editor), Benjamin/Cummings, Redwood City, CA, 1993, pp. 418–432.

[KSS97] Korth, H.F., Silberschatz, A., and Sudarshan, S. *Database System Concepts* (3rd Ed.), McGraw-Hill, New York, 1997.

[KTF95] Kumar, A., Tsotras, V.J., and Faloutsos, C. "Access Methods for Bitemporal Databases," *Proc. Intl. Workshop on Temporal Databases,* 1995, pp. 235–254.

[Kuni95] Kunii, T.L., Shinagawa, Y., Paul, R.M., Khan, M.F., and Khokhar, A.A. "Issues in Storage and Retrieval of Multimedia Data," *Multimedia Systems* 3 (1995), pp. 298–304.

[Lars95] Larson, J.A. *Database Directions: From Relational to Distributed, Multimedia, and Object-Oriented Database Systems,* Prentice Hall, Upper Saddle River, NJ, 1995.

[LeMu92] Leung, T.Y.C., and Muntz, R.R. "Generalized Data Stream Indexing and Temporal Query Processing," *2nd Intl. Workshop on Research Issues in Data Eng: Transaction and Query Processing,* 1992.

[LoRa94] Lo, M-L. and Ravishankar, C.V. "Spatial Joins Using Seeded Trees," *Proc. ACM SIGMOD Intl. Conf. on Mgt. of Data,* R.T. Snodgrass and M. Winslett (editors), 1994, pp. 209–220.

[LoRa96] Lo, M.-L., and Ravishankar, C.V. "Spatial Hash Joins," *Proc. ACM SIGMOD Intl. Conf. on Mgt. of Data,* 1996, pp. 247–258.

[LoSa93] Lomet, D., and Salzberg, B. "Transaction Time Databases," *Temporal Databases: Theory, Design, and Implementation,* Chapter 16, A. Tansel (editor), Benjamin/Cummings, Redwood City, CA, 1993, pp. 388–417.

[Melt95] Melton, J. "Accommodating SQL3 and ODMG," ANSI X3H2-95-161/ DBL:YOW-32, April 15, 1995, *http://www.jcc.com/sql_s3h2_95_161.html.*

[MeMa95] Melton, J., and Mattos, N.M. "An Overview of the Emerging Third-Generation SQL Standard," *Proc. ACM SIGMOD Intl. Conf. on Mgt. of Data,* 1995.

[MeMa96] Melton, J., and Mattos, N.M. "An Overview of SQL3—the Emerging New Generation of the SQL Standard," *Tutorials of the 22nd Intl. Conf. on VLDB,* 1996.

[MeYu95] Meng, W., and Yu, C. "Query Processing in Multidatabase Systems," *Modern Database Systems,* W. Kim (editor), ACM Press, New York, 1995, pp. 551–572.

[MuPo97] Mueck, T.A., and Polaschek, M.L. *Index Data Structures in Object-Oriented Databases,* Kluwer, Norwell, MA, 1997.

[NaAh93] Navathe, S.B., and Ahmed, R. "Temporal Extensions to the Relational Model and SQL," *Temporal Databases: Theory, Design, and Implementation,* A. Tansel (editor), Benjamin/ Cummings, Redwood City, CA, 1993.

[ODBC] *ODBC 2.0 Programmer's Reference and SDK Guide,* ISBN 1-55615-658-8.

[ORS97] Ozden, B., Rastogi, R., and Silberschatz, A. "Architecture Issues in Multimedia Storage Systems," *Performance Evaluation Review* 25, 2 (Sept. 1997), pp. 3–12.

[OzSn95] Ozsoyoglu, G., and Snodgrass, R.T. "Temporal and Real-Time Databases: A Survey," *IEEE Trans. for Knowledge and Data Engr.*, 7, 4 (Aug. 1995), pp. 513–532.

[Papi97] Papiani, M. "Generic Web Interfaces for Accessing and Browsing Federated Databases," MSc. mini-thesis, ECS Dept., Univ. of Southampton, Sept. 1997.

[PBE95] Pitoura, E., Bukres, O., and Elmagarmid, A. "Object Orientation in Multidatabase Systems," *ACM Computing Surveys* 27, 2 (1995), pp. 141–195.

[PDH97] Papiani, M., Dunlop, A.N., and Hey, A.J.G. "Automatic Web Interfaces and Browsing for Object-Relational Databases," *Advances in Databases: Proc. 15th British National Conf. on Databases, BNCOD15*, 1997, pp. 131–132.

[Prab96] Prabhakaran, B. *Multimedia Database Management Systems*, Kluwer, Norwell, MA, 1996.

[Rama96] Ramamritham, K., Sivasankaran, R., Stankovic, J.A., Towsley, D.T., and Xiong, M. "Integrating Temporal, Real-Time, and Active Databases," *SIGMOD Record* 25, 1 (March 1996), pp. 8–12.

[Robi81] Robinson, J.T. "The k-D-B-Tree: A Search Structure for Large Multidimensional Dynamic Indexes," *Proc. ACM SIGMOD Intl. Conf. on Mgt. of Data*, 1981, pp. 10–18.

[Same90] Samet, H. *The Design and Analysis of Spatial Data Structures*, Addison-Wesley, Reading, MA, 1990.

[SaTs98] Salzberg, B., and Tsotras, V.J. "A Comparison of Access Methods for Time Evolving Data," *ACM Computing Surveys* (to appear 1998).

[ScWy97] Schloss, G.A., and Wynblatt, M.J. "Providing Definition and Temporal Structure for Multimedia Data," *Multimedia Systems* 3 (1995), pp. 264–277.

[Simo95] Simon, A.R. *Strategic Database Technology: Management for the Year 2000*, Morgan Kaufmann, San Francisco, 1995.

[SKS96] Soparkar, N.R., Korth, H.F., and Silberschatz, A. *Time-Constrained Transaction Management*, Kluwer, Norwell, MA, 1996.

[Snod90] Snodgrass, R. "Temporal Databases: Status and Future Directions," *SIGMOD Record* 19, 4 (Dec. 1990), pp. 83–89.

[SOL94] Shen, H., Ooi, B.C., and Lu, H. "The TP-Index: A Dynamic and Efficient Indexing Mechanism for Temporal Databases," *10th Intl. Conf. on Data Engineering*, 1994, pp. 274–281.

[SQL3] SQL standards home page: *http://www.jcc.com/sql_stnd.html.*

[SRF87] Sellis, T., Roussopoulos, N., and Faloutsos, C. "The R+-Tree: A Dynamic Index for Multi-Dimensional Objects," *Proc. 13th Intl. Conf. on Very Large Data Bases*, Brighton, UK, 1987, pp. 507–518.

[StMo96] Stonebraker, M., with Moore, D. *Object-Relational DBMSs: The Next Great Wave*, Morgan Kaufmann, San Francisco, 1996.

[Ston98] Stonebraker, M. (editor) *Readings in Database Systems* (3rd Ed.), Morgan Kaufmann, San Francisco, 1998.

[Subr98] Subrahmanian, V.S. *Principles of Multimedia Database Systems*, Morgan Kaufmann, San Francisco, 1998.

[Tans93] Tansel, A., Clifford, J., Gadia, S., Jajodia, S, Segev, A., and Snodgrass, R. (editors). *Temporal Databases: Theory, Design, and Implementation*, Benjamin/Cummings, Redwood City, CA, 1993.

[TeWi97] Texel, P.P., and Williams, C.B. *USE CASES Combined with BOOCH/OMT/UML: Process and Products*, Prentice Hall, Upper Saddle River, NJ, 1997.

[TGH94] Tsotras, V.J., Gopinath, B., and Hart, G.W. "Efficient Management of Time-Evolving Databases," *IEEE Trans. on Knowledge and Data Engineering*, 1994.

[Zani97] Zaniolo, C., Ceri, S., Faloutsos, C., Snodgrass, R., Subrahmanian, V.S., and Zicari, P. *Advanced Database Systems*, Morgan Kaufmann, San Francisco, 1997.

[ZdMa90] Zdonik, S., and Maier, D. *Readings in Object-Oriented Database Systems*, Morgan Kaufmann, San Francisco, 1990.

Appendix A

Review of SQL

Structured Query Language, or SQL, is the ISO-ANSI standard data definition language and data manipulation language for relational database management systems. Individual relational database systems use slightly different dialects of SQL syntax and naming rules, and these differences can be seen by consulting the SQL user guides for those systems. In this text, where we explore each step of the logical and physical design portion of the database life cycle, many examples of database table creation and manipulation make use of SQL syntax.

SQL is, first of all, relational; its queries operate only on tables in a relational database and produce only tables as the result. Similarly, SQL updates modify relational tables. Second, SQL is nonprocedural; each statement in the language specifies an atomic act to be carried out involving a set of rows. As a language, it is based more on relational calculus, which specifies what the result of the query looks like, than on the procedure-oriented relational algebra, which specifies the sequence of steps needed to obtain a database result. Third, SQL is unified; database administrators (DBAs), programmers, and system administrators all learn and use a single language and set of constructs, and use the same language on-line, in either batch files or individual programs.

The basic use of SQL can be learned quickly and easily by reading this appendix. More advanced features, such as statistical analysis and presentation of data, require more study and are beyond the reach of the typical nonprogrammer. However, SQL views can be set up by the DBA to help the nonprogrammer set up repetitive queries, and other languages such as forms are being commercially sold for nonprogrammers. For the advanced database programmer, embedded SQL (in C programs, for instance) is widely available for the most complex database applications that need the power of procedural languages.

This appendix introduces the reader to the basic constructs for SQL-92 (sometimes called SQL2) database definition, queries, and updates through a sequence of examples with some explanatory text. We start with a definition of SQL-92 terminology for data types and operators. This is followed by an explanation of the SQL-92 data definition language (DDL) constructs using the "create table" commands and including a definition of the various types of integrity constraints such as foreign keys and referential integrity. Finally, we take a detailed look at the SQL-92 data manipulation language (DML) features through a series of both simple and complex practical examples of database queries and updates.

A.1 SQL Names and Operators

This section gives the basic rules for SQL-92 data types and operators according to the ISO-ANSI standard [MeSi93].

- SQL-92 names have no particular restrictions, but vendor-specific versions of SQL do have some restrictions. For example, in Oracle, names of tables and columns (attributes) can be up to 30 characters long, must begin with a letter, and can include the symbols (a–z, 0–9,_,$,#). Names should not duplicate reserved words or names for other objects (attributes, tables, views, indexes) in the database.
- Data types for attributes: character, character varying, numeric, decimal, integer, smallint, float, double precision, real, bit, bit varying, date, time, timestamp, interval.
- Logical operators: and, or, not, ().
- Comparison operators: =, <>, <, <=, >, >=, (), in, any, some, all, between, not between, is null, is not null, like.
- Set operators:

  union—combines queries to display any row in each subquery

  intersect—combines queries to display distinct rows common to all subqueries

  except—combines queries to return all distinct rows returned by the first query but not the second (this is "minus" or "difference" in some versions of SQL)
- Set functions: count, sum, min, max, avg.

- Advanced value expressions: CASE, CAST, row value constructors. The CASE is similar to the CASE expressions in programming languages in which a select command needs to produce different results when there are different values of the search condition. The CAST expression allows you to convert data of one type to a different type, subject to some restrictions. Row value constructors allow you to set up multiple column value comparisons with a much simpler expression than is normally required in SQL (see [MeSi93] for detailed examples).

A.2 Data Definition Language (DDL)

The basic definitions for SQL objects (tables and views) are

- *create table*—defines a table and all its attributes
- *alter table*—adds new columns, drops columns, or modifies existing columns in a table
- *drop table*—deletes an existing table
- *create view, drop view*—defines/deletes a database view (see Section A.3.4)

Some versions of SQL also have create index/drop index, which defines/deletes an index on a particular attribute or composite of several attributes in a particular table.

The following table creation examples are based on a simple database of three tables: **customer**, **item**, and **order**. (Note that we put table names in boldface throughout the book for readability.)

```
create table customer
    (cust_num numeric,
    cust_name char(20),
    cust_addr varchar(256),
    credit_num numeric,
    check (credit_num >= 1000),
    primary key (cust_num));
```

Note that the attribute cust_num could be defined as "numeric not null unique" instead of explicitly defined as the primary key, since they have the same meaning. However, it would be redundant to have both forms in the same table definition. The check rule is an important integrity constraint that tells SQL to automatically test each insertion of credit_num value for something greater than or equal to 1000. If not, an error message should be displayed.

```
create table item
        (item_num numeric,
        item_name char(20),
        item_price numeric,
        item_wt numeric,
        primary key (item_num));

create table order
        (ord_num       char(15),
        cust_num       numeric not null,
        item_num numeric not null,
        quantity numeric,
        total_cost numeric,
        primary key (ord_num),
        foreign key (cust_num) references customer
            on delete no action on update cascade,
        foreign key (item_num) references item
            on delete no action on update cascade);
```

SQL-92, while allowing for the preceding format for primary key and foreign key, recommends a more detailed format, shown here for table **order**:

```
constraint pk_constr primary key (ord_num),
constraint fk_constr1 foreign key (cust_num) references customer
            (cust_num)
        on delete no action on update cascade,
constraint fk_constr2 foreign key (item_num) references item
            (item_num)
        on delete no action on update cascade);
```

where pk_constr is a primary key constraint name, and fk_constr1 and fk_constr2 are foreign key constraint names. The word "constraint" is a keyword, and the object in parentheses after the table name is the name of the primary key in that table referenced by the foreign key.

The following constraints are common for attributes defined in the SQL create table commands:

- *Not null.* A constraint that specifies that an attribute must have a nonnull value.
- *Unique.* A constraint that specifies that the attribute is a candidate key—that is, that it has a unique value for every row in the table. Every attribute that is a candidate key must also have the constraint not null. The constraint unique is also used as a clause to designate composite candidate keys that are not the primary key. This is particularly useful when transforming ternary relationships to SQL.
- *Primary key.* The primary key is a set of one or more attributes, which, when taken collectively, allows us to identify uniquely an entity or table. The set of attributes should not be reducible (see Section 5.1.2). The designation "primary key" for an attribute implies that the attribute must be "not null" and "unique," but the SQL keywords NOT NULL and UNIQUE are redundant for any attribute that is part of a primary key, and need not be specified in the create table command.
- *Foreign key.* The referential integrity constraint specifies that a foreign key in a referencing table column must match an existing primary key in the referenced table. The references clause specifies the name of the referenced table. An attribute may be both a primary key and a foreign key, particularly in relationship tables formed from many-to-many binary relationships or from n-ary relationships.

Foreign key constraints are defined for row deletion on the referenced table and for the update of the primary key of the referenced table. The referential trigger actions for delete and update are similar:

- *on delete cascade*—the delete operation on the referenced table "cascades" to all matching foreign keys.
- *on delete set null*—foreign keys are set to null when they match the primary key of a deleted row in the referenced table. Each foreign key must be able to accept null values for this operation to apply.
- *on delete set default*—foreign keys are set to a default value when they match the primary key of the deleted row(s) in the reference table. Legal default values include a literal value, "user," "system user," or "no action."

- *on update cascade*—the update operation on the primary key(s) in the referenced table "cascades" to all matching foreign keys.
- *on update set null*—foreign keys are set to null when they match the old primary key value of an updated row in the referenced table. Each foreign key must be able to accept null values for this operation to apply.
- *on update set default*—foreign keys are set to a default value when they match the primary key of an updated row in the reference table. Legal default values include a literal value, "user," "system user," or "no action."

The "cascade" option is generally applicable when either the mandatory existence constraint or the ID dependency constraint is specified in the ER diagram for the referenced table, and either "set null" or "set default" is applicable when optional existence is specified in the ER diagram for the referenced table (see Chapters 2 and 4).

Some systems such as DB2 have an additional option on delete or update, called "restricted." Delete restricted means that the referenced table rows are deleted only if there are no matching foreign key values in the referencing table. Similarly, "update restricted" means that the referenced table rows (primary keys) are updated only if there are no matching foreign key values in the referencing table.

Various column and table constraints can be specified as "deferable" (the default is "not deferrable"), which means that the DBMS will defer checking this constraint until you commit the transaction. Often this is required for mutual constraint checking.

The following examples illustrate the alter table and drop table commands. The first alter table command modifies the cust_name data type from char(20) in the original definition to varchar(256). The second and third alter table commands add and drop a column, respectively. The add column option specifies the data type of the new column.

```
alter table customer
        modify (cust_name varchar(256));
alter table customer
        add column cust_credit_limit numeric;
alter table customer
        drop column credit_num;
drop table customer;
```

A.3 Data Manipulation Language (DML)

Data manipulation language commands are used for queries, updates, and the definition of views. These concepts are presented through a series of annotated examples, from simple to moderately complex.

A.3.1 SQL Select Command

The SQL select command is the basis for all database queries. We look at a series of examples to illustrate the syntax and semantics for the select command for the most frequent types of queries in everyday business applications. We use the indentation form of select command to emphasize readability and consistency.

1. Display the entire **customer** table. The asterisk (*) denotes that all records from this table are to be read and displayed.

   ```
   select *
       from customer;
   ```

2. Display customer number and credit number for all customers in Toronto with credit number greater than 5. Order by ascending sequence of customer numbers (the order by options are asc, desc). Note that the first selection condition is specified in the "where" clause and succeeding selection conditions are specified by "and" clauses. Character type data and other nonnumeric data are placed inside single quotes, but numeric data is given without quotes.

   ```
   select cust_num, credit_num
       from customer
       where cust_addr = 'Toronto'
       and credit_num > 5
       order by cust_num asc;
   ```

3. Display all customer and ordered item information (all columns), but omitting customers with credit number of 40. In this query the "from" clause shows the definition of abbreviations c and o for tables **customer** and **order**, respectively. The abbreviations can be used anywhere in the query to denote their respective table names. This example also illustrates a join between table **customer** and table **order** using the common attribute name cust_num, as shown in the "where" clause. The join finds matching cust_num values from the two tables and

displays all the data from the matching rows, except where the credit number is 40.

```
select c.*, o.*
    from customer as c, order as o
    where c.cust_num = o.cust_num
    and c.credit_num <> 40;
```

4. Which items are ordered by customer 1 or customer 2? This query can be answered in two ways, one with a set operator (union) and the other with a logical operator (or).

```
select item_num, cust_num
    from order
    where cust_num = 1
union
select item_num, cust_num
    from order
    where cust_num = 2;
```

```
select item_num, cust_num
    from order
    where (cust_num = 1 or cust_num = 2);
```

5. Which items are ordered by both customers 1 and 3? All the rows in table **order** that have customer 1 are selected and compared to the rows in **order** that have customer 3. Rows from each set are compared with all rows from the other set, and those that have matching item numbers have the item numbers displayed.

```
select item_num
    from order
    where cust_num = 1
intersect
select item_num
    from order
    where cust_num = 3;
```

6. Display the total number of customers. This query uses the SQL function "count" to count the number of rows in table **customer**.

```
select count(*)
    from customer;
```

7. Display the total number of customers actually shipping items. This is a variation of the count function that specifies that only the distinct number of customers are to be counted. The "dis-

tinct" modifier is required because duplicate values of customer numbers are likely to be found and because a customer can order many items and appear in many rows of table **order**.

```
select count (distinct cust_num)
    from order;
```

8. Display the maximum quantity of an order of item number 31. The SQL "maximum" function is used to search the table **order**, select rows where the item number is 31, and display the maximum value of quantity from the rows selected.

```
select max (quantity)
    from order
    where item_num = 31;
```

9. For each type of item ordered, display the item number and total order quantity. Note that item_num in the select line must be in a "group by" clause. In SQL any attribute to be displayed in the result of the select command must be included in a "group by" clause when the result of an SQL function is also to be displayed. The "group by" clause results in a display of the aggregate sum of quantity values for each value of item_num. Item_num could appear in many different rows in table **order**, so the aggregate sums are taken over all rows with the same value of item_num.

```
select item_num, sum(quantity)
    from order
    group by item_num;
```

10. Display item numbers for all items ordered more than 10 times. This query requires the use of the "group by" and "having" clauses to display data that is based on a count of rows from table **order** having the same value for attribute item_num.

```
select item_num
    from order
    group by item_num
    having count(*) > 10;
```

11. Display item numbers and customer numbers and their largest quantity ordered, and group by item number as primary and customer number as secondary columns.

```
select item_num, cust_num, max(quantity)
    from order
    group by item_num,cust_num;
```

12. Display customer names for customers who order item 32. This query requires a join (equijoin) of tables **customer** and **order** in order to match customer names with item number 32. The equijoin is the most common type of join, and the only one we discuss here, but the reader may note that SQL-92 defines several other types [MeSi93].

```
select c.cust_name
    from customer as c, order as o
    where c.cust_num = o.cust_num
    and o.item_num = 32;
```

This query can be equivalently performed with a *subquery* (sometimes called *nested subquery*) with the following format. The select command inside the parentheses is a nested subquery and is executed first, resulting in a set of values for customer number (cust_num) selected from the **order** table. Each of those values is compared with cust_num values from the **customer** table, and matching values result in the display of customer name from the matching row in the **customer** table. This is effectively a join between tables **customer** and **order** with the selection condition of item number 32.

```
select c.cust_name
    from customer as c
    where c.cust_num in
    (select cust_num
    from order as o
    where o.item_num = 32);
```

13. Display customer names who order at least one item priced over $500.00. This query requires a three-level nested subquery format. Note that the phrases "in," "= some," and "= any" in the "where" clauses are often used as equivalent comparison operators; see [MeSi93].

```
select c.cust_name
    from customer as c
    where c.cust_num in
    (select o.cust_num
        from order as o
        where o.item_num = any
        (select i.item_num
            from item as i
            where i.item_price > '$500.00'));
```

14. Which customers have not ordered any item over $20? Note that you can equivalently use "not in" instead of "not any." The query first selects the customer numbers from all rows from the join of tables **order** and **item** where the item price is over $20. Then it selects rows from table **customer** where the customer number does not match any of the customers selected in the subquery, and displays the customer names.

```
select c.cust_name
    from customer as c
    where c.cust_num not any
    (select o.cust_num
        from order as o, item as i
        where o.item_num = i.item_num
        and i.item_price >'$20.00');
```

15. Which customers have only ordered items weighing more than 1000? This is an example of the universal quantifier "all." First the subquery selects all rows from table **item** where the item weight is over 1000. Then it selects rows from table **order** where all rows with a given item number match at least one row in the set selected in the subquery. Any rows in **order** satisfying this condition are joined with the customer table and the **customer** name is displayed as the final result.

```
select c.cust_name
    from customer as c, order as o
    where c.cust_num = o.cust_num
    and o.item_num = all
    (select i.item_num
        from item as i
        where i.item_wt > 1000);
```

16. Find all items that have the word "video" in their name. This requires the use of the "like" predicate, which locates the character string 'video' anywhere in the string. Note that a % before and/or after a character string satisfies this query. An underscore specifies a particular position in a character string, but the value is unknown. An example of this would be '_xyz', which specifies a four-character string with unknown first value; '%abcde_fg' specifies a variable-length string in which the last eight characters are 'abcde', followed by an unknown character, and ending with 'fg'.

```
select item_name
    from item
    where item_name like '%video%';
```

17. How much has Schmidt made while working for this company? This illustrates a more complex query involving computation of an aggregate total from individual row data. Let us assume a new table, **salary_history**, with attributes last_name, monthly_salary, start_date, and end_date. (The special functions in this query are from Oracle SQL*Plus.)

```
select sum(monthly_salary*months_between
        (end_date,start_date))
    from salary_history
    where last_name = 'Schmidt';
```

A variation of this query checks to see if the last end date is null. *Note:* the null value test function nvl(expr1, expr2) = expr1 if it is not null, or expr2 if expr1 is null.

```
select sum (monthly_salary*
        (months_between (nvl (end_date,sysdate),
            start_date)))
    from salary_history
    where last_name = 'Schmidt';
```

A.3.2 SQL Update Commands

The following SQL update commands relate to our continuing example and illustrate typical usage of insertion, deletion, and update of selected rows in tables.

```
insert into customer
    values (35,'Smith','Detroit,MI',10);
delete from customer
    where credit_num < 2;
update order
    set quantity = 450
    where quantity = 500
    and cust_num = 3
    and item_num = 31;
```

A.3.3 Referential Integrity

The following update to the **item** table resets the value of item_num for a particular item, but because item_num is a foreign key in the **order** table, SQL must maintain referential integrity by triggering the execution sequence named by the foreign key constraint "on update cascade" in the definition of the **order** table (Section A.2). This means that, in addition to updating a row in the **item** table, SQL will search the **order** table for values of item_num equal to 53300 and reset each value to 53327.

```
update item
    set item_num = 53327
    where item_num = 53300;
```

If this update had been a "delete" instead, such as the following:

```
delete from item
    where item_num = 53300;
```

then the referential integrity trigger would have caused the additional execution of the foreign key constraint "on delete set default" in order (as defined in Section A.2), which finds every row in order with item_num = 53300 and takes the action set up in the default. A typical action for this type of database might be to set item_num to either null or a predefined literal value to denote that the particular item has been deleted; this would then be a signal to the system that the customer needs to be contacted to change the order. Of course, the system would have to be set up in advance to check for these values periodically.

A.3.4 SQL Views

A view in SQL is a named, derived (virtual) table that derives its data from base tables, the actual tables defined by the "create table" command. While view definitions can be stored in the database, the views (derived tables) themselves are not stored but derived at execution time when the view is invoked as a query using the SQL select command. The person who queries the view treats the view as if it were an actual (stored) table, unaware of the difference between the view and the base table.

Views are useful in several ways. First, they allow complex queries to be set up in advance in a view, and the novice SQL user is only required to make a simple query on the view. This simple query invokes the more complex query defined by the view. Thus, nonprogrammers are allowed to utilize the full power of SQL without having to create complex queries. Second, views provide greater security for a database because the DBA can assign different views of the data to different users and control what any individual user sees in the database. Third, views provide a greater sense of data independence—that is, even though the base tables may be altered by adding, deleting, or modifying columns, the view query may not need to be changed. While view definition may need to be changed, that is the job of the DBA, not the person querying the view.

Views may be defined hierarchically, that is, a view definition may contain another view name as well as base table names. This allows for some views to become quite complex.

In the following example, we create a view called "orders" that shows which items have been ordered by each customer and how many. The first line of the view definition specifies the view name and (in parentheses) lists the attributes of that view. The view attributes must correlate exactly with the attributes defined in the select statement in the second line of the view definition:

```
create view orders (customer_name, item_name, quantity) as
        select c.cust_name, i.item_name, o.quantity
              from customer as c, item as i, order as o
              where c.cust_num = o.cust_num
              and o.item_num = i.item_num;
```

The "create view" command creates the view definition, which defines two joins among three base tables **customer**, **item**, and **order**; and SQL stores the definition to be executed later when invoked by a query. The following query selects all the data from the view "orders." This query causes SQL to execute the select command given in the preceding view definition, producing a tabular result with the column headings for customer_name, item_name, and quantity.

```
select *
        from orders;
```

Views are usually not allowed to be updated because the updates would have to be made to the base tables that make up the definition of the view. When a view is created from a single table, the view update is often unambiguous, but when a view is created from the joins of multiple tables, the base table updates are very often ambiguous and may have undesirable side effects. Each relational system has its own rules about when views can and cannot be updated.

As an example of an ambiguous update situation, consider the two tables, **table1** and **table2**, with columns named one, two, three, and four:

table1	one	two	three	**table2**	three	four
	a	b	e		e	k
	a	d	f		e	m
	a	d	e		f	n

```
create view view1 (one, two, three, four) as
    select t1.one, t1.two, t1.three, t2.four
        from table1 as t1, table2 as t2
        where t1.three = t2.three;
```

The resulting view produced by a query "select * from view1" would be displayed as

view1	one	two	three	four	
	a	d	f	n	/* row 1 */
	a	b	e	k	/* row 2 */
	a	b	e	m	/* row 3 */
	a	d	e	k	/* row 4 */
	a	d	e	m	/* row 5 */

If we try to delete row 2 from view1, there are serious problems in trying to delete the corresponding data from the base tables, **table1** and **table2**. One approach is to delete row 1 in **table1**, but this has the unintended side effect of deleting row 3 in view1 as well as row 2. Similarly, deleting row 1 in **table2** has the side effect of deleting row 4 in view1 as well as row 2. Deleting row 1 in both **table1** and **table2** makes matters even worse, deleting rows 3 and 4 in view1.

If we try to update row 2 in view1, attribute three from "e" to "f," we have more problems. If we update row 1 of **table1** to be (a,b,f) and update row 1 of **table2** to be (f,k), the join of these two updated rows in the view query will produce several superfluous rows as a result, and view1 will be incorrect. As a result, deleting or updating of rows from view1 is not recommended!

Literature Summary

[ISAN89] *ISO-ANSI Database Language SQL2 and SQL3,* ANSI X3H2-89-110, ISO DBL CAN-3 (working draft), J. Melton (editor), February 1989.

[ISAN92] ANSI X3.135-1992 Database Language SQL and ISO/IEC 9075:1992 Database Language SQL.

[MeSi93] Melton, J., and Simon, A.R. *Understanding the New SQL: A Complete Guide,* Morgan Kaufmann, San Francisco, 1993.

Exercises

Problem A-1

Given the following schema for a presidential database, write SQL queries (in correct syntax) for each of the following three queries:

```
create table president
        (identifier integer not null unique,
        last_name char(16),
        first_name char(16),
        middle_init char(2),
        political_party char(16),
        state_from      char(16));
create table administration
        (pres_identifier integer,
        start_date date not null unique,
        end_date date,
        vp_last_name char(16),
        vp_first_name char(16),
        vp_middle_init char(2));
create table state
        (state_name char(16)      not null unique,
        date_admitted date not null,
        area integer,000000
        population integer,
        capital_city char(16));
```

Queries

Q1. Which presidents were from the state of Ohio and also members of the Republican party?

Q2. Which states were admitted when President Andrew Johnson was in office?

Q3. Which vice presidents (vp's) did not later become president? Assume that no one could be president and then vice president, but could be vice president and then president.

Please see page 352 for the solution to Problem A-1.

Problem A-2

For the following relational table definitions, write the SQL queries and updates for the English queries and updates specified.

Queries

Q1. Who does Bill Joy manage?

Q2. Is there a manager who manages both Ed Birss and Leo Horvitz? If so, who is it?

Q3. Display employee names and room numbers of those individuals who work in the "special funds" department.

Q4. Which employees work in either the "engineering" or "data processing" departments?

Q5. Display the names of project managers who are also department heads.

Q6. Display all projects, sorted (ascending) by project name. Specify who manages each project, which employees work on it, and what department the project manager is in. Within a project, sort employees by employee name.

Q7. Which programmers are not assigned to the "new computers" project?

Q8. How much money has Mike Wilens made while working for this company?

Q9. Which employees make over $5000/month and have no project management responsibility?

Q10. Who are the first-, second-, and third-level managers above Beverly Kahn? Use the "manager" attribute in the employee table. Create three "views," one for the first-level manager, another for the second-level manager, and yet another for the third-level manager. Then specify three separate queries in terms of these three "views."

Updates

U1. Create a new table that has your last name and first initial as its name prefix and that lists employee names and three hobbies. Make up four rows for this table. (Example table name: **deppe_m_hobbies**.) In this way each member of the class can add to the database without damaging the existing database. See if you can print out a nonredundant list of hobbies for those employees working in the "special funds" department.

U2. Delete one of the rows in your table.

U3. Modify one of the remaining rows to change one of the hobbies.

```
create table dept (dept_no char(6),
      dept_name char(20),
      dept_head char(10),
      primary key (dept_no));
create table employee (emp_no char(10),
      emp_name char(20),
      room_no char(8),
      dept_no char(6),
      manager char(10),
      primary key (emp_no),
      foreign key (dept_no) references dept
            on delete set null on update cascade,
      foreign key (manager) references employee
            on delete cascade on update cascade);
create table salary (salary_level integer,
      mon_salary float,
      primary key (salary_level));
create table job (job_code char(5),
      job_title char(15),
      primary key (job_code));
```

```
create table salary_hist (emp_no char(10),
    salary_level integer,
    job_code char(5),
    start_date char(8),
    end_date char(8),
    primary key (emp_no, salary_level),
    foreign key (emp_no) references employee
        on delete cascade on update cascade,
    foreign key (salary_level) references salary
        on delete cascade on update cascade);
create table project (proj_code char(6),
    proj_name char(15),
    start_date char(8),
    end_date char(8),
    proj_mgr char(10),
    primary key (proj_code),
    foreign key (proj_mgr) references employee
        on delete set default on update cascade);
create table workson (emp_no char(10),
    proj_code char(6),
    primary key (emp_no, proj_code),
    foreign key (emp_no) references employee
        on delete cascade on update cascade,
    foreign key (proj_code) references project
        on delete cascade on update cascade);
```

Appendix B

Database Performance Tuning

This appendix looks at the various parameters associated with relational database tuning in terms of what the database user can control and what the database administrator usually manages. For each parameter, we define how the concept works and what choices are possible, including trade-offs that should be considered. Some of the specific parameters and their values are taken from Oracle [OR89a,b], but the concepts can be applied to many commercial relational systems.

B.1 User-Defined Parameters

Relational database users typically have control over the table definitions, including primary and foreign keys, normalization, and denormalization. However, they also have a significant amount of control over the indexing and clustering of tables.

1. *Indexing.* An index is a method for speeding up the access to database tables compared to a full table scan. In general, it is better to build an index when fewer than 10–15% of the rows will be accessed. A full table scan is typically faster for greater than 10–15% of the rows scanned because of multiblock sequential access techniques (single reads of 64 KB or more).
   a. *Number of indexes per table*—more than one index per table allows a greater variety of efficient accesses for different types of queries. This flexibility and efficiency is created at the expense of greater space overhead and index update overhead.

b. *Unique index*—an index created for primary keys only, with pointers to individual (unique) rows. This is very often implemented as a hashing table but also can be implemented as a B^+-tree (sometimes referred to as a B* tree).

c. *Nonunique index (secondary index)*—an index based on nonkey attributes, requiring a pointer array to possibly many rows that satisfy the attribute value(s) given in the search argument. This type of index is very efficient and flexible for complex Boolean queries involving several nonkey attribute values.

d. *Concatenated index*—an index created on more than one column, that is, based on a concatenated key of more than one column. This index is typically much larger than a single column index because of the many possible values for the combined keys. It tends to give faster database access for queries based on the concatenated key, but is less flexible than a simple index, requires more space, and has greater index update overhead. It is used for certain dominating queries in terms of frequency of execution.

e. *Compressed index*—any index that is stored in compressed mode, thus having more index entries per B^+-tree node than a noncompressed index. Oracle does both front and rear compression, which is based on storing only the key value characters that are different from the value of the previous entry and an integer representing the number of overlapping characters between the current key value and the previous one. Compressed indexes require much less space (typically a 3 or 4 to 1 reduction) and thus less I/O, but at the expense of somewhat higher CPU cost to compress and decompress the entries.

f. *Percent free*—a numeric value that specifies how much free space will be allocated to B^+-tree leaf nodes during index creation. Typically, values of 10–15% are used to allow for expansion for new rows after the initial allocation of index values.

2. *Clustering.* The main idea of clustering is to physically store together data that is often queried together. Clustering has no effect on the type of SQL statements used to access the data, only on the efficiency of those statements. Tables selected for clustering are those that are frequently joined to satisfy queries. These tables typically have one or more columns in common, and the redundant data is eliminated in the cluster.

a. *Cluster key*—designates which columns are overlapping between two tables in a cluster and thus indicates which data will be stored nonredundantly.

b. *Logical block size*—the logical unit of clustered data that encompasses data from both tables in the cluster. This is typically smaller than the physical block size of the database and is used for conserving space and minimizing the I/O calls during cluster scans.

B.2 Database Administrator and System-Defined Parameters

1. *Blocks*. The physical block is the basic unit of I/O for many systems and thus is an important parameter for database storage.

   a. *Block size*—typical block size for most environments (UNIX, IBM, etc.) is either 2048 or 4096 bytes. However, multiblock scans of 64 KB per I/O have been used to increase the sequential processing efficiency of certain systems.

   b. *Row length*—bytes per row, including overhead such as row sequence number and column id number and compressed data such as null values.

   c. *Percent free*—a numeric value that specifies how much free space will be allocated to data blocks to allow for expansion due to insertions and updates. (Updates cause expansion when null values are replaced by nonnull values.)

   d. *Blocking factor (bf)*—the number of rows (records) per block. This number takes into account the row length, all overhead for headers, and percent free space in the block.

   $$\text{bf} = \text{integervalue}[(1 - \text{freespace\_fraction}) * (\text{blocksize} - \text{headersize})/\text{rowsize}]$$

   For example, if percent free is 20%, block size is 2048 bytes, header size is 76 bytes, and row size is 150 bytes, then the blocking factor is integer[(1 – .2) * (2048 – 76)/150] = 10.

   e. *Blocks per table*—the number of rows in the table divided by the the blocking factor, taken to the next higher integer if a fractional value.

2. *Buffers*. A buffer is the space allocated in main memory to hold data accessed from I/O devices.

a. *Buffer size*—size of individual buffers, typically preset by the I/O block size, standardized for a given system; for example, UNIX uses 2048-byte blocks, whereas MVS uses 4096-byte blocks.
b. *Buffer pool size*—the number of buffers allocated in main memory for a database application; for example, Oracle defaults to 50 buffers in the buffer pool. The greater the number of buffers cached in main memory, the greater the likelihood that a record you need is in main memory and the lesser that you will need an I/O to get it. This probability is highly dependent on the locality of the database queries and the way the data is clustered.

Literature Summary

[OR89a] *Oracle Database Administrator's Guide,* Part No. 3601-V5.1, 1989.

[OR89b] *Oracle RDBMS Performance Tuning Guide,* Part No. 5317-V6.0, 1989.

Appendix C

Dependability Estimation

This appendix shows how to estimate the availability, reliability, and mean transaction time (response time) for repairable database configurations, centralized or distributed, in which each service component is continuously available for repair. Reliability—the probability that the entire transaction can execute properly without failure—is computed as a function of mean time to failure (MTTF) and mean time to repair (MTTR). Mean transaction time in the system is a function of the mean service delay time for the transaction over all components, plus restart delays due to component failures, plus queuing delays for contention. These estimates are potentially applicable to more generalized distributed systems.

C.1 Introduction

The increasing availability and importance of centralized, distributed, and multidatabases raise serious concerns about their dependability in a fragile network environment, much more so than with centralized databases. Although the major impetus for distributed data is to increase data availability, it is not always clear whether the dependability of the many hardware and software components of a distributed system is such that the level of availability desired is actually provided. Performance of a database system is closely related to dependability, and it cannot be good if the dependability is low.

Failures occur in many parts of a computer system: at the computer sites, the storage media (disk), the communication media, and in the database transactions [Duga90, Gray90, MaFe90, BeGa92]. Site failures may be due to hardware (CPU, memory, power failure) or software system problems. Disk failures may occur from operating system software bugs, controller problems, or head crashes. In the network, there may be errors in messages, including lost messages and improperly ordered messages, and line failures. Transaction failures may be due to bad data, constraint failure, or deadlock [GrRe93]. Each of these types of failures contributes to the degradation of the overall dependability of a system.

A significant amount of research has been reported on the subject of dependability of computer systems, and a large number of analytical models exist to predict reliability for such systems [JoMa88, SaMe86, SaTr87]. While these models provide an excellent theoretical foundation for computing dependability, there is still a need to transform the theory to practice. The goal here is to provide the initial step in such a transformation with a realistic set of system parameters, a simple analytical model, and comparison of the model predictions with a discrete event simulation tool [TeNg98].

Based on the definitions in [SiSw82, JoMa88], the dependability of any system can be thought of as being composed of three basic characteristics: availability, reliability, and serviceability. *Steady-state availability* is the probability that a system will be operational at any random point of time, and is expressed as the expected fraction of time a system is operational during the period it is required to be operational. *Reliability* is the probability that a system will perform its intended function properly without failure and satisfy specified performance requirements during a given time interval [0,t] when used in the manner intended. *Serviceability* or *maintainability* is the probability of successfully performing and completing a corrective maintenance action within a prescribed period of time with the proper maintenance support.

We look at the issues of availability and reliability in the context of simple database transactions (and their subtransactions) in a network environment where the steady-state availability is known for individual system components: computers, networks, the various network interconnection devices, and possibly their respective subcomponents. A transaction path is considered to be a sequential series of resource acquisitions and executions, with alternate parallel paths allowable. We assume that all individual system components, software and hardware, are repairable [JoMa88]. A *nonrepairable* distributed database is one in which transactions can be lost and the system is not available for repair. In a *repairable* distributed database all components are assumed to be continuously available for repair, and any aborted transaction is allowed to restart from its point of origin. We only consider repairable databases here.

Serviceability is assumed to be deterministic in our model, but the model could be extended for probabilities less than 1 that the service will be successfully completed on time.

C.2 Availability

Availability can be derived in terms of the mean time to failure (MTTF) and the mean time to repair (MTTR) for each component used in a transaction. Note that from [SiSw82] we have the basic relationship for mean time between failures (MTBF):

$$MTBF = MTTF + MTTR \tag{C.1}$$

The steady-state availability of a single component i can be computed by

$$\begin{aligned} A_i &= MTTF_i/(MTTF_i + MTTR_i) \\ &= MTTF_i/MTBF_i \end{aligned} \tag{C.2}$$

Let us look at the computation of steady-state availability in the network underlying the distributed or multidatabase. In Figure C.1a two sites, S1 and S2, are linked with the network link L12. Let A_{S1}, A_{S2}, and A_{L12} be the steady-state availabilities for components S1, S2, and L12, respectively.

Assuming that each system component is independent of all other components, the probability that path S1/L12/S2 is available at any randomly selected time t is the product of the individual availabilities in series:

$$A_{S1/L12/S2} = A_{S1} * A_{L12} * A_{S2} \tag{C.3}$$

Extending the concept of availability to parallel paths (Figure C.1b), we factor out the two components, S1 and S2, that are common to each path:

$$A_{S1//S2} = A_{S1} * A_{S2} * [\text{availability of the connecting paths between S1 and S2}] \tag{C.4}$$

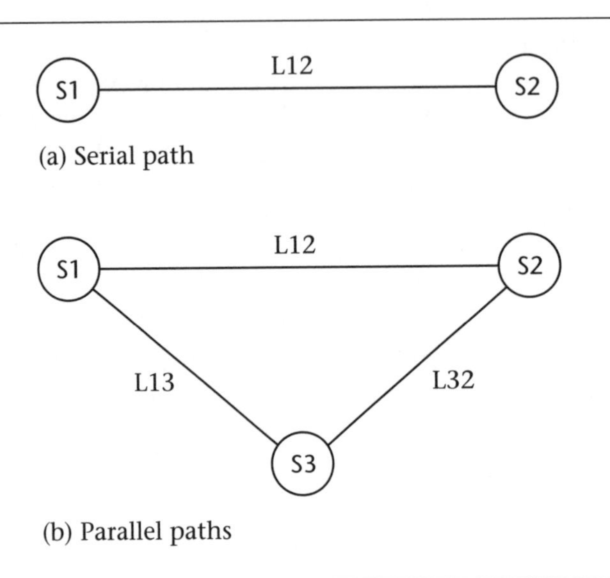

Figure C.1 Network paths for a distributed database: serial (a) and parallel (b)

Equation C.2 states that the total path from site S1 to site S2 has three serial components: S1, S2, and the two possible connecting paths between the sites. We simply partition the whole path into three serial parts and apply Equation C.1 to them to determine the total path availability. Now we need to determine the actual value of the third component of availability, the connecting paths. This is determined by the well-known relationship for parallel independent events, which states that the total availability of a parallel path is the sum of the serial availability of each of the two separate paths, minus the product of their serial availabilities.

$$A_{S1//S2} = A_{S1} * A_{S2} * [A_{L12} + A_{L13} * A_{S3} * A_{L32} - A_{L12} * A_{L13} * A_{S3} * A_{L32}] \tag{C.5}$$

We now have the basic relationships for serial and parallel paths for steady-state availability. We note that if query optimizers pick the shortest path without regard to availability, the system could reverse the decision if the selected path is not available. Because of the extreme complexity of computing reliability for parallel paths, the remaining discussion focuses on serial paths only, to illustrate the basic concepts of combining reliability and performance into a single measure.

C.3 Reliability

An estimate of availability is limited to a single point in time. We now need to estimate the reliability for an entire transaction (including queries and/or updates), and (in Section C.4) the mean transaction completion time for a repairable distributed or multidatabase that has automatic restarts. Reliability is the probability that the entire transaction can execute properly (over a given time interval) without failure, and we need to compute the estimated mean reliability over a time duration [0,t], where t is the mean delay experienced over the system during the transaction execution.

For tractability we first assume that the number of failures of each system component is exponentially distributed:

$$P_i(k,t) = (mt)^k * e^{-mt/k!} \qquad \text{(C.6)}$$

This is the probability that there are exactly k failures of component i in time interval t, where m is the mean number of failures per unit time. The probability that there are no failures of component i in time interval t is:

$$P_i(0, t) = e^{-mt} \qquad \text{(C.7)}$$

Let

$MTTF_i$ = mean time to failure on component i,
$MTTR_i$ = mean time to repair for component i, and
D = mean service delay time for the transaction.

We can now compute the reliability of the transaction at component i, that is, the joint probability that the transaction has no failures while actively using component i, which is equal to the conditional probability that the component i is reliable over the interval (0, D) times the probability that the component i is available at the beginning of the same interval. That is,

$$P_i(0, D) = e^{-m_i * D} * A_i \qquad \text{(C.8)}$$

where m_i = failure rate = expected number of failures per unit time = $1/MTTF_i$. The reliability of the entire transaction is the product of the (assumed independent) reliabilities of the transaction for each component.

Let us now apply the relationship on Equation C.8 to the serial path database configuration over the network in Figure C.1a. The transaction reliability is equal to the probability that the transaction can be completed without failure from initiation at site S1, obtaining local access to the data in site S2, and returning with the result to site S1. We assume that the transaction is successful only if all components are active during the entire time required to service the transaction. We are given the mean delay experienced by each subtransaction on each component resource, derived from known characteristics of the network and database system.

$$P(0, D) = \text{transaction reliability} = P_{S1}(0, D)*P_{L12}(0, D)*P_{S2}(0, D) \quad (C.9)$$

Let

QIT	=	query initiation time(CPU) = 1 ms
PTT	=	packet transmission time = 8 ms (T1 link @ 1.544 Mb/s, packet size 1544 bytes)
PD	=	packet propagation delay = 10 ms (assumed 2000 km distance, degraded electronic speed 200 km/ms)
QPT	=	query processing time(CPU and I/O) = 200 ms
n	=	number of packets in the result of the query = 5
QRDT	=	query result display time (CPU and I/O) = 60 ms
$MTTF_i$	=	10 hours (36,000 seconds) for each component i
$MTTR_i$	=	.5 hour (1800 seconds) for each component i ($MTBF_i$ = 10.5 hours)
A_i	=	10/(10.5) = .9524

Let us define the mean service delay time as the sum of all the non-overlapped delays from site S1 to site S2, returning the result to site S1:

$$\begin{aligned} D &= QIT + PTT + PD + QPT + n*PTT + PD + QRDT \\ &= 1 + 8 + 10 + 200 + 5*8 + 10 + 60 \text{ ms} \\ &= 329 \text{ ms } (.329 \text{ seconds}) \end{aligned}$$

Applying Equation C.9 we obtain the transaction reliability:

$$\begin{aligned} P(0, D) &= [e^{-.329/36,000}(.9524)]^3 \\ &= .8639 \end{aligned}$$

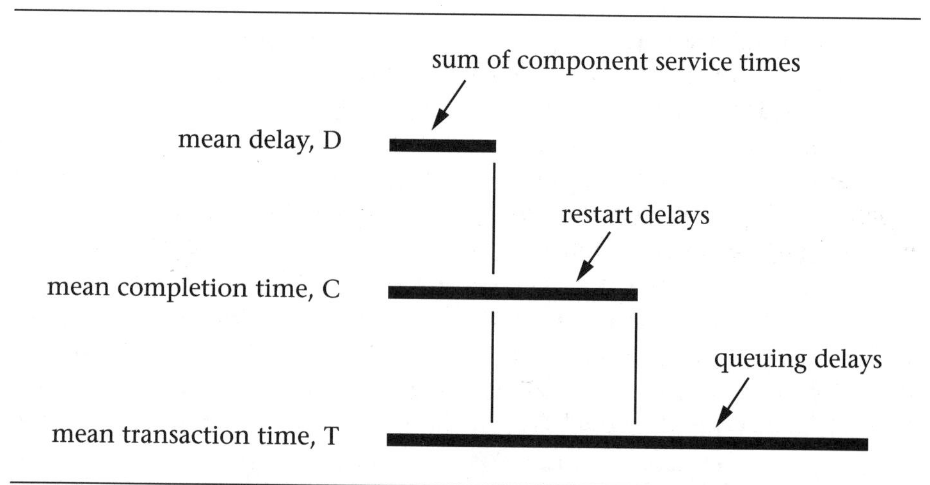

Figure C.2 Components of mean transaction time

C.4 Mean Transaction Time

The mean transaction time in the system is a function of the mean service delay time for the transaction over all components, plus restart delays, plus queuing delays for contention (Figure C.2). Once the mean service delay time (D) is known, we can then compute the mean completion time (C), taking into account the restart delays. Finally, we compute the mean transaction time in the system (T) from known queuing formulas.

If there are no queuing delays, we can easily estimate mean completion time C, the combination of mean service and restart delays, by computing the probability of different completion times possible. For example, if D is the mean service delay time, C can be easily derived assuming p, the reliability of a transaction, and for every failure, an average time to failure and recovery, D/2 + MTTR, where D/2 is the mean time to failure of the transaction, given random failures of a collection of components over which that transaction must successfully execute.

$$
\begin{aligned}
C &= p*D + q*p*(D + D/2 + MTTR) + q^{2}*p*(D + 2*D/2 + 2*MTTR) \\
&\quad + q^{3}*p*(D + 3*D/2 + 3*MTTR) + \ldots \\
&= p*D + q*p*D + q^{2}*p*D + q^{3}*p*D + \ldots + q*p*(D/2 + MTTR) \\
&\quad + 2q^{2}*p*(D/2 + MTTR) + 3q^{3}*p*(D/2 + MTTR) + \ldots \\
&= p*D*(1 + q + q^{2} + q^{3} + \ldots) + q*p*(D/2 + MTTR) \\
&\quad *(1 + 2q + 3q^{2} + 4q^{3} + \ldots) \\
&= D + (q/p)*(D/2 + MTTR) \qquad \text{(C.10)}
\end{aligned}
$$

by noting that (1 + q + q2 + q3 + . . .) = 1/(1 – q) = 1/p

and $(1 + 2q + 3q^2 + 4q^3 + \ldots) = 1/(1 - q)^2 = 1/p^2$.

If, on the other hand, queuing delays do exist (e.g., in any shared resource system), the simple model of Equation C.10 breaks down, and mean transaction time T can be derived by noting the similarity between queues with breakdowns and preemptive priority queues [FeGr86]. We model our reliability problem with a preemptive priority queue. Consider a queuing system with two priority classes in which the high-priority jobs can preempt any low-priority job. This is equivalent to our reliability problem, where the transaction process corresponds to the low-priority job (2) and the failure process corresponds to an arrival of a high-priority job (1). The mean transaction time is thus the mean service time of the low-priority job, and the exact solution [BeGa92] is:

$$T = \frac{(1/\mu_2)(1 - \rho_1 - \rho_2) + R_2}{(1 - \rho_1 - \rho_2)(1 - \rho_1)} \tag{C.11}$$

where is the mean residual time

$$R_2 = \frac{\lambda_1 \overline{X_1^2} + \lambda_2 \overline{X_2^2}}{2} \tag{C.12}$$

ρ_1 and ρ_2 are the utilization of the failture and transaction processes, respectively, μ_2 is the transaction service rate, and $\overline{X_j^2}$ is the second moment of service time. Equation C.11 is valid for any general service time.

Since each component is assumed to fail independently, the k independent Poisson failure processes on each component on the network can be combined into a single process with the arrival rate equal to the sum of the rates of each individual process [BeGa92]. We assume that the transaction is successful only if all components are active during the entire time required to service the transaction, so the tandem network in Figure C.1a can be simplified to a single server with mean transaction time given in Equation C.11.

Literature Summary

[BeGa92] Bertsekas, D., and Gallager, R. *Data Networks*, Prentice Hall, Englewood Cliffs, NJ, 1992.

[Duga90] Dugan, J.B. "On Measurement and Modeling of Computer Systems Dependability: A Dialog among Experts," *IEEE Transactions on Reliability* 39, 4 (Oct. 1990), pp. 506–510.

[FeGr86] Federgruen, A., and Green, L. "Queueing Systems with Service Interruptions," *Operations Research*, 34, 5 (Sept.–Oct. 1986), pp. 752–768.

[Gray90] Gray, J., "A Census of Tandem System Availability between 1985 and 1990," *IEEE Transactions on Reliability* 39, 4 (Oct. 1990), pp. 409–418.

[GrRe93] Gray, J., and Reuter, A. *Transaction Processing: Concepts and Techniques*, Morgan Kaufmann, San Francisco, 1993.

[JoMa88] Johnson, A.M., Jr., and Malek, M. "Survey of Software Tools for Evaluating Reliability, Availability, and Serviceability," *ACM Computing Surveys* 20, 4 (Dec. 1988), pp. 227–269.

[MaFe90] Maxion, R.A., and Feather, F.E. "A Case Study of Ethernet Anomalies in a Distributed Computing Environment," *IEEE Transactions on Reliability* 39, 4 (Oct. 1990), pp. 433–443.

[SaMe86] Sanders, W.H., and Meyer, J.F. "METASAN: A Performability Evaluation Tool Based on Stochastic Activity Networks," *Proc. 1986 Fall Joint Computer Conference*, 1986, AFIPS, New York, pp. 807–816.

[SaTr87] Sahner, R.A., and Trivedi, K.S. "Reliability Modeling Using SHARPE," *IEEE Transactions on Reliability* 36, 2 (June 1987), pp. 186–193.

[SiSw82] Siewiorek, D.P., and Swarz, R.S. *The Theory and Practice of Reliable System Design*, Digital Press, Bedford, MA, 1982.

[TeNg98] Teorey, T.J., and Ng, W.-T. "Dependability and Performance Measures for the Database Practitioner," *IEEE Transactions on Knowledge and Data Engineering* 10, 3 (May–June 1998). pp. 499–503.

Appendix D

Data Warehousing Technology Vendors

This appendix lists most of the major players in data warehousing, OLAP, and data mining, as well as a summary of the larger relational database vendors. This list is by no means exhaustive and no priorities are implied—all are alphabetically arranged within each category. It is hoped that enough data is presented to give readers motivation to follow up on their own and narrow the list of potential vendors of interest to them. More complete descriptions are given in the references, including several World Wide Web sites to start a more detailed search.

The basic format of each listing is

business-name, city, state, country if not in the U.S.—sample products (comments)

D.1 Data Warehousing

Business Objects, San Jose, CA—BusinessObjects, Metadata Repository

EMC Corporation, Hopkinton, MA—Integrated Cached Disk Array, Symmetrix (very large DW platform)

IBM, Armonk, NY—DB2 Universal Database

Informix Software, Inc., Menlo Park, CA—various DW products

Micro Strategy, Vienna, VA—DSS Agent, DSS Web (Java based)

Microsoft Corporation, Redmond, WA—various DW products coming out in 1998/1999

NCR, Dayton, OH—Teradata Database System (used by Wal-Mart, largest known user)
Oracle Corporation, Redwood Shores, CA—Applications DW, Data Mart Suites
Red Brick Systems, Inc., Los Gatos, CA—StarIndex, StarJoin
SAS Institute, Cary, NC—CFO Vision, several other DW products
Sybase, Inc., Emeryville, CA—Sybase IQ (data mart)

D.2 OLAP

Andyne Computing Ltd., (Hummingbird Comm. Ltd.), Canada—PaBLO (MDD, OLAP on the desktop)
Arbor Software Corp., Sunnyvale, CA—Essbase (MDD, MOLAP)
Brio Technology, Palo Alto, CA—BrioQuery Server
Business Objects Americas, San Jose, CA—BusinessObjects, Mercury (MDD, OLAP on the desktop)
Cognos, Burlington, MA—PowerPlay (MDD, OLAP on the desktop)
Comshare, Inc., Ann Arbor, MI—BOOST, Commander Decision and OLAP, Arthur products
Dimensional Insight, Inc., Burlington, MA—CrossTarget
Gentia Software, Wakefield, MA—"networked BI OLAP environment"
Holistic Systems, Inc., Edison, NJ—Holos (MDD high-end tools)
Hyperion Software, Stamford, CT—Hyperion OLAP, Enterprise, Pillar
Information Advantage, Inc., Minneapolis, MN—DecisionSuite (ROLAP), WebOLAP
Informix Software, Inc., Menlo Park, CA—INFORMIX MetaCube (ROLAP), INFORMIX MetaCube Explorer, Warehouse Manager, Warehouse Optimizer
Infospace, San Mateo, CA—OLAP Server (100% Java)
IQ Software Corporation, Norcross, GA—IQ/Vision
Kenan Systems Corp., Cambridge, MA—Acumate Enterprise Solution products (MDD high-end tools)
Micro Strategy, Inc., Vienna, VA—DSS Server products (ROLAP)
Microsoft Corporation, Redmond, WA—Excel (additional OLAP products in 1998/1999)
NetCube Corporation, Edgewater, NJ—NetCube Product Suite products

Oracle Corporation, Redwood Shores, CA—Oracle Express (MDD high-end tools)
PeopleSoft Inc., Pleasanton, CA—future products in OLAP
Pilot Software, Inc., Cambridge, MA—Pilot Desktop, Pilot Analysis Server, Pilot Designer, Pilot Analysis Library, Pilot Excel Add-in
PLATINUM Technology, Inc., Oakbrook Terrace, IL—PLATINUM Info-Beacon (ROLAP)
Red Brick Systems, Inc., Los Gatos, CA—Red Brick Warehouse (ROLAP)
SAS Institute, Cary, NC—Orlando II (MDD high-end tools)
Seagate, Vancouver, BC, Canada—Holos OLAP/Crystal Info
Sterling Software, Woodland Hills, CA—Clear:Access
TM/1 Software, Warren, NJ—TM1 Server products, Sinper (MDD, MOLAP)
Verity, Sunnyvale, CA—various OLAP products

D.3 Data Mining

Angoss Software, Toronto, ON, Canada—KnowledgeSEEKER
Business Objects Americas, San Jose, CA—Business Miner
Cirrus Recognition Systems, Reading, MA—DataSage
Cognos, Burlington, MA—Scenario, 4Thought
Data Mining Technologies, Inc., Melville, NY—The Data Mining Power Toolkit
DataMind, San Mateo, CA—DataCruncher
IBM, Armonk, NY—Intelligent Miner
Information Discovery, Inc., Hermosa Beach, CA—The DataMining Suite
NCR Corporation, Dayton, OH—KDW
NeoVista Software, Cupertino, CA—The Decision Series suite
Red Brick Systems, Los Gatos, CA—Red Brick Data Mine Option, Data Mine Builder
SAS Institute, Cary, NC—SAS Enterprise Miner
SPSS, Chicago, IL—SPSS
Trajecta, Austin, TX—dbProphet
WhiteCross Systems Ltd., Bracknell, England—HeatSeeker (pattern matching)

D.4 Relational Databases (Largest Vendors)

Compaq/Tandem Computers, Houston, TX, and Cupertino, CA—Non-Stop SQL/MX
IBM, Armonk, NY—DB2 Universal Database
Informix Software, Inc., Menlo Park, CA—Informix
Microsoft Corporation, Redmond, WA—Access, SQL Server NT (new)
Oracle Corporation, Redwood Shores, CA—Oracle
Sybase Inc., Emeryville, CA—Sybase

D.5 Acronyms

BI—business intelligence (systems)
MDD—multidimensional database
MOLAP—multidimensional OLAP
OLAP—on-line analytical processing
ROLAP—relational (SQL-oriented) OLAP

Literature Summary

[BaEd97] Barquin, R., and Edelstein, H. (editors). *Planning and Designing the Data Warehouse*, Prentice Hall, Upper Saddle River, NJ, 1997, Chapter 10 (OLAP).

[Stod97] Stoddard, D. "The Database Dozen," *Database Prog. & Design* 10, 13 (Dec. 1997), pp. 8–24.

[Thom97c] Thomsen, E. *OLAP Solutions*, John Wiley & Sons, New York, 1997.

Web sites: *www.yahoo.com/Business_and_Economy/Companies/Software/ Databases/Data_Mining/* (*Note:* It is easy to search on OLAP or data warehousing from this site as well.) and *scanner-group.mit.edu/DATAMINING/Datamining/DMProducts.html*

Appendix E

Connecting Databases to the World Wide Web

One of the most dramatic changes in business has been the rapid expansion of electronic commerce through the World Wide Web. Early use of the Web involved file access, but many businesses today use databases as their information repositories. If you could combine easy-to-use Web browser interfaces with the sophisticated database storage and retrieval facilities of DBMSs, you would have a very powerful tool for doing business efficiently. A recent study by Austrian researchers has developed and tested a thorough taxonomy of concepts associated with Web connectivity [EKR97], which is summarized here.

Requirements for interfacing databases from the Web have been proposed as follows:

- *Harmonized user interface*—user interface provides integration of data types within the client, for example, static text and images (multimedia).
- *Interactive Web model*—the ability to change the content as a reaction to a user's input, which allows the client to control the input and reduces the load on the server; for instance, using Java applets or JavaScript pages.
- *Consistency and integrity*—WWW browsers have problems with integrity due to the stateless nature of the HyperText Transfer Protocol (HTTP) and must be enhanced as part of the integration with the database system.

- *Performance and scalability*—scalability can be measured by database size and number of simultaneous users. Most performance comparison at this level is bottleneck detection and avoidance.

Although the technologies for integrating Web browsers with databases are constantly changing, we can take a snapshot of those technologies to get a good sense of the variety of approaches possible.

1. *CGI—Common Gateway Interface.* This is a standard for external gateway programs to interface with servers and is the best-known approach to add services to the WWW. A browser (such as Netscape or Microsoft Explorer) requests an executable to be started at the server site, via HTTP, and the server application (CGI program) performs the database access. This approach allows a wide variety of database access languages to be used. The disadvantages are that the server can be heavily loaded since each invocation of a CGI program starts a new server process, and transaction management is poor due to the stateless nature of HTTP.
2. *SSI—Server Side Include.* This approach involves a server that understands database commands (e.g., Netscape's LiveWire), which are embedded as comments within HTML or are included with special tags that are ignored by the browser. The server then does the database access when serving the documents to the browser. The database access functions are included at the server, thus the name Server Side Include. The main advantage is the potentially improved performance due to the server directly accessing the database. The disadvantages include poor transaction management and possibly scalability at the server, which must serve both the database and the WWW.
3. *Databases "speaking" HTTP.* This approach involves a database system that understands HTTP requests so that all data manipulation is expressed in HTML and parsed by the database's interface. The main advantage is that the browser speaks directly to the database, so concurrency and transaction management is easier. The disadvantages include the bottleneck problem similar to SSI (except the database is the bottleneck due to its service of WWW requests), the lack of openness because the HTTP interface is database specific, and the lack of real interactivity of Web pages.
4. *Direct access using Java.* This approach uses the recent development of Java Database Connectivity (JDBC) so that databases can

be connected to/from/within the WWW. This could also be known as "client side includes." It is based on the concept that a browser loads a dedicated program (applet), either via the Web or locally, and the applet then does the database access. Thus, the Web server is no longer needed for database access—only for HTTP communication—so once the applet has been loaded, the session control is with the browser. The main advantages are full concurrency and transaction management, the platform independence of Java (thus heterogeneity), fancier user interfaces, and potential performance improvements due to the separation of WWW server and database functions. JDBC also allows access to either relational or object-oriented databases. Problems include being able to fully integrate Java and HTML, and scalability for large distributed applications.

5. *External viewers for accessing databases*. In this approach, a browser requests a document from a WWW server; the document of a specific type arrives and the browser launches an external viewer, which in turn performs the database access. The database command must be embedded in a document that can be loaded by a simple mouse click, and the browser must be configured in order to deal with the document. It has the advantage of a dedicated viewer and full transaction management and concurrency control. Performance is also better due to the separation of WWW service and database access. However, there is no integration between the Web and database data, and there is additional overhead for installing an external viewer at each site.
6. *Extending the browser's capabilities with plug-ins*. Plug-ins are programs that extend the capabilities of browsers in various ways, for example, to play video files. This is similar to an external viewer except that program control stays with the browser. Plug-ins are, however, platform specific and must be installed at each site.
7. *Proxy-based services*. This approach redirects the browser's requests to HTTP proxy servers, which access the database and deliver the results to the browser. The proxy server performs the database access while the WWW server is separate. The database manipulation commands must be embedded in the HTML documents, and the proxy server recognizes them by parsing the browser's request. Advantages include interactivity of Web pages, performance, and scalability. The downside is the lack of transaction management or concurrency control.

8. *Database connectivity in HyperWave(TM).* Hyperwave(TM) uses a gateway server between the WWW server and the database. This three-tiered structure allows connection to multiple databases and cache mechanisms for performance improvement. There are no serious disadvantages.

In summary, the most promising solutions that allow querying, editing, and collaboration suffer from the mixing of control code and formatting instructions, mainly due to the stateless nature of HTTP as well as (at present) insufficient Java-to-HTML integration. Furthermore, the availability and properties of tools for integrating the Web with databases are constantly changing; this requires a generalized middleware architecture for Web-to-database connectivity.

Literature Summary

[EKR97] Ehmayer, G., Kappel, G., and Reich, S. "Connecting Databases to the Web: A Taxonomy of Gateways," *Proc. 8th Intl. Conf. on Database and Expert Systems Applications (DEXA97)*, Springer LNCS 1308, Toulouse, France, Sept. 1997.

References

[Abri74] Abrial, J. "Data Semantics," Data Base Management, *Proc. IFIP TC2 Conf.*, North-Holland, Amsterdam, 1974.

[ACM90] *ACM Computing Surveys (Special Issue on Heterogeneous Databases)* 22, 3 (Sept. 1990), pp. 173–293.

[Adal96] Adali, S., Candan, K.S., Chen, S.-S., Erol, K., and Subramanian, V.S. "The Advanced Video Information System: Data Structures and Query Processing," *Multimedia Systems* 4 (1996), pp. 172–186.

[AdZa96] Adriaans, P., and Zantinge, D. *Data Mining*, Addison-Wesley Longman, Reading, MA, 1996.

[AnTa95] Ang, C., and Tan, K. "The Interval B-Tree," *Information Processing Letters* 53, 2 (1995), pp. 85–89.

[Aper88] Apers, P.M.G. "Data Allocation in Distributed Database Systems," *ACM Trans. Database Systems* 13, 3 (Sept. 1988), pp. 263–304.

[Aria86] Ariav, G.A. "A Temporally Oriented Data Model," *ACM Trans. Database Systems* 11, 4 (Dec. 1986), pp. 499–527.

[ASS93] Al-Taha, K., Snodgrass, R.T., and Soo, M.D. "Bibliography on Spatiotemporal Databases," *SIGMOD Record* 22, 1 (March 1993).

[BaBu84] Batory, D.S., and Buchmann, A.P. "Molecular Objects, Abstract Data Types, and Data Models: A Framework," *Proc. 10th Intl. Conf. on Very Large Data Bases,* Aug. 1984, pp. 172–184.

[Bach69] Bachman, C.W. "Data Structure Diagrams," *Database* 1, 2 (1969), pp. 4–10.

[Bach72] Bachman, C.W. "The Evolution of Storage Structures," *Comm. ACM* 15, 7 (July 1972), pp. 628–634.

[Bach77] Bachman, C.W. "The Role Concept in Data Models," *Proc. 3rd Intl. Conf. on Very Large Data Bases,* Oct. 6–8, 1977, IEEE, New York, pp. 464–476.

[BaEd97] Barquin, R., and Edelstein, H. (editors). *Planning and Designing the Data Warehouse,* Prentice Hall, Upper Saddle River, NJ, 1997, Chapter 10 (OLAP).

[BaLe84] Batini, C., and Lenzerini, M. "A Methodology for Data Schema Integration in the Entity Relationship Model," *IEEE Trans. on Software Engr.* SE-10, 6 (Nov. 1984), pp. 650–664.

[BaMc72] Bayer, R., and McCreight, E. "Organization and Maintenance of Large Ordered Indexes," *Acta. Inf.* 1, 3 (1972), pp. 173–189.

[Banc96] Bancilhon, F. "Object Databases," *ACM Computing Surveys* 28, 1 (1996), pp. 137–140.

[Bane87] Banerjee, J., Chou, H.T., Garza, J.F., Kim, W., Woelk, B., and Ballou, N. "Data Model Issues for Object-Oriented Applications," *ACM Trans. on Office Information Systems* 5, 1 (Jan. 1987), pp. 3–26.

[BaSu97] Barbara, D., and Sullivan, M. "Quasi-Cubes: Exploiting Approximations in Multidimensional Databases," *SIGMOD Record* 26, 3 (Sept. 1997), pp. 12–17.

[BBG78] Beeri, C., Bernstein, P., and Goodman, N. "A Sophisticated Introduction to Database Normalization Theory," *Proc. 4th Intl. Conf. on Very Large Data Bases,* Sept. 13–15, 1978, IEEE, New York, pp. 113–124.

[BCN92] Batini, C., Ceri, S., and Navathe, S. *Conceptual Database Design: An Entity-Relationship Approach,* Benjamin/Cummings, Redwood City, CA, 1992.

[Beec93] Beech, D. "Collections of Objects in SQL3," *Proc. 19th Intl. Conf. on VLDB,* 1993, pp. 244–255.

[BeGa92] Bertsekas, D., and Gallager, R. *Data Networks,* Prentice Hall, Englewood Cliffs, NJ, 1992.

[BEGL95] Bukres, O.A., Elmagarmid, A.K., Gherfal, F.F., and Liu, X. "The Integration of Database Systems," *Object-Oriented Multibase Systems,* O.A. Bukhres and A.K. Elmagarmid (editors). Prentice Hall, Upper Saddle River, NJ, 1995.

[BeGo81] Bernstein, P.A., and Goodman, N. "Concurrency Control in Distributed Database Systems," *ACM Computing Surveys* 13, 2 (June 1981), pp. 185–222.

[BeGr92] Bell, D., and Grimson, J. *Distributed Database Systems,* McGraw-Hill, New York, 1992.

[BeKi89] Bertino, E., and Kim, W. "Indexing Techniques for Queries on Nested Objects," *IEEE Trans. on Knowledge and Data Engineering* 1, 2 (1989), pp. 196–214.

[BenZ82] Ben-Zvi, J. "The Time Relational Model," Ph.D. dissertation, UCLA, 1982.

[Bern76] Bernstein, P. "Synthesizing 3NF Relations from Functional Dependencies," *ACM Trans. Database Systems* 1, 4 (1976), pp. 272–298.

[Bert97] Bertino, E., Ooi, B.C., Sacks-Davis, R., Tan, K.-L., Zobel, J., Shidlovsky, B., and Catania, B. *Indexing Techniques for Advanced Database Systems*, Kluwer, Norwell, MA, 1997.

[BeSm97] Berson, A., and Smith, S.J. *Data Warehousing, Data Mining, & OLAP*, McGraw-Hill, New York, 1997.

[Best96] Bestavros, A. "Advances in Real-Time Database Systems Research," *SIGMOD Record* 25, 1 (March 1996), pp. 3–7.

[BFH77] Beeri, C., Fagin, R., and Howard, J.H. "A Complete Axiomization for Functional and Multivalued Dependencies in Database Relations," *Proc. 1977 ACM SIGMOD Int'l. Conf. on Management of Data,* Toronto, 1977, pp. 47–61.

[BHHS85] Braind, H., Habrias, H., Hue, J., and Simon, Y. "Expert System for Translating an E-R Diagram into Databases," *Proc. 4th Intl. Conf. on Entity-Relationship Approach,* IEEE Computer Society Press, Silver Spring, MD, 1985, pp. 199–206.

[BKSS90] Beckman, N., Kriegel, H.-P., Schneider, R., and Seeger, B. "The R*-Tree: An Efficient and Robust Access Method for Points and Rectangles," *Proc. ACM SIGMOD Intl. Conf. on Mgt. of Data*, 1990, pp. 322–331.

[BlEs77] Blasgen, M.W., and Eswaran, K.P. "Storage and Access in Relational Data Bases," *IBM Syst. J.* 16, 4 (1977), pp. 363–377.

[BLN86] Batini, C., Lenzerini, M., and Navathe, S.B. "A Comparative Analysis of Methodologies for Database Schema Integration," *ACM Computing Surveys* 18, 4 (Dec. 1986), pp. 323–364.

[BlPr98] Blaha, M., and Premerlani, W. *Object-Oriented Modeling and Design for Database Applications*, Prentice Hall, Englewood Cliffs, NJ, 1998.

[BMS84] Brodie, M.L., Mylopoulos, J., and Schmidt, J. (editors). *On Conceptual Modeling: Perspectives from Artificial Intelligence, Databases, and Programming Languages,* Springer-Verlag, New York, 1984.

[Booc86] Booch, G. "Object-Oriented Development," *IEEE Trans. on Software Engineering* SE-12, 2 (Feb. 1986), pp. 211–221.

[Booc91] Booch, G. *Object Oriented Design with Applications,* Benjamin/Cummings, Redwood City, CA, 1991.

[BoSa96] Bontempo, C.J., and Saracco, C. *Database Management: Principles and Products,* Prentice Hall, Upper Saddle River, NJ, 1996.

[BPP76] Bracchi, G., Paolini, P., and Pelagatti, G. "Binary Logical Associations in Data Modelling," *Modelling in Data Base Management Systems,* G.M. Nijssen (editor), North-Holland, Amsterdam, 1976.

[Bran96] Branchman, R.J., Khabaza, T., Kloesgen, W., Piatetsky-Shapiro, G., and Simoudis, E. "Mining Business Databases," *Comm. ACM* 39, 11 (Nov. 1996), pp. 42–48.

[BRJ98] Booch, G., Rumbaugh, J., and Jacobson, I. *UML User's Guide,* Addison-Wesley, Reading, MA, 1998.

[Bruc92] Bruce, T.A. *Designing Quality Databases with IDEF1X Information Models,* Dorset House, New York, 1992.

[Bube77] Bubenko, J. "The Temporal Dimension in Information Modelling," *Architecture and Models in Data Base Management Systems,* G. Nijssen (editor), North-Holland, Amsterdam, 1977.

[Bulo96] Bulos, D. "OLAP Database Design: A New Dimension," *Database Prog. & Design* 9, 6 (June 1996), pp. 33–37.

[CACM92] *Comm. ACM* (Special Issue: *Analysis and Modeling in Software Development*) 35, 9 (Sept. 1992), pp. 35–171.

[CACM96] *Comm. ACM* (Special Issue: *Data Mining and Knowledge Discovery in Databases*), Fayyad, U., and Uthurusamy, R. (editors), 39, 11 (Nov. 1996), 24–68.

[Card85] Cardenas, A.F. *Data Base Management Systems* (2nd Ed.), Allyn & Bacon, Boston, 1985.

[Case72] Casey, R.G. "Allocation of Copies of a File in an Information Network," *Spring Joint Computer Conf.,* 1972, AFIPS Press, Washington D.C., Vol. 40.

[Cata97] Cataldo, J. "Care and Feeding of the Data Warehouse," *Database Prog. & Design* 10, 12 (Dec. 1997), pp. 36–42.

[Catt95] Cattell, R.G.G. (editor). *The Object Database Standard: ODMG–93,* Morgan Kaufmann, San Francisco, 1995.

[CBFP91] Ceri, S., Baralis, E., Fraternali, P., and Paraboschi, S. "Design of Active Rule Applications: Issues and Approaches," *Proc. Intl. Conf. on Deductive and OO Databases,* 1995, pp. 1–18.

[CBS96] Connolly, T., Begg, C. and Strachan, A. *Database Systems: A Practical Approach to Design, Implementation, and Management: Version 2*, Addison-Wesley, Reading, MA, 1996.

[CeFr92] Ceri, S., and Fraternali, P. *Designing Database Applications with Objects and Rules: The IDEA Metholology, Series on Database Systems and Applications*, Addison-Wesley, Reading, MA, 1997.

[CePe84] Ceri, S., and Pelagatti, G. *Distributed Databases: Principles and Systems*, McGraw-Hill, New York, 1984.

[CFT84] Cobb, R.E., Fry, J.P., and Teorey, T.J. "The Database Designers Workbench," *Information Sciences* 32, 1 (Feb. 1984), pp. 33–45.

[CGO97] Chan, C., Goh, C., and Ooi, B.C. "Indexing OODB Instances Based on Access Proximity," *Proc. 13th Intl. Conf. on Data Engineering*, 1997, pp. 14–21.

[CGP80] Coffman, E.G., Gelenbe, E., and Plateau, B. "Optimization of the Number of Copies in Distributed Databases," *Proc. of the 7th IFIP Symposium on Computer Performance Modelling, Measurement and Evaluation*, Springer-Verlag, New York, May 1980, pp. 257–263.

[Cham96] Chamberlin, D. *Using the New DB2*, Morgan Kaufmann, San Francisco, 1996.

[ChDa97] Chaudhuri, S., and Dayal, U. "An Overview of Data Warehousing and OLAP Technology," *SIGMOD Record* 26, 1 (March 1997), pp. 65–74.

[Chen76] Chen, P.P. "The Entity-Relationship Model—Toward a Unified View of Data," *ACM Trans. Database Systems* 1, 1 (March 1976), pp. 9–36.

[Chen87] Chen and Associates, Inc. *ER Designer* (user manual), 1987.

[Chu69] Chu, W.W. "Optimal File Allocation in a Multiple Computer System," *IEEE Trans. on Computers* C-18, 10 (Oct. 1969), pp. 885–889.

[Chu84] Chu, W.W. *Distributed Data Bases, Handbook of Software Engineering*, C.R. Vick and C.V. Ramamoorthy (editors), Van Nostrand Reinhold, New York, 1984.

[ClWa83] Clifford, J., and Warren, D. "Formal Semantics for Time in Databases," *ACM Trans. Database Systems* 8, 2 (1983), pp. 214–254.

[CMCL95] Chen, C.Y.R., Meliksetian, D.S., Chang, M.C.-S., and Liu, L.J. "Design of a Multimedia Object-Oriented DBMS," *Multimedia Systems* 3 (1995), pp. 217–227.

[CNP82] Ceri, S., Negri, M., and Pelagatti, G. "Horizontal Data Partitioning in Database Design," *Proc. ACM-SIGMOD Int'l. Conf. on Management of Data,* 1982, pp. 128–136.

[CNW83] Ceri, S., Navathe, S.B., and Wiederhold, G. "Distribution Design of Logical Database Schemes," *IEEE Trans. on Soft. Engr.* SE-9, 4 (1983), pp. 487–504.

[Codd70] Codd, E. "A Relational Model for Large Shared Data Banks," *Comm. ACM* 13, 6 (June 1970), pp. 377–387.

[Codd74] Codd, E. "Recent Investigations into Relational Data Base Systems," *Proc. IFIP Congress,* North-Holland, Amsterdam, 1974.

[Codd79] Codd, E.F. "Extending the Database Relational Model to Capture More Meaning," *ACM TODS* 4, 4 (Dec. 1979), pp. 397–434.

[Codd90] Codd, E.F. *The Relational Model for Database Management: Version 2,* Addison-Wesley, Reading, MA, 1990.

[Codd95] Codd, E.F. "Twelve Rules for On Line Analytical Processing," *Computerworld* (April 13, 1995).

[Cole94] Coleman, D., Arnold, P., Bodoff, S., Dollin, C., and Gilchrist, H. *Object-Oriented Development: The Fusion Method,* Prentice Hall, Upper Saddle River, NJ, 1994.

[Coll96] Colliat, G. "OLAP, Relational, and Multidimensional Database Systems," *SIGMOD Record* 25, 3 (Sept. 1996), pp. 64–69.

[Conk87] Conklin, J. "Hypertext: An Introduction and Survey," *Computer* 20, 9 (1987), pp. 17–41.

[CoYo90] Coad, P., and Yourdon, E. *Object-Oriented Analysis,* Prentice Hall, Englewood Cliffs, NJ, 1990.

[CPW87] Ceri, S., Pernici, B., and Wiederhold, G. "Distributed Database Design Methodologies," *Proc. of the IEEE,* May 1987, pp. 533–546.

[Date84] Date, C.J. *A Guide to DB2,* Addison-Wesley, Reading, MA, 1984.

[Date87] Date, C.J. "The Twelve Rules for a Distributed Data Base," *Computerworld,* June 8, 1987.

[Date89] Date, C.J. *A Guide to the SQL Standard* (2nd Ed.), Addison-Wesley, Reading, MA, 1989.

[Date95] Date, C.J. *An Introduction to Database Systems, Vol. 1* (6th Ed.), Addison-Wesley, Reading, MA, 1995.

[DBMS93] *DBMS* (Special Issue: *Database Buyer's Guide*) 6, 7 (Sept. 1993).

[Deer90] Deerwester, S., Dumais, S.T., Furnas, G.W., Kandauer, T.K., and Harshman, R. "Indexing by Latent Semantic Analysis," *J. American Society for Information Science* 41, 6 (1990), pp. 391–407.

[DeMa78] De Marco, T. *Structured Analysis and System Specification,* Yourdon Press, New York, 1978.

[Devl97] Devlin, B. *Data Warehouses: From Architecture to Implementation,* Addison-Wesley, Reading, MA, 1997.

[DGL86] Dittrich, K.R., Gotthard, W., and Lockemann, P.C. "Complex Entities for Engineering Applications," *Proc. 5th ER Conf.,* North-Holland, Amsterdam, 1986.

[DKM86] Dittrich, K.R., Kotz, A.M., and Mulle, J.A. "An Event/Trigger Mechanism to Enforce Complex Consistency Constraints in Design Databases," *SIGMOD Record* 15, 3 (Sept. 1986), pp. 22–36.

[DKS92] Du, W., Krishnamurthy, R., and Shan, M-C. "Query Optimization in Heterogeneous DBMS," *Proc. 18th Intl. Conf. on VLDB,* 1992, pp. 277–291.

[DPH96] Dunlop, A.N., Papiani, M., and Hey, A.J.G. "Providing Access to a Multimedia Archive Using the World-Wide Web and an Object-Relational Database Management System," *IEE Computing and Control Engineering Journal* 7, 5 (Oct. 1996), pp. 221–226.

[Duga90] Dugan, J.B. "On Measurement and Modeling of Computer Systems Dependability: A Dialog among Experts," *IEEE Transactions on Reliability* 39, 4 (Oct. 1990), pp. 506–510.

[DuHa89] Dutka, A.F., and Hanson, H.H. *Fundamentals of Data Normalization,* Addison-Wesley, Reading, MA, 1989.

[EHW85] Elmasri, R., Hevner, A., and Weeldreyer, J. "The Category Concept: An Extension to the Entity-Relationship Model," *Data and Knowledge Engineering* 1, 1 (1985), pp. 75–116.

[EKR97] Ehmayer, G., Kappel, G., and Reich, S. "Connecting Databases to the Web: A Taxonomy of Gateways," *Proc. 8th Intl. Conf. on Database and Expert Systems Applications (DEXA97),* Springer LNCS 1308, Toulouse, France, Sept. 1997.

[ElNa94] Elmasri, R., and Navathe, S.B. *Fundamentals of Database Systems* (2nd Ed., Chap. 25), Benjamin/Cummings, Redwood City, CA, 1994.

[ElWi79] Elmasri, R., and Wiederhold, G. "Data Model Integration Using the Structural Model," *Proc. ACM SIGMOD Conf.,* Boston, 1979, ACM, New York, pp. 319–326.

[Ever86] Everest, G.C. *Database Management: Objectives, System Functions, and Administration,* McGraw-Hill, New York, 1986.

[Ever96] Evernden, R. "The Information FrameWork," *IBM Syst. J.* 35, 1 (1996), pp. 16–27.

[EWK90] Elmasri, R., Wuu, G.T., and Kouramajian, V. "The Time Index: An Access Structure for Temporal Data," *Proc. 16th Intl. Conf. on VLDB,* 1990, pp. 1–12.

[Fagi77] Fagin, R. "Multivalued Dependencies and a New Normal Form for Relational Databases," *ACM Trans. Database Systems* 2, 3 (1977), pp. 262–278.

[Fagi79] Fagin, R. "Normal Forms and Relational Database Operators," *Proc. 1979 ACM SIGMOD Conf. on Mgmt. of Data,* pp. 153–160.

[Falo92] Faloutsos, C. "Signature Files," *Information Retrieval: Data Structures and Algorithms,* W.B. Frakes and R. Baeza-Yates (editors), Prentice Hall, Upper Saddle River, NJ, 1992.

[Falo96] Faloutsos, C. *Searching Multimedia Databases by Content,* Kluwer, Norwell, MA, 1996.

[Fayy98] Fayyad, U. "Diving into Databases," *Database Prog. & Design* 11, 3 (March 1998), pp. 24–31.

[FeGr86] Federgruen, A., and Green, L. "Queueing Systems with Service Interruptions," *Operations Research,* 34, 5 (Sept.–Oct.), 1986, pp. 752–768.

[FeMi86] Feldman, P., and Miller, D. "Entity Model Clustering: Structuring a Data Model by Abstraction," *Computer Journal* 29, 4 (Aug. 1986), pp. 348–360.

[Ferg85] Ferg, S. "Modeling the Time Dimension in an Entity-Relationship Diagram," *Proc. 4th Intl. Conf. on the Entity-Relationship Approach,* IEEE Computer Society Press, Silver Spring, MD, 1985, pp. 280–286.

[FHJS85] Fong, E., Henderson, M., Jefferson, D., and Sullivan, J. *Guide on Logical Database Design,* NBS Spec. Pub. 500–122, U.S. Dept. of Commerce, 1985.

[FHS80] Fisher, P., Hollist, P., and Slonim, J. "A Design Methodology for Distributed Databases," *Proc. IEEE Conf. Distributed Computing,* 1980, IEEE, New York, pp. 199–202.

[FHS96] Fayyad, U., Haussler, D., and Stolorz, P. "Mining Scientific Data," *Comm. ACM* 39, 11 (Nov. 1996), pp. 51–57.

[FiHo80] Fisher, M.L., and Hochbaum, D. "Database Location in Computer Networks," *J. ACM* 27, 4 (Oct. 1980), pp. 718–735.

[FiKe92] Fichman, R.G., and Kemerer, C.F. "Object-Oriented and Conventional Analysis and Design Methodologies," *IEEE Computer* 25, 10 (Oct. 1992), pp. 22–39.

[FlvH89] Fleming, C.C., and von Halle, B. *Handbook of Relational Database Design,* Addison-Wesley, Reading, MA, 1989.

[FoDu92] Foltz, P.W., and Dumais, S.T. "Personalized Information Delivery: An Analysis of Information Filtering Methods," *Comm. ACM* 35, 12 (Dec. 1992), pp. 51–60.

[FoSc97] Fowler, M., with Scott, K. *UML Distilled: Applying the Standard Modeling Language,* Addison-Wesley, Reading, MA, 1997.

[FPS96] Fayyad, U., Piatetsky-Shapiro, G., and Smyth, P. "The KDD Process for Extracting Useful Knowledge from Volumes of Data," *Comm. ACM* 39, 11 (Nov. 1996), pp. 27–34.

[FPSU96] Fayyad, U.M., Piatetsky-Shapiro, G., Smyth, P., and Uthurusamy, R. (editors). *Advances in Knowledge Discovery and Data Mining,* MIT Press, Cambridge, MA, 1996.

[Fren95] French, C.D. "'One Size Fits All' Database Architectures Do Not Work for DSS," *Proc. 1995 ACM SIGMOD Intl. Conf. on Management of Data,* M. Carey and D. Schneider, (editors), *SIGMOD Record* 24, 2 (1995), pp. 449–450.

[Gadr87] Gadre, S.H. "Building an Enterprise and Information Model," *Database Prog. & Design* 1, 1 (Dec. 1987), pp. 48–58.

[GaSa79] Gane, C.P., and Sarson, T. *Structured System Analysis: Tools and Techniques,* Prentice Hall, Englewood Cliffs, NJ, 1979.

[GBJP97] Gray, J., Bosworth, A., Jayman, A., and Pirahesh, H. "Data Cube: A Relational Aggregation Operator Generalizing Group-by, Cross-Tab and Sub Totals," *Data Mining and Knowledge Discovery* 1, 1 (1997), pp. 29–53.

[GJM97] Grosky, W.I., Jain, R., and Mehrotra, R. *The Handbook of Multimedia Information Management,* Prentice Hall, Upper Saddle River, NJ, 1997.

[GLOT96] Goh, C.H., Lu, H., Ooi, B.C., and Tan, K.L. "Indexing Temporal Data Using B^+-Tree," *Data and Knowledge Engineering* 18 (1996), pp. 147–165.

[GrAn87] Gray, J.N. and Anderson, M. "Distributed Computer Systems: Four Cases," *Proc. IEEE* 75, 5 (May 1987), pp.719–729.

[Gray81] Gray, J. "The Transaction Concept: Virtues and Limitations," *Proc. 7th Intl. Conf. on Very Large Data Bases,* Sept. 1981, IEEE, New York, pp. 144–154.

[Gray90] Gray, J. "A Census of Tandem System Availability between 1985 and 1990," *IEEE Transactions on Reliability* 39, 4 (Oct. 1990), pp. 409–418.

[Grim98] Grimes, S. "The New Face of Data Access," *Database Prog. & Design* 11, 2 (Feb. 1998), pp. 35–40.

[Gros86] Grosshans, D. *File Systems Design and Implementation,* Prentice Hall, Englewood Cliffs, NJ, 1986.

[Grov98] Groves, S. "Business Intelligence Products," Savant, *http://www.sgroves.demon.co.uk/bi_products.html.*

[GrRe93] Gray, J., and Reuter, A. *Transaction Processing: Concepts and Techniques,* Morgan Kaufmann, San Francisco, 1993.

[GrWa98] Gray, P., and Watson, H.J. *Decision Support in the Data Warehouse,* Prentice Hall, Upper Saddle River, NJ, 1998.

[GST96] Gardarin, G., Sha, F., and Tang, Z.-H. "Calibrating the Query Optimizer Cost Model of IOR-DB, an Object-Oriented Federated Database System," *Proc. 22nd Intl. Conf. on VLDB,* 1996, pp. 378–389.

[GuSe93] Gunadhi, O., and Segev, A. "Efficient Indexing Methods for Temporal Relation," *IEEE Trans. on Knowledge and Data Engineering* 5, 3 (1993), pp. 496–509.

[Gutt84] Guttman, A. "R-trees: A Dynamic Index Structure for Spatial Searching," *Proc. ACM SIGMOD Intl. Conf. on Mgt. of Data,* B. Yormack (editor), 1984, pp. 47–57.

[HaCa97] Hamilton, G., and Cattell, R. "JDBC: A JAVA SQL API," Version 1.20, JavaSoft Inc., January 10, 1997.

[HaMc82] Hammer, M., and McLeod, D. "Database Description with SDM: A Semantic Database Model," *ACM Trans. Database Systems* 6, 3 (Sept. 1982), pp. 351–386.

[Harb88] Harbron, T.R. *File Systems Structures and Algorithms,* Prentice Hall, Englewood Cliffs, NJ, 1988.

[Hawr84] Hawryszkiewycz, I. *Database Analysis and Design,* SRA, Chicago, 1984.

[Hawr90] Hawryszkiewycz, I. *Relational Database Design,* Prentice Hall, Upper Saddle River, NJ, 1990.

[Heba77] Hebalkar, P.G. "Logical Design Considerations for Distributed Database Systems," *IEEE COMPSAC,* Nov. 1977, pp. 562–580.

[Hern97] Hernandez, M.J. *Database Design for Mere Mortals,* Addison-Wesley, Reading, MA. 1997.

[HeYa87] Hevner, A.R., and Yao, S.B. "Querying Distributed Databases on Local Area Networks," *Proc. IEEE* 75, 5 (May 1987), pp. 563–572.

[HHW97] Hellerstein, J.M., Haas, P.J. and Wang, H.J. "Online Aggregation," *Proc. 1997 ACM SIGMOD Conf, on Mgt. of Data*, Tucson, AZ, pp. 171–182.

[HRU96] Harinarayan, V., Rajaraman, A., and Ullman, J. "Implementing Data Cubes Efficiently," *Proc. 1996 ACM SIGMOD Conf. on Mgt. of Data*, Montreal, pp. 205–216.

[HsKa89] Hsiao, D.K., and Kamel, M.N. "Heterogeneous Databases: Proliferations, Issues, and Solutions," *IEEE Trans. on Knowledge and Data Engineering* 1, 1 (March 1989), pp. 45–62.

[HuBr95] Hurson, A.R. and Bright, M.W. "Object-Oriented Multidatabase Systems," *Object-Oriented Multiase Systems*, O.A. Bukres and A.K. Elmagarmid (editors), Prentice Hall, Upper Saddle River, NJ, 1995.

[HuKi87] Hull, R., and King, R. "Semantic Database Modeling: Survey, Applications, and Research Issues," *ACM Computing Surveys* 19, 3 (Sept. 1987), pp. 201–260.

[IBM94] IBM. "IFW Financial Services Data Model Description," IFW 03101, IBM Corporation, San Jose, CA, 1994.

[IEEE92] *IEEE Computer* (Special Issue: *Inheritance and Classification in Object-Oriented Computing*) 25, 10 (Oct. 1992), pp. 6–90.

[Inmo87] Inmon, W.H. "Optimizing Performance with Denormalization," *Database Prog. & Design* 1, 1 (Dec. 1987), pp. 34–39.

[Inmo92a] Inmon, W.H. *Building the Data Warehouse*, Wiley-QED Publishing Group, Somerset, NJ, 1992.

[Inmo92b] Inmon, W.H. "Should We Rewrite History?" *Database Prog. & Design* 5, 3 (March 1992), pp. 70–71.

[IrKh81] Irani, K.B., and Khabbaz, N.G. "A Combined Communication Network Design and File Allocation for Distributed Databases," *2nd Intl. Conf. on Distributed Systems*, IEEE Computer Society Press, April 1981.

[ISAN89] *ISO-ANSI Database Language SQL2 and SQL3*, ANSI X3H2-89-110, ISO DBL CAN-3 (working draft), J. Melton (editor), February 1989.

[ISAN92] ANSI X3.135-1992 Database Language SQL and ISO/IEC 9075:1992 Database Language SQL.

[ISO82] ISO/TC97/SC5/WG3-N695 Report. "Concepts and Terminology for the Conceptual Schema and the Information Base," J. van Griethuysen (editor), ANSI, New York, 1982.

[Jaco87] Jacobsen, I. "Object Oriented Development in an Industrial Environment," OOPSLA'87 as *ACM SIGPLAN* 22, 12 (Dec. 1987), pp. 183–191.

[JaKo84] Jarke, M., and Koch, J. "Query Optimization in Database Systems," *ACM Computing Surveys* 16, 2 (June 1984), pp. 111–152.

[JaNg84] Jajodia, S., and Ng, P. "Translation of Entity-Relationship Diagrams into Relational Structures," *J. Systems and Software* 4, 2–3 (1984) pp. 123–133.

[Java96] Java database access, Sun Microsystems Inc., 1996, *http://splash.javasoft.com/jdbc/jdbc.databases.html.*

[Jens94] Jenson, C.S., Clifford, J., Elmasri, R., Gadia, S.K., Hayes, P., and Jajodia, S. (editors). "A Glossary of Temporal Database Concepts," *SIGMOD Record* 23, 1 (March 1994), pp. 52–64.

[JeSn96] Jensen, C.S., and Snodgrass, R.T. "Semantics of Time-Varying Information," *Information Systems* 21, 4 (1996), pp. 311–352.

[JoMa88] Johnson, A.M., Jr., and Malek, M. "Survey of Software Tools for Evaluating Reliability, Availability, and Serviceability," *ACM Computing Surveys* 20, 4 (Dec. 1988), pp. 227–269.

[JWBT91] Janakiraman, J., Warack, C., Bhal, G., and Teorey, T.J. "Progressive Fragment Allocation," *Proc. 10th Int'l. Conf. on the Entity Relationship Approach*, ER Institute, San Mateo, CA, 1991, pp. 543–560.

[KeMo94] Kemper, A., and Moerkotte, G. *Object-Oriented Database Management*, Prentice Hall, Upper Saddle River, NJ, 1994.

[Kent78] Kent, W. *Data and Reality*, Elsevier, Amsterdam, 1978.

[Kent81] Kent, W. "Consequences of Assuming a Universal Relation," *ACM Trans. Database Systems* 6, 4 (1981), pp. 539–556.

[Kent83] Kent, W. "A Simple Guide to Five Normal Forms in Relational Database Theory," *Comm. ACM* 26, 2 (Feb. 1983), pp. 120–125.

[Kent84] Kent, W. "Fact-Based Data Analysis and Design," *J. Systems and Software* 4 (1984), pp. 99–121.

[KhBa96] Khoshafian, S., and Baker, A.B. *Multimedia and Imaging Databases*, Morgan Kaufmann, San Francisco, 1996.

[KiLo89] Kim, W., and Lochovsky, F. *Object-Oriented Concepts, Databases, and Applications,* Addison-Wesley, Reading, MA, 1989.

[Kimb96] Kimball, R. *The Data Warehouse Toolkit,* John Wiley & Sons, New York, 1996.

[Kolo93] Kolovson, C. "Indexing Techniques for Historical Databases," *Temporal Databases: Theory, Design, and Implementa-*

tion, A. Tansel (editor), Benjamin/Cummings, Redwood City, CA, 1993, pp. 418–432.

[Kroe95] Kroenke, D.M. *Database Processing: Fundamentals, Design, and Implementation* (5th Ed.), Prentice Hall, Upper Saddle River, NJ, 1995.

[KSS97] Korth, H.F., Silberschatz, A., and Sudarshan, S. *Database System Concepts* (3rd Ed.), McGraw-Hill, New York, 1997.

[KTF95] Kumar, A., Tsotras, V.J., and Faloutsos, C. "Access Methods for Bitemporal Databases," *Proc. Intl. Workshop on Temporal Databases*, 1995, pp. 235–254.

[Kuni95] Kunii, T.L., Shinagawa, Y., Paul, R.M., Khan, M.F., and Khokhar, A.A. "Issues in Storage and Retrieval of Multimedia Data," *Multimedia Systems* 3 (1995), pp. 298–304.

[Lars95] Larson, J.A. *Database Directions: From Relational to Distributed, Multimedia, and Object-Oriented Database Systems*, Prentice Hall, Upper Saddle River, NJ, 1995.

[LeMu92] Leung, T.Y.C., and Muntz, R.R. "Generalized Data Stream Indexing and Temporal Query Processing," *2nd Intl. Workshop on Research Issues in Data Eng: Transaction and Query Processing*, 1992.

[LeSa83] Lenzerini, M., and Santucci, G. "Cardinality Constraints in the Entity-Relationship Model," *The Entity-Relationship Approach to Software Engineering*, G.C. Davis et al. (editors), Elsevier, North-Holland, Amsterdam, 1983, pp. 529–549.

[LiCe96] Lin, T.Y., and Cercone, N. *Rough Sets and Data Mining*, Kluwer, Norwell, MA, 1996.

[Lien81] Lien, Y. "Hierarchical Schemata for Relational Databases," *ACM Trans. Database Systems* 6, 1 (1981), pp. 48–69.

[Lien82] Lien, Y. "On the Equivalence of Data Models," *J. ACM* 29, 2 (1982), pp. 333–362.

[Ling85] Ling, T. "A Normal Form for Entity-Relationship Diagrams," *Proc. 4th International Conf. on the ER Approach*, IEEE Computer Society Press, Silver Spring, MD, 1985, pp. 24–35.

[LiWa96] Li, C., and Wang, X.S. "A Data Model for Supporting On-Line Analytical Processing," *Proc. CIKM Conf.*, 1996.

[Loom83] Loomis, M.E.S. *Data Management and File Processing*, Prentice Hall, Englewood Cliffs, NJ, 1983.

[LoRa94] Lo, M.-L., and Ravishankar, C.V. "Spatial Joins Using Seeded Trees," *Proc. ACM SIGMOD Intl. Conf. on Mgt. of Data*, R.T. Snodgrass and M. Winslett (editors), 1994, pp. 209–220.

[LoRa96] Lo, M.-L., and Ravishankar, C.V. "Spatial Hash Joins," *Proc. ACM SIGMOD Intl. Conf. on Mgt. of Data*, 1996, pp. 247–258.

[LoSa93] Lomet, D., and Salzberg, B. "Transaction Time Databases," *Temporal Databases: Theory, Design, and Implementation*, Chapter 16, A. Tansel (editor), Benjamin/Cummings, Redwood City, CA, 1993, pp.388–417.

[Maci89] Maciaszek, L. *Database Design and Implementation,"* Prentice Hall, Upper Saddle River, NJ, 1989.

[MaFe90] Maxion, R.A., and Feather, F.E. "A Case Study of Ethernet Anomalies in a Distributed Computing Environment," *IEEE Transactions on Reliability* 39, 4 (Oct. 1990), pp. 433–443.

[Maie83] Maier, D. *Theory of Relational Databases,* Computer Science Press, Rockville, MD, 1983.

[MaRi76] Mahmood, S., and Riordan, J. "Optimal Allocation of Resources in Distributed Information Networks," *ACM Trans. Database Systems* 1, 1 (March 1976), pp. 66–78.

[Mark87] Mark, L. "Defining Views in the Binary Relationship Model," *Inform. Systems* 12, 3 (1987), pp. 281–294.

[Mart82] Martin, J. *Strategic Data-Planning Methodologies,* Prentice Hall, Englewood Cliffs, NJ, 1982.

[Mart83] Martin, J. *Managing the Data-Base Environment,* Prentice Hall, Englewood Cliffs, NJ, 1983.

[MaSh89a] Markowitz, V.M., and Shoshani, A. "Name Assignment Techniques for Relational Schemas Representing Extended Entity-Relationship Schemas," *Proc. 8th Intl. Conf. on the Entity-Relationship Approach,* 1989, pp. 21–39.

[MaSh89b] Markowitz, V.M., and Shoshani, A. "On the Correctness of Representing Extended Entity-Relationship Structures in the Relational Model," *Proc. ACM SIGMOD Conf. on Management of Data,* 1989, pp. 430–439.

[MaTe88] Mantei, M.M., and Teorey, T.J. "Cost/Benefit Analysis for Incorporating Human Factors into the Software Lifecycle," *Comm. ACM* 31, 4 (April 1988), pp. 428–439.

[Matt96] Mattison, R. *Data Warehousing: Strategies, Technologies, and Techniques,* McGraw-Hill, New York, 1996.

[McGe74] McGee, W. "A Contribution to the Study of Data Equivalence," *Data Base Management,* J.W. Klimbie and K.L. Koffeman (editors), North-Holland, Amsterdam, 1974, pp. 123–148.

[McKi79] McLeod, D., and King, R. "Applying a Semantic Database Model," *Proc. 1st Intl. Conf. on the Entity-Relationship Approach to Systems Analysis and Design*, North-Holland, Amsterdam, 1979, pp. 193–210.

[MeKh96] Meredith, M.E., and Khader, A. "Divide and Aggregate: Designing Large Warehouses," *Database Prog. & Design* 9, 6 (June 1996), pp. 24–30.

[Melt95] Melton, J. "Accommodating SQL3 and ODMG," ANSI X3H2-95-161/ DBL:YOW-32, April 15, 1995, *http://www.jcc.com/sql_s3h2_95_161.html.*

[MeMa95] Melton, J., and Mattos, N.M. "An Overview of the Emerging Third-Generation SQL Standard," *Proc. ACM SIGMOD Intl. Conf. on Mgt. of Data*, 1995.

[MeMa96] Melton, J., and Mattos, N.M. "An Overview of SQL3—the Emerging New Generation of the SQL Standard," *Tutorials of the 22nd Intl. Conf. on VLDB*, 1996.

[MeSi93] Melton, J., and Simon, A.R. *Understanding the New SQL: A Complete Guide*, Morgan Kaufmann, San Francisco, 1993.

[Meye88] Meyer, B. *Object-Oriented Software Construction*, Prentice Hall Hertfordshire, England, 1988.

[MeYu95] Meng, W., and Yu, C. "Query Processing in Multidatabase Systems," *Modern Database Systems*, W. Kim (editor), ACM Press, New York, 1995, pp. 551–572.

[Mitt91] Mittra, S.S. *Principles of Relational Database Systems*, Prentice Hall, Upper Saddle River, NJ, 1991.

[MMR86] Makowsky, J.A., Markowitz, V.M., and Rotics, N. "Entity-Relationship Consistency for Relational Schemas," *Proc. Intl. Conf. on Database Theory*, G. Ausiello and P. Atzeni (editors), Springer-Verlag, New York, Sept. 1986, pp. 306–322.

[MoLe77] Morgan, H.L., and Levin, K.D. "Optimal Program and Data Allocation in Computer Networks," *Comm. ACM* 32, 5 (May 1977), pp. 345–353.

[MQM97] Mumick, I.S., Quass, D., and Mumick, B.S. "Maintenance of Data Cubes and Summary Tables in a Warehouse," *Proc. 1997 ACM SIGMOD Intl. Conf. on Mgt. of Data*, pp. 100–111.

[MSOP86] Maier, D., Stein, J., Otis, A., and Purdy, A. "Development of an Object-Oriented DBMS," *OOPSLA 1986 Proc.*, Sept. 1986, pp. 472–482.

[MTM91] Moyne, J.R., Teorey, T.J., and McAfee, L.C. "Time Sequence Ordering Extensions to the Entity Relationship Model and Their Application to the Automated Manufacturing Process," *Data and Knowledge Engr.* 6, 5 (Sept. 1991), pp. 421–433.

[MuPo97] Mueck, T.A., and Polaschek, M.L. *Index Data Structures in Object-Oriented Databases*, Kluwer, Norwell, MA, 1997.

[NaAh93] Navathe, S.B., and Ahmed, R. "Temporal Extensions to the Relational Model and SQL," *Temporal Databases: Theory, Design, and Implementation*, A. Tansel (editor), Benjamin/Cummings, Redwood City, CA, 1993.

[NaCh83] Navathe, S., and Cheng, A. "A Methodology for Database Schema Mapping from Extended Entity Relationship Models into the Hierarchical Model," *The Entity-Relationship Approach to Software Engineering,* G.C. Davis et al. (editors), Elsevier, North-Holland, Amsterdam, 1983.

[NaGa82] Navathe, S., and Gadgil, S. "A Methodology for View Integration in Logical Database Design," *Proc. 8th Intl. Conf. on Very Large Data Bases,* 1982, IEEE, New York, pp. 142–152.

[NEL86] Navathe, S., Elmasri, R., and Larson, J. "Integrating User Views in Database Design," *IEEE Computer* 19, 1 (1986), pp. 50–62.

[NiHa89] Nijssen, G.M., and Halpin, T.A. *Conceptual Schema and Relational Database Design: A Fact Oriented Approach,* Prentice Hall, New York, 1989.

[NSE84] Navathe, S., Sashidhar, T., and Elmasri, R. "Relationship Merging in Schema Integration," *Proc. 10th Intl. Conf. on Very Large Data Bases,* 1984, pp. 78–90.

[NvS79] Nijssen, G., van Assche, F., and Snijders, J. "End User Tools for Information Systems Requirement Definition," *Formal Models and Practical Tools for Information System Design,* H. Schneider (editor), North-Holland, Amsterdam, 1979.

[ODBC] *ODBC 2.0 Programmer's Reference and SDK Guide*, ISBN 1-55615-658-8.

[OHE96] Orfali, R., Harkey, D., and Edwards, J. *The Essential Client/Server Survival Guide* (2nd Ed.), John Wiley & Sons, New York, 1996.

[ONei94] O'Neil, P. *Database: Principles, Programming, Practice,* Morgan Kaufmann, San Francisco, 1994.

[ONGr95] O'Neil, P., and Graefe, G. "Multi-Table Joins through Bitmapped Join Indices," *SIGMOD Record* 24, 3 (Sept. 1995).

[OR89a] *Oracle Database Administrator's Guide,* Part No. 3601-V5.1, 1989.

[OR89b] *Oracle RDBMS Performance Tuning Guide,* Part No. 5317-V6.0, 1989.

[Oren85] Oren, O. "Integrity Constraints in the Conceptual Schema Language SYSDOC," *Proc. 4th Intl. Conf. on the Entity-Relationship Approach,* Chicago, IEEE Computer Society Press, Silver Spring, MD, 1985, pp. 288–294.

[ORS97] Ozden, B., Rastogi, R., and Silberschatz, A. "Architecture Issues in Multimedia Storage Systems," *Performance Evaluation Review* 25, 2 (Sept. 1997), pp. 3–12.

[Ossh84] Ossher, H.L. "A New Program Structuring Mechanism Based on Layered Graphs," *Proc. 11th Annual ACM SIGACT-SIGPLAN POPL,* 1984, pp. 11–22.

[OzSn95] Ozsoyoglu, G., and Snodgrass, R.T. "Temporal and Real-Time Databases: A Survey," *IEEE Trans. for Knowledge and Data Engr.*, 7, 4 (Aug. 1995), pp. 513–532.

[OzVa91] Ozsu, M.T., and Valduriez, P. *Principles of Distributed Database Systems*, Prentice Hall, Englewood Cliffs, NJ, 1991.

[Papi97] Papiani, M. "Generic Web Interfaces for Accessing and Browsing Federated Databases," MSc. mini-thesis, ECS Dept., Univ. of Southampton, Sept. 1997.

[Parn72] Parnas, D.L. "On the Criteria to be Used in Decomposing Systems into Modules," *Comm. ACM* 15, 12 (1972), pp. 1053–1058.

[Pars97] Parsaye, K. "OLAP and Data Mining: Bridging the Gap," *Database Prog. & Design* 10, 2 (Feb. 1997), pp. 30–37.

[PaSp86] Parent, C., and Spaccapietra, S. "Enhancing the Operational Semantics of the Entity-Relationship Model," in *Database Semantics (DS-1),* T.B. Steel, Jr. and R. Meersman (editors), Elsevier, North-Holland, 1986, pp. 159–173.

[PBE95] Pitoura, E., Bukres, O., and Elmagarmid, A. "Object Orientation in Multidatabase Systems," *ACM Computing Surveys* 27, 2 (1995), pp. 141–195.

[PDH97] Papiani, M., Dunlop, A.N., and Hey, A.J.G. "Automatic Web Interfaces and Browsing for Object-Relational Databases," *Advances in Databases: Proc. 15th British National Conf. on Databases, BNCOD15*, 1997, pp. 131–132.

[PeCr95] Pendse, N., and Creeth, R. *The OLAP Report: Succeeding with On-Line Analytical Processing*, Business Intelligence Ltd., London, 1995.

[PeMa88] Peckham, J., and Maryanski, F. "Semantic Data Models," *ACM Computing Surveys* 20, 3 (Sept. 1988), pp. 153–190.

[Poe96] Poe, V. *Building a Data Warehouse for Decision Support*, Prentice Hall, Upper Saddle River, NJ, 1996.

[PoKe86] Potter, W.D., and Kerschberg, L. "A Unified Approach to Modeling Knowledge and Data," *IFIP WG 2.6 Working Conf. on Knowledge and Data,* Elsevier, North-Holland, Amsterdam, Sept. 1986.

[Prab96] Prabhakaran, B. *Multimedia Database Management Systems,* Kluwer, Norwell, MA, 1996.

[Rama96] Ramamritham, K., Sivasankaran, R., Stankovic, J.A., Towsley, D.T., and Xiong, M. "Integrating Temporal, Real-Time, and Active Databases," *SIGMOD Record* 25, 1 (March 1996), pp. 8–12.

[Rama97] Ramakrishnan, R. *Database Management Systems,* McGraw-Hill, New York, 1997.

[Rein85] Reiner, D., Brodie, M., Brown, G., Friedell, M., Kramlich, D., Lehman, J., and Rosenthal, A. "The Database Design and Evaluation Workbench (DDEW) Project at CCA," *Database Engineering* 7, 4 (1985), pp. 10–15.

[Rein86] Reiner, D., Brown, G., Friedell, M., Lehman, J., McKee, R., Rheingans, P., and Rosenthal, A. "A Database Designer's Workbench," *Proc. 5th ER Conference,* North-Holland, Amsterdam, 1986, pp. 347–360.

[RKR97] Roussopoulos, N., Kotidis, Y., and Roussopoulos, M. "Cubetree: Organization of and Bulk Incremental Updates on the Data Cube," *Proc. 1997 ACM SIGMOD Intl. Conf. on Mgt. of Data,* pp. 89–99.

[Robi81] Robinson, J.T. "The k-D-B-Tree: A Search Structure for Large Multidimensional Dynamic Indexes," *Proc. ACM SIGMOD Intl. Conf. on Mgt. of Data,* 1981, pp. 10–18.

[Rodg89] Rodgers, U. "Denormalization: Why, What, and How?" *Database Prog. & Design* 2, 12 (Dec. 1989), pp. 46–53.

[RoSt87] Rowe, L., and Stonebraker, M. "The Postgres Data Model," *Proc. 13th Intl. Conf. on Very Large Data Bases,* Sept. 1–4, 1987.

[Rumb91] Rumbaugh, J., Blaha, M., Premerlani, W., Eddy, F., and Lorensen, W. *Object-Oriented Modeling and Design,* Prentice Hall, Englewood Cliffs, NJ, 1991.

[Sacco87] Sacco, G.M. "The Fact Model: A Semantic Data Model for Complex Databases," *ESPRIT 86: Results and Achievements,* Elsevier, North-Holland, Amsterdam, 1987, pp. 587–594.

[Saka83] Sakai, H. "Entity-Relationship Approach to Logical Database Design," *Entity-Relationship Approach to Software Engineering,* C.G. Davis, S. Jajodia, P.A. Ng, and R.T. Yeh (editors), Elsevier, North-Holland, New York, 1983, pp. 155–187.

[SaMe86] Sanders, W.H., and Meyer, J.F. "METASAN: A Performability Evaluation Tool Based on Stochastic Activity Networks," *Proc. 1986 Fall Joint Computer Conference*, 1986, AFIPS, New York, pp. 807–816.

[Same90] Samet, H. *The Design and Analysis of Spatial Data Structures*, Addison-Wesley, Reading, MA, 1990.

[SaTr87] Sahner, R.A., and Trivedi, K.S. "Reliability Modeling Using SHARPE," *IEEE Transactions on Reliability* 36, 2 (June 1987), pp. 186–193.

[SaTs98] Salzberg, B., and Tsotras, V.J. "A Comparison of Access Methods for Time Evolving Data," *ACM Computing Surveys* (to appear 1998).

[ScSo80] Schkolnick, M., and Sorenson, P. "Denormalization: A Performance Oriented Database Design Technique," *Proc. AICA 1980 Congress,* AICA, Brussels, pp. 363–377.

[ScWy97] Schloss, G.A., and Wynblatt, M.J. "Providing Definition and Temporal Structure for Multimedia Data," *Multimedia Systems* 3 (1995), pp. 264–277.

[Seli79] Selinger, P. G., Astrahan, M.M., Chamberlin, D.D., Lorie, R.A., Price, T.C. "Access Path Selection on a Relational Database Management System," *Proc. 1979 ACM SIGMOD Internatl. Conf. on Management of Data,* ACM, New York, pp. 23–34.

[Senk73] Senko et al. "Data Structures and Accessing in Data-base Systems," *IBM Syst. J.* 12, 1 (1973), pp. 30–93.

[Shee89] Sheer, A.-W. *Enterprise-Wide Data Modelling,* Springer-Verlag, Berlin, 1989.

[ShMe88] Shlaer, S., and Mellor, S. *Object-Oriented Systems Analysis: Modeling the World in Data*, Yourdon Press, Englewood Cliffs, NJ, 1988.

[Simo95] Simon, A.R. *Strategic Database Technology: Management for the Year 2000,* Morgan Kaufmann, San Francisco, 1995.

[SiSw82] Siewiorek, D.P., and Swarz, R.S. *The Theory and Practice of Reliable System Design,* Digital Press, Bedford, MA, 1982.

[SiTe95] Simovici, D.A., and Tenney, R.L. *Relational Database Systems*, Academic Press, San Diego, CA, 1995.

[SKS96] Soparkar, N.R., Korth, H.F., and Silberschatz, A. *Time-Constrained Transaction Management*, Kluwer, Norwell, MA, 1996.

[SMC74] Stevens, W., Myers, G., and Constantine, L. "Structured Design," *IBM Syst. J.* 13, 2 (1974), pp. 115–139.

[Smit85] Smith, H. "Database Design: Composing Fully Normalized Tables from a Rigorous Dependency Diagram," *Comm. ACM* 28, 8 (1985), pp. 826–838.

[SmSm77] Smith, J., and Smith, D. "Database Abstractions: Aggregation and Generalization," *ACM Trans. Database Systems* 2, 2 (June 1977), pp. 105–133.

[Snod90] Snodgrass, R. "Temporal Databases: Status and Future Directions," *SIGMOD Record* 19, 4 (Dec. 1990), pp. 83–89.

[SOL94] Shen, H., Ooi, B.C., and Lu, H. "The TP-Index: A Dynamic and Efficient Indexing Mechanism for Temporal Databases," *10th Intl. Conf. on Data Engineering,* 1994, pp. 274–281.

[SQL3] SQL standards home page: *http://www.jcc.com/sql_stnd.html.*

[SRF87] Sellis, T., Roussopoulos, N., and Faloutsos, C. "The R+-Tree: A Dynamic Index for Multi-Dimensional Objects," *Proc. 13th Intl. Conf. on Very Large Data Bases*, Brighton, UK, 1987, pp. 507–518.

[SSW80] Scheuermann, P., Scheffner, G., and Weber, H. "Abstraction Capabilities and Invariant Properties Modelling within the Entity-Relationship Approach," *Entity-Relationship Approach to Systems Analysis and Design,* P. Chen (editor), Elsevier, North-Holland, Amsterdam, 1980, pp. 121–140.

[StMa88] Stein, J., and Maier, D. "Concepts in Object-Oriented Data Management," *Database Prog. & Design* 1, 4 (April 1988), pp. 58–67.

[StMo96] Stonebraker, M., with Moore, D. *Object-Relational DBMSs: The Next Great Wave,* Morgan Kaufmann, San Francisco, 1996.

[Stod97] Stoddard, D. "The Database Dozen," *Database Prog. & Design* 10, 13 (Dec. 1997), pp. 8–24.

[Ston98] Stonebraker, M. (editor) *Readings in Database Systems* (3rd Ed.), Morgan Kaufmann, San Francisco, 1998.

[StRo86] Stonebraker, M., and Rowe, L.A. "The Design of Postgres," *Proc. ACM-SIGMOD Intl. Conf. on Management of Data,* 1986, pp. 340–355.

[Su83] Su, S.Y.W. "SAM*: A Semantic Association Model for Corporate and Scientific Statistical Databases," *Inform. Sciences* 29, 2–3 (May–June 1983), pp. 151–199.

[Subr98] Subrahmanian, V.S. *Principles of Multimedia Database Systems,* Morgan Kaufmann, San Francisco, 1998.

[Swee85] Sweet, F. "Process-Driven Data Design," *Datamation* (first of a series of 14 articles), 31, 16 (1985), pp. 84–85.

[Tans93] Tansel, A., Clifford, J., Gadia, S., Jajodia, S, Segev, A., and Snodgrass, R. (editors). *Temporal Databases: Theory, Design, and Implementation*, Benjamin/Cummings, Redwood City, CA, 1993.

[TCOU89] Teorey, T.J., Chaar, J., Olukotun, K., and Umar, A. "Distributed Database Design: Some Basic Concepts and Strategies," *Database Prog. & Design* 2, 4 (April 1989), pp. 34–42.

[TeFr82] Teorey, T., and Fry, J. *Design of Database Structures*, Prentice Hall, Upper Saddle River, NJ, 1982.

[TeHe77] Teichroew, D., and Hershey, E.A. "PSL/PSA: A Computer Aided Technique for Structured Documentation and Analysis of Information Processing Systems," *IEEE Trans. Software Engr.* SE-3, 1 (1977), pp. 41–48.

[TeNg98] Teorey, T.J., and Ng, W.-T. "Dependability and Performance Measures for the Database Practitioner," *IEEE Transactions on Knowledge and Data Engineering* 10, 3 (May/June 1998) pp. 499–503.

[Teor89] Teorey, T.J. "Distributed Database Design: A Practical Approach and Example," *SIGMOD Record* 18, 4 (Dec. 1989), pp. 23–39.

[TeWi97] Texel, P.P., and Williams, C.B. *USE CASES Combined with BOOCH/OMT/UML: Process and Products*, Prentice Hall, Upper Saddle River, NJ, 1997.

[TeYa91] Teorey, T.J., and Yang, D. "Usage Refinement for ER-to-Relation Design Transformations," *Information Sciences* 55, 1–3 (June 1991), pp. 49–67.

[TGH94] Tsotras, V.J., Gopinath, B., and Hart, G.W. "Efficient Management of Time-Evolving Databases," *IEEE Trans. on Knowledge and Data Engineering*, 1994.

[Thom97a] Thomsen, E. "Dimensional Modeling: An Analytical Approach," *Database Prog. & Design* 10, 3 (March 1997), pp. 29–35.

[Thom97b] Thomsen, E. "Mining Your Way to OLAP," *Database Prog. & Design* 10, 9 (Sept. 1997), pp. 101–103.

[Thom97c] Thomsen, E. *OLAP Solutions*, John Wiley & Sons, New York, 1997.

[TsLo82] Tsichritzis, D., and Lochovsky, F. *Data Models*, Prentice Hall, Englewood Cliffs, NJ, 1982.

[TWBK89] Teorey, T.J., Wei, G., Bolton, D.L., and Koenig, J.A. "ER Model Clustering as an Aid for User Communication and Documentation in Database Design," *Comm. ACM* 32, 8 (Aug. 1989), pp. 975–987.

[TYF86] Teorey, T.J., Yang, D., and Fry, J.P. "A Logical Design Methodology for Relational Databases Using the Extended Entity-Relationship Model," *ACM Computing Surveys* 18, 2 (June 1986), pp. 197–222.

[Ullm88] Ullman, J. *Principles of Database and Knowledge-Base Systems, Vols. 1 and 2,* Computer Science Press, Rockville, MD, 1988.

[UlWi97] Ullman, J., and Widom, J. *A First Course in Database Systems,* Prentice Hall, Upper Saddle River, NJ, 1997.

[VeVa82] Verheijen, G., and Van Bekkum, J. "NIAM: An Information Analysis Method," *Information Systems Design Methodologies,* T.W. Olle, et al. (editors), North-Holland, Amsterdam, 1982, pp. 537–590.

[WaGr97] Watson, H.J., and Gray, P. *Decision Support in the Data Warehouse,* Prentice Hall, Upper Saddle River, NJ, 1997.

[WeIn98] Weiss, S.M., and Indurkhya, N. *Predictive Data Mining,* Morgan Kaufmann, San Francisco, 1998.

[Wied83] Wiederhold, G. *Database Design* (2nd Ed.), McGraw-Hill, New York, 1983.

[Wied86] Wiederhold, G. "Views, Objects, and Databases," *IEEE Computer,* Dec. 1986, pp. 37–44.

[Wied87] Wiederhold, G. *File Organization for Database Design,* McGraw-Hill, New York, 1987.

[Wilm84] Wilmot, R. "Foreign Keys Decrease Adaptability of Database Designs," *Comm. ACM* 27, 12 (Dec. 1984), pp. 1237–1243.

[WoKa79] Wong, E., and Katz, R. "Logical Design and Schema Conversion for Relational and DBTG Databases," *Proc. Intl. Conf. on the Entity-Relationship Approach,* 1979, pp. 311–322.

[WPM89] Wasserman, A.I., Pircher, P.A., and Muller, R.J. "An Object-Oriented Structured Design Method for Code Generation," *Software Eng. Notices* 14, 1 (Jan. 1989), pp. 32–55.

[Yao85] Yao, S.B. (editor). *Principles of Database Design,* Prentice Hall, Upper Saddle River, NJ, 1985.

[YoCo79] Yourdon, E., and Constantine, L.L. *Structured Design,* Prentice Hall, Englewood Cliffs, NJ, 1979.

[YuCh84] Yu, C., and Chang, C. "Distributed Query Processing," *ACM Computing Surveys* 16, 4 (Dec. 1984), pp. 399–433.

[ZaMe81] Zaniolo, C., and Melkanoff, M. "On the Design of Relational Database Schemas," *ACM Trans. Database Systems* 6, 1 (1981), pp. 1–47.

[Zani97] Zaniolo, C., Ceri, S., Faloutsos, C., Snodgrass, R., Subrahmanian, V.S., and Zicari, P. *Advanced Database Systems*, Morgan Kaufmann, San Francisco, 1997.

[ZdMa90] Zdonik, S., and Maier, D. *Readings in Object-Oriented Database Systems,* Morgan Kaufmann, San Francisco, 1990.

[ZDN97] Zhao, Y., Deshpande, P.M., and Naughton, J.F. "An Array-Based Algorithm for Simultaneous Multidimensional Aggregates," *Proc. 1997 ACM SIGMOD Conf. on Mgt. of Data*, pp. 159–170.

Solutions to Selected Exercises

Problem 2-3 (page 43)

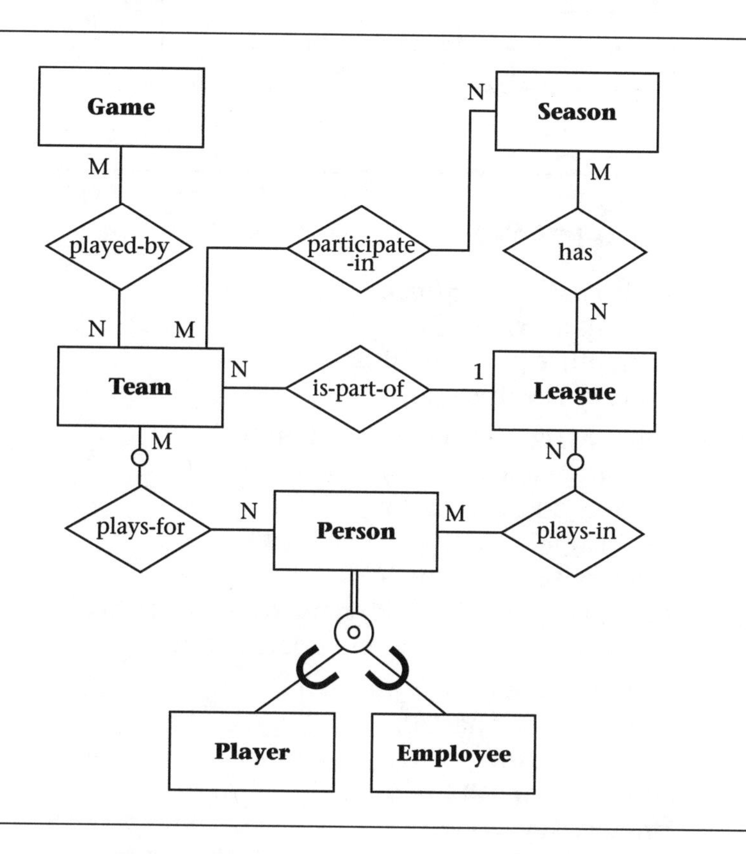

Problem 3-2 (page 77)

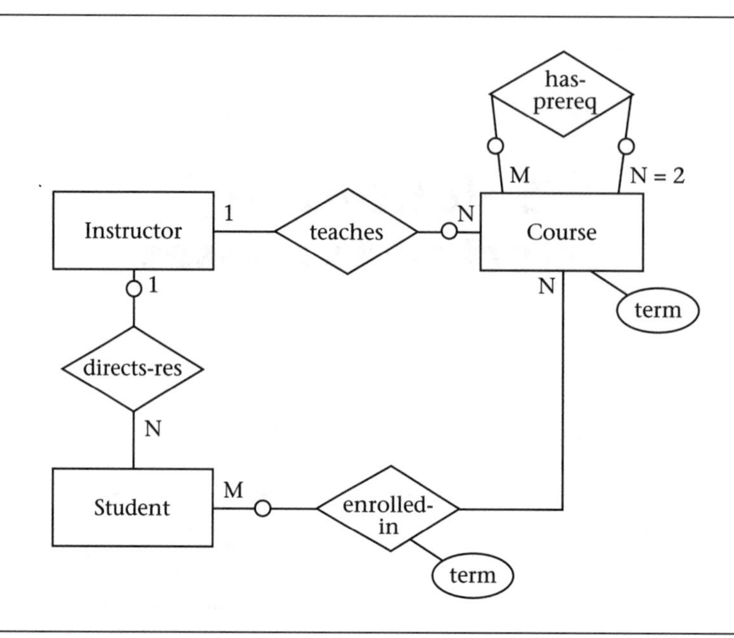

Problem 4-2 (page 94)

```
create table instructor (instr_id char(10),
        instr_name char(20),
        instr_office_no char(10),
        primary key (instr_id));
create table student (student_id char(10),
        student_name char(20),
        student_address char(30),
        res_instr_id char(10),
        primary key (student_id),
        foreign key (res_instr_id) references instructor
              on delete set null on update cascade);
create table course (course_id char(9),
        course_name char(20),
        term char(10),
        instr_id char(10) not null,
        primary key (course_id),
        foreign key (instr_id) references instructor
              on delete set default on update cascade);
```

```
create table enrolled_in (student_id char(10),
        course_id char(10),
        term char(10),
        primary key (student_id, course_id),
        foreign key (student_id) references student
            on delete cascade on update cascade,
        foreign key (course_id) references course
            on delete cascade on update cascade);
create table has_prereq (course_id char(10),
        prereq_course_id char(10),
        primary key (course_id, prereq_course_id),
        foreign key (course_id) references course
            on delete cascade on update cascade,
        foreign key (prereq_course_id) references course
            on delete cascade on update cascade);
```

Problem 5-2 (page 132)

1. No, R is not in 3NF because of the transitive functional dependencies.
2. Yes, R is in 3NF because A is a prime attribute (part of the candidate key AB).
3. Yes, R is in BCNF because BC is a candidate key, determining the only other attribute.
4. Yes, BC is a candidate key.
5. No, non–fully functional dependency exists.
6. Yes, if A–>C, then AB–>C.
7. No, because the transitive dependency A–>C–>B exists.

Problem 5-3 (page 132)

1. Functional dependencies
   course_id –> instructor_id
   student_id –> instructor_id (optional)
   student_id, course_id –> term (optional)
2. Level of normalization when implemented as a single table with no repeating columns: 1NF
3. Convert to BCNF: use separate relations for instructor, student, course, enrollment, and prerequisite (see solution to Problem 4-2).

Problem 5-6 (page 135)

Minimum set of 3NF relations. R1–R4 are BCNF; R5 is 3NF.

R1: AB with key A and functional dependency A –> B

R2: BCD with keys B and D and functional dependencies B –> CD and D –> B

R3: AEF with composite key AE and functional dependency AE –> F

R4: EJ with key E and functional dependency E –> J

R5: EGH with composite key EG and functional dependencies EG –> H and H –> G

Problem 5-8 (page 136)

Minimum set of 3NF (and BCNF) relations:

R1: ABC with key A (A –> BC)

R2: BDEFG with keys B, E (B –> DEFG, E –> B)

Problem 6-3 (page 174)

1. Sequential search of the student records:

   Disk access times: seek(disk) = 40 ms, rot = 20 ms, tr = 200 KB/sec

   Sequential block access time: Tsba = rot/2 + bks/tr = 20/2 + 1000/200 KB/sec = 15 ms

   Random block access time: Trba = Tsba + seek(disk) = 15 ms + 40 ms = 55 ms

   Sequential access is to be computed for a single pass through 20,000 records:

   blocking factor: bf = floor(1000 bytes per block /64 bytes per student record) = 15

   lra = 20,000 logical record accesses

   sba = ceiling(lra/bf) = ceiling(20,000/15) = 1334 sequential block accesses

   iotime = tsba*sba = 15 ms * 1334 sba = 20.0 seconds

2. Secondary index access to student records:

   We assume that the foreign key research_instr_id in student records has a secondary index.

   We also assume that the attribute name index is small and fits into a single block in main memory.

   Attribute value index size: 2500 instructors*9 bytes = 22,500 bytes => 23 blocks (thus a successful search requires an average of 12 blocks).

   Accession list size = 10 (given each instructor has an average of 10 research students).

   Pointer size = 5 bytes (assumed).

   iotime = time1 (access the index of attribute types)
   + time2 (access the index of attribute values)
   + time3 (access the accession list for a given instructor id)
   + time4 (access the 10 target records)
   = 0 (attribute type index in RAM)
   + 12 rba*Trba (attribute value index search)
   + 1 rba*Trba (accession list has 10 entries of 5B each, fitting into a single block)
   + 10 rba*Trba (target data block accesses)
   = 23*55 ms
   = 1265 ms

Problem 8-1 (page 206)

Best fit nonredundant allocation:

Table **R1** is allocated to site S2 (total local frequency of 100: 100 for update 1)

Table **R2** is allocated to site S3 (total local frequency of 60: 10 for query 2 and 50 for update 2)

Table **R3** is allocated to site S1 (total local frequency of 20: 10 for query 1 and 10 for query 2)

All beneficial sites allocation (where to replicate after the initial allocation):

Table **R1** is to be replicated at S1 (benefit of 101.2 seconds exceeds cost of 27 seconds).

No other replications are recommended: Cost exceeds or equals benefit in all other cases.

Benefit computation for the replication of table **R1** at site S1:

Query 1 accesses table **R1** at site S1 with frequency of 10. Remote minus local query eliminates the local disk I/O.

Time per transaction = [request propagation delay + transmission of request packet + result propagation delay + result of the query (100 packets at 100 ms/packet)]*frequency

= [10 + 100 + 10 + 100*100]*10
= 101,200 ms (101.2 seconds)

Cost computation for the replication of table **R1** at site S1:

Update 1 accesses table **R1** at site S1 with frequency of 100.
Time per transaction = [request propagation delay + transmission of request packet + local update disk I/O (random read plus rewrite) + result propagation delay + result of the update (1 packet at 100ms)]*frequency
= [10 +100 + (40 + 40) + 10 + 100]*100
= 30,000 ms (30 seconds)

Problem A-1 (page 296)

Query 1.

```
select first_name, middle_init, last_name
    from president
    where political_party = 'Republican'
    and state_from = 'Ohio';
```

Query 2.

```
select s.state_name
    from state as s, president as p, administration as a
    where p.first_name = 'Andrew'
    and p.last_name = 'Johnson'
    and p.identifier = a.pres_identifier
    and a.start_date <= s.date_admitted
    and a.end_date >= s.date_admitted;
```

Query 3.

```
select a.vp_first_name, a.vp_middle_init, a.vp_last_name
       from administration as a
minus
select a.vp_first_name, a.vp_middle_init, a.last_name
       from administration as a, president as p
       where p.first_name = a.vp_first_name
       and p.middle_init = a.vp_middle_init
       and p.last_name = a.vp_last_name;
```

Index

About the Author

Toby J. Teorey received his B.S. (1964) and M.S. (1965) degrees in electrical engineering from the University of Arizona and his Ph.D. (1972) in computer science from the University of Wisconsin.

He served as an EDP officer in the U.S. Air Force from 1965 to 1969 and was a White House social aide for President Lyndon Johnson from 1966 to 1968. At the University of Wisconsin (1969 to 1972), he became coordinator of the Operations Research Group in the Madison Academic Computing Center. He is currently professor of electrical engineering and computer science at the University of Michigan, Ann Arbor, and served as associate chair of the departement from 1994 to 1997. He also served as the program chair for the 1991 Entity-Relationship Conference and as general chair of the 1981 ACM SIGMOD Conference. This is his second book on database design.

Professor Teorey's current research interests are data modeling, data warehousing, OLAP, advanced databases, and network configuration and performance tools. In 1992, he led an effort resulting in the development of NetMod, a Windows-based analytical tool for predicting the performance of large-scale, interconnected local area networks. He is a member of the ACM and the IEEE Computer Society.

Professor Teorey has consulted widely in the area of database design, including work with General Motors, Apple Computer, IBM, Northern Telecom, the World Bank, and NSA, as well as other corporations and agencies of the U.S. government.